contributed their time and talents in recommending improvements to the text.

I am most appreciative of criticism and materials received from the National Association of Independent Insurance Adjusters, and particularly from Robert B. Irwin, chairman of the publications committee. I also acknowledge with thanks those materials received from Irvin E. Williamson, chairman of the GAB Business Services, Inc.

Special thanks are expressed to my friends at the Insurance Institute of America, Inc., including Edwin S. Overman, and particularly to Frederick R. Hodosh, who spent many hours reviewing the manuscript of the new edition, making important changes, and who solicited critiques and recommendations from many people in the insurance claims handling community. In addition, I appreciate the help provided by Christopher Pitt, who reviewed the manuscript and furnished important suggestions and assistance.

Finally, I acknowledge the patience and forbearance of my wife and family, who have long understood the demands that my research and writing activities have made on holidays, vacations, and other family time. In addition I thank Pat DeLancey for her stenographic assistance.

Willis Park Rokes

HUMAN RELATIONS IN HANDLING INSURANCE CLAIMS

Know then thyself; presume not God to scan;
The proper study of mankind is man.

Alexander Pope (1688–1744)
Essay on Man

To my wife, Catherine;
my sons, John, Mark & Adam;
And to my mother and late father.

ISBN 0-256-02504-5
Library of Congress Catalog Card No. 80–85063

Printed in the United States of America

1 2 3 4 5 6 7 8 9 0 MP 8 7 6 5 4 3 2 1

Human relations in handling insurance claims

Revised edition

WILLIS PARK ROKES, J.D., Ph.D., C.L.U., C.P.C.U.

Professor, College of Business Administration
University of Nebraska at Omaha

1981

RICHARD D. IRWIN, INC.   Homewood, Illinois   60430
Irwin-Dorsey Limited   Georgetown, Ontario   L7G 4B3

Preface

Fundamental and significant changes have occurred during the past 15 years in the field of insurance claims handling. Since the publication of the first edition of this book, we have seen incorporated in claims handling a number of important innovations. Particularly significant has been the means by which the claims investigation is conducted, utilizing the telephone claims handling techniques. The advent of the miniaturized, reliable, and inexpensive recording device has played an important role in the realization of economies and efficiency in most claims offices of today. Many firms now report that they handle most claims by telephone and obtain most statements by the recorded telephone interview technique.

In addition, when the first edition of this book was published some 15 years ago, the occupation of insurance claims handling was almost exclusively the province of male claims personnel. Since then, however, women claims persons have become a highly important and essential phenomenon in the insurance claims handling picture. The claims offices today have a sizable number of women employed, and in some cases women constitute the majority of claims handling personnel.

Other significant changes have taken place in claims handling practice. The use of advance payments techniques was a new phenomenon 15 years ago; today, however, such techniques are in common use. In addition, claims are paid today under "open-end" releases, and in many cases the "no-release" technique is being used. The liberality of these new claims handling techniques reflects a modern-day adjustment and adaptation of the insurance industry to the rising expectations of the insuring public to be treated in a fair and conscientious manner, providing for the expediting of insurance claims. These same public expectations and a popular sense of justice regarding the handling of insurance claims have resulted in the enactment of "unfair claims practices" acts with a legislative mandate which must be followed by insurers and their claims personnel. Outlined in these statutes are rules of conduct and fair play which transcend traditional contract responsibilities and impose upon insurers the legal duty to treat insureds and claimants in a "socially responsible" manner, irrespective of contract obligations.

As in the first edition of the book, I received assistance and contributions from many people who contributed to the preparation of the revised edition. I particularly acknowledge the valuable technical materials and assistance provided by Robert H. Woody, professor of psychology, University of Nebraska at Omaha. The criticism, advice, guidance, and hours of conversation provided by P. Knute Peterson, Continental Agency Company, are gratefully acknowledged. His contributions and those of Dr. Woody on the rapidly developing subject of forensic psychology have been invaluable to me.

Thanks also are due to Carl E. Schultz, senior vice president and claims counsel, and also Dick Jordon, Inez Gonzales and Bob Gottschalk of the Claims Training Division of Fireman's Fund Insurance Companies. Their generosity, assistance, and advice during a week's communications workshop were most helpful in the preparation of the manuscript.

A special debt of gratitude is owed to the many individual claims persons and adjuster education instructors who have utilized the first edition of this book in their classes. Their recommendations have resulted in many modifications and the inclusion of new materials has been stimulated by their criticism, advice, and suggestions. I gratefully acknowledge the contributions of these individuals, including: Gordon L. Berger, GAB National Education Center; Reno H. Forsythe, Jr., C.P.C.U.; Richard H. Greene, The Maryland; Louise Grubbs, C.P.C.U., Merritt & McKenzie; Richard Guthrie, Employers Casualty Company; Herbert H. Hildebrand, C.P.C.U., Reliance Insurance Companies; B. David Hinkle, Crawford & Company; Richard W. Knipping and Richard Manson, Metropolitan Property & Liability Insurance Company; J. W. Lanning, Employers Mutual Companies; Earl LeRoy Rankin, C.P.C.U., Nationwide Insurance; James A. Sadler, American Mutual Fire Insurance Company; Henry Sager, Jr., Celina Insurance Group; Steven Utrata, C.P.C.U., State Automobile Group; M. E. Verbeck, Kemper Insurance Companies; Suzanne Wilkinson, Aetna/Cravens, Dargan and Company; and the many anonymous individuals who

Preface to the first edition

This book was written to meet the increasing demand for a definitive treatment of the psychology of handling insurance claims—principles of human relations to be applied by the insurance claims representative. The book also was intended to accommodate the needs of the Insurance Institute of America, Inc., program in insurance claim adjusting.

Claims men, insurance counsel, and those agents who handle claims are confronted daily with demanding situations which require the most skillful use of communication and motivation techniques. As front-line representatives of the insurance industry, these people have the vital function of handling complex legal matters arising out of contractual obligation and tort liability. At the same time, they must present the insurance industry as a socially conscious and responsible institution in contemporary society. Their responsibility to investigate and to negotiate insurance claims require a sophisticated application of good human relations and practical salesmanship if the claims handling functions are to be accomplished properly.

Much has been written to guide the insurance agent or the general salesman of manufactured goods to help him to present his product in its most favorable light. Salesmen have been instructed in communication and selling principles and techniques to improve their abilities to induce sales prospects to purchase goods and services of every conceivable variety. The demanding area of insurance claims handling, however, has been marked by a dearth of helpful literature designed specifically to meet the needs of the claims representative in the vital subjects of human behavior, communication, motivation, and philosophy—human relations in handling insurance claims.

Human Relations in Handling Insurance Claims was written to satisfy these needs. Although the book is oriented toward a specialized readership, it should be interesting and informative reading for anyone engaged in the insurance business and anyone interested in the subject of insurance claims handling.

The author acknowledges the assistance and contributions of the many people who have helped in the inspection and the preparation of this book. He is indebted to Dr. William E. Jaynes, professor and chairman of the psychology department, Oklahoma State University. Dr. Jaynes collaborated with the author on a monograph which served as a basis for this book, and he has provided helpful advice in connection with the present volume.

Valuable technical advice was given by Dr. A. H. Malo, resident psychologist of Kemper Insurance. Dr. Malo provided criticism and review of the entire manuscript. The author also acknowledges the technical assistance of Dr. Richard W. Nicholson, professor of psychology, University of Omaha.

Painstaking editorial criticism was given by Dr. Robert M. Crowe, assistant vice president, University of South Carolina, and Dr. Jack A. Hill, professor of business administration, University of Omaha.

A number of claims men and insurance counsel have played an important part in influencing the final form of the manuscript. They have read all or a part of the material and have stimulated modification and the inclusion of new materials by their criticism, advice, and suggestions. The author especially recognizes the contributions of Mr. Charles F. Berryman, Milwaukee Mutual Insurance Company and Mr. Corydon T. Johns, Johns and Company, who read the entire manuscript and suggested editorial, substantive, and organizational changes.

In addition, the author gratefully acknowledges the advice of others, including the following, who provided ideas and guidance in the preparation of the manuscript: Mr. Paul K. Clayton, C.P.C.U., Continental National American Group; Mr. E. A. Cowie, Hartford Insurance Group; Mr. H. L. Handley, Jr., Farmers Insurance Group; Mr. B. D. Hinkle, Crawford and Company; Mr. Frank P. Horner, American Family Insurance Group; Mr. John A. Mayes, C.P.C.U., Texas Employers' Insurance Association; Mr. Meredith Nelson, State Farm Group; Mr. Arthur J. Nevins, Royal-Globe Insurance Companies; Mr. P. Knute Peterson, Continental Agency Company; Mr. G. H. "Jack" Sawyer, Continental National American Group; Mr. John H. Wallace, C.P.C.U., Northwestern Mutual Insurance

Company; and Mr. Thomas W. Wassell, Texas Employers' Insurance Association.

The author does not infer that the foregoing concur in whole or in part with the contents of the book. Rather, he merely thanks them most sincerely.

The constructive criticism of members of the Educational Committee of the National Association of Independent Insurance Adjusters is gratefully acknowledged. In addition, advice and materials furnished by the General Adjustment Bureau and the Federation of Insurance Counsel have been of utmost value.

Special thanks is expressed to the author's friends at the Insurance Institute of America, Inc., and particularly to Dr. Harry J. Loman, Dr. Edwin S. Overman, Dr. James J. Chastain, and Mr. Evan E. Clingman. Their suggestions and encouragement stimulated the effort which culminated in this book. Dr. Chastain especially has served as a demanding critic. His continued encouragement has been much appreciated.

To his wife, Catherine, the author expresses thanks for moral support and hours of practical assistance. Finally, he is grateful for the stenographic assistance of Mrs. Judy Benecke and Miss Susan C. Joseph.

Willis Rokes

Contents

PART II   FOUNDATION FOR INFLUENCING PEOPLE

PART III   INFLUENCING PEOPLE

ciples: *Equilibrium states of people. Motives and motive appeals.* Motives and claims handling: *Pride. Fear. Anger and aggression. Competition and aggression. Acquisition and saving.* Wants versus needs. Frustration and conflict: *Conflicting attractions. Conflicting repulsions. Repulsion-attraction conflict. Situational reactions—traumatic neuroses.*

Human behavior

1

Understanding human relations

The job of the claims person is unique. As claims representatives who handle first-party and liability claims, we must receive notice of claims, verify possible insurance coverage and investigate the circumstances which give rise to claims. We must ascertain the monetary amount of losses sustained by insureds and third-party claimants, and we must assemble the facts and circumstances of the losses (usually in evidential form). After analyzing contracts and the evidence accumulated to determine whether and to what extent coverage and liability exist, we then may negotiate settlements with insureds and with third-party claimants and/or their legal counsel. Occasionally we must appear in court to assist the insurance company's trial counsel in establishing and corroborating evidence. In handling these claims functions we find that, more so than in almost any other line of work, conflict and adversary relations with other people can develop. There is a discovery that in the great variety of claims situations, one factor is dominant—we are dealing with people during almost every hour of the workday. To be successful we must understand human relations.

Most of the people we meet in claims situations have lost something of value. In these meetings, we sometimes deal with people who are sophisticated in insurance matters, who understand the nature of damages and the principle of indemnity. Most of the time, however, we discover that people are unfamiliar with the legal technicalities involved in insurance claims, and they don't understand much about liability and the law of negligence. Their background of education and training is foreign to the world of insurance claims. Into this strange world they often bring a complete naïveté, a distrust of unfamiliar things, and an irrationality of approach which is often aggravated by the event which gave rise to their claim. It is within this environment of human behavior that the claims person must work.

The keynote to the entire insurance claims handling process, consequently, is the claims person's association with people—all types of people. We deal with all ages and all nationalities. Some people can't write their names; others are highly educated. We must use an interpreter to talk to some individuals. We enter the homes of the wealthy and the hovels of the slumdwellers. Many homes are immaculate; others are dirty. We talk to the professional man who, in his spare hours, is weeding his garden. At other times, we chat with the day laborer who is slouched in fatigue in front of his television set.

In our relationships with these people we must serve as the contact, the trained investigator, the counselor, the salesperson, and oftentimes the judge. We must provide the service which will best accomplish the claims handling job. The approach must be rational and objective, and we must understand that we oftentimes will not be dealing with rational and objective people (owing to the unfamiliar and aggravating nature of claims situations). As claims representatives, we also must realize that many times we may appear to be irrational to other people.

The claims person must enter the foregoing arena armed with the knowledge and skills to meet obstacles that are confronted. A knowledge of human relations principles and the skill to motivate other people will assure success in the demanding task of insurance claims handling.

NEED FOR FORMAL STUDY

Everyone likes to think of himself or herself as somewhat of a psychologist. In a way, everyone is and should be. The claims person particularly needs to be a practical psychologist in performing the everyday functions of the claims handling job. Oftentimes, however, use of "common sense," "down-to-earth" applications of human relations ideas (currently referred to as *pop-psychology*) are merely reflections of the claims person's own personal opinions and are severely handicapped by limited experience and observation and by the peculiarities of the individual's own "frames of reference."

The idea that good human relations in insurance claims handling is "just common sense"—something learned by experience—is a popular misconception. Some claims people become skilled at human relations through experience, but most do not. Nothing bears this out more clearly than the wide variations of opinion of claims representatives as to what constitutes good human relations practice in the handling of insurance claims. To understand the human factor in claims handling usually requires something more than experience. As Keith Davis states:

> Human relations requires the learning of technical knowledge about people, the development of social skills, development of a philosophy, and research into conditions affecting each situation. All these things must be sought through study and experience, because they are not a natural inheritance.[1]

No actuary of right mind would base predictions of claims losses of his or her insurance company on the extremely limited loss experience of one small insured. Data is collected on the losses experienced by thousands of insureds in order to predict future losses. Only by employing the law of large numbers can the actuary make meaningful predictions of future losses. Only by gathering the combined experiences of a large number of insureds can actuarial science formulate useful principles which largely eliminate uncertainty in the underwriting process.

An insurance claims person, similarly, is ill advised to formulate human relations principles based only upon limited data. It is questionable that personal experiences and observations of the individual claims person or that the opinions and experiences of a few of his or her friends and acquaintances in the claims field provide sufficient data upon which to make ironclad assumptions. Like the actuary, the claims representative will find it invaluable to rely on the principles formulated from the observations and experience of thousands of other people.

Too many books and articles have been written with a how-to approach, containing a proliferation of the experiences of one claims

---

[1] Keith Davis, *Human Relations at Work* (New York: McGraw-Hill, 1962), p. 12.

person and a few acquaintances. The conclusions, more often than not, are meaningless and unintelligible and produce as many opinions as there are contributors to the material. Any meaningful human relations book for claims personnel must start with well-established psychological principles supported by sufficient data to lend validity and credibility to specific claims handling applications. This is the only logical way to approach the subject.

The behavioral scientists—psychologists, cultural anthropologists, economists, and others—have assembled an impressive body of scientific data from which important human relations principles have been formulated. This information is readily available to us and will provide us with meaningful and valid assumptions upon which we can justify many day-to-day claims handling decisions.

In this book, therefore, we will start with established theory and examine the many influences which cause people to act as they do. This will require an examination of roles played by heredity and environment on human behavior. Further, we will analyze the characteristics of human behavior and the aspects of personality development which account for human behavior. Of particular interest to the insurance claims representative will be the chapter dealing with "The imperfect human" in which the many variations of a human being's perception, narration, recollection, and integrity are explored and explained. This chapter is important to the claims person because it helps to account for the discrepancies which exist in testimony of several witnesses. It also explains why insureds, claimants, and witnesses act as they do in various insurance claims situations.

The foregoing material will be followed by chapters which present principles of communication and motivation. Throughout the book the basic theory presented is related to actual insurance claims handling situations. With this practical application, the claims person is able to relate some of the problems of the claims handling job to established human relations principles.

WHAT INFLUENCES HUMAN BEHAVIOR

The human being is a complex species of animal life. Unlike most forms of animals, however, the human has the ability to use complex reasoning in his or her day-to-day existence. This makes it more difficult to comprehend the meaning behind our various activities. The complexity of a human being's mental makeup and the vast sophistication and range of his or her activities produce many situations which require imaginative adjustment. We need every available means to ferret out the answers to the problems which confront us in our complex society.

In our quest we discover that science serves both as a faithful servant and as a cruel master. Science both aids us in finding solutions, and it aggravates our situations by presenting problems which create ponderous complications to our very existence. Every time we make some new and frightful discovery and create a revolutionary instrument of warfare or a laborsaving, automated device, we are faced with the problem of the human factor—how to use these instruments and devices for the benefit of our society rather than for its destruction.

Human beings live today in an age in which the findings and technology of science have aggravated our ability to live harmoniously with each other. We are threatened by self-extinction by that same technology. Clearly, we must acquire greater comprehension of the nature of science and its modern application to the vital area of human relations, for it is the human being's lack of understanding of science in relation to human behavior which poses the very problems which endanger us.

Scientists are trying to understand human behavior in order to achieve an element of control over the use of the expanding technology of natural sciences. As scientists' important work of experimentation progresses, important principles regarding communication, group dynamics, and individual motivation are exposed. Many of these principles have found important practical application in American business enterprise. Businesspersons today, for example, are aware that customers do not remember complex, wordy slogans and sales appeals. People tend to remember only simple insignias and symbols. As a consequence, many companies (including a number in the insurance business) have simplified their trademarks and letterheads. In the area of market research, companies spend vast sums to determine the motives behind human behavior. These companies find that it often pays to identify their products with things which stimulate human needs or wants. The study of human behavior shows, for instance, that soaps, soft drinks, and deodorants are more easily sold if identified with romance.

Claims persons frequently call upon experts in other fields to help them understand the great variety of claims situations and problems. Thus, the claims representative employs the medical expert, the legal expert, the body-shop expert, and the person who understands the construction business. Why should he or she not learn something from the behavioral scientist?

Many practical applications of the behavioral sciences have direct application to insurance claims handling. Thus, as insurance claims representatives, we must be concerned with the behavioral sciences—psychology, economics, anthropology, sociology, political science, history, and related subjects. The behavioral sciences can help provide an understanding of the society in which we live. If we understand the factors which cause other people's behavior, insight can be gained of the nature of motivation. This will help us to influence others.

By understanding the factors which have molded our own ideas, values, attitudes, urges, and motives, we can understand ourselves and realize why we react in a given situation as we do. In knowing ourselves, we can cope with our own attitudes and potential reactions which might arise because of the differences in such things as sex, appearance, nationality, social class, and religion of other people. This is particularly important for the insurance claims representative.

In acquiring self-knowledge and an understanding of others, the claims person must know something about the dynamics of human association—how people interact. He or she should understand the role that his or her association with other people plays in the formation of patterns of thought and behavior. This subject, together with a consideration of the influence of heredity, will be explored in this chapter.

HOW PEOPLE INTERACT

Some people have considerable ability in understanding others and in using that understanding to accomplish desired objectives. Men such as the Pharaohs of Egypt, the emperors of Rome, Alexander the Great, Napoleon, and Hitler have swayed the behavior of millions of people, thereby changing the course of history.

There are always the rulers and the ruled. Why one individual or group should possess great power over other people within a society, controlling social, political, and economic activity, is a fascinating subject. It is a state of affairs which at times appears to defy reason.

Even in the animal world the idea of equality is a myth. Probably there, more so than in the human world, the individual is born equal to his or her contemporaries. Soon, however, the individual becomes a leader and a wielder of power or is relegated to an inferior position of subservience through the dynamics of group association.

A baboon troop, for example, consists of as many as 200 members and is firmly led by a male. This dominant boss male is not necessarily the best fighter but has acquired his position of leadership because of his ability to attract supporters—one or two other males that will back him up against challengers. There is a descending order of importance among the rest of the males of the troop, who, having found early in life their particular niche, rarely try to move up. Females, too, have their place in the social hierarchy of the troop. There are dominant females, and there are subservient females. Members of a baboon troop establish social rank by the force of individual character and personality.

Chickens provide another example of social structure in animals. Among chickens there is a *pecking order*. The most powerful chicken can peck any of the other chickens in the yard. The latter, in turn, can peck less-important chickens until the bottom of the social order is reached. The chicken at the bottom of the order dares not peck other chickens. That individual, although hatched from the same type of egg as the leader chicken, occupies a decidedly inferior station in the social world of chickens.

In the world of humans, as in the animal world, there seems to be a pecking order. It appears to be the "natural" state of affairs that some men and women will dominate others. Some individuals are born into positions of power because their families have the wealth, prestige, and status, coupled with association with other powerful individuals, which perpetuates power. They possess authority because they are strategically situated. It is a peculiar characteristic of the human society that status, prestige, and power are inherited and perpetuated, in formal groupings, irrespective of the intelligence, talent, knowledge, or other personal characteristics of the individuals involved. Most animals attain rank by the force of ability, character, and personality, unaided by inherited wealth, power, and status.

The event of birth plays an important part in the ultimate ranking of man and woman in the hierarchy of society. Nevertheless, a significant number of humans do move out of their class into a "higher" class.[2] They create and grasp power and acquire rank because of their

---

[2] Joseph Schumpeter, *Imperialism and Social Classes* (New York: Meridian Books, 1955), pp. 126, 130.

ability to dominate, understand, and influence others through their individual character and personality. Throughout the world the individual man or woman jockeys for position, transcending class lines or attempting to acquire superior rank in his or her own social class.

This elemental ranking process can be observed easily in the play activities of children. For example, a group of schoolboys playing together soon establishes its hierarchy of rank. Two individuals who are the most aggressive and authoritative in their approach, often supported by one or two other boys who are vocal in their opinions, announce that they are the captains who will choose up sides to play a game of baseball. Through this informal but extremely influential process the hierarchy of rank is established. The last boy chosen by the team captains is relegated to the lowest level of the pecking order. On the other hand, this boy may be top man in his class. He is at the top in the pecking order in scholarship. This success, usually, does not elevate his ranking in his baseball activities.

The human pecking order is a phenomenon that has fascinated human beings throughout the ages. That the myth of equality cannot be substantiated by the harsh world of reality is self-evident to even the casual observer. The reader no doubt observed that all through school some classmates occupied positions of influence and power sheerly because of the peculiarities of their individual personalities. During the school years and thereafter, people's personalities and behaviors have a most important bearing upon whether they become leaders or followers.

The leader

Without leadership, the efforts and energies of a group cannot be channeled into cooperative activities. A group without a leader experiences confusion and chaos. Only through a leader can the individual behavior of each member of the group be controlled and directed toward the group's common goals and objectives. Effective leadership determines the success of any group. It requires that the individual assuming the role of leader be able to influence the others to behave in a manner consistent with common objectives of the group.

In situations where there is not ingrained or inherited power and leadership, however, the dynamics of the leadership process are bound to the personal characteristics of the individual. An individual person, like the leader of the baboon troop, often acquires the role of leader by successfully attracting supporters. These supporters are acquired because the leader is perceived as the individual who will be most effective in helping the supporters and perhaps the whole group in setting and acquiring common goals—social objectives.

To become a leader, therefore, it is apparent that we must be able to influence others to believe in us, to have confidence in our ability, and to support our position of leadership. Others judge us through our behavior, for it is there that our qualities are revealed. It is through our past behavior that our future behavior can be predicted, and it is this future behavior which is vital to the welfare of the group.

Since leadership allows a person to occupy a position from which to influence the behavior and activities of other people, what characteristics and qualities must be displayed in order to qualify for the leadership role? Experiments reveal that being a leader requires better than average intelligence and social adjustment. It demands self-confident, decisive, extroverted, dominant, *and socially sensitive behavior.*[3] To be a leader, one must be *sensitive to the needs of others.* If one is to influence others, one must have an awareness of social responsibility.[4] When we ignore that responsibility, we lose the privilege to lead. The leader, therefore, must acquire traits which demonstrate that he or she can best serve the interests of supporters.[5] An awareness of the characteristics of leadership and the qualities possessed by the leader is important to the insurance claims person. If we seek to lead others and to influence their actions, we must acquire and develop leadership characteristics and qualities.

History is rich with examples of successful leaders. One of the most influential of leaders in recent years was Hitler. Even he displayed social sensitivity. In a Germany torn with political dissension and burdened with war reparations and a sense of national despair, his "cult of the superman" and his martial organization gave hope to

---

[3] R. M. Stogdill, "Personal Factors Associated with Leadership," *Journal of Psychology* (1948), pp. 25, 35–71; Howard H. Kendler, *Basic Psychology* (New York: Appleton-Century-Crofts, 1963), p. 570.

[4] Floyd L. Ruch, *Psychology and Life,* 4th ed. (Chicago: Scott, Foresman, 1953), p. 343.

[5] Clifford T. Morgan, *Introduction to Psychology* (New York: McGraw-Hill, 1956), p. 319.

a large number of dispirited young people. They identified with his ideology and had great faith in his abilities to carry out his ideas—he could lead them to greatness. With his loyal cadre of supporters he was in time able to acquire the power to control a great nation and to affect the destiny of tens of millions of people in the world.

Personality, and its power to influence others, is a highly important factor in the success of the individual leader. It is the key to success in influencing and motivating others. Since the claims person is vitally concerned with achieving success in dealing with others, he or she must be an ardent student of the human personality—how it relates to insurance claims handling, how it develops, and how it can be modified to produce different patterns of behavior. The following pages will explore the subject in depth.

A person's need for association

Independence? That's middle class blasphemy. We are all dependent upon one another, every soul of us on earth.
    ——George Bernard Shaw

The human, like the ants, bees, termites, and many other animals, thrives on association with his or her fellow creatures. We rely upon others for almost all of our needs. We would find it difficult to live alone. As a matter of fact, we believe it to be one of the worst punishments to commit a human to a life of isolation. For centuries penal institutions have used solitary confinement as a drastic form of punishment.

Man or woman withers in isolation. We draw our whole reason for existence from other people. Our efforts are almost always directed toward activities which will result in recognition, commendation, and acceptance by other people. We obtain from others love, warmth, sympathy, recognition, and all of those things which we value most.

Even the social outcast, the misfit, needs the recognition of society. If circumstances retard normal personality development, the ability to adjust to the society which is so desperately needed is seriously impaired. Being unable to obtain acceptance and recognition through normal channels of activity and achievement, this person may commit socially unacceptable, and often shocking, acts to draw attention to himself or herself. Although the satisfaction is perverted, a feeling of importance is derived by this individual. When attention is directed to the enormity of this person's action, he or she then obtains recognition, however adverse.

It has been theorized that the assassination of the late President John F. Kennedy was prompted by just such a motivation. Lee Harvey Oswald apparently had withdrawn into a shell of self-exile and isolation. Antisocial acts helped him to obtain a strange sense of self-importance. This sorely disturbed person's need for recognition, at any price, festered his own terrible inability to attune himself to his fellow man. The assassin's widow reportedly stated to newsmen that her husband killed President Kennedy because Oswald "wanted to be a big shot."[6]

A human being's obsessive need for recognition and acceptance is so elemental that it is important for the individual person to understand others in order to gain their goodwill. If we are to be successful in a chosen vocation, we must know how to win acceptance and to influence customers, fellow workers, employers, and all others.

Relation to insurance claims handling

As claims representatives, we must have the ability to meet people under varying circumstances. We must know how to secure their cooperation so that we can perform the functions of the claims handling job. To acquire competence in dealing with other people, the claims person must know and understand why other people act as they do. To accomplish this, we must obtain competence in observing and analyzing other people's actions. Through their actions, humans best reveal how they think or feel.

Variations in the behavior of individual people are readily apparent and pose baffling questions. If we are to influence other people, we must comprehend what forces mold the individual's personality and cause the individual to act as he or she does. Without such understanding many of the phenomena in the everyday world will be most puzzling. Why, for example, do juries in one section of the United States grant awards appreciably higher than those awarded by juries in another part of the country? It is not uncommon to observe jury

---

6 *Time*, June 19, 1964, p. 21.

verdict amounts that deviate on the average as much as 40 percent to 60 percent on comparable cases, all depending upon the state or city in which a case is tried. The differences in jury awards all over the nation are only one example of the behavior variations which exist in the United States.

Insurance claims representatives find variations in human behavior within their immediate area of operations. For instance, whether a person lives or has lived in a rural community seems to have a bearing on that person's personality and is reflected in his or her behavior, although regional differences are not as marked as they were in years past. According to some experienced claims representatives, it is not uncommon to find a more easy-going, less contentious, and less claims-minded individual living in a farming community outside a major city. His or her urban contemporary, by contrast, may be a difficult person with whom to negotiate an insurance settlement. As U.S. society becomes more urbanized and mobile in character, and as urban centers become more readily accessible to rural dwellers, it is likely that individual differences, such as the foregoing, will be hardly discernible.

The key to variation in human behavior has to do with the interplay of society upon each individual, as well as hereditary influences which help to shape the personality of the individual, resulting in a particular type of human behavior. The claims person, consequently, can sometimes roughly predict human behavior by having a knowledge of an individual's background and the society in which that person lives or has lived. More important, the knowledge provides the claims representative with information to utilize in influencing the behavior of the people with whom he or she must work.

Influencing human behavior

To suggest that one person is able to manipulate the behavior of another in sort of a puppet fashion may shock the reader's sensitivities. Manipulation, nevertheless, plays an important part in the everyday schemes of men and women. We, like the baboons and chickens, attempt to dominate our contemporaries. Successful propagandists, politicians, salespersons, trial counsel, and others become expert in the subtle art of inducing other people to do their bidding.

The confidence man is a perfect example of one who manipulates the behavior of others. One such human predator called at the home of a woman, flashed a badge, and said that he was investigating the shortage of funds at a savings and loan company. He asked to see the woman's passbook listing her deposits in the firm and requested that she withdraw the entire amount, $800, and turn it over to him; he then would immediately redeposit the sum. She complied with his request. As soon as the man had the money in his possession, he disappeared. Although the strings of the puppet were not literally pulled, the puppeteer utilized his understanding of human nature and supplied the stimulus which produced the desired reaction.

The trial attorney admittedly uses his or her knowledge of others to influence their actions. If the attorney understands the judge's habits of thought and bent of mind in the examination of evidence, the attorney can better present the case. The attorney stands a much better chance of influencing the judge with the merits of a case than does the inexperienced practitioner.

There need not be anything insidious about the process of influencing others. The problem is one of being able to present ideas and information to a recipient in such a way that the person receives the material in the most favorable light. The process of influencing others is merely using knowledge of human personality in order to communicate best and to motivate others to act in a desired fashion.

PERSONALITY

The claims person can learn much about human behavior through the study of personality and the interaction of human beings. *Personality* is defined as the traits, the adjustments, and the behavior which characterize the individual and his or her relation to others. The function of our personality is to enable us to produce behavior advantageous to us under the conditions imposed by our environment. One's personality often works to one's disadvantage.

Our personality is molded by the influences which play upon us during our lifetime. What we are and how we think and act can often be traced to the particular society within which we live. The personal development of the individual is a function of our own conditioning history—those things in our background which cause us to think, speak, and act as we do. The laws and customs to which we subscribe, our value judgments, attitudes, and ideas of what is or is not "normal" or acceptable behavior depend upon each individual's conditioning in the society of which he or she is a member.

Important influences have been at work long before our birth. The ways in which we think and act during our lifetime often are determined by factors which were predetermined, as far as we are concerned. For example, a man may be born in a certain country of parents of a certain economic and social class. He inherits distinctive physical characteristics, including coloration of skin, eyes, and hair. These social and hereditary factors greatly influence the development of his personality following his birth.

Much effort has been spent in an attempt to ascertain the relative importance of heredity as compared to environment in the development of an individual's personality. It is impossible to specifically pinpoint cause and effect relationships in human development. Society, nevertheless, constantly attempts to establish relationships in order to explain human behavior. For example, in the classic legal case of Loeb and Leopold,[7] counsel referred repeatedly to the background influences which molded the personalities of the two defendants and caused them to kill. The defense attorney's purpose was to convince the judge and jury that the two youths were not solely responsible for their act. Rather, it was argued, they were products of their biological inheritance and social environment.

The defense of heredity and environment is similarly applied in many other cases where defendants are charged with antisocial behavior. The success of these defenses proves that contemporary society places great reliance upon the cause and effect relation between an individual's background and behavior. The evidence to support this relation is present in abundance. From statistics based upon individual case studies, behavioral scientists have been able to identify and to describe the principal influences on personality development.

Heredity

Certain human qualities are inherited. The most typical of these are physical characteristics, such as body build and facial features.

---

[7] A 1924 Chicago murder case involving two young men convicted of a "thrill" killing of a 14-year-old boy.

There is also ample reason to believe that talent is passed on from generation to generation. It has been theorized that such talent sometimes skips a generation, so that today's prominent man probably had a famous grandfather, but his father may have been comparatively obscure. The theory is difficult to prove with conclusive documentation. There nevertheless is convincing evidence that talent or the propensity to excel at certain activities is hereditary in a large number of cases.

It generally is concluded that an innate biological predisposition influences personality development in many ways. Scientists believe there is a definite relation between body build and personality. There are some compelling reasons why one's physical makeup influences one's personality formation. For example, being born with physical characteristics which attract the opposite sex makes it possible for one high school student to achieve attention and a social acceptance which are not readily available to a less attractive one. The latter, consequently, may devote more time to developing personality characteristics which will win social acceptance. It often is the case that the homely student's efforts to acquire an attractive personality will result in more successful and longer-enduring social acceptance than that achieved by the superficially glamorous one.

The influence of heredity on human development has been borne out by extensive studies conducted on extremely intelligent children.[8] Such children are physically stronger, healthier, more stable emotionally, and better adjusted than normal children. This superiority carries over into adulthood. Better health and greater physical strength no doubt produce a better functioning nervous system and higher intelligence. These, in turn, probably bring about better social adjustments and personality development. It is difficult to assess thoroughly the hereditary and biological influences on personality, but they, nevertheless, obviously play their part in molding the human personality.

The insurance claims representative should take the factor of heredity into account in claims situations when attempting to understand and predict human behavior. It is worth noting, however, that although the role of heredity should not be underemphasized, it perhaps is not the most important factor to consider in the development

---

[8] See, for example, L. M. Terman, *Genetic Studies of Genius*, vol. 1—*Mental and Physical Traits of a Thousand Gifted Children* (Stanford, Calif.: Stanford University Press, 1925).

of the human personality. Differences in personality and resultant behavior probably are more influenced by socioenvironmental factors. These factors make up the culture of the individual.

Culture

The relation of a man or a woman to society is most important. It is the association of individual men and women which makes up society, and an individual is a by-product of that society because of his or her association with it and reliance upon it. In each society many factors form the human personality and cause individual persons to think and act in more or less predictable patterns.

In studying human society and in surveying the influences which account for human behavior, the claims person must be concerned with the behavioral sciences—particularly those of psychology and anthropology. The two disciplines are interrelated and overlapping. The psychologist is concerned with the analysis of individual behavior and the explanation of the factors causing individual behavior. The anthropologist, on the other hand, is concerned with the general behavior of a society and the factors causing that behavior. The anthropologist is concerned with *culture*.

Culture is defined as "the integrated pattern of human behavior that includes thought, speech, action, and artifacts and depends upon man's capacity for learning and transmitting knowledge to succeeding generations."[9] It is these patterns of behavior that constitute the characteristic features of a society's culture. The cultural anthropologist's conception of culture is consistent with this definition. Culture is not restricted to the visible product of human society—the fine arts, for example. Rather, a culture is made up of the overt, patterned ways of behaving, feeling, and reacting.[10] It is a way of thinking and believing. It is the stored-up knowledge of a *society*—a group of people who have learned to live together. Culture, in the classic definition, refers to "That complex whole which includes knowledge, belief, art, morals, law, custom, and any other capabilities and habits acquired by man as a member of society."[11]

---

[9] *Webster's New Collegiate Dictionary*, 1977.

[10] Alfred L. Kroeber and Clyde Kluckhohn, "Culture: A Critical Review of Concepts and Definitions," *Papers of the Peabody Museum*, vol. 47, no. 1a (1952), p. 157.

[11] Edward B. Taylor, *Primitive Culture*, 3d English ed. (Murray, 1891), p. 1.

The significance of culture is in its influence on the behavior of the individual within a society. Culture helps us to live together, giving us solutions to problems and helping us to predict the behavior of others.

Each society tends to stylize the behavior of its members. Individuals in that society thus are taught to think, feel, believe, and act in certain ways that are approximately the same for the whole group. An illustration of this sameness in thinking is afforded by the eating habits and the manner in which individual societies look at different types of foods. A fat, juicy grasshopper, for example, causes the African Bushman's mouth to water. It is questionable, however, whether we could find many people in the United States who enjoy eating grasshoppers.

This difference in behavior patterns is due to the conditioning influences exerted by each person's society upon the individual. Insects may be perfectly edible, nutritious, and tasty, but, in the United States, people have acquired an abhorrence at the thought of eating "bugs." Besides, there are other more attractive things to eat. The Bushman, however, living in the harsh environment of the Kalahari Desert of southwest Africa, is constantly threatened by famine and drought. A nice, fat bug is a delicacy to him. He isn't crazy. Rather, he is confronted by an entirely different set of environmental factors which condition his thinking and motives and result in his characteristic behavior.

To the extent that certain behavior of a group becomes rather uniform and is passed on from generation to generation, it is called the *culture* of that group. It is possible, consequently, to expect a certain type of behavior from most members of a given society. This is because each society shapes the individual's activities by defining the range of each member's permissible behavior. Certain responses are encouraged by the society; others are discouraged by withholding rewards or meting out punishment.

Certain popular conceptions exist regarding the characteristic behavior of members of different national groups. The tight and frugal nature of the Scot, for example, is legend. The Western movies depict the American Indian as a person who never lied and invariably accused the white man of talking with a "forked tongue." This trait of absolute honesty, however, is not borne out by the facts. According to anthropologists, the Navajo, for example, at the turn of the century was no more truthful than people in contemporary society. Like every

culture, Navajo culture, nevertheless, has its distinguishing characteristics. During World War II when occasionally a young man sought to
evade the military draft in response to the wishes of his mother, the
Navajo community applauded. Loyalty to one's family takes precedence over all other loyalties in Navajo culture.[12]

In marine insurance underwriting it has long been observed that
certain nations produce more skillful mariners than others. Culture
appears to play a dominant role. Citizens of certain nations appear to
possess an innate ability to respond correctly in times of crisis on the
high seas. Capabilities, habits, and attitudes have been passed down
from generation to generation and have created a seafaring people.

It also is apparent that culture plays an important role in the matter
of honesty. William D. Winter points out in his book, *Marine Insurance*,[13] that marine underwriters are aware that the standards of
business ethics are low with some societies of people, whereas other
societies have a better-developed sense of commercial honor and integrity. The standards of integrity are established by each society's
pattern of thinking and believing, and some peoples are more ethical
in their business dealings than others.

It would be meaningless to ascribe a single set of standard characteristics to the people of the United States—a land of contrasts.
Marked cultural differences exist in this nation. Some ethnic groups
have not been absorbed completely into "the melting pot of the world"
—the United States. These groups often tend to retain a considerable
amount of the culture of the place of their origin. Cities, in particular,
have ethnic groups which have their own distinguishing cultural
characterstics.

We can see from the evidence presented that there is strong reason
to believe that membership in a social group can make people suffi-
ciently similar in psychological respects so as to enable the observer to
determine how they will respond in a given situation. Appreciable
differences are observed between economic classes within the United
States. It is well recognized that the economically lower-class people
seem to live a more physical existence. Kinsey's famous reports,[14] for

[12] Clyde Kluckhohn, *Culture and Behavior* (New York: Free Press of Glencoe,
1962), pp. 168–71.

[13] William D. Winter, *Marine Insurance*, 3d ed. (New York: McGraw-Hill, 1952),
p. 231.

[14] Alfred C. Kinsey, Wardell B. Pomeroy, Clyde E. Martin, and Paul H. Gebhard,

example, indicate that members of the economically lower class have sexual experience earlier, more openly, and more often than people of the upper economic classes. Furthermore, lower socioeconomic groups are more inclined to respond in physically aggressive behavior. Physical strength and capabilities and a sense of bravado seem to play a more dominant role in this social class. Controversies frequently are resolved by contests of physical strength and violence. These people, as a consequence, have come to accept bodily injury as a matter of course. Often the evidence of such injury serves as a badge of courage for the injured person.

To the extent that the claims person or insurance counsel can ascertain the differences, peculiarities, and traits of a given culture, the knowledge has obvious practical value in handling claims of individual claimants who belong to that culture.

Modifying cultural patterns

All men feel something of an honorable bigotry for the objects which have long continued to please them.

————William Wordsworth

The conditioning influence of society upon the behavior pattern of the individual is so strong that a culture is extremely difficult to change. Any attempt made to modify cultural patterns is met with resistance because it interferes with firmly established habits and strong motivation. Changing a cultural pattern is essentially a problem of education, and its implications are highly important to societies today.

Today the prospects of over-population give great cause for worry, and a number of countries have attempted to do something about birth control in order to avoid famine and other undesirable consequences of too much population. In these attempts to adjust future population growth, countries are confronted by almost insurmountable ingrained cultures which resist change.

History is full of futile attempts of governments to attempt to change human behavior by instituting new cultural patterns by force.

Sexual Behavior in the Human Female (Philadelphia, Pa.: Saunders, 1953); and Alfred C. Kinsey, Wardell B. Pomeroy, and Clyde E. Martin, *Sexual Behavior in the Human Male* (Philadelphia, Pa.: Saunders, 1948).

Sweeping programs of social change fail when they ignore the long-established customs and traditions of a society. The Soviet government, for example, following the revolution of 1918, was forced to abandon sweeping programs of social change because it failed to conform to Russian traditions. India, likewise, experienced bloody riots in which scores of people were killed when attempts were made to reduce the number of cattle which roam the nation in the millions and aggravate the country's food problems. The Indian Hindu considers cattle to be sacred.

The revolutionist has learned that time must be devoted to change; goals must be compromised. The old social order must be destroyed not by edict but by cutting the chief link by which the old culture is transmitted—education of the younger generation by the older. In the Soviet Union, in China, and in Cuba, the revolutionists have taken over the education of children and have attempted to overcome the influence exerted by parents in the home. It is a slow and time-consuming task.

The educational process, as slow as it is, nevertheless is the key to the problem of modifying cultural patterns. Laws alone do not automatically bring about cultural changes. Civil rights legislation in the United States did not sweep away overnight the deeply entrenched traditions and patterns of behavior between blacks and whites. Time, education, and the mobilization of strong support to the American traditions of obedience to the law are causing change and will continue to bring about significant changes in the cultural pattern and behavior of individuals most affected by the legislation. It is only through education that any public attitude will undergo change.

Changing attitudes toward the insurance business

This nation's insurance industry has awakened belatedly to the fact that the culture of the United States embodies a permissive and somewhat hostile attitude toward the insurance business. Extensive efforts are now being undertaken to change the image of the business, thus modifying cultural patterns and producing human behavior more compatible to the continued existence of the private insurance industry as an important and continuing institution for human betterment. Organizations such as the Insurance Information Institute (organized in 1959 and representing over 300 insurance companies), have undertaken to attain better public understanding and acceptance of the insurance business. The institute's work in contacting young, precollege-age people is particularly important for a business which for many years largely ignored advertising and public relations activities which were not directly related to the immediate sale.

Other organizations are busily engaged in upgrading the insurance practitioner so that he or she will know the insurance business thoroughly and will recognize that continued livelihood depends upon socially sensitive conduct and resultant public acceptance. Important organizations in this category are the Insurance Institute of America, Inc. (I.I.A.), the American Institute for Property and Liability Underwriters, Inc., and the American College of Life Underwriters. Meanwhile, hundreds of American colleges and universities offer courses in risk and insurance. Colleges and universities account for millions of student hours of instruction each year. In addition, many company educational programs offer basic as well as intermediate and advanced courses in risk and insurance. Their influence and that of the professional educational organizations and the colleges and universities in the United States have an important impact upon public attitudes.

The tremendous influence of this education in modifying the cultural patterns of the United States cannot be overemphasized. Insurance Information Institute surveys conducted by the Opinion Research Center of Princeton, New Jersey, reveal that public understanding of property-liability companies has improved appreciably in recent years, primarily among college-educated persons. At the same time, public attitudes are undergoing perceptible change, and formal education reflects, documents, alters, and sometimes leads that change. The impact of education on the societal expectations of the American insurance consumer is a critically significant factor in today's insurance marketing environment. Consumerism has had a marked influence on today's business practices—an influence that is drastically affecting relations between business and its customers. This influence is nowhere more apparent than in the insurance industry. Long-standing contract and property law principles are breaking down and are being replaced by a "revolution of rising entitlement,"[15] where

---

[15] Martin C. Schnitzer, *Contemporary Government and Business Relations* (Chicago: Rand McNally, 1978), p. 501.

anyone who needs insurance is entitled to it, and anyone who is sick or injured is entitled to medical care, irrespective of traditional legal rights.

An entitlement is a right—a moral right and/or a legal right. When society begins to believe strongly that a person is *entitled* to something, this right usually manifests itself as a moral entitlement. "People generally, and probably correctly, look upon moral rights as the proper basis for legal rights in a just society."[16] When society begins to view certain services as entitlements, it is not long thereafter that the moral right is translated into an institutional guarantee, a legal right. Society's educational institutions constantly examine the concepts of rights and responsibilities and reflect and document trends and changes in a society's value system. No area of business and society relationships is more critical to the insurance industry than the changes that are occurring in public expectations and the effect that this revolution of rising entitlement is exerting on historic contract and private property law. The formal education programs provide the tools for examining the past, analyzing the present, and forecasting the future.

Rising expectations and higher levels of public education and awareness make it incumbent upon insurance claims persons to "aggressively pursue a path of continuing education," according to Frederick R. Hodosh of the American Institute for Property and Liability Underwriters and the Insurance Institute of America. Dr. Hodosh believes that success in insurance claims handling in the coming decades will be restricted to those men and women who are "willing to live up to tough educational as well as ethical standards demanded by society."[17] Change will be the norm, and business people must keep up with that change in order to survive. The growing demands on insurance claims representatives to exercise skill in human interaction in a changing environment as well as to demonstrate technical knowledge in loss handling necessitates intensifying the emphasis placed upon continuous formal education programs.

Any insurance executive who fails to recognize the significance of these formal education programs to his or her livelihood and to the

---

16 Ronald Yezzi, *Medical Ethics* (New York: Holt, Rinehart & Winston, 1980), pp. 22–23.

17 "Role for Adjusters to be More Important in 1980's—Hodosh," *Insurance Adjuster* (January 1980), pp. 8, 36–37, on page 36.

future of the insurance industry is truly shortsighted. The executive must realize that individuals behave within society as they are conditioned to behave by that society. Faith begets faith; confidence begets confidence; and sharp dealing begets sharp dealing. Each person's personality and his or her resultant patterns of behavior develop within the conditioning framework of society, and an intense study of that society is the individual's best guide to understanding human relations.

SUMMARY

A theory has been presented in this chapter that all human behavior is purposive—that is, it is not accidental or fortuitous. It results when men and women respond to the stimuli which act upon their drives and urges—the physical and social motives. These motives may be out in the open or they may be buried deep within a person's subconscious mind. Whichever the case, they are the key to human behavior, for human behavior is responsive to underlying human motives.

Perhaps the starting point in learning about human behavior, therefore, is to examine the "climate" within which the human mind develops, for it is here that our motives are formed and acquired. That climate is our environment, and that together with our heritage of genetic peculiarities, or heredity, is responsible for the formation of the individual's motives, which cause a pattern of behavior or adjustment which is called the *human personality*.

In this chapter an attempt has been made to examine this climate of heredity and environment and to explore the general and specific background influences which mold the mental peculiarities of individuals and make us respond in a characteristic manner. By exploring the climate within which a man or woman lives, the scientific observer is able to see that certain individual human behavior can be traced directly to that person's hereditary and environmental background, the breeding-place for human urges, desires, and wishes—the motives. The supposition is that by knowing the characteristics of a broad society, or of narrow subsocieties within the broad society, which generate human motives, the scientific observer can gain insight into the expected human behavior of any individual who is a member of the social group studied.

This process of tracing behavior back to its underlying causes is the essential problem confronted by any psychological theory. Further, that problem is to specify the conditions that will lead to a certain kind of behavior before it occurs, that is, to predict it.

Attempts to establish a formal science which will enable us to predict the behavior of our contemporaries have met with some success. This success has been achieved by the identification and establishment of the basic principles of human behavior. These principles, in turn, have been discovered only through the tedious process of systematic and laborious study and experimentation conducted by the behavioral scientists. The tool they have utilized has been the scientific method. Through its application scientists have analyzed the phenomena of human behavior, discovered the underlying factors giving rise to that behavior, and have grouped behavior into classifications to serve as a foundation for the establishment of principles of human motivation. The following chapter examines this application of the scientific method and the classification of human behavior. It sets the stage for the discussion in later chapters of communication, motivation, and the specialized techniques which can be utilized by the insurance claims representative in accomplishing the claims handling objectives.

2

Science and human behavior

Some seasoned claims representatives have become excellent students of human behavior. This has occurred only after years of trial and error and often-modified conclusions. Experience can be a painful teacher. The new or relatively new claims representative perhaps can avoid some of the hard knocks of experience by learning early some of the fundamental principles of human behavior which have been developed through the application of the scientific method.

To provide the reader with such an understanding, this chapter will examine methods whereby human behavior has been investigated, analyzed, and classified.

USING SCIENCE TO STUDY BEHAVIOR

Behavior is the key to human personality. To understand its complexities, we have developed the subject of psychology—the study of behavior. Because behavior is the subject of psychology, the latter has come to be called a *behavioral science* along with anthropology, sociology, and other related fields. To understand the behavioral sciences, we have had to develop and employ a controlled, orderly, and systematic method by which behavior can be observed, recorded, classified, and analyzed. This is called the *scientific method.*

The scientific method has evolved because of our need to establish facts and to formulate useful principles. Throughout history, humans have sought to explain phenomena in the often strange and disturbing world in which they have had to live. Primitive humans, for instance, gazing at the mysterious and capricious happenings of nature, sought to explain the forces which struck terror and wonder to their unsophisticated minds. The only means at their disposal to provide an explanation for such phenomena was simple observation and the logic and fertile imagination of impressionable minds.

Since simple observation did not provide primitive man with much explanation, he came to depend greatly upon his reasoning ability and his active imagination. He became so impressed with the value of reasoning, moreover, that he often paid scant attention to the source of the facts from which he reasoned. Out of his necessity to provide explanations which would afford him security from the uncertainties of his environment, he evolved his theories which provided him with comforting answers to the ever-arising questions which his mysterious world presented.

Even a few hundred years ago this process was about the only means available to humans to explain human environment. At the time of Columbus, for example, many people believed the earth to be flat and to be enclosed by a cover called the firmament of the heavens. If a mariner ventured too far into the seas, he would fall off the earth. Likewise, rain would occur whenever the firmament was opened.

By experience and the self-same logic of the mind, humans developed the scientific method. This method provided a control which enabled the scientist to disprove the conclusions which he or she formulated from simple observation. Experience and the work of scientists have disproved the ancient concepts that the earth is flat and that the heavens have a firmament. In like manner other facts have been established which disprove previous concepts. Oftentimes, however, the findings of scientists are subject to severe criticism when they contradict contemporary attitudes and beliefs. Darwinian geology and biology challenged the literal truth of Genesis, and Darwin's theories are unacceptable to many people in the United States. In like manner, since The Holy Bible (e.g., chapter 1 of Genesis) mentions the firmament of the heavens, some people believe there is such a firmament and consider it sacrilegious for others to question its existence.

The scientific method has for many years been applied to the natural sciences such as physics and chemistry. From such use have come the modern-day miracles of medical technology and space exploration. The use of the scientific method in the behavioral sciences has been relatively recent, and it is accurate to say that considerably less is known about the nature of human beings and the mysteries of the human mind than about the environment in which we live. Nevertheless, men and women have reached the frontier in the study of the human mind.

To understand the principles discovered in the study of humans and human behavior, we must familiarize ourselves with the scientific method itself and with the environment within which it operates. This will provide us with a greater appreciation of the value and the reliability of the psychological principles which have been formulated by behavioral scientists.

The scientific method

The scientific method is designed to enable us to handle a subject matter more efficiently. The environment in which the scientific method is employed is popularly pictured as a spotless laboratory replete with white coats, test tubes, and complicated apparatus. While this idea is not completely erroneous, it can be misleading. Legitimate and important scientific research can be conducted in many cases with no more equipment than a pen and a piece of paper. This is especially true in the behavioral sciences.

In applying the scientific method, we follow three steps:

1. We form a conjecture, i.e., a hypothesis, regarding some problem or question which has not been answered or which has been only partially or imperfectly answered.
2. We then investigate the phenomenon and experiment with it, utilizing scientific control of the factors or variables under observation.
3. Finally, we interpret and formulate principles which serve to explain the phenomenon which gave rise to the problem or question which stimulated the inquiry.

The scientific method itself is probably best viewed as a refinement of the "common sense" approach which is used in handling everyday problems. The refinement introduced into the scientific method is a special safeguard known as *experimental control*. In the introduction of the element of control to the course of an experiment, the scientist attempts to isolate one factor that may have some direct influence on a given phenomenon. The scientist hopes to determine conclusively whether that factor is truly significant. Consequently, when the scientist employs the scientific method, attempts are made to hold constant all factors which might conceivably be responsible for producing the phenomenon, except the one factor whose effects are being examined.

Utilizing this method of experimental control, the scientist often employs an experimental group and a control group when he or she conducts the inquiry. An attempt is made to assure that both groups are identical except in respect to the experimental variable. For example, if a group of school children of the same age, attending the same school, living in essentially the same type of neighborhood, with essentially the same standard of living, is split into two groups of equal number, it can be concluded that the two groups are substantially similar.

The next step is to introduce the experimental variable. This is what was done when scientists tested the new polio vaccines. Two substantially similar groups of people were obtained. The experimental group received the vaccine; the control group did not. Relative absence of polio among the first group was apparent. Thus, it was concluded that the presence of the experimental variable, the polio vaccine, prevented contraction of polio by individuals who received the vaccine. The spectacular success of these early experiments led to the widespread adoption of the polio vaccines.

In the behavioral sciences, unfortunately, it is difficult for us to control the human mind and behavior in a laboratory setting. Humans are not inert as are the materials of physics and chemistry. Because of the dynamic nature of the human mind and human behavior, and the difficulty in analyzing both, it often is difficult to obtain perfect control when applying the scientific method to behavioral phenomena. In other words, it would be erroneous to assume that we can apply perfect laboratory control to all of our experiments in the behavioral sciences and come up with some hard and fast rules, which, if applied, unerringly will produce certain results. Nevertheless, although we often cannot manipulate the variables in our research of human behavior, we often can recognize and measure these variables in light of their effect.

We apply the scientific method in our study of human behavior by utilization of *controlled observation*. Again, it is the factor of control which is all-important. It is the systematic methodology of science with its controls which makes the difference between simple, often faulty observation and scientific observation. Prediction, control, and formulation of general principles all must depend upon our accurate observation of facts.

Controlled observation

It is quite possible to apply experimental control in behavioral sciences, utilizing controlled observation. An example illustrates the point. A small boy drank some of his mother's perfume. He was rushed to the poison center of a nearby children's hospital where he was relieved of the contents of his stomach. One of the physicians mentioned the fact that the hospital had made it a practice in the past to give gifts to small children upon their release from all departments of the hospital. The staff discovered, however, that a disturbing number of the children admitted to the poison center repeated their previous errant behavior and again had to be rushed to the hospital.

Someone on the staff theorized that the expectation of receiving a gift might serve as a sufficient stimulus to motivate a child to repeat the previous behavior. The hospital decided to apply the scientific method in an experiment to test the theory. A control group and an experimental group were chosen. The control group was made up of all admissions to the children's hospital, with the exception of those children who came to the poison center. The latter made up the experimental group. The hospital discontinued the practice of giving gifts to those children who came to the poison center. Child patients in all of the other departments of the hospital continued to receive gifts upon discharge. The incidence of repeaters admitted to the poison center dropped sharply; there was no significant change in the pattern of children admissions in the other departments.

The principal variable factor in this case was the presence or absence of the gift. Its isolation and study by use of the scientific method proved the presence of the gift to be a significant factor in causing children to repoison themselves. The hospital continues to give gifts to discharged child patients in all departments except the poison center. Application of the scientific method to this particular phase of human behavior led to favorable results. Here the use of science was nothing more than controlled observation.

By using this type of controlled observation the scientist seeks to identify the uniformities in the behavior of people. The practicality of the theories of human behavior formulated by the scientist rests upon the ability of those theories to predict the behavior of an individual in real-life situations. Striving to gain insight into the subject of science and human behavior, the scientist is careful not to engage in the common practice of attributing to human behavior a single cause. This is a gross oversimplification, for, as mentioned previously, the human mind and behavior do not lend themselves to the ideal laboratory experiment.

Even with ideal conditions for controlled observation, the exact prediction of an individual's behavior is complicated because of numerous interacting variables. No matter how much we may long for simple explanations, we are faced with the realization that human behavior is complexly determined. Uncertainty, therefore, must exist when we attempt to predict individual behavioral phenomena.

It is important, however, for us to use the techniques at our disposal, for even though we are unable to predict phenomena with complete accuracy, approximations are of considerable value. For example, an actuary cannot predict mortality experience exactly, but because he or she is able to eliminate most of the error in predictions made, error can be compensated for by introducing a safety factor into the insurance mortality tables. Because of an ability to predict with some accuracy, the actuary has been able to create the highly essential institution of life insurance to lend security to our way of life.

Similarly, the engineer cannot rely upon the "exact" science of physics to reveal the exact maximum load-bearing strength of the bridge under construction. The bridge, too, is subject to variables. Because of the many interacting variations of stresses and strains, it is impossible to estimate the maximum load precisely. With the introduction of an adequate safety factor, however, the bridge can be used with confidence by the public.

In the behavioral sciences, likewise, approximations are of utmost value, and despite the variables which confound the best of theories, the principles deduced from application of the scientific method can be most helpful in the prediction of individual human behavior. Despite the limitations, applied scientific methodology can yield definite beneficial results in many areas of human activity.

SCIENTIFIC METHOD AND CLAIMS HANDLING

Psychology can be used by the millions, for the millions, or on the millions.
———Abraham P. Sperling

Some readers of the first edition of this book have expressed impatience and intolerance for the behavioral science approach to insurance claims handling, suggesting instead that the chapter be based upon "case histories" furnished by experienced claims people. Thus, we would turn to the "common sense" approach, "what everyone knows", "fireside induction," or "pop psychology." Let us examine the suggestions.

The "common sense" approach

In the early 1960s the author was asked to write some materials on the subject of the psychology of insurance claims handling. With a legal background and years of experience in handling claims, and with extensive aid from a practicing academic psychologist, the task seemed approachable. The author's first step in approaching the subject was to review the existing claims literature dealing with the subject. Here the research came to a dead end—the existing literature presented an irresolvable conflict of a variety of recitations of widely differing techniques and practices of experienced claims personnel. Of the literature reviewed, virtually every book or company manual written on the subject of insurance claims handling since the 1930s incorporated each author's personal experiences and philosophy regarding proper claims handling psychology, with little reference to authenticated behavioral research. In a typical claims handling book, for example, the author recounted the factual situations of a variety of claims episodes confronted, described how the author handled the situation, and then arrived at the conclusion that the author's claims investigation, negotiation, and settlement techniques were generally suitable for similar claims situations. The implication was that experience and "common sense" were the best teachers and were the most accurate guides to successful insurance claims handling. The episodal approach to teaching human relations and claims handling was entertaining, but few clear and concrete principles of human relations emerged to guide the claims representative who was reading such a book.

The psychology of insurance claims handling, however, like any other of the subareas of human psychology is an appropriate and fertile field for scientific research and principle formulation. Behavioral principles from other fields of human endeavor have clear and definite application to insurance claims handling. Mere recitation of experience, on the other hand, is sometimes repetitious and often without pedagogical or practical value. From recitations of experience it is particularly difficult to present an organized framework of rules and principles governing insurance claims handling. Further, "common sense" is not so common.

Reliance on the simple recitation of case histories furnished by experienced claims people without controlled observation and formulation of general behavioral principles suggests that we have nothing to learn from the behavioral scientists, ignoring their rich store of controlled laboratory research on human behavior. We understandably distrust the extrapolation of controlled laboratory findings to "real-world" situations because of the inherent ambiguities present in laboratory hypothesis and methodology. "Common sense" often seems to to be more reliable.

Scientific method: A guide

A prevailing conflict between the behavioral scientist and the common sense practitioner is the former's distrust of common knowledge concerning human conduct and the latter's reliance on it. Neither has a perfect solution to understanding human behavior. A clinical psychologist, Paul E. Meehl, admits, "While the sources of error in 'common knowledge' about behavior are considerable, the behavioral sciences are plagued with methodological problems that often render their generalized conclusions equally dubious."[1] In fact, the scientific method and its associated statistical paraphernalia do not insure a precise test of quantitative hypotheses, but rather allow

---

[1] Paul E. Meehl, "Law and the Fireside Inductions," *Law, Justice, and the Individual in Society*, edited by June Louin Tapp and Felice J. Levine (New York: Holt, Rinehart, & Winston, 1977), p. 10.

the scientist some basis for stating whether the evidence supports a particular hypothesis. It is common, however, for psychologists to report statistical probabilities at the 0.05 and 0.01 levels of confidence, indicating that they are certain 95 to 99 times out of 100 that their prediction is confirmed.[2]

We must not suggest that science provides absolute principles in forecasting and manipulating programmed human behavior. The scientific method is only a guide and an approximation. Nevertheless, it has value, and it has application which is frequently superior to the seat-of-the-pants, trial-and-error approach to insurance claims handling that depends upon years of experience before competence is acquired by the individual. Even universally held generalizations about the origins and control of human conduct should be subjected to quantitative documentary research and, where feasible, to systematic experimental testing. Since the balance of this book is based largely upon claims handling techniques derived from principles established by behavioral scientists, it is important and appropriate to spend some time discussing the scientific method and its relationship to the establishment of human behavior principles.

The occupation of insurance claims handling affords a rich field for us to observe, record, and analyze human behavior. Emotional experiences, resulting from bodily injury and loss of life and property, together with the adversary relationships created in insurance claims situations, produce a wide variety of behavior among the people involved. It is possible, therefore, to accumulate a considerable body of useful empirical evidence (observations from experience).

By using the scientific method and controlled observation certain conclusions or theories can be developed. The establishment of such theories enables the behavioral scientist to set forth principles which can be used to predict human behavior in a wide variety of circumstances. A knowledge of such principles and resultant ability to predict human behavior have unquestionable value for the insurance claims representative.

Controlled observation

The use of controlled observation in insurance claims handling is not something new. The claims person has over the years deliberately

---

[2] A. Daniel Yarmey, *The Psychology of Eyewitness Testimony* (New York: Free Press, 1979), p. 33.

or inadvertently applied some behavioral science methods to claims handling work. A simple case will help illustrate. When the claims person relies upon written statements, rather than upon recordings to record information, his or her equipment is a pen and a piece of paper. Suppose during a five-year period the claims person divides all witnesses encountered into two groups. Assume that the division is at random (i.e., not handpicked or preselected in any way). The claims person attempts to obtain signed statements from all of the witnesses. If an assumption is made that the claims person's approach is the same in all personal acts and language, then the percentage of signed statements obtained from each group is probably fairly identical (if it is further assumed that the claims person has a fairly large number of witnesses).

Suppose, however, that the clams person hands the pen to each witness in the control group and states, "Sign here, please." The language used when speaking to witnesses in the experimental group, however, is different. The claims representative hands the pen to witnesses with the words, "Would you please write your name here at the bottom?" He or she observes that more witnesses in the experimental group than in the control group sign statements. The experimental variable is the difference in language used in closing the transaction. Therefore, the claims person concludes that people have an aversion to the word *sign*.

In the simple illustration the experienced claims person, over a period of many months of trial and error, formulated a principle. Observation revealed that the most significant variable in the procedure of obtaining a signed statement seemed to be a simple matter of the language used. When the claims person said "Sign here, please," a proportionately larger number of witnesses balked at signing their statements than when the claims representative said, "Would you please write your name here at the bottom?"

When the claims person formulated this principle, he or she no doubt was intrigued by the fact that the first approach elicited different behavior from that which resulted when the second approach was used. The claims representative probably asked, "Why do people act so differently in two cases that are identical when all I have done is to change slightly the wording in my request? The only variation seems to be the word 'sign.' When I use it, I stimulate a negative response."

This curious claims person then began to explore why people responded negatively to the word *sign*. In his or her investigations it was discovered that people have been educated to fear the word. They have been told not to sign this and not to sign that. Movies, for example, have for years bombarded the public with scenes in which one of the characters announced firmly and melodramatically, "I'm not signing until I see my lawyer." Through simple observation the insurance claims representative formulated a principle which stated simply, "A person does not like to *sign* a paper; tell each person instead to write his or her name."

It is interesting to note that people have less reluctance to have their voices recorded than to agree to sign a written statement. According to figures obtained by the Dictaphone Corporation, approximately only 1 percent of witnesses refuse to be recorded, and this is a considerably lower figure than the percentage who refused to sign statements before recording equipment was introduced.[3] Witnesses seem to respond favorably when they are assured that recordings are more accurate than written statements and "you won't be misquoted."

Despite the growing importance of sound recordings, there remain many instances where signatures must be obtained in insurance claims work—written statements are taken under some circumstances, releases and other forms must be signed, etc. The new claims person, therefore, should be informed of the simple principle—that people don't like to "sign" papers. Equally important, the underlying reason for the principle should be explained to the new claims representative. The reason is simply that when the word "sign" is used, it triggers the emotions of fear and anxiety, which result in defensive behavior.

Similarly, people react with fear to the language used by the claims person when the latter seeks to obtain recorded statements. If the claims person approaches a witness with the remark, "I would like to record your statement," or if he or she states, "I would like to take your deposition," difficulty may be experienced in obtaining cooperation. The objectionable words are *statement* and *deposition*. They are "red flag" words and cause reactions of fear or anxiety. The word *statement,* while not objectionable to some people, tends to frighten others by the connotation of a formalized, legalistic undertaking. The use of the

---

[3] Letter from Eric A. Lamont, Executive Assistant, Dictaphone Corporation, November 10, 1964.

word *deposition* should be avoided for the same reason. Rather than using the objectionable words, the claims person would do well to say "I would like to record our interview" or "I will record our discussion."[4]

When the new claims person is taught the foregoing principles relating to these red flag words and the underlying reasons for the principles, knowledge is acquired about human behavior, and there is a greater understanding of how people will act and why people will act in a certain way in a given set of circumstances. Through a lengthy process of trial and error experience with such red flag words, insurance claims representatives have stumbled upon some important common sense stimulus-response relations which have practical application in claims work.

In drawing common sense conclusions, unfortunately, much error results. People are sometimes too hurried or careless to take the precautions provided by experimental control. Once they stumble upon what seems to be a solution, they are satisfied. They have not accumulated enough empirical evidence to arrive at meaningful conclusions. They formulate principles which are not solidly grounded in a large number of controlled observations.

A hypothetical example of a hastily drawn theory will illustrate the point. A man may see two events occur in sequence and may mistakenly conclude that the first event leads to the second. He may not bother to determine if the second event also occurs when the first is absent. A man in his use of an elevator may make this error. Suppose that he has used the elevator for the past year. Each time the door has opened, the elevator has been waiting there for him. One day, however, he rushes out of his office, observes that the elevator door is open, steps in and plunges five floors to his death. The elevator wasn't there. It was being repaired three stories higher.

The man always had observed previously that two events occurred in sequence. The first event was the arrival of the elevator. The second event was the opening of the door. He concluded that the two were related. The mistake that he made was assuming that because the second event (the door opening) had occurred, the first event (arrival of the elevator) necessarily had taken place. He mistakenly concluded

---

[4] See John L. Cote, "Recorded Statements," *Insurance Law Journal,* no. 449 (June 1960).

that the two events would always occur in sequence. He had formulated an erroneous theory.

In the foregoing example unwarranted conclusions were drawn from simple observations which lacked the essential element of control. Such trial and error mistakes are common and contribute greatly to the confused and sometimes contradictory nature of the ideas provided by common sense. The claims person's absolute reliance on common sense principles is fraught with danger. The difficulty in using common sense is that it is as uncommon in the insurance claims handling job as it is elsewhere. Human relations principles must be formulated from *controlled* observation. As a Harvard psychologist has stated: "The intuitive wisdom of the old-style diagnostician has been largely replaced by the analytical procedures of the clinic . . . scientific analysis of behavior will eventually replace personal interpretation."[5]

The scientist, through the use of the scientific method, largely eliminates trial and error mistakes. The scientist resembles others in that he or she attempts to describe and to explain the events that take place in the surrounding environment. The basic difference between these methods, however, and those used in the "common sense" approach is in the scientist's utilization of the scientific method and its important element of experimental control as a safeguard against inaccurate description and erroneous explanation.

A further example illustrates the difference between simple observation and scientific control. You may make it a point never to attempt to settle liability claims during the morning hours. You may have observed that compared to other claims persons who attempt to settle liability claims during any hour of the day that you are unusually successful. You may attribute this personal success to the fact that you never attempt to settle claims during the morning hours. You have concluded that the afternoon or evening hours are best.

From the standpoint of the behavioral scientist this conclusion is unwarranted because you have failed to use experimental control. Until you make an equal attempt to settle a corresponding number of claims during a corresponding number of morning hours, there is no justification for the conclusions that you have made from personal experience. Through scientific experimentation, you may find that

---

[5] B. F. Skinner, *Science and Human Behavior* (New York: Macmillan, 1958), p. 19.

morning hours are excellent for settling claims and that your relative success is due to other factors. On the other hand, you may discover that scientific experimentation bears out the previous conclusions reached from personal experience.

STIMULUS-RESPONSE RELATIONS

The scientific method is important to us in the study of human behavior because of its use in uncovering elemental principles which serve to explain human behavior. Since psychologists, such as Freud, Adler, and Jung, have concluded that all behavior is purposive—caused by some motive or human drive—it should be possible to make some progress in identifying motives or drives which cause behavior. Some success should be realized in identifying motives or drives and in tracing these causative factors to their effects, the resultant human behavior.

This, essentially, is what the behavioral science of psychology attempts to do. In trying to identify causes and in predicting effects, psychologists attempt to establish *stimulus-response relations*. These relations define and explain the responses which can be expected to result when certain stimuli are introduced in close enough proximity so that an individual's sense organs can be employed.

To suggest that a given stimulus will always create a given response or effect is admittedly presumptuous. Human behavior and its causes cannot be reduced to such simplicity. We can push a button on a vending machine and usually get what we order but to produce certain predictable human behavior is not so simple. A person cannot always push the right button, or use a certain stimulus, and produce a predictable response. We can frequently anticipate a predictable response to a certain stimulus. For example, a claims person can offer to pay a claim in full (the stimulus), and the response is quite predictable—the other person is relieved and pleased. We can almost label this a *programmed stimulus-response reaction*. The more unpredictable reactions are more difficult to handle.

Despite the obvious shortcomings, the reader is again reminded that human behavior is purposive and is caused by certain factors, which if stimulated, will produce behavior. The mechanistic approach, therefore, has definite theoretical application in the study of human behavior and in the motivation of other people. As for its value in insurance claims handling, a theory becomes valuable to us as soon as it raises the accuracy level of the predictor to any extent.

If we can predict human behavior roughly by knowing ahead of time which stimuli usually produce which types of responses, we are well on the way toward exercising greater influence over other people. If human behavior can be predicted within the stimulus-response framework, an understanding of the framework will help educate the claims person to be more effective in the insurance claims handling job.

The starting point in learning human behavior principles is to understand the nature of stimuli and the possible resultant responses. Since repeated reference will be made to these two terms, it will be helpful at this time to provide a definition and some examples. A *stimulus* is something which changes in a person's physical environment and excites his or her sense organs, resulting in some sort of response. A *response* is a manifestation of human behavior. An alarm bell, for example, is a stimulus; the person responds by jumping out of bed. Criticism of a particular claims person by an immediate supervisor probably will prove to be a stimulus; the response, however, may be somewhat unpredictable. The criticized person may buckle down and try to improve personal performance, or he or she may counter with some criticism of the claims supervisor and quit the job. A bullfighter may use a red cape and considerable movement as a stimulus; the bull responds by charging.

There are useful stimulus-response relations which can help the claims person. For instance, an insurance claims representative may display the company's check prominently in one hand and a pen in the other; this often serves to stimulate a claimant to settle the insurance claim, the sought-after response—the behavior.

BEHAVIOR

Behavior is not limited to human behavior but includes the behavior of all organisms. The scope of the study of psychology embraces a wide range of phenomena, dealing not only with human behavior but also with the behavior of a variety of other living organisms. Lower animals are studied in the hope that facts and principles may be discovered which will be applicable to the human organism and will shed some light on the character of human beings and their complex behavior.

Behavior itself is defined as the observable responses of the organism under study. The term *observable* is important, for human personality is judged by observation, and the scientific method is based upon the foundation of controlled observation. Through observation behavior can be recorded, analyzed, and classified, and then useful principles can be formulated from such observation.

One of the big problems in studying behavior is the complexity of the task. A complete description of an organism's behavior is impossible. Fortunately, it is not necessary to record all of an organism's activities for the study to be meaningful. The psychologist only needs to record those responses which have significant implication and lead to fruitful hypotheses. Only those responses which are recurrent and have apparent relation to recognized stimuli are truly significant. Thus, controlled observation permits fairly reliable conclusions to be drawn from these connected or related phenomena.

Behavior traits

In controlled observation the behavioral scientist tries to determine which behavior events or responses are distinctive and characteristic of the organism under study. Aspects of a person's observed behavior, for example, which are judged to be reasonably distinctive and characteristic, are considered to be the substance of his or her personality.

These distinctive and characteristic responses (behavior patterns) are called human *traits*. They are persisting characteristics of personality which, in principle at least, can be measured. A person's personality, therefore, is the aggregate of his or her traits, and other people's judgment of a person's personality is based upon their concept, whether erroneous or not, of what traits a person possesses.

This process of judging human personality according to observable behavior traits is an integral part of the ranking function which goes on in a society. The individual who is most skilled at demonstrating or revealing either actual traits or feigned traits and is most successful in conveying an image of favorable personality, will often rise in the human pecking order because of personal skill in communication and persuasion. Another individual, who "hides his or her light under a bushel basket" because of inability or unwillingness to communicate, is judged according to the traits which are observable to other people. Thus, the first person may be judged by contemporary society to be "high-powered" while the second person is "low-powered" and usually is relegated to the lowest level of the pecking order.

Describing human behavior

One of the apparent problems in categorizing personalities is to establish a meaningful list of behavior traits. The unabridged dictionary contains approximately 18,000 adjectives that are used to describe how people act, think, perceive, feel, and behave.[6] Another 4,000 words might be accepted as possible traits. When synonyms and rare words are culled, the list is reduced to about 170 words. This still produces room for considerable disagreement in any attempt made to reduce the number to *the* final list. As a matter of fact, if there is anything about which psychology textbook writers seem to disagree, it is in their listing of characteristic behavior traits.

It will not be unusual, therefore, if the reader discovers that the listing of behavior traits used in this book may not completely correspond to the trait categorization used by some other writers. The author's choice of traits, however, includes those which are mentioned most frequently by many writers and which are particularly relevant to the field of insurance claims handling. A study of these traits should open the door to the development of useful stimulus-response relations which will be helpful in the work of the claims representative.

Classifying stimuli and responses. A starting point in the discussion of behavior traits is to proceed with a classification system. Since any attempt to make a complete classification of behavior traits would be foolhardy, the discussion will be limited to a few important general traits. These traits, suggested by William E. Jaynes, involve three different kinds of stimuli.[7] The stimuli and examples of each are shown in Table 2–1.

---

[6] Taken from a psychological study which lists in alphabetical order no less than 17,953 names of human traits. G. W. Allport and H. S. Odbert, "Trait Names" *Psychological Monographs*, 1936, vol. 47, no. 1, whole no. 211.

[7] Willis Rokes and William E. Jaynes, *The Human Factor in Insurance Claim Adjusting* (Bryn Mawr, Pa.: Insurance Institute of America, 1963), pp. 40–42.

Table 2–1

Stimuli	Examples
Personal contacts	Questioning another person.
No personal contacts	
Complex problem	The problem of computing your income tax.
	The problem of dictating an analytical investigation report.
Simple problem	The problem of how to file a daily report or a claims form.
	The problem of how to sharpen a pencil.

Analysis of Table 2–1 indicates that there are essentially two types of stimuli—those which come from personal contact with other individuals and those encountered in isolation. The latter are divided into two subcategories—complex problems and simple, routine problems (both noncontact stimuli).

Although the distinction between complex problems and simple problems is not clear-cut, it serves as a rough guide for classification. Since the personal contact stimuli are so important to the area of insurance claims handling, discussion of them will be reserved until the next section where they can be explored in detail. The noncontact stimuli will be explained briefly here. Although they are important, they do not involve the complex interaction of human personalities found in the personal contact situations.

Complex problems are solved when an individual uses the personality traits of comprehension or imagination. These traits, when applied to problems, result in certain types of responses. The trait of *comprehension* is a tendency to grasp problems effectively and to find solutions quickly if ready-made answers are available. The person who is high in comprehension is sensitive to problems and rational in attempts to solve problems. He or she has considerable reasoning ability usually coupled with a large vocabulary. As a consequence, this person may be characterized as being *intelligent* or having high *general mental ability.*

Imagination, on the other hand, is the tendency to produce ideas in the attempt to solve the complex problem. Alternative approaches will be used to solve the problem. Some of these approaches will be highly novel or unusual. People of this sort often are characterized as *idea people.* If the trait of imagination is not balanced by comprehension, the person may be seen as one who is full of wild ideas or who is highly eccentric.

Simple problems are the other noncontact stimuli, and they usually are handled when an individual uses one or the other of two personality traits: (1) attention to detail and (2) manipulative skill. *Attention to detail* is a trait involving rapid detection of flaws through visual inspection and a good short-term memory. A person who scores high in this regard is well-suited for jobs involving much routine paperwork or a great deal of close inspection of objects. This trait sometimes is called *clerical skill* or *perceptual ability.*

Manipulative skill is the tendency to be well coordinated in moving about and in handling objects. Two important forms of this trait are finger and manual dexterity. A person with manipulative skill is well suited for physical activity or work in the trades. When a person has a high degree of this trait, coupled with a great deal of attention to detail, he or she is referred to as a *craftsman* or *artisan.*

Noncontact stimuli and responses are quite important in insurance claims handling. Much of the work of the claims person is noncontact work—preparation and evaluation of investigation reports, inspection of damage and the physical aspects of a claims situation, perhaps some typing, and so forth. The area of human behavior which most concerns the claims representative, however, is that relating to personal contact stimuli and the resultant responses. It is the traits and responses encountered in personal contact which present the claims person with the problems of communicating with and of motivating other people.

Traits encountered in personal contact.   It is in the area of personal contact with insureds, claimants, witnesses, and other people that the claims person experiences the greatest challenges, frustrations, and measure of success or failure. All of the noncontact functions of the claims handling job are merely corollaries to the principal function— that of contacting people, communicating with people, and influencing people. It is this fundamental fact which makes it important for the claims representative to understand the nature of the behavior traits, and the resultant responses, which are stimulated by personal contact in insurance claims situations.

As mentioned earlier, we could list a large number of adjectives which describe how people act, think, perceive, feel, and behave in a personal contact relation with other people. Such an approach has little to commend it. To have value to the claims person, a simpler approach will be used, making it easier to classify traits and to establish simple claims handling principles. To have practical value they must relate to the basic objective of communicating and influencing people in claims situations.

To accomplish this objective, consequently, it is self-evident that the claims person must be dealing with people who are amenable to the claims person's efforts at communication and persuasion. If a claimant, for example, is submissive and considerate when approached by the claims representative, the claims handling job will be much simpler than if the claimant is inconsiderate and highly assertive. Thus, two extremes of behavior confront the claims person—extreme submissiveness and extreme assertiveness—and these will be combined with variations of considerate or inconsiderate behavior traits on the part of the other person. The relationship is depicted in the behavior model in Figure 2–1.

The trait of *assertiveness* is the tendency to dominate personal contacts with others, particularly by talking most of the time. The highly assertive individual finds it easy to put ideas into words, and this person tends to keep the air filled with the sound of his or her voice. While this individual feels comfortable in any social situation, he or she gets the greatest amount of enjoyment out of being in the

FIGURE 2–1.   Behavior model

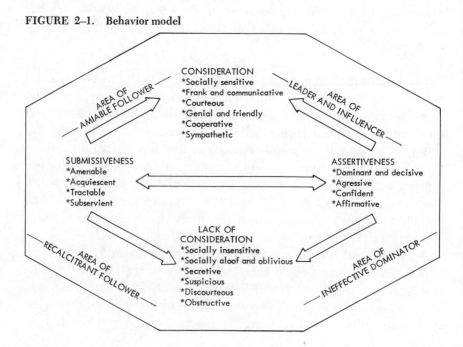

spotlight. If this assertive tendency is not balanced with consideration, this person can become obnoxious to others.

If, however, the "right" blend of consideration is mixed with this trait of assertiveness, this individual will be a natural leader, capable of communicating with and influencing other people. If his or her social sensitivities are highly developed, and these are combined with unusual communicative and persuasive abilities (assertiveness), this leader is said to possess *charisma,* an extraordinary personal and "spiritual" power conceived of as belonging to those exceptional individuals capable of securing the allegiance of large numbers of people.

In leadership, therefore, the trait of consideration is highly important, as was observed in an earlier section in Chapter 1 dealing with "The leader." If we wish to lead, influence, and motivate others, we must be sensitive to the needs of other people. We must be considerate. The considerate person, by being friendly, courteous, attentive to, and sincerely interested in the comfort and well-being of other people, has demonstrated traits of consideration that make other people feel good. Through such traits the considerate person attracts followers, for he or she appeals to the self-interests of others.

The prototype of the successful claims person, then, is one who combines assertiveness with consideration. This person's antithesis, or opposite, is the meek, submissive, and withdrawn individual who dislikes personal contact and who seeks emotional outlet in introvertive pursuits. On the other hand, the perfect claimant, insured, or witness, from the claims person's viewpoint, is the submissive, highly considerate individual. If the latter is highly assertive and inconsiderate, the claims representative's efforts to communicate and motivate probably will meet with considerable difficulties.

Behavioral trait approach and claims handling

All the world's a stage, and all the
  men and women merely players.
They have their exits and their entrances;
And one man in his time plays many parts ....
              ——Shakespeare

There is considerable evidence to the effect that personality traits in a given individual have a certain degree of constancy. William James concluded that "by the age of thirty, the character has set like plaster, and will never soften again."[8] Freud believed that an individual's personality was molded by the end of childhood, a view shared by many psychologists.

There are a number of recent studies, however, that suggest that the constancy of personality is not as great as was once generally believed. Although basic traits of submissiveness and assertiveness have a certain constancy and we carry throughout our lifetime many of the traits acquired during childhood, it should not be concluded that a person's personality is static and always fits into a certain niche. Human personality has its dynamic aspects. Our individual responses differ according to each of the situations which confront us, our emotions at a particular time, our physical condition, and a host of other circumstances.

It is this very factor which affords the claims representative a fertile ground upon which he or she can use personal knowledge of human behavior. If, for example, the claims person can develop personality traits of consideration and assertiveness and can develop skill in utilizing these traits to communicate with and to motivate others, these efforts will assure success in the claims handling job and in all of the claims person's human relations. If through skillful maneuvering we can reduce the assertiveness of a claimant and at the same time induce the latter to behave with more consideration, efforts expended in handling an insurance claim are much more likely to meet with success.

The significance of the behavioral trait approach to the claims representative, therefore, is its value in everyday application. If a stimulus can be classified, and if it is known that the stimulus usually will elicit a certain response, we may well use this knowledge to gain some control over the behavior of those people with whom we must deal from day to day. In other words, the claims representative can bring about a certain response by employing a certain stimulus.

In contacts with others, therefore, the claims person must develop skill in observation. He or she must be able to understand the nature of the human traits observed; they provide a useful thumbnail sketch of the people the claims person meets. If a claimant is inconsiderate, highly assertive, and completely lacking in comprehension, it is obvious that the claims person will have to employ an entirely different

---

8 William James, *The Principles of Psychology* (New York: Dover, 1950), p. 121.

approach than that used in talking to a considerate and completely unassertive person who has presented a claim.

The observations made above are nothing more than a restatement of the techniques which have been used by successful people in any field of endeavor. In fact, they merely reiterate basic principles of human dynamics which have been employed by human beings for thousands of years. Unfortunately, however, the basic, familiar things often are taken for granted, so that their importance is obscured. Reading about those things causes us to think and to analyze them and to evaluate our comprehension, awareness, and current use of important principles which are so vital to our daily existence.

SUMMARY

As humans developed, explanations were sought for the things which were observed and experienced through the human's elemental senses. His or her physical world, the strange and mysterious manifestations of the elements, or "mother nature," particularly gave cause for concern and insecurity. The person's inquiring mind sought answers. Order, security, and certainty were needed in the harsh world in which humans eked out a livelihood.

Having no rational explanations available, the human depended upon personal powers of observation and individual reasoning ability to supply "reasonable" answers. More often than not, simple observation did not provide adequate explanations, and the person resorted to a highly active imagination to explain the things observed. Through imagination primitive humans were able to formulate comforting explanations for the apparently hostile forces which added hardship to everyday life. If a storm, an earthquake, or some other force of nature threatened, for example, the person reasoned that it was because he or she had offended the gods. The individual's unsophisticated mind reasoned that amends would have to be made to placate these deities by doing something that would please them. Accordingly, elaborate rituals were fashioned which paid homage to the gods, and things of value—property or human sacrifices—were offered.

Still relying upon observation as the primary tool, over the centuries humans developed a methodology, a "scientific" method, which permitted the individual to introduce controls to observation so that unwarranted conclusions could be guarded against. As the person observed, recorded, classified, and analyzed a vast number of events, he or she was able to disprove many early conclusions which were nothing more than fantasies born out of uncontrolled imagination. As the person learned more and more about the surrounding physical environment, this knowledge permitted the individual to harness many of the forces which previously were not understood and were feared.

As individuals gained competence in understanding the external world in which people lived, each person also turned inward to the strange internal world of the workings of his or her mind and those of contemporaries. The individual sought to explain why people behave as they do. The scientific method appeared to be the best means by which answers might be acquired. Through controlled observation attempts were made to record, classify, and analyze behavioral phenomena. Men and women developed the behavioral science of psychology—the study of behavior.

This relatively new science presented people with many obstacles. Rather than physical phenomena, the individual was now dealing with things which came about because of the workings of the mind. The problem of controlling variables within a reliable framework was difficult. Holding all elements constant while one variable was extracted and examined presented formidable problems.

Despite difficulties, however, the behavioral scientist has been able to amass a reliable body of empirical facts relating to human behavior. The scientist has applied the scientific method in controlled observation of these facts; the facts have been classified; and reliable principles have been formulated which provide guideposts for understanding the behavioral phenomena. These guideposts help the scientist to explain why people think as they do, why some people see and hear things that other people do not perceive, why people forget things they have seen or heard, and why people resort to so many variances of human behavior under different circumstances.

The guideposts formulated by the behavioral scientists have direct application to the work of the claims person. Rules relating to the proper taking of written or recorded statements, the avoidance of "red flag" words which may generate negative reactions in other people, and other "do's and "don'ts" of claims work are founded upon well-defined psychological principles. Many of these principles have been adopted by claims representatives only after much trial-and-error experience.

Such trial-and-error experience often can be avoided by the claims person if he or she will become familiar with some of the basic principles of human behavior. For example, if we as insurance claims representatives have a rudimentary knowledge of what specific things (stimuli) cause certain behavior (responses), we are well on the way toward exercising greater influence over other people. By selecting appropriate stimuli, we often can motivate others to respond in a desirable fashion. To do so, we must have a comprehension of elemental behavior traits. We also must understand what characteristics we ourselves should have in order to motivate insureds, claimants, witnesses, and other people. By developing and utilizing appropriate personality characteristics, we will possess valuable tools to perform the functions of the claims handling job. Further, through comprehension of human behavior principles, we will be better qualified to observe and to analyze other people, and our efforts to influence others are much more likely to meet with success.

In the following chapter some of the scientific findings relating to claims handling will be explored. It will be seen that many of the variations existing in human behavior result from differences in acuity of a human's elemental senses. Other variations result from the manner in which people interpret phenomena which have been experienced. Still other variations have a bearing upon human value judgments and an individual's personal concept of and standards of human integrity.

3

The imperfect human

*Don't tell me of facts, I never believe facts; . . . nothing is so fallacious
as facts, except figures.*

——Sydney Smith

One of the most peculiar phenomena which has plagued and
fascinated lawyers, judges, and juries for centuries has been the
fantastic variation in "fact" appearing in the testimony of people
involved in legal controversies. Some of these variations are no doubt
accounted for by the deliberate falsification of testimony—perjury.
Most of them, however, are honest variations caused by the inherent
nature of human beings. We are imperfect creatures. We have senses
of smell, touch, taste, hearing, and sight, but they play tricks on us.
Furthermore, we have the ability to reason—to think—a unique and
highly desirable ability which has permitted us to build superb civil-
izations and to master our environment.

Unfortunately, our ability to think is not always advantageous. Our
thought processes do not always permit us to record and to relate
accurately the true character of those images or stimuli which affect
our senses. Through our reasoning processes, we interpret a stimulus—
we think about it and color it because we interpret it according to our
own background of experiences, thoughts, and emotions. In so doing,
we modify or completely change what was originally perceived. As a
consequence, imperfections in human sensitivity, our peculiar mental
processes, and dishonesty, result in wide distortions and differences in
perception, recollection, and narration.

The foregoing is most important to the business of insurance claims handling, for it accounts for many of the difficulties which confront us as claims persons in disposing of insurance claims. Sometimes what a person hears or sees and what he or she reports are entirely different. Likewise, recollections of an earlier event may be so intermingled with the memory of subsequent events that a narration of the earlier event will be distorted. To illustrate, we may recall a point which helps to support an insured's case. We review the claims file, recollecting that witness number one will corroborate the fact. When we read or listen to the statement of witness number one, we find no mention of the fact. Reviewing two more statements, we finally find the fact mentioned in the statement of witness number four. Irritated, we mutter, "I could have sworn that it was witness number one who said it."

Such an occurrence is not uncommon for a claims person who is reviewing a stale file. He or she probably has handled dozens of other claims since last reviewing the stale file. The factual information of subsequent cases alters the claims person's recollection of the case in hand.

The new claims representative is often baffled when discovering that several witnesses to the same accident have widely differing versions of what happened. When witnesses have different versions of an accident or when someone changes a personal account of an event, the distortion process is probably at work.

People differ in ability to perceive what has happened, and they differ in their recall of the "facts" of an accident or an occurrence. These differences result because people have varying degrees of awareness of the stimuli which influence their behavior.

The new claims person must be familiar with the nature of this distortion problem and be acquainted with the many factors that distort "facts." He or she will soon discover that truth is obscure and relative; "facts" vacillate; and evidence is fleeting. If the claims person will become familiar with the imperfections of humans, he or she will be better equipped to go about the claims handling work. Equally important, the claims representative will not be so bewildered when experiencing the manifestations that characterize the imperfect human.

To acquaint the reader with "the imperfect human," this chapter analyzes some of the psychological explanations for differences that exist in a person's perception, recollection, and narration. It also examines individual variations in human integrity. These differences and variations are the natural phenomena of mankind.

IMPERFECTIONS IN HUMAN SENSITIVITY

Between the idea and the reality
. . . Falls the shadow.
————T. S. Eliot

The human senses do not always give us a correct impression of actuality. People sometimes think they have seen things which never existed. This is perfectly natural—it is common in every person to experience distortions because of the imperfections of his or her own senses. Likewise, we frequently fail to see or fail to hear things which are there to be seen and heard. These failures spring from the imperfections of our elemental senses. They result in what psychologists call *breakdowns in reality contact*.

Sense imperfections, distortions, or weaknesses fall into two broad classes—passive and active. Passive distortions will be discussed in this section. They are called *passive* because they are for the most part unavoidable. Examples are those things which we *fail to notice* through our senses and the things which we *forget*.

The sudden, split-second happening of accidents, accompanied by distracting stimuli, militate against attention. The human mind experiences great difficulty in focusing intently upon all of the circumstances that transpire in the course of such a brief moment of time. There is not sufficient time for a person to pinpoint attention on one thing so that the sense receptors can be fully employed. The result, understandably, is relative inattention and imperfect perception. The person, as a consequence, fails to perceive much of what transpired.

We are attentive to stimuli, and we see and hear, more or less, according to the circumstances of each individual situation. We may react to a stimulus but at the same time have no appreciation of its source and no memory of its occurrence. A person in a state of sleep, for example, may start at a loud sound, or turn away from a bright light. We are aware of the sensation and we respond to the stimuli, but our perception is poor and our recollection may be nonexistent. In this case, there is complete inattention.

The above example suggests that a person's state of attention or intensity of attention is extremely important in determining the quality of perception and recollection. If our mind is ready—that is, if we are motivated—to devote our entire attention to a certain stimulus, the quality of our perception and our recollection probably will be relatively good. This very fact explains why people don't perceive and recollect the factual circumstances of accidents and occurrences which give rise to insurance claims—they may be unable, unprepared, or unwilling to concentrate on a stimulus.

Another factor that influences perception is an individual's past experiences. In some respects people are born with the ability to perceive some phenomena. For example, it is generally believed that perceptions of space and motion are innate characteristics. In other respects, however, what an individual perceives will to a great extent be dependent upon the person's past experiences—frames of reference. Thus, experience has a profound influence on the individual's susceptibility to the perceptual constancies and the optical illusions, both of which are discussed later in this chapter.

Poor reception

Poor reception is the failure to notice a stimulus when it is initially presented. A sensation is not received. A person fails to see what is there to be seen, fails to hear what is there to be heard, fails to smell what is there to be smelled, and so forth.

Poor reception sometimes results when the stimulus is so weak or lacking in intensity that a person fails to notice it no matter how hard he or she tries. The stimulus may be so weak that no one could possibly notice it. A whispered remark, for instance, would not be noticed by a person standing 200 yards away.

Likewise, poor reception results when an individual lacks the necessary sensitivity—our sight may be bad; our hearing may be imperfect; and so forth. There is the story about an Army sergeant at an induction center who once asked an inductee to read an eye chart. The sergeant asked, "What is that first letter on the chart on the wall?" The recruit supposedly squinted and replied, "What wall?" In this case necessary sensitivity or acuity was totally lacking.

In other cases failure to notice a stimulus results when the stimulus occurs in combination with a number of other distracting stimuli. A witness to an auto accident, even though he or she has an unobscured view of the accident scene, often will miss seeing much of what happened because the witness is watching something else. The sleight-of-hand expert recognizes this type of distortion when drawing attention to the left hand while the right hand is accomplishing the sleight of hand. In the eye chart example the stimulus received was so weak that the individual failed to notice it no matter how hard he tried, while in the auto accident and the sleight-of-hand examples, the witness' attention was focused elsewhere.

Receptor organs.   A starting point in exploring sensitivity or acuity is provided by noting that the body is equipped with a variety of receptor organs, such as the eye and the ear. These organs are located in the nose, mouth, skin, and other parts of the body. Each receptor is particularly sensitive to one specific stimulus which is most likely to activate a given receptor. This is known as the *adequate stimulus* for that receptor. Light is the adequate stimulus for the eye, and sound is the adequate stimulus for the ear, for example.

Receptors may respond to stimuli that are not in the adequate category. When receptors respond in this fashion, the sensation experienced by the individual is the same as that ordinarily derived from the receptor. In this way pressure on the eye can lead to the sensation of light even though the eyelid is closed.

Thresholds.   More important, however, is the existence of the threshold or limen. This is the point at which a decrease in stimulation results in the individual's failure to identify the stimulus even though some stimulation is still present. If a sound of a specific pitch is relayed to an individual through a set of earphones and then made softer and softer, the threshold is the point at which the individual no longer hears anything.

The significance of the threshold to the insurance claims representative is that it helps explain why witnesses see things differently and why people behave differently. Thresholds can be measured, and these measurements show marked differences between people. Some people can see better than other people; some have better hearing.

Highly sensitive detection devices measure relative hearing abilities of a person on sound pitch and tone. One person can appreciate a wide range of sound produced by modern high-fidelity phonograph records and equipment. A second person is really no better off than he or she would have been in the days of the old wind-up phonographs.

Thresholds place limits on reception by completely eliminating our ability to detect and report some of the events that occur around us. The nearsighted individual without glasses and facing the scene of an accident some distance away cannot give a good account of what happened because of his or her visual threshold. An insurance claims representative may have a witness who renders an excellent account of the "facts" of an accident, even though the witness was some distance from the accident scene. The witness perhaps has excellent long-range vision. On the other hand, he or she may have merely a flair for histrionics and a good imagination. The claims person must determine which is the case.

A special kind of threshold which deserves some mention is the *differential threshold*. This is the smallest difference that an individual can reliably detect between two similar stimuli. For instance, the smallest difference that we can detect between two weights is our differential threshold for these weights. The size of the differential threshold is directly proportional to the magnitude of the stimuli involved in determining the threshold. Thus, with small weights most people can detect a very slight difference accurately, but with large weights—such as two heavy suitcases—the difference must be sizable before it can be detected accurately.

Span of attention.   Another kind of failure to notice stimuli has to do with limits to *span of attention*. Most people cannot perceive more than about six or seven separate stimuli at one time. For example, if you throw a handful of marbles on the floor, you will find it difficult to view at once more than six marbles, or seven at the most, without confusion. Consequently, where an accident occurs in a few seconds, it is not unusual that a witness will miss many of the things that happened. Another witness will observe some of the things missed by the first witness, but the second witness, too, will fail to notice everything. *Perception is always selective.* "We see that which interests us, and we become aware of details we have earlier learned to discern."[1]

When stimuli can be grouped, some of the disadvantages of limits to span of attention can be eliminated. For example, the task of the general trying to determine the position of his army would be insurmountable if he had to think of 30,000 separate units. The task be-

---

[1] Arne Trankell, *Reliability of Evidence* (Stockholm: Beckmans, 1972), p. 17.

comes manageable, however, when he thinks of three divisions, each composed of various smaller groups.

Forgetting

Forgetting is the second type of imperfection in human sensitivity. This passive distortion of stimuli results when memories decay or deteriorate. It results primarily because of the passage of time. It is not, however, merely the passage of time that determines the extent of forgetting which takes place. Rather, it is what happens during the time that has passed. When a thing is learned, it will be retained and remembered well if nothing new is learned immediately thereafter. For this reason, retention is best when a person sleeps immediately after learning. While ordinary daily activities bring sizable losses in memory with disturbing rapidity, forgetting is greatly reduced during sleep.

Because of this phenomenon, there may be good reason for a student who is preparing for an examination to do his or her studying the night before the exam, and then get a good night's sleep, and review the material in the morning rather than to attempt to study early in the morning before the examination. If we attempt to learn early in the morning and then drive to campus, park the automobile, talk to classmates, and then sit down to take the examination, we may discover that the subsequent experiences immediately following the learning of the subject material may inhibit our ability to recall that material. This process is called *retroactive inhibition*, which means "we forget because what we do inhibits retroactively what we have learned."

Considerable scientific evidence suggests that old memories are displaced or impaired by new memories rather than simply being erased by the mere passage of time. Francis L. Wellman, the eminent authority on cross-examination, has written: "Not only does our idea of the past become inexact by the mere decay and disappearance of essential features; it becomes positively incorrect through the gradual incorporation of elements that do not properly belong to it . . . extraneous ideas become imported into our mental representation of a past event."[2] Courts are aware of the interaction between memory of

---

[2] Francis L. Wellman, *The Art of Cross-Examination*, 4th ed. (Garden City, N.Y.: Garden City Publishing, 1936), p. 158.

events and imagined memory of these events, and they accept the statement made by William James in 1890 that "Ere long fiction expels reality from memory and reigns in its stead alone."[3]

The memory curve. It is possible to graph the memory process. This can be done with a memory curve which represents quantitatively the extent of forgetting and the extent of retention present over a period of days since the original learning. The illustration in Figure 3–1 presents a typical example of a memory curve. The curve reveals that forgetting takes place at a rapid rate initially and then falls off as time elapses. The rate of forgetting decreases so that the curve becomes rather flat after the expiration of several days.

Memory image clarity. Courts are concerned with the clarity of a witness's memory image. *Memory image clarity* describes how distinctly a witness can give an account of an episode observed earlier. The deterioration of images caused by forgetting is a serious problem for the claims investigator.

Figure 3–1. Ebbinghaus memory curve

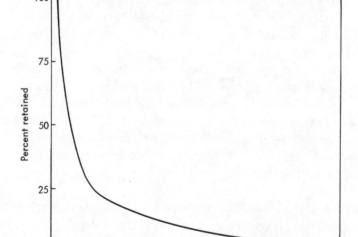

Time in days since learning

---

[3] William James, *The Principles of Psychology* (New York: Dover, 1950), p. 373.

Memories of experiences fade away. Memories of mundane, every-day data, such as dates, time of day, day in the week, or place of occurrence fade rapidly. "With a further lapse of time the sequence of events begins to become rearranged. At the same time the details become confused or fuse together to form new units."[4] When considerable time has elapsed, only the core of the experience remains.

The best way to bring forth "the lost anchorage" of certain events is to preserve the facts with a witness's statement. This can only be done if the claims representative is timely in securing the statement. Delay dims memory image clarity.

The timely statement.   In the ordinary waking state most forgetting takes place immediately after perceiving or learning. This explains why it is so critical for the insurance claims representative to investigate promptly. We must obtain statements while the information perceived is still fresh in a witness's mind, before time and the happening of subsequent events dim the latter's memory and impair his or her ability to recollect. Edgar James Swift, a professor of psychology at Washington University, wrote: "My experiments have proved to me that, in general, when the average man reports events or conversations from memory and conscientiously believes that he is telling the truth, about one-fourth of his statements are incorrect, and this tendency to false memory is the greater the longer the time since the original experience."[5]

As more time intervenes, the process of memory deterioration slows down. There is even an indication in some cases that something perceived will never be completely forgotten. This fact has caused courts of law to permit the introduction of statements for their evidential value in legal proceedings. A statement, taken promptly, can be used and will be of considerable value in refreshing the memory of a witness.

Rule of past recollection recorded.   Even where something has been completely forgotten by a witness, the statement preserves the evidence. This is made possible by a peculiar doctrine of law adopted in England by the middle of the 18th century, and in America by 1814.

---

[4] Trankell, *Reliability of Evidence*, p. 21.

[5] Edgar James Swift, *Psychology and the Day's Work* (New York: Scribner, 1918).

This doctrine established the "Rule of Past Recollection Recorded."[6] The rule takes care of a situation where a witness recorded the facts witnessed soon after their occurrence, but the witness does not now recall the fact from memory.

It further provides that if the witness recalls that the report was accurate when made, his or her statement may be admitted as direct evidence. The majority of cases and the Model Code of Evidence take the view that the written record is a more accurate source for obtaining the truth than the partially refreshed memory of the witness. The Rule of Past Recollection Recorded may be said to be in complete harmony with the view held by psychologists that a person may recognize a fact as being true, although the person does not now recall the fact from memory.[7] This rule should be of interest to the reader, for some claims representatives believe that statements can be used only to "refresh" the memory of witnesses.

When a witness is not present in court, however, a statement that does not qualify as a deposition usually is not admissible as direct evidence. The witness must be present to testify that, according to his or her best information and belief, the facts recorded in the statement were accurate when the statement was taken, although the facts are no longer remembered.

A timely statement, therefore, has value in refreshing the memory of a witness whose memory of an earlier event has deteriorated (under the Rule of Present Recollection Revived),[8] and under the Rule of Past Recollection Recorded, a statement may be admitted as direct evidence. A third value of the timely statement is its use in impeaching a witness whose testimony of facts is inconsistent with the recitation of facts which appear in the witness's statement. The statement will serve to discredit the oral testimony by reflecting on the credibility of the witness.

Doctrine of recent fabrication. Another peculiar rule of law also is relevant to the subject of memory deterioration. This is the Doctrine

---

[6] *Shove* v. *Wiley*, 35 Mass. (18 Pick.) 558 (1836); *Haig* v. *Newton*, 1 Mill Const. 423 (S.C., 1817); *Pearson* v. *Wightman*, 1 Mill Const. 336 (S.C., 1817); 3 Wigmore, Evidence Section 735, 3d ed. (1940).

[7] For discussion, see Robert M. Hutchins and Donald Slesinger, "Some Observations on the Law of Evidence—Memory," *Harvard Law Review 41,* 860 (1928); C. W. Luh, "The Conditions of Retention," *Psych. Monogr.,* vol. 31, no. 142 (1922).

[8] See 3 Wigmore, Evidence, Section 725, 3d ed. (1940).

of Recent Fabrication.[9] This rule of law recognizes that memory decays and sometimes deteriorates completely. The rule reflects the fact that courts view with considerable suspicion the testimony of a witness who remembers the minute details of an occurrence of, for example, two or three years previous, giving the location and speed of colliding vehicles, the actions and relative positions, and distances apart of the objects and persons, all with assumed photographic accuracy. A witness's testimony (unsupported by a memorandum to refresh a memory) of specific, detailed "facts" related to an event which occurred months or years previously is suspect as proper evidence.

The foregoing adds more reason to the mandate that the insurance claims representative must make immediate contact with witnesses and obtain timely statements, untainted by the passage of time and new memories. It also permits the claims person to evaluate objectively the oral remarks of claimants who report minutely the detailed facts of their cases after considerable lapses of time.

SUMMARY

In the previous sections we have examined the inherent imperfections in human senses. We may not see things or hear things because of the limitations of our sense receptors. It is only when stimuli reach those receptors with sufficient intensity that an adequate impression is made. Likewise, the perceptivity of the sense receptors must be adequate to pick up stimuli which have the necessary intensity. In addition, the proper receptors must be "tuned in" to respond to those stimuli. Attention must be focused on those stimuli. Unless an adequate stimulus reaches an adequate sense receptor, there is little likelihood that the reality of a situation will be perceived by anyone.

Imperfections in human sensitivity present obvious negative implications for the quality of a person's ability to sense and remember the circumstances of an accident or an occurrence. Equally important, however, are the further aberrations which distort actuality when the person's peculiar reasoning process records and interprets a stimulus which it has received. These aberrations are the "active distortions" that result in "breakdowns in reality contact." They are our mental

---

[9] *Robb* v. *Hackley*, 23 Wend. 50 (N.Y., 1840); see discussion in William T. Fryer, *Selected Writings on the Law of Evidence and Trial* (St. Paul, Minn.: West Publishing, 1957), pp. 367–71.

peculiarities, the mental distortions that influence perception, recollection, and narration.

MENTAL DISTORTIONS

In controversial moments
My perception's very fine;
I always see both points of view,
The one that's wrong—and mine!
————Anonymous

Our reasoning process can do much to alter the "facts" of a situation. Our hearing and our sight may be excellent; we may have had an unobscured view of everything that transpired during the happening of an accident. Adequate stimuli may have reached our sense receptors with sufficient intensity so that we should have received an accurate image of what actually happened.

Nevertheless, when we receive the stimuli in the form of a "sensation," our minds then begin to interpret the phenomena that we have witnessed. Through our own mental peculiarities we introduce *active distortion*, and we color the things seen and heard. We give them a new flavor or tone. Our interpretation actively distorts original impressions received and can produce completely erroneous results, or "breakdowns in reality contact." The same impressions, moreover, will be interpreted differently by two different individuals and by the same individual at different times, and result in varying degrees of distortion.

Such distortion shows up in a number of forms. Examples of

Table 3–1. Mental distortions

Common active distortions	Uncommon active distortions
Perceptual constancies:	Delusions
Color constancies	Hallucinations
Size constancies	
Shape constancies	
Illusions	
Defense mechanisms:	
Repression	
Projection	
Identification	
Rationalization	
Displaced aggression	

common forms of active distortion are perceptual constancies, illusions, and defense mechanisms. Uncommon forms of active distortion include the delusions and hallucinations which are sometimes found in the behavior of persons with severe emotional disturbances (see Table 3–1). The common and uncommon forms of distortion wreak havoc upon a person's ability to report reality.

Because we color sensory impressions according to our own experiences, attitudes, beliefs, and background, we often see things as we think they appear and want them to appear, rather than as they actually appear. This manifestation was recognized many years ago by Sir John Romilly when he wrote:

> It must always be borne in mind how extremely prone persons are to believe what they wish. It is a matter of frequent observation that persons dwelling for a long time on facts which they believe must have occurred, and trying to remember whether they did so or not, come at last to persuade themselves that they do actually recollect the occurrences of circumstances which at first they only begin by believing must have happened. What was the result of imagination becomes in time the result of recollection. Without imputing anything like willful and corrupt perjury to witnesses of this description, they often in truth bona fide believe that they have heard and remembered conversations and observations which in truth never existed, but are the mere offspring of their imaginations.[10]

Imagination plays an important role. Edgar James Swift wrote: "Imagination reconstructs evidence with many omissions and substitutions, and the final outcome is likely to be so different from the original as to be almost unrecognizable."[11]

Thus, psychological distortion results from our mental interpretations of the stimuli we have received. In this process of *perception* each individual attempts to "make sense" out of the sensations received by his or her sense receptors. We "perceive," or comprehend, according to our individual mental interpretations of sensory impressions received by us. Through an unconscious process the original impression received by the individual will take on all of the color of frames of reference, motives, past experience, and all of the peculiarities and character of the individual mind that received the impression.

---

10 16 Beavan, 105.
11 Swift, *Psychology and the Day's Work.*

Frames of reference

Frames of reference have to do with all of the background experiences, education, mental conditioning, ideas, prejudices, and moods that influence a person when he or she interprets phenomena. Our orientation to life affects our ability to perceive, or comprehend, the sensory impressions received by our sense receptors. Our ability to interpret such impressions is limited by our own peculiar mental makeup—our own personal way of looking at things. We, unfortunately, are restricted in our interpretation to the tools at our command—our frames of reference.

Language and the extent of one's vocabulary probably have a strong influence on how individual persons view their environment.[12] The number of descriptive words—nouns or adjectives—that a witness can command to interpret and narrate phenomena have a definite bearing on the witness's reported perception of an event. Thus, a witness with extensive familiarity with automobiles—makes, models, years of manufacture, special features, and so on—may appear much more perceptive in describing an automobile accident than a witness who can not recall much about the motor vehicles except their color. Similarly, an English-speaking person who reports that there was snow on the ground at the time of an accident is more limited in perception and interpretation of the weather and physical conditions than an Eskimo would be, for Eskimos have seven separate words in their language for "snow" and are more apt to provide a better description of the snow conditions that are present at the scene of an accident.

Sometimes we will have our own individual and unique interpretation of a sensory impression. At other times, we and a group of other individuals all will interpret a phenomenon in a similar manner because we all have been subjected to the same orientation or conditioning process. We "see things the same way."

An interesting experiment illustrates how a group has been conditioned by its society to interpret things in the same manner. A group of students was shown a photograph of a bearded man. Before they were shown the photograph, they were informed that the man was a skid row bum who had been arrested for drug addiction. After a brief showing of the photograph, it was withdrawn and then the

---

[12] B. L. Whorf, *Language, Thought, and Reality*, ed. by J. B. Carroll (Cambridge, Mass.: M.I.T. Press, 1956).

students were asked to describe in writing the man's physical features, the clothes he wore, and any physical surroundings which appeared in the photograph.

The written descriptions typically characterized the man to be of dissolute appearance and of poor health. He was described as having unkempt hair and beard. His clothing was described as being worn and of apparent poor quality. The physical surroundings and background in the photograph were described in vague terms or in terms as having some relation to the typical locale of a skid row bum. After the descriptions had been read to the students, they were informed that the man was in reality a member of a mountain-climbing team that had just returned from scaling a well-known mountain peak. The man was a picture of obvious health and strength; he was wearing expensive outdoor clothing; his hair and beard had been recently trimmed; and the photograph was taken in front of a cottage at a mountain resort.

Thus, through past experiences and training the group had been conditioned to interpret according to preconceived attitudes that actively distorted each individual's ability to perceive accurately. In this example, suggestion conditioned the group to interpret in light of their previous knowledge, experience and prejudices, regarding the subject suggested. They built a mental picture of what they *expected* something *should* look like. In the process, they completely misinterpreted the actual visual impression received by their sense of sight.

Principle of expectancy—Mind-set

Expectancy frequently distorts perception and interpretation, and this is common in the phenomenon known as *stereotyping*. In one study the researcher had subjects briefly view a pictorial scene of people riding a subway train, in which a black man stood facing a white man. The white man held a razor in his hand. When the subjects were asked to indicate who on the train held the razor, half of the observers reported that the razor was in the hand of the black man. Some subjects reported that the black man was brandishing the razor wildly and others remember him as "threatening" the white man.[13]

---

[13] G. W. Allport, and L. F. Postman, "The Basic Psychology of Rumor," *Transactions of the New York Academy of Sciences, Series 11*, vol. 8, (1945), pp. 61–81.

When the claims representative asks a witness to explain what happened in a given situation, and the witness proceeds with his or her narration, there are three mental processes involved: (1) memory obviously becomes important, but it is the memory of the witness's (2) perception, and (3) interpretation of that perception. Because of the witness's frames of reference, an expectancy mind-set is present. Consequently, a witness will interpret a personal observation according to what the witness has learned in the past and what the witness expects to happen in the future.[14] Thus, so-called credible witnesses often report what they believed must have happened according to their expectancy mind-set, rather than what they actually observed.[15]

This *principle of expectancy* creates serious distortions. Rather than seeing what is there to be seen, people see what they expect to see. Thomas F. Staton suggests that this tendency upon the part of mankind is no doubt responsible for some of the hunting accidents which occur. He uses a deer hunting accident as an example. During the off-season men spend the long days talking about their deer hunting adventures. They look forward to the hunting season in the fall of the year. As the season approaches, their excitement and expectations for an exciting hunt increase. This excitement and expectation reaches a climax as the hunter walks quietly through a grove of trees, shouldering his rifle. Ahead he sees movement and a dim silhouette. He wants to see a deer, and he expects to see a deer. Staton says: "He honestly believes that he actually sees a deer, not realizing that he only sees a hazy silhouette which reminds him of the shape of a deer."[16] When he shoots, a human scream corrects his misperception. This reliance on expectations is well demonstrated in the perceptual constancies, which will be discussed next.

Perceptual constancies

And finds with keen discriminating sight,
Black's not so black—nor white so very white.
                    ——Canning

---

[14] A. Daniel Yarmey, *The Psychology of Eyewitness Testimony* (New York: Free Press, 1979), p. 49.

[15] R. Buckhout, "Eyewitness Testimony," *Scientific American*, vol. 231, no. 6 (1974), pp. 23–31.

[16] Thomas F. Staton, "What People See and Why," *Psychological Factors In Insurance Law* (Houston, Texas: Federation of Insurance Counsel Foundation, 1963), p. 41.

The *perceptual constancies* cause people to describe a phenomenon more in terms of the properties that it ought to have rather than in terms of those that it actually has. Because of the constancies, we build mental pictures of the way we think things should be in the world around us. For example, a white shirt viewed in a shadow is described as white despite the fact that it really appears blue. The grass seems green at night despite the fact that at low levels of illumination everything is gray. Both of these mistakes are illustrations of *color constancy*.

In addition to color constancy, there are two other types of perceptual constancies—*size constancy* and *shape constancy*. Size constancy leads to incorrect reports of the relative size of familiar objects when these objects are viewed under unusual circumstances. A familiar face, for example, tends to seem larger and closer than it in fact is.[17]

Shape constancy causes the observer to expect that objects will not change their expected nature. This helps the magicians. Even a beginning Houdini can switch hats, for example, and his audience will tend to think that he is still using the same hat without the eggs, rabbit, and assorted odds and ends.

A story attributed to Cordell Hull[18] tells of a veteran attorney who was seated on a porch late one afternoon with two other men. A sheep trotted by. One of the attorney's companions remarked, "That sheep has been freshly shorn."

To this the attorney countered, "We know only that it has been shorn on *this* side." He refused to concede a condition that he could not see. The other side of the sheep was not visible. His companion because of his reliance upon constancies did not question any other possibility but that the sheep had been fully shorn. In his experience a sheep had always been fully shorn or it was unshorn. The idea that it might be shorn on only one side did not enter his mind.

His observation and remark were natural because of the reliance people place upon the constancy of a familiar state of facts. The truth is, however, that if the sheep had been shorn on only one side, the perception of the observer easily could have been distorted because of his reliance upon constancies. The attorney might well

17 See Clifford T. Morgan, *Introduction to Psychology* (New York: McGraw-Hill 1956), pp. 176–77.

18 U.S. Secretary of State, 1933–44; Nobel Prize winner for his work in building the organization that resulted in the United Nations.

have asked his friend, "Did you really see a fully shorn sheep or did you merely rely upon a partial view to make your conclusion that it was fully shorn? In other words, did you allow constancies to distort your perception, thus causing you to believe you saw something which may not have been present?"

The various constancies can at times produce highly erroneous descriptions of environment. They are not, however, entirely without value. To live in a world without these constancies would be a frightening experience. Every change in stimulation would give rise to a completely new description. A house viewed from one side would not appear to be the same house if it were viewed from the other side. It would be nearly impossible to say what color anything was, and so on. The best conclusion, then, seems to be that the constancies are a mixed blessing. At times they give comfort and produce correct descriptions. On other occasions they foster a belief in continuity which is unjustified.

Suggestion and leading questions

Our perception also is susceptible to suggestion. Ideas can be implanted in a person's mind so that his or her perception of sensory impressions will be influenced by preconceptions. These cause interpretations that will result in complete distortions of reality. The power of suggestion cannot be overemphasized in this process of extracting reliable information from witnesses.

Experiments demonstrate the great influence that context exerts upon the choice of the reaction word. In other words, the nature of the questions put to a witness can predetermine his or her response. Preliminary interviews with police officers, insurance claims representatives, friends, and relatives, all afford full play to suggestion and evoke verbalization on the part of a witness. This verbalization can, in effect, be so distorted by suggestion and leading questions that it will replace the original sensory impressions received by the witness. By the time the person reaches the witness stand, attorneys can well question whether the witness's verbalizations at that time are based upon his or her recall of the event or upon recall of the former verbalizations.

For this reason an insurance claims representative interested in securing another person's version of facts must be most careful that ideas and impressions are not implanted in the other's mind. Despite the fact that the question and answer method has been so extensively, almost invariably, used in legal proceedings, obviously it can distort reality. Modern thinking on the part of the courts and the bar commends the use of the narrative form in eliciting information from witnesses. The practice of recent years to require a witness to respond to questions only and to prevent the witness from "telling his or her own story" has thus turned full circle to the practice recommended in 1810 by Judge Zephaniah Swift in his *Digest* in which he wrote: "In the examination of witnesses admitted to testify, the proper mode is to permit them in the first place to tell their stories in their own language."[19] Because of the psychological effects of suggestion and leading questions, a witness's own narrative will be much closer to the truth than his or her version of the facts usually brought forth by question and answer.

The question and answer process is of unquestionable value in the claims handling process, however, in keeping a witness on the subject and in developing and extracting information from the witness. The claims person, nevertheless, must be ever-mindful of the distortion that can be introduced into the picture if questions are colored in such a way that they implant new interpretations in the minds of the witness.

Principle of closure—logical completion mechanism

Closely related to the subject of perceptual constancies and the principle of expectancy is the *principle of closure*. Our ability to see an object is affected by a tendency to "make sense" out of whatever we see. This tendency is explained by the principle of closure. In the absence of information which we need to "round out the picture," we tend to make up or guess at the facts. We tend to fill in the gaps. Arne Trankell calls this tendency *the mechanism of logical completion*. He states:

> Since we can only cope with a limited number of signals that reach us, there will always remain gaps to be filled with appropriate material in order to make the observations conceivable to us. This is usually attained by means of arbitrarily chosen details with which we combine

---

[19] Zephaniah Swift, *Digest* (1871 ed.; first published in 1810), p. 771.

Figure 3–2   Figure 3–3

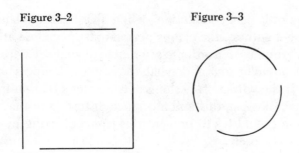

the authentic fragments into chains of events which are logically understandable. However, such chains need not necessarily correspond with the real course of events.[20]

Rather than leave something incomplete and fragmentary, we will unconsciously supply what we have not actually seen, or do not remember, in order to have a satisfyingly complete picture. Figure 3–2 and 3–3 illustrate how closure works. Although Figure 3–2 is not a square, the reader sees it as a square, because he or she fills in the blank spaces. Figure 3–3 is perceived as a circle.

This principle has definite application to insurance claims handling situations. A witness may think he or she saw something when in fact only fragments of the entire picture were seen. In filling in the gaps, the witness may come up with some erroneous conclusions. In one case, for example, eyewitnesses reported that they saw an automobile driven onto a frozen lake, and while racing at a high rate of speed, break through the ice and disappear. Three or four people reportedly were in the car at the time that it went under.

The report touched off an all-night search by skin divers. They discovered that no one was in the vehicle nor did it appear that any one had gone down with it. The automobile had been driven onto the ice, and possibly it had been driven at high rates of speed along the ice. From all appearances, however, the occupants had left the vehicle before it went through the ice. Although the witnesses did not see this latter part of the incident, they attempted to provide a complete explanation of what had happened by filling in the gaps in what they had actually seen. It resulted in some mistaken conclusions.

The insurance claims representative must always be mindful of this

---

[20] Trankell, *Reliability of Evidence*, p. 18.

"mechanism of logical completion" while investigating claims. While interviewing a witness, the claims person must pay close attention to the witness's responses in order to attempt to distinguish between what the witness *actually saw* and what the witness believes *must have* happened. If the witness is fleshing out the fact situation in order to make it appear logical, this will introduce distortion to the facts. The claims person should try to prevent this from occurring by questioning the witness closely.

In an actual case, a witness was riding in a taxi, and an automobile in front of the taxi came to an abrupt halt. The left rear door of the vehicle flew open; a man lay unconscious on the street.

The witness reported that the man either fell out of or was thrown from the vehicle. What actually occurred was different. The vehicle driver had tried unsuccessfully to avoid hitting the man who was crossing the street without looking. The witness saw the open door of the car, and he saw a man lying in the street. He fleshed out the fact situation and arrived at a totally logical, but erroneous, conclusion.

To guard against this phenomenon or tendency of a witness to fill in the missing gaps requires close attention to detail and an alert awareness on the part of the claims person. He or she must be ever watchful for signs that the witness is fleshing out the story. When it appears that the witness may be reporting something that *probably* happened, the claims representative should inquire, "But, did you actually *see* that?" A step-by-step breakdown of the logical sequence of events reported by the witness should be undertaken by the claims representative, inquiring at each step whether the witness actually witnessed each event.

Illusions

Illusions, like constancies, are caused by the distortion that a person's reasoning process introduces into a situation. Although a phenomenon is perceived clearly, we make a mistake in judgment when we interpret that phenomenon. This judgment is not a conscious evaluation; rather, it is caused by the manner in which a person's nervous system is structured. In certain circumstances a misleading stimulus causes the mind to be deceived.

The most common of the illusions are visual or auditory in nature, but other senses are subject to illusions. Two of the optical illusions

Figure 3–4   Figure 3–5

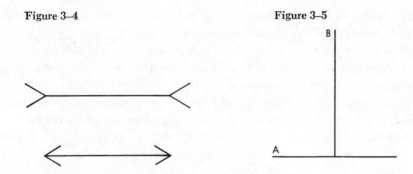

appear in Figures 3–4 and 3–5. In Figure 3–4, most people would estimate that the top horizontal line is the longer of the two. A simple
measurement will reveal that both lines are of the same length. In like
fashion, line A of Figure 3–5 appears to be shorter than line B. They,
too, are of the same length. In both examples the observer's judgment
has been deceived by the misleading nature of the visual stimuli.

Other illusions affect a person's perception of distance or affect his
or her depth perception. For example, an object partially covering
another is seen as closer. The more detailed and salient the features
of an object, the closer it appears to be. The lower of two objects is
also perceived as being closer. Light and shadows on edges and curves
promote the appearance of depth.[21] Illusions can materially affect
motor-vehicle driving performance by creating visual distortions,
resulting in distance or depth misjudgments on the part of the driver.
The effects of these illusions on the perception and interpretation of
phenomena by witnesses should be quite apparent.

Defense mechanisms

The defense mechanisms present by far the richest store of examples where we actively distort the impressions received by our sense
receptors. These special behavior patterns have come to be called
defense mechanisms because they serve to defend or protect us against
the anxiety which we might otherwise suffer from our true motives.
The claims representative should be interested particularly in these
special forms of human behavior, because he or she often is confronted

---

[21] A. Daniel Yarmey, *The Psychology of Eyewitness Testimony* (New York: Free
Press, 1979), p. 38.

with manifestations of defense mechanisms in day-by-day dealings with insureds, claimants, and witnesses.

The use of defense mechanisms is common. Much of the irrational behavior which the claims person sees during the course of claims handling work can be explained by these peculiar mental distortions. Furthermore, since behavior is purposive, a claims representative's familiarity with the types and nature of the defense mechanisms will aid considerably in understanding why people act as they do in the various situations encountered. Knowing the cause or the purpose of the unusual or "irrational" behavior of others should be invaluable to the claims person who seeks to bring an insurance claim to a successful conclusion.

Six specific defense mechanisms deserve special attention: repression, perceptual defense, projection, identification, rationalization, and displaced aggression. These will be discussed in turn, and appropriate claims handling examples will be used to illustrate these distortions.

Repression.   Repression is probably the simplest of the defense mechanisms. It is a type of forgetting. Earlier in this chapter the subject of forgetting was discussed in some detail. It was described as being a *passive* process which took place by the passage of time and by the influence of subsequent experiences. In repression there is an *active* type of distortion which results in forgetting.

The phenomenon of repression was first discovered by Freud. Out of this discovery developed the practice of psychoanalysis. Freud reasoned that the mental distress suffered by his patients was caused by traumatic experiences which persisted in their subconscious minds. Although his patients apparently could not remember the disturbing experiences, the technique of psychoanalysis enabled his patients to recall the forgotten events. Freud therefore concluded that the events originally had caused such distress and anxiety that his patients had pushed them from their conscious minds. To avoid anxiety, a patient would forget an experience—the patient repressed the memory of the event from the conscious mind.

In this form of forgetting, a person denies ever having received a stimulus—an impression of some happening. We do this not only in talking to others but also in our own thinking. It is this peculiar behavior on the part of others which sometimes complicates the work of the claims representative. For example, the claims person may be questioning the passengers of an insured motor vehicle following an accident. Improper driving on the part of the insured may have caused the accident. A passenger, when friendly to the insured driver, may experience distress and anxiety over the prospect of having to "tattle," or inform on the insured.

Instead of pointing the finger of guilt at the insured driver, the passenger will rise to the defense of the driver. The passenger subconsciously represses the actual facts of the accident. In place of the actual circumstances, he or she may relate a general belief that the insured driver, a personal friend, was driving carefully, is a careful driver, and has always driven carefully on previous occasions, even though other evidence completely refutes these statements.

It is difficult to determine when a witness is lying deliberately and when he or she simply has repressed memory of what actually did take place. There are cases, nevertheless, where repression, rather than deliberate falsification accounts for distorted "facts." While repression is easily distinguished from the other defense mechanisms, it is not so easily separated from forgetting. The repression label is usually applied when loss of memory is much more rapid and complete than in the usual passive process of forgetting.

An extreme form of repression is illustrated by the *hysterical reaction.* This is one of the psychoneuroses and occurs when a person converts motivational conflict into physical symptoms. The symptoms have no biological basis; they simply are devices for coping with conflict and anxiety. The person represses conflict by resorting to physical symptoms which effectively dispose of conflict and anxiety. The particular symptom that the hysteric employs may first occur by accident or may follow real physical illness or trauma.[22] For example, a man may sustain disabling injuries in an automobile accident. Long after he has recovered from the injuries, he, nevertheless, may complain of them. They serve to satisfy other wants. They have given him the love, care, and attention that he had lacked prior to the injuries. They also may serve as a means to punish those who have the work and expense of caring for him, or they may protect him from anxiety-producing situations, such as a job, school, or social relations.

Perceptual defense.   Closely related to repression is the phenomenon of *perceptual defense.* In repression the man or woman uses the

---

[22] Morgan, *Introduction to Psychology,* p. 267.

device of forgetting to reject the things that cause anxiety or discomfort. In perceptual defense, however, the person does not see things which are personally unpleasant.

People tend to become "blind" to objects they prefer not to know about. Don E. Dulany, Jr., has demonstrated that people's ability to perceive a triangle diminished gradually if they received an electrical shock at the same time the triangle was flashed before their eyes.[23] The unpleasantness of the electrical shock which accompanied the viewing caused the subjects to see the triangle less clearly. As Staton observes, "Extrapolation of this fact to draw the conclusion that a witness will tend not to see what is unpleasant to him or what he would prefer not to see is reasonable, and is substantiated by investigations in the field of clinical psychology."[24]

Researchers suggest that witnesses engage in multiple levels of perceptual processing. A witness will stop looking at something which he or she considers to be stressful or upsetting. A threatening or unpleasant stimulus already received is rapidly processed in the mind and rejected, and further threatening or unpleasant stimuli are perceptually avoided.[25]

It would be impossible in a given situation for a claims representative to ascertain whether poor perception of a witness was caused by repression or by perceptual defense. It is important, however, for the claims person to recognize that these two psychological phenomena may account for the fact that a witness is unable to relate the circumstances of an accident in which he or she had a clear and unobstructed view.

Projection. Projection is a somewhat more distinct form of behavior than either repression or perceptual defense. In projection, we attribute our own feelings to other people or objects. This is done without any real awareness on the part of the individual that such a process has been set in motion.

Projection is called a defense mechanism, because we protect ourselves against our own anxiety-producing characteristics by projecting

23 Don E. Dulany, Jr., "The Place of Hypotheses and Intentions: An Analysis of Verbal Control in Verbal Conditioning," in Charles W. Eriksen, ed., *Behavior and Awareness* (Durham, N.C.: Duke University Press, 1962), pp. 102–29.

24 Staton, *Psychological Factors in Insurance Law*, p. 38.

25 P. Suedfeld, M. H. Erdelyi, and C. R. Corcoran, "Rejection of Input in Processing of an Emotional Film," *Bulletin of the Psychonomic Society* 5 (1975), 30–32.

those characteristics to other people. Thus, a person who is not a good mixer, who is not interested in other people, and who is unfriendly and indifferent to other people, will conclude that other people are unfriendly and hostile. This tendency to project one's own faults to other people is a common malady. A person who attributes his or her social inadequacies to the unfriendliness of others does not fully realize that *people like people who like people.*

Everyone has bad days when other people seem to be impatient, grouchy, ill-tempered, inconsiderate, unfriendly, uncooperative, and mean. If a man walks into a store with a sullen look and an impatient manner, he will probably walk out of the same store with a poor opinion of the sales personnel of that store. He has been the author of any misfortune which befell him in the store. If, however, he walks in with a big smile, a cheery greeting, and a considerate and friendly manner, the chances are much better that he will receive considerate treatment.

A claims representative in an untalkative, gloomy mood one day may keep an appointment to discuss settlement with a male claimant. Although the claimant may act the same on that day as he did on two or three previous occasions, the claims person may conclude, "He is certainly in a poor mood today. He won't smile, and he seems on edge. I had better put off settlement negotiations until later." The claims person has projected his or her own feelings to the claimant. This has resulted in a distorted interpretation of actuality.

Identification. Where repression and projection often cause personal difficulties, identification can be a most desirable form of response. Identification is similar to projection but is, in a sense, its opposite. In identifying with another person, we take on the other person's feelings as if they were our own, and we behave accordingly.

True identification involves complete acceptance of the other's feelings and a total failure to comprehend the actual origin of the feelings. A good example of this type of behavior is the sharing of the feelings of friends and relations. Because of the necessity to defend one's own motives and emotions, a person will adopt completely the viewpoints of others which may be entirely contradictory to impressions received by that person's sense receptors.

Identification can cause problems for anyone attempting to obtain fair and impartial testimony of the facts of an accident or occurrence. Wellman calls this tendency of witnesses to identify as "unconscious partisanship."[26] Because of it, witnesses in and out of court, in "the cause of righteousness," conceal some facts and color or change other facts, resulting in serious distortions of reality.

The insurance claims representative will find that through identification close friends and relatives of an insured or a third party claimant become so involved in a case that it hinders the claims person's efforts to secure evidence and dispose of claims. For example, a claims person, accompanied by a court reporter, may enter a hospital room and begin to question a party. A visiting relative, who was nowhere near the accident scene and knows nothing about the accident (except through hearsay), will inject himself or herself into the conversation and proceed to answer the claims representative's questions, render opinions, and in general complicate the latter's job. The same friends and relatives also will feel so strongly about the case that they will advise a claimant freely about the merits of the claim, its monetary value, and the best procedure to follow in extracting a settlement.

When we identify so closely with a given situation that we lose contact with reality, we tend to indulge in flights of fancy and imagination. In other words, we permit personal mental processes to interpret phenomena in such a manner that the original impressions received by our sense receptors are completely ignored. Through imagination, artificial impressions are substituted in place of the original impressions. Before long, fiction expels reality and reigns in its stead. Because of the psychological phenomenon of identification, we actively distort our interpretations of sensory impressions to believe what we want to believe. As a consequence, we are highly amenable to suggestions supporting our preacquired inclinations, beliefs, and dispositions. With the prejudice of identification and the tendency of wanting "to make sense" out of things we have sensed, we permit a freewheeling imagination to distort reality.

Even in cases where there is not an active substitution of imaginary facts for real impressions, "when the images of memory become dim, our present imagination helps to restore them, putting a new patch in the old garment."[27] This results because of our desire to make sense

---

26 Francis L. Wellman, *The Art of Cross-Examination,* 4th ed. (Garden City, N.Y.: Garden City Pub. Co., Inc., 1936), p. 161.

27 Ibid., p. 146.

out of a situation we have observed—the principle of closure. Probably as important, however, is our unconscious partisanship—our desire to champion a cause and to identify with another person and a situation. Wellman writes: "Witnesses in court are almost always favorable to the party who calls them, and this feeling induces them to conceal some facts and to color others which might, in their opinion, be injurious to the side for which they give their testimony."[28] This unconscious partisanship, the tendency to identify with others, obviously creates serious distortions in our perception and in our narration of the things that we have seen or heard.

Without identification, nevertheless, much of the sympathy, compassion, and warmth would disappear from human behavior. A certain amount of identification is absolutely necessary for the claims person. He or she must have sympathy, compassion, and warmth in everyday dealings with people. Otherwise a claims representative could generate little confidence from another person. People like to deal with a person who possesses some of the so-called milk of human kindness.

The claims representative, furthermore, needs a degree of identification with other people so that he or she is better able to understand them and to influence them. This is nothing more than *consideration*, that socially sensitive behavior trait discussed in the preceding chapter. The considerate claims person identifies through *empathy*— the ability to sense and appreciate the feelings of others. This does not mean *sharing* the feelings of others, however. By being able to identify with the situation of another person, the claims representative is able to *understand* the feelings and attitudes of others.

This matter of identification and empathy brings out a well-recognized principle of forensics—the area of argumentation and debate. That principle is: the skilled contest debater thoroughly understands and is prepared to debate either side of a proposition. A debater is not confined to knowing one side of an issue. A good debater knows the strengths and weaknesses of each side of the question. Further, he or she knows how to exploit the strengths of his or her side of the issue and how to attack the weaknesses of the adversary's side of the issue. The lyrics of a popular song of some years past declare, "You've got to accentuate the positive, eliminate the negative, latch on to the affirmative—don't mess with Mr. In-between."

---

[28] Ibid., p. 161.

This, essentially, is the job of the successful debater or the successful claims person. He or she must identify enough with a claimant to be able to anticipate the latter's attitudes, demands, grounds, and contentions. Being aware of the claimant's feelings, the merits of the claimant's case, and a probable evaluation of the case will forearm the claims person, making it possible to deal with the strengths of the claimant's case. When the strong points cannot be avoided, the claims representative has through identification been able to anticipate these points and has planned carefully how best to deal with them.

The claims person should not in any sense disparage the claimant's case by glossing over its strengths. Any attempt to present the claimant's case in its worst light usually will be apparent to the claimant, creating hostility in the claimant, and destroying the confidence the claims representative is attempting to maintain. Rather, the claims representative should anticipate these strengths and show that he or she fully understands the claimant's position, but the claims person will be prepared to cope with the strong points (if they come up) of the claimant's case effectively and convincingly. Walter Lippmann stressed the importance of identification, of understanding another person's viewpoint, when he wrote: "The ability to put himself in other men's places, and to argue their case as well as they can argue it themselves, is disarming and most persuasive. . . . It is the method of effective negotiation. The last stage of art is to induce the [other person] to welcome the accommodation, having persuaded [him] to feel that it is [his] very own."[29]

A word of warning, however, should be injected here. The claims representative must recognize that identification nevertheless distorts reality in the same way as the other defense mechanisms. The claims representative who identifies too much with other people's feelings will fail in insurance claims handling work. Insurance claims still must be settled with the head and not the heart—with reason and not with emotion.

Rationalization. Rationalization is a commonly used type of defense mechanism. The distortions resulting from rationalization often are similar to those made in identification or projection, because the rationalizer errs either in his or her description of personal feelings or

---

[29] A syndicated column, "Johnson's Art Is Accommodation," appeared in *The Benson Sun*, Omaha, Nebraska (September 3, 1964), p. 5–A. Copyright 1964, by The Washington Post Co.

the feelings of others. He or she conceals the motive for personal behavior by assigning some other motive to it. We give an incorrect explanation for our actions, rather than admit the real reason or motive behind our behavior. This allows us to adjust to the anxiety of the motive which actually caused our behavior. The explanation we select is more acceptable to us, because it serves to justify our actions.

A male student, for example, may fail a course in college because he is not motivated to study and because he devotes most of his time to part-time work and to dating. The student will not give the real reason for his failure. Instead, he will rationalize with another explanation. His "official" explanation will be that the professor was a poor teacher who didn't cover the text in his lectures and whose examinations were unreasonable. To strengthen his explanation for his failure, the student also may mention the fact that the professor was prejudiced against him. This tendency to rationalize is a common human failing—making excuses to oneself for oneself.

Because of rationalization we sometimes fail to obtain statements from claimants and from some witnesses. Rather than go to the bother of contacting a claimant, we tell ourselves that the claimant is hostile and wouldn't talk even if we made the effort to approach the claimant. Likewise, rather than take the trouble to contact a witness, we may conclude that the witness's testimony will be of no value to our investigation. The truth may be that because of the particular circumstances of each case, we shrink from performing the claims handling duty. By rationalizing, we are able to obscure the real reasons for our dereliction. It may require some courage to approach the claimant, and it may involve considerable effort and inconvenience to search out the witness. We, consequently, use rationalization to excuse ourselves from contacting either person. In the sometimes unpleasant situations encountered in insurance claims handling, it frequently takes considerable effort and courage, or intestinal fortitude, to carry out a diligent and thorough investigation, and the claims representative must always guard against the self-rationalization phenomenon. "To thine ownself be true" is valuable advice for the claims person. Is a task left undone because it is truly unimportant, or is the claims person avoiding a difficult, unpleasant duty and justifying a dereliction of duty through the rationalization process?

Claims representatives often see examples of rationalization among insureds or third party claimants. People don't lock their automobiles "because we never have had any trouble in this neighborhood," or "there was nothing of value in it." The truth of the matter is, rolling up the windows and locking the car requires a certain amount of effort. Moreover, the interior of a locked automobile in the summertime becomes unpleasantly hot by the time its owner returns to the vehicle. Similarly, when a person overturns a car or collides with some object off the highway, it is because "I was blinded by approaching headlights," rather than the fact that the person was intoxicated, sleepy, or driving too fast for existing conditions.

Displaced aggression. Displaced aggression is a most interesting form of defense mechanism. When aggression is displaced, anger and perhaps even physical force are turned away from the original source of frustration and redirected toward some more suitable victim. This ordinarily occurs when it would be dangerous to attack openly the person who provoked the anger and when a vulnerable scapegoat is near at hand. The *Saturday Evening Post* cover once depicted a sequence of events in which an executive severely criticized a subordinate; the subordinate then yelled at his wife; the wife browbeat her child; and the child ended up scolding the family cat.[30] The last three of the four steps of this sequence are excellent illustrations of displaced aggression.

A claims person may dislike his or her insurance company because of a sincere belief that the job is inadequately compensated. We may dislike our immediate supervisor because the latter constantly looks over our shoulder to see that the work is being done properly. Further, we may feel hostility toward our boss because the boss expects us to check in at the office promptly at 8:30 each morning irrespective of the fact that we have been up half the night every night for a week working on some important claim.

Realizing that a direct assault on the supervisor probably would be futile, if not dangerous to our job security, we practice displaced aggression. We vent our resentment against the insurance company and against the supervisor by letting it color our relations with insureds, claimants, and other people. In being rude to an insured, we punish our employer. The general inefficiency, coupled with high turnover, of a particular claims supervisor's field personnel may be a manifestation of displaced aggression which reflects upon the wisdom

---

[30] May 20, 1954, issue.

of the supervisor's own behavior and ability to conduct his or her supervisory duties.

The list of defense mechanisms could be expanded, but the more common varieties have been discussed here.

Delusions

A delusion is an uncommon form of active mental distortion. It is a groundless, irrational belief or thought, usually of grandeur or of persecution. In cases involving delusions the individual has a severe emotional problem, and may need a great deal of care. In extreme form delusions are a manifestation of a mental disorder or psychosis called *paranoia*.

In the personality disorder of paranoia the individual is extremely suspicious of the motives of other people. The paranoiac frequently will resort to use of the defense mechanism of projection. For example, a paranoiac man might protect himself against the anxiety-producing characteristics of his own disturbed mind by projecting his own feelings to other individuals. Consequently, he is completely suspicious and hostile toward the society in which he lives. He reacts with aggression in his attitudes, acts, and thoughts.

This aggression often erupts unexpectedly and in a most irrational manner. The person suffering from delusions has the belief, no matter how groundless, that all actions are directed against him or her. For example, in his early college years the author worked part-time in a factory that employed a woman deaf-mute. She would see people laughing around her and would imagine that they were laughing about her condition. As a consequence, she often acted explosively, throwing her work into the air and gesturing wildly at her supposed tormentors. Several bewildered co-workers received strange and accusing notes from her. The great inadequacy that she felt from her physical condition had generated paranoiac tendencies in the poor woman.

Although the average person seldom must deal with persons suffering from delusions, the insurance claims representative occasionally has contact with these people. There is nothing quite like a claim for money to bring out delusions of persecution in persons subject to these manifestations. For example, a man entered an insurance office one day and inquired about a life insurance policy in which he had been named beneficiary. According to him, his wife (the insured) had died, leaving a substantial sum of insurance money. The man believed that his guardian had misappropriated the money to his own use. Whenever the man inquired about the money, he suspected that everyone had lied to him.

He, therefore, came to the insurance company to find out how much money had been paid and to whom. He was later shown a letter from the insurer's home office indicating that the policy in question had expired without forfeiture values prior to the woman's death and that no amount had been paid as a death claim. The man left the insurance office abruptly, convinced that the insurance company, too, probably was part of the conspiracy.

In those cases in which the claims representative is confronted by a person with paranoiac tendencies, the situation must be handled with extreme care. In some cases a paranoiac can be extremely dangerous, requiring custody in order to protect society from his or her irrational behavior.

Hallucination

A hallucination is another manifestation of mental distortion which divorces the individual from reality. In the hallucination the person simply sees or hears someone or something not actually present. This results in a completely erroneous description of physical reality. The classic example of hallucination in American folklore, of course, is the pink elephant or the huge, fuzzy caterpillars supposedly observed by the heavy drinker suffering from delirium tremens.

The claims person sometimes thinks that many people suffer from hallucinations. Usually, however, he or she is observing the manifestations of other distortions which result from imperfections in a human being's senses or from more common and normal mental peculiarities of humankind as a whole. It is rare that the claims representative will meet people who are bothered with hallucinations. People suffering from such obvious mental aberrations usually are in hospitals or mental institutions.

THE ROLE OF STRESS

Distortion enters the picture in every phase of human sensitivity, perception, recollection, and narration. In stressful situations distortion is magnified considerably. We know that stress is obviously a factor that contributes to the mental distortions, such as the defense mechanisms. Stress plays an important role in repression and perceptual defense, displaced aggression, and the other defense mechanisms. It is always a major factor in the quality of human sensitivity. Stress is discussed here separately to emphasize the inordinate influence that it plays in the physiological and psychological aspects of stimulus reception, interpretation, and recitation (narration).

We have already observed that in threatening or unpleasant situations a person tends to reject stimuli received and perceptually to avoid disturbing stimuli. This is perceptual defense—the perceptual processing of a stimulus and rejecting it or the literal failure to perceive the stimulus.

Stress produces other manifestations of behavior. Any threat to a person creates a narrower perceptual field; a person may concentrate attention on the danger to the exclusion of all else. The threat of danger and the fear produced in an individual may create a rigidity that results in decreased efficiency on intellectual and visual tasks. For example, Robert Buckhout in his studies of air force flight-crew members, reported that even highly trained subjects, under stress, are poor observers.[31]

Stress produces disorganization, disorientation, and a blunted awareness of one's surroundings. The effect of stress is directly proportional to the degree or severity of the stress, its duration, and the tolerance level of the individual experiencing the stress. People in a highly relaxed state can become competent observers, but as stress intensifies, it causes a narrowing down of our perceptual field, with a substantial loss of details. "While a threat to our well-being can bring about dramatic changes that provide us with extra-ordinary physical ability, it cripples us as reliable observers. With a quickened heartbeat, high blood pressure, irregular breathing, and high levels of adrenalin in circulation, our attention is drawn inward, reducing our awareness of the surroundings."[32]

Aside from the fact that stress creates poor observers, observations actually made by persons under stress are unreliable. Individuals

---

[31] Robert Buckhout, "Eyewitness Testimony," *Scientific American*, vol. 231 (1974), pp. 23–31.

[32] Thomas Sannito and James F. Whalen, *Courtroom Psychology and Techniques*, a trial advocacy series seminar, Utah State Bar, 1979, p. 11.

overestimate the passage of time under conditions of stress; time seems to pass slowly. A motorist who is in danger will overestimate the distance he or she has travelled. As threat and fear exacerbate stress, a motorist will believe that more time has elapsed and more distance has been travelled.[33]

Consequently, statements secured from insureds, claimants, or witnesses who recount the details of events while they themselves were in highly stressful circumstances are to be viewed with circumspection. The insurance claims representative should not be surprised if a person has little recollection of the details of a stressful situation. Further, the claims person must exercise caution in placing too much reliance on the statement of an insured or witness that provides a detailed account of a personally stressful accident or situation, particularly where testimony of other people is contradictory. Evaluation of the liability and the measure of damages depends upon the credibility of the insured, claimant, and witnesses involved, and the determination of that credibility must be affected by the claims representative's assessment of the effects of stress on the testimony of the people involved.

IMPERFECTIONS IN HUMAN INTEGRITY

Examine man's integrity;
Is it real or is it not?
Does honesty spring from conscience
Or the fear of being caught?
——Willis Park Rokes

Human integrity is a subject which continually plagues the insurance claims person. Many claims representatives will argue vehemently that most people have some larceny in their souls. Claims persons also will argue that insurance companies are constant targets of this larceny, because it is so easy to fabricate damages and claims in insurance. Moreover, it is sometimes believed that there is a general attitude of permissiveness in society regarding the public's dealings with insurance companies. As a consequence, *the claims person is cautioned to maintain an attitude of alert and healthy skepticism*

---

[33] H. Werner and S. Wapner, "Changes in Psychological Distance under Conditions of Danger," *Journal of Personality*, vol. 24 (1955), pp. 155–67.

about human integrity as he or she performs the claims handling functions.

Some of the factors which enter to distort reality, resulting in variations in perception, recollection, and narration already have been considered. These come about because of our inherent sensory imperfections and because of the fact that our peculiar mental processes serve to distort what was originally perceived. Deliberate falsification because of dishonesty serves to alter further the "facts" of a given situation. Some of this deliberate falsification obviously is only a step removed from the unconscious partisanship which takes place when a witness so identifies with one of two parties that he or she unconsciously colors testimony in favor of that party.

The claims person must consider this factor of deliberate falsification which crops up in the claims handling process. As the claims representative interviews a witness, he or she must be concerned with the veracity of that witness. Is the witness telling the truth? Is the witness honest? If dishonest, is he or she completely faithless in narrating what was perceived and is now recollected? Perhaps the witness is telling only a half-lie or perhaps he or she has "bent" the truth only slightly? How is the claims representative to know? It is this conundrum confronting the claims person which causes him or her to want to know more about human integrity. What is it? When does it exist and when is it absent? How can a knowledge of the nature of human integrity enable the insurance claims representative to better accomplish the claims handling job?

Nature of human integrity

The Christian ideal, it is said, has not been tried and found wanting; it has been found difficult and left untried.
———Harold Begbie

Human integrity is a subject about which no accurate generalizations can be made. When an insured, a claimant, or a witness obviously relates a false story or deliberately conceals important information, it is because, *in that particular case,* he or she is lacking in the characteristic which is called honesty or integrity. It is this last statement which pinpoints the nature of human integrity and dictates the obvious conclusion—the only safe thing to say about human honesty is that it is relative.

Significant psychological research has led to the conclusion that a general trait of honesty or dishonesty does not exist. For example, studies by Leonard Keeler, of Northwestern University, reveal that a majority of people will take small sums if the situation is such that there is no immediate danger of being caught.[34] Most of these people are scrupulously "honest" in other situations. Our honesty depends upon the circumstances—the situation in which we find ourself and our viewpoint and sense of values relating to that situation.

It is not inaccurate to say that every person is "honest," under certain circumstances. Likewise, it is equally accurate for one to say that every person is "dishonest" under certain circumstances. The words, "honest" and "dishonest" are placed in quotes because they are merely topical terms which help to reflect contemporary standards of integrity of a society.

Conduct which is dishonest in the eyes of one person may be perfectly proper from another person's viewpoint. One's conduct depends upon the circumstances. A military officer who has served for years in other countries was appalled by what he considered to be a low sense of morality and honesty in one place where he was stationed. The native population made an occupation of stealing from American personnel and from their military installations. One native, when questioned about this apparently low "moral" character of his people, replied, "If we steal your television set, we merely inconvenience you. You will grumble about the incident, but because you have money, you will go to the the the PX and replace your set. The money we get from selling your stolen set will keep our babies from starving."

Since society, as such, is a social order or system which restricts the individual, society's standards of honesty or dishonesty may or may not reflect the individual's standards of human integrity formulated from his or her own value judgments. Our standard of honesty often derives from what we believe will yield "justice" under a given situation. We cheat the parking meter because we do not really believe it is fair to us. We underdeclare on our income tax, because we feel victimized by a complex, inequitable system which we believe was perpetrated upon us without our consent. We cheat the insurance company because we are angered at the premiums we must pay, or

---

[34] Abraham P. Sperling, *How to Make Psychology Work for You* (Greenwich, Conn.: Fawcett Publications, 1957), p. 14.

because we believe insurance companies make too much money, or because we believe an insurer will cheat us on a justifiable claim. In all of the foregoing cases our sense of "justice" has been outraged and this serves as a rationale for our asocial behavior.

Thus, a person's judgment may justify committing a "dishonest" act. A person rationalizes when he or she commits the act. That rationalization is a defense reaction for the individual, and it conceals some "irrational" determinant of conduct. It is irrational, because that person's society dictates that it is irrational. The person has justified in his or her own mind why it is proper to do an act which to other people is wrong.

Many "God-fearing" people, for example, believe that they follow scrupulous standards of conduct. They religiously profess to observe the Ten Commandments, and particularly the one which stipulates that "thou shalt not steal." This, according to their value judgments, means that it is unconscionable to break into safes, rob banks, and hijack the cargoes of trucks. It may not, however, include other types of stealing (stealing is defined as the misappropriation of another person's property with the intent permanently to deprive that person of ownership). A man who would frown at robbing a little old lady of her life savings or at taking money from his church's collection box will rationalize that it is all right to carry away a few ash trays, towels, blankets, pillows, and pieces of glassware and silverware from the hotels in which he stays on business trips. One large hotel loses some $50,000 worth of such items each year to guests. Many of these guests are unquestionably good, religious, God-fearing people; they also steal several thousand Gideon Bibles yearly.

Standards of a society

Regardless of the inescapable differences of opinion regarding right and wrong which individuals formulate according to their own value judgments, the only available criteria and starting point for determining human integrity or the absence thereof are those standards prescribed by one's society. It must be one's own society, for societies, like individuals, differ tremendously in their concepts of right and wrong.

In one society, for example, it is wrong to eat any meat; in a second society, the eating of human flesh is most acceptable, and, in fact, is accompanied by celebrating and rejoicing. The act placates the gods of the second society and avenges wrongs visited upon departed warriors. The custom of kissing takes many forms in various societies. Some people rub noses; others employ the tongue in a manner considered quite unacceptable to still other societies. The natives of the Honduras Islands don't kiss each other; they look upon kissing as a rather mild form of cannibalism. As another example of cultural difference, one society believes it is most honorable for the head of a household to invite an honored guest to sleep with the former's wife. In the United States this quaint custom is not condoned.

The cultures of the American Indian have their concepts of right and wrong. Clyde Kluckhohn in his writings indicates that the Navaho Indian at the turn of the century did not punish the individual for theft; the thief was required only to make reparation. As a matter of fact, theft and fraud on the part of supernaturals were pictured approvingly in the Navajo culture. The terrible crimes in that society were incest and witchcraft.[35]

The typical individual desires to be accepted by his or her society. We must maintain our reputation and self-respect. Thus, we are driven by social pressure to conform to the standards of right and wrong of our society. More important, we feel particularly obliged to conform to those standards which are especially emphasized and enforced in our society. This conclusion gives rise to an interesting question: is it dishonest or wrong, according to contemporary standards of human integrity in the United States, to cheat "a little" or to steal from insurance companies?

Stealing from insurance companies

A corruption of the heart resulting from a confusion of the head.
                                            ——Anonymous

Penal codes in the United States are specific in a few cases in prohibiting acts which might be directed against insurance companies. An example is the specific statute prohibiting arson to defraud an insurer. Arson has become a major problem for insurance companies. Property claims specialists report that the increased volume of arson claims reflects the existence of more fraud-oriented claimants today than in the past. Indeed, during 1979 the National Fire Data Center

---

[35] Clyde Kluckhohn, *Culture and Behavior* (New York: Free Press of Glencoe, 1962), pp. 168–69.

reported that incendiary fires were currently accounting for 26.7 percent of the number of non-residential fires and 35.7 percent of the dollars lost to non-residential fires.[36]

The general fraud and theft statutes provide prohibitions against a host of different activities which affect insurance companies. Professional practitioners of personal injury fraud, automobile theft rings, and claims persons who fabricate fictional claims in order to collect insurance, occasionally are prosecuted.

There is no question that flagrant cases of "serious" criminal activity, such as the foregoing, are frowned upon by society in this country. It is difficult, however, to attempt to draw a profile of the integrity of the "average" person who has dealings with insurance companies. One would have to know the general standard of integrity followed by the public in its dealings with insurance companies. Is it one of moral laxity and permissiveness, or is it one which still recognizes the "golden rule?" If there is moral laxity in the public's dealings with insurance companies, is it merely a reflection of the general level of human integrity in our contemporary society as it relates to all sectors of economic, social, and political activity?

If it is not the foregoing, does the public adopt a more lax and permissive standard of honesty in dealing with insurance companies than that adopted for other areas of activity? *If* the latter conclusion is the case (and this possible conclusion is for the sociologists to decide), then further conclusions are in order. Since "honesty" is relative, depending upon a person's individual value judgment of right and wrong (standard of "justice"), then if the individual deals sharply with insurance companies, it is because insurers have a poor image in this person's eyes. The various surveys and studies over the years indicate that such an image does exist in the eyes of many people in this country. Findings from a number of Insurance Information Institute surveys (conducted during both profitable and unprofitable underwriting periods over a 20-year period) indicate that the public perpetually views property and casualty insurance rates as being too high and insurers as making too much profit.[37]

---

[36] National Fire Data Center, U.S. Fire Administration, U.S. Department of Commerce, based on studies in eight states during 1977 and an additional seven states in 1978. Reported in *Insurance Facts* (New York: Insurance Information Institute, 1980–81 edition), p. 44.

[37] See *Trends in Public Appraisal of the Property and Casualty Insurance Business—1961–1964* (New York: Insurance Information Institute, December 1964) and *Pricing, Profits and Regulation* (New York: Insurance Information Institute, January 1980).

Whether this indication of bad reputation is justified or not, it is incumbent upon the insurance industry to improve the image. The claims representative is in an outstanding position to help accomplish this task. He or she can do so by practicing good public relations—the art of making friends—being fair and selling an image of fairness to the public.

Handling the problem of dishonesty

Irrespective of the broad philosophical issues relating to human integrity, what it is, and how it can be improved upon, today's insurance claims representative is confronted with the day-by-day problem of dishonesty which he or she finds in some of the insureds, claimants, and witnesses encountered in claims handling work. Variations in human integrity are psychological distortions that enter a claims handling situation and obscure reality. We must have practical means by which we can ferret out the truth.

Particularly when the claims person's initial impression of a loss gives reason to suspect the legitimacy of a claim, the claims representative will wish to learn as much as possible about the insured, including the latter's business history and prior losses. Conversation with the insured's agent and inquiries regarding the insured's business reputation may turn up facts regarding the credibility of the insured and the legitimacy of the claim.

It is particularly essential to have a clear picture of the insured's business history in those claims where there is a suspicion of fraud or arson. In such cases, the insured's business history may be particularly revealing. Fire set by insureds are common during periods of economic recession, for through a fraudulent fire, assets are converted to cash, embarrassment of bankruptcy is eliminated, credit ratings are protected, and the insured is in a position to refinance the business.

Fraudulent property losses also may occur because of other motives. For example, insureds sometimes start fires to hide other crimes, and the claims person sometimes has a complex job seeking motives for arson-related losses.

Since moral hazard or financial difficulties of an owner or tenant have historically been present in most cases of suspicious fires, the claims person must question the insured at length and seek as much outside information—financial records, credit reports, witnesses's reports, and so on—as is available. In addition, the claims representative should consult with the insured's agent and secure as much information on the financial position of the insured and the insured's business affairs as is obtainable.

Where fraud is not suspected, the investigation required is minimal. Nonetheless, the value of statement-taking is becoming more evident as losses become more complex, frequently involving several insurance policies. The claims person should secure statements particularly in those situations:

1. Where the cause of loss is of suspicious origin.
2. Where coverage of liability is questionable.
3. Where insurable interest is questioned.
4. Involving possible cancellation of the policy.
5. In which the insurer's rights have been prejudiced.
6. Where the claim is excessive or borders on attempted fraud.
7. Where the claims person wishes to preserve evidence or place on record the story of the insured or witnesses.
8. That indicate possibilities of subrogation against third parties.[38]

Besides arson, there are a number of losses that may arouse the suspicion of the claims representative. Examples of such suspicious losses are falsified book claims, claims for property intentionally damaged, lost, or destroyed, or claims for nonexistent property. Fraudulent losses and many bona fide loss situations present questions of liability, coverage, and compliance with requirements in case of loss. Thus, it is necessary for the claims person to act in a manner consistent with any defenses that an insurer may have against an insured.[39]

The successful claims person does not discover dishonesty by intuition, inspiration, and flashes of telepathic insight. The best defense against the dishonesty of insureds, claimants, and witnesses is a thorough investigation in those instances where from all indications a complete inquiry appears warranted. The claims person must be continually on the alert for clues which suggest deliberate distortion.

The evidence the claims representative collects on many claims is usually assembled bit by bit like a huge jigsaw puzzle. Frequently,

---

[38] Paul I. Thomas and Prentiss B. Reed, *Adjustment of Property Losses*, 4th ed. (New York: McGraw-Hill, 1977), p. 84.

[39] Bernard L. Webb, J. J. Launie, Willis Park Rokes, and Norman A. Baglini, *Insurance Company Operations*, vol. 2 (Malvern, Pa.: American Institute for Property and Liability Underwriters, 1978), pp. 350–51.

some of the pieces do not fit. These pieces often are distortions of reality caused inadvertently by the various psychological phenomena which have been discussed already, or they may be deliberate untruths.

For example, a woman insured made a collision claim for extensive damages allegedly caused by one accident. The only witness was the insured's girl friend, passenger in the insured vehicle, who corroborated the insured's story. Upon investigation, it was found that *four* accidents, not just one, caused the insured's damages.

First, she had backed out of her driveway into a tree opposite her driveway, damaging the rear of her automobile. Second, she damaged the front end of her automobile in an intersection accident. Third, the tow truck, responding to her call, skidded on ice and slid into the side of her car, damaging it. Fourth, partial repairs subsequently had been made so that the vehicle was driveable, but the damaged hood was secured only by a couple of strands of fine wire. The insured made a short trip before contacting her insurance company, and while proceeding along the highway at about 50 miles per hour, the wires broke. The hood flipped up and smashed the car top and windshield.

The claims man in this case did an inordinate amount of investigation of this claim (for a simple collision case). This was prompted partially by the peculiar character of the damage—front, top, sides and rear of the vehicle were damaged—from what appeared to be merely a front-end collision. The most suspicious aspect of the case, however, was the witness's account of the accident. She gave an unusually complete and clear account of the most minute details of the case. It sounded like a memorized speech. The claims man explored various parts of her story in more detail, requestioning her and asking her to explain or expand upon her previous story—having her retell various parts of her story several times. She couldn't tell the same story twice. Her narration was full of inconsistencies and contradictions. It was apparent that she was lying, and she finally admitted to the deliberate falsification.

Trial lawyers employ similar techniques in cross-examining witnesses during legal hearings. The purpose of cross-examination is to test the witness's story by exploring its details and implications, in the hope of disclosing inconsistencies or impossibilities, and to develop the truth further. Oftentimes the layman's concept of cross-examination is derived from the melodramas of the movies and television. The hero of the story, an attorney, hammers away mercilessly at some villainous witness on the stand. Through an amazing display of histrionics, the lawyer tears the witness's story to shreds, discredits the witness before the entire court, and reduces him or her to tears. All of this is accomplished by unusually perceptive, piercing, and cutting questions, delivered in staccato-like fashion.

The above representation of legal cross-examination is an exaggeration and misconception of what usually takes place in court. The foregoing technique may be used by some attorneys, but it has rare and limited proper use. Better results with a person on the witness stand usually will flow from tact and consideration rather than from bulldozing and ridicule. Francis L. Wellman, a well-known authority on legal cross-examination, wrote: "I just want to say this one thing to you: It pays to be a gentleman."[40]

In the proper handling of insurance claims, too, it pays to be a "gentleman" (or "gentlewoman"). Little is to be gained by telling an insured, a claimant, or a witness that he or she is a liar. The other person's pride—the person's great concern for self-reputation and self-esteem—must be respected at all times. To attack another person's story by attacking the person's integrity generally is not wise. Rather, the claims person always should maintain a courteous and conciliatory manner. Obvious falsification can be handled in most cases as if it were an unconscious mistake. A person is willing to admit to mistakes, but don't call him or her a liar!

Early in his claims handling years the author settled a claim involving an obvious falsification on the part of the claimant. The claimant was walking along a sidewalk. Two men employed by an insured gas company were repairing a broken gas main adjacent to the sidewalk. An explosion ensued, and a flare-up of flame seared the claimant, scorching his suit and overcoat. In addition, his eyebrows were singed, and he suffered a mild case of "sunburn" on his face. The author talked to him at his place of employment, some 20 miles from his home. He had his suit with him, but his overcoat was at his home. He described the overcoat as being in new condition. The man was well-known, respectable, and a brother of a high official in the author's own church. His evaluation of his special damages was

<hr>

[40] Wellman, *The Art of Cross-Examination*, p. 18.

accepted by the author and an additional amount was paid to cover general damages for the minor personal injuries involved.

As he motored back to his office, the author began to have some doubts as to whether he had discharged his responsibilities in a proper manner. The amount paid for the ruined, new overcoat was appreciable, and the author had not seen it before settling the claim. Since the claimant's home was, more or less, on his route back to his office, he stopped and talked to the claimant's wife. She brought out the overcoat. It was shiny and worn. The buttonholes were ragged, and the cuffs and lapels were threadbare.

Rather than stopping payment on the settlement check, the author telephoned the claimant that evening. The claimant, whose wife had informed him of the author's visit, was noticeably distraught and disturbed. Figuratively speaking, the claimant had been caught with the jam on his face and his hand in the cookie jar. The author suggested that perhaps some mistake had been made; that the claimant had possibly mistaken the damaged overcoat for one which had been recently purchased. The claimant replied, "I think definitely that I made a mistake on this. The damaged overcoat was not new."

"Well, Mr. Jones," continued the author, "since we were talking about a different overcoat when we figured out a settlement figure, do you think it would be proper if we adjusted the amount I paid you?"

"Yes, I certainly do," replied the claimant.

"What do you think would be a fair figure on the damaged coat?" asked the author. The claimant, in a most anxious attempt to redress the wrong he had committed, named a perfectly reasonable figure. He returned the check, and a new set of releases and a new check were prepared. The author thanked the claimant for his cooperation and fairmindedness. The author also made it a point on subsequent claims always to verify damages carefully.

Telephone voice stress analyzers

As we move more and more into the era of computers and electronic gadgetry, it is inevitable that we will find increasing application of sophisticated techniques to assist the claims representative to accomplish the claims handling functions. One device that has seen practical application is the telephone "voice stress" analyzer, which determines if the person being interviewed is under stress—and therefore, is with-holding information or is lying.

The voice stress analyzer essentially is a lie detector (polygraph), and the concept has been with us for some time now. Law enforce-ment agencies, for example, have used lie detectors for many years, and in recent years heavy reliance has been placed on polygraph tests by retail businesses. Some firms have used them extensively to detect employee theft.[41] However, a number of states have reacted to this practice by enacting laws prohibiting the use of such tests.

An increasing demand for sophisticated gadgetry has developed in the security industry. Heads of multinational oil companies and banks, the superrich, and other VIPs routinely travel in bombproof limousines equipped with a variety of antiterrorist and antikidnapping devices. Vehicles are outfitted with elaborately concealed transmitters, elec-tronic "watchdogs" that reveal if anyone has tampered with the car, black boxes that sniff out explosives, and electronic devices that will start the auto a quarter-mile away with no one in it. In addition, electronic "nite-finders" enable drivers to see through fog, smoke, and total darkness at long range; "electronic handkerchiefs" on the car's telephone render the speaker's voice unrecognizable, while telephone voice stress analyzers make it possible to check out whether people at a passenger's destination are under stress or lying, posing a threat to the car's occupants.[42]

Some insurance companies today are utilizing telephone voice stress analyzers to aid in the conduct of claims investigations. Bearing the name *Psychological Stress Evaluations (PSE)*, the technique in-volves taking a person's recorded telephone statement and then eval-uating it by the PSE analysis. As in the case of the polygraph test used on employees, however, severe criticism has been directed at the prac-tice of telephone voice stress analysis, and the legality of the technique as an insurance claims handling practice is in question. Until and unless state laws, court decisions, and insurance department rulings establish the acceptability of this technique as a proper and valid practice for securing and evaluating evidence, the use of voice stress

---

[41] Leonard W. Prestwich, "Impact of Employee Attitudes on Employee Theft," *The Plains Business Review*, vol. 7, no. 1 (Winter–Spring 1980), p. 1.

[42] Leonard Katz, "Terror-Proof Limousines Become a Lucrative Business," *Omaha World Herald* (July 23, 1980).

analyzers must be surreptitious. If claims offices can resolve whatever personal ethical questions the technique may pose, it is clear that a claims representative can gain valuable insight regarding the credibility of the telephone narration of an insured, claimant, or witness by using the analyzer. As long as its use is restricted strictly to a surreptitious office use to assist the claims person in judging the evidence gathered by telephone, it is a useful tool. If used openly, incurring public and insurance department wrath, it may prove to be much more trouble than it is worth.

ROLE AND CREDIBILITY OF WITNESSES

And who is the reliable witness?
Just thee and me, and I am not so
sure about thee and thee is not so
sure about me.
           ——Ralph Slovenko

Witnesses played no important role in litigation for hundreds of years in judicial history. Until the 16th century the independent witness was considered a meddler, and if he intervened, was in peril of being held guilty of the crime of maintenance—an unauthorized and officious interference in a lawsuit in which he had no interest. Information regarding the matters at issue in a case was furnished by the jury. In fact, the original meaning of the word *juror* is one who took an oath and swore to declare truly what he knew or believed in a given case. An inquiry into how the juror acquired his knowledge of the case was not made.[43]

The Elizabethan Act of 1562 required that the facts of the case be presented by outside witnesses, rather than jurors. Attendance of witnesses was mandatory, and severe penalties for perjury were imposed. Because of the historic reluctance to employ witnesses in litigation, however, they were still viewed with some suspicion, and broad categories were established, designating certain persons who were considered incompetent to serve as witnesses.

Today, some of that suspicion persists, and for good reasons, as we have observed in our examination of the imperfections in human sen-

---

[43] A. Goodhart, "A Changing Approach to the Law of Evidence," *Virginia Law Review,* vol. 51 (1965), pp. 759, 761.

sitivity and integrity and the various mental distortions. Distortions and differences in perception, recollection, and narration are enormous, and eyewitness testimony—a psychologically spurious phenomenon—is viewed by psychologists as unreliable, inaccurate, and seriously distorted. "Considering the ephemeral nature of perception, the problems of short term memory, the limitations of recall, the subjectivity and suggestibility of the testimony, and the raw effects of stress, eyewitness testimony must be viewed askance."[44]

Nevertheless, eyewitness testimony plays a crucial role in the legal arena. Jurors are convinced by a witness who authoritatively recounts the "facts" of a case. Moreover, the early rules on witness competency have been broadened so that any person of "proper understanding" is considered to be a competent witness. The credibility of the witness can be questioned, however, by showing (1) present testimony is inconsistent with prior statements made; (2) other evidence refutes the witness's testimony; (3) the eyewitness is biased because of kinship with one party or hostility to a party, or because of a monetary interest in the case; (4) the witness lacks the capacity to observe, remember, or recount the matters about which he or she testifies; and/or (5) the witness's character is deficient, materially affecting credibility.[45]

SUMMARY

By now you may have concluded that an undistorted appearance of reality is nonexistent because there are so many possibilities for distortion. You probably have recognized that some of your own behavior belongs in some of the categories of distortion mentioned. Be comforted, however, with the knowledge that perfection is as undesirable as it is unattainable. Achievement of maximum contact with all of the details of reality would on one hand be so burdensome that we would never have time to accomplish anything. Likewise, the inability to identify with others would deprive us of the warmth and sympathy which everyone needs.

The human is a remarkably complex and talented creature possessed of more or less well-developed senses. Because of the senses of sight,

---

[44] Thomas Sannito and James S. Whalen, *Discrediting Eyewitness Testimony* (Dubuque, Iowa: Thomas and C. J. Sannito, 1979), p. 15.

[45] Ralph Slovenko, *Psychiatry and Law* (Boston: Little, Brown, 1973), p. 42.

hearing, taste, touch, and smell, we know that we are quite well attuned to our environment. Moreover, with our superior intellect and reasoning ability, compared to other living organisms, we are able to interpret and formulate judgments regarding the sensations and impressions obtained through the human senses.

Despite the fact that we possess these senses, we experience definite limitations to our individual human sensitivity. Because of these limitations, our sensory impressions are not always strong, clear, and accurate. Our sight, for example, is limited. We cannot see distant objects too clearly; our width or peripheral vision is not completely adequate; we cannot see things behind us; and we cannot see many things simultaneously. Our limited span of attention makes it possible for us to focus on only a few things at a time; attempting to perceive many things within our field of vision causes confusion.

Not only do people tend to react differently to the same stimulus because of differences in human sensitivity, but their reaction is determined largely by the peculiarities of their mental processes—how they go about interpreting stimuli. We may have recognized the stimuli, but because of the factors of active distortion, we respond in an apparently unconnected manner, probably because of the perceptual constancies, illusions, defense mechanisms, and so forth, which distort our interpretation of the impressions perceived. In addition, the factor of human integrity enters the picture.

It is obvious, after studying the nature of the human's imperfect senses and peculiar mental processes, that these factors bring about many of the distortions in reality. It, therefore, is an obvious over-simplification to say that people have failed to tell the truth when witnesses come up with several versions of the "facts" of a case. Human integrity and the problem of deliberate falsification of facts, neverthe-less, are important matters for the insurance claims representative. When there is reason to suspect that dishonesty lurks in the back-ground, the claims person's best defense is a thorough investigation of that particular claim.

In dealing with insureds, third-party claimants, and witnesses, the insurance claims representative must always be aware of the possibility of distortion resulting from the foregoing factors. Fortunately, the claims person probably scores relatively high in reality contact. This is because he or she is able to approach each claim dispassionately and with relative disinterest. This is one of the requirements of the job.

The other person is unlikely to react in the same fashion. The latter is under tension in many situations so that anxiety builds up to a troublesome degree, causing the person to forget, repress, project, and rationalize in an attempt to reduce tension. The person may even regress and become openly belligerent. The claims representative must be prepared to cope with these responses. He or she must be able to recognize distortions that are likely to create obstacles in the relations and transactions with others.

Thus, if a claims representative arrives at the scene of an automobile accident and discovers that the insured has backed recklessly out into a stream of traffic, the claims person needn't wonder what happened. Although the insured may rationalize by stating that his brakes didn't hold, he perhaps had a fight with his wife. Instead of belting his wife, he kicked the dog, stepped on the cat's tail, and backed his automobile recklessly into the street, working off his frustration through displaced aggression.

Feeling cross and out of sorts, he projects his feelings to the driver of the automobile with which he collided and warns the claims person, "Don't try to talk to that guy; he's mean as a bear!" Although the third-party claimant, owner of the automobile, apparently hasn't been hurt and does not seem particularly distressed, his wife identifies herself with him and exclaims, "The poor dear probably has hurt his back, and look at his nice, new automobile!" A witness who had a clear view of the accident but an inordinate fear of testifying as a witness represses her memory and declares, "I never saw the accident."

Foundation
for influencing people

CHAPTER

4

Communication

The subject of communication has received much attention. Books on selling and human behavior commonly contain discussions of it. Business and industry leaders explore it with a consuming interest. Colleges and universities teach the topic in depth. The reader might well inquire why so much emphasis should be placed on the subject. Isn't communication an activity which a person masters as a matter of course? Why should there be any formal discussion about it? Is it necessary to spend time reading about something that everyone practices every day? Almost since birth, don't people exchange ideas, feelings, and experiences with their contemporaries? We do, indeed, spend our lifetimes in communication activities. Despite our reliance on the communication process, nevertheless, we often feel inadequate in our attempts to make ourselves understood. We conclude that communication is a most difficult activity.

The restraints imposed by society and the nature of the process itself cause people to communicate imperfectly. Social pressures cause us to restrain ourselves from saying exactly what we mean. We shade our meaning or we use innuendo to express ourselves. Double meaning may protect us from social repercussions, but it distorts the communication process.

Not only must we contend with constant social pressure and refrain from saying exactly what we are thinking, a further obstacle confronts us—the nature of the communication process itself. If we want to be completely understood, we must use language which clearly reflects our true meaning, and we must transmit that language in such a manner that the meaning will not be lost in the transmission. If we can accomplish the foregoing, there is still the likelihood that what we have just said will be misconstrued, misinterpreted, or not heard in whole or in part. These obstacles frustrate us, for the need to communicate is basic to human well-being.

IMPORTANCE OF COMMUNICATION

Communication is indeed important. We shape our relations with other people through the transmission of thought, belief, opinion, and information. Communication embraces the whole universe of human relations and activities. It has shaped history and given contemporary men and women a knowledge of their predecessors. We have greater understanding and insight into our origins and our environment through communication. We have discovered evidence of our existence on earth dating back 3.5 million years.[1] The human skeletons, footprints and artifacts have communicated the message that humans did in fact exist that long ago. This object language has aided the physical anthropologist particularly to trace the development of human beings for hundreds of thousands of years.

As human beings developed, they began to express themselves symbolically by engraving, drawing, and painting upon the walls of caves. Complete records of this type date back some 40,000 years. The first records of a written language, however, are no more ancient than 4,000 B.C. when the Sumerian language was spoken and written in the Mesopotamian valley of southwest Asia.

The human's ability to communicate the lessons of history was appreciably enhanced with the emergence of written language. Through

---

[1] According to some experts, the first creature that could rightfully be called Homo—a human being—must have emerged longer ago than 3.5 million years, the age of fossils whose classification as human is still controversial. See *New York Times* (April 12, 1975), pp. 29 and 54; *Time* (November 7, 1977), p. 69; and *New York Times* (March 22, 1979), p. A16. Whatever the age of the fossils, early humans, by leaving fossilized remains, footprints, and other artifacts, inadvertently have communicated significant information to modern-day humans.

writings and other forms of communication people have developed and have passed on a rich heritage of language, custom, law, philosophy, religion, technology and all of the other things which have been invented and have evolved through the centuries. Only through history and precedent have humans been able to create a civilization. Without the ability to record our history and to communicate with our fellow beings, we would still be base animals living a primitive existence, unable to profit from the accumulated knowledge of preceding generations.

We are social animals who feel compelled to communicate. We are capable of passing information to our contemporaries and to succeeding generations. Because of our gregarious nature and our ability to communicate, we have developed specialized skills and brought about division of labor and all of the manifestations of civilization. Like other gregarious species of animals, humans practice the principle of mutual aid in their activities. Were it not so, humans never would have thought of the group principle and the law of large numbers, which have spawned the insurance institution.

Communication, accordingly, is the crux of the whole area of human endeavor, achievement, and existence. The ability of individual men and women to communicate effectively with one another determines in large part the degree to which they achieve success and realization of their goals. The nature of the process deserves study and analysis.

NATURE OF COMMUNICATION

The communication process is broad in its scope. It includes every device used by men and women to convey meaning. People are inclined to think of communication and its process in a rather narrow sense. Communication through language—the art of public speaking and the fundamentals of written communication—often receives predominant attention. Colleges and universities offer specialized courses labeled "business communication." Some of these courses are devoted exclusively to the subject of business letter and report writing. Other "communications" courses are limited to the subject of speech —oral communication.

Considerable attention is devoted by business and industry to the subject of communication—both "upward" and "downward." The boss must know how to communicate through speaking and writing. As a supervisor, we are told how to conduct interviews and how to listen to grievances. We are trained to make instructions clear. We must know the important uses of the bulletin board, the public address system, the meetings with employees, and the house organ. We are told to keep an "ear to the ground"—we should know what is going on via the "grapevine." To demonstrate to employees that we are interested in a two-way exchange of communication, we let it be known that we are adopting the "open-door policy." Presumably, if any employee has the nerve to do so, that employee can walk in on us and express his or her thoughts and opinions. Obviously, we actually must be approachable and must be attentive and sympathetic listeners.

These are all important methods for conveying meaning, but speech and writing are only part of the communication process. The process is not limited to the transmission of language which men or women speak and write. Communication takes place on many levels and in a variety of ways. Facial expressions, posture, accent, manner of dress, and behavior all convey meaning. Silence often speaks eloquently. The artist communicates through form and color; a musician is able to pass along meaning through the emotion, rhythm, and flow of the music.

Meaning can be communicated unintentionally as well as intentionally: A look, an involuntary expression, and a quiver to the voice often betray a person's real feelings and meaning. People often convey negative impressions because of their reputation, their manner of speech, and their appearance. What they say will be distorted and interpreted in light of the negative impression. The popular expression "clothes make the man" is merely a reflection of the fact that the poorly dressed individual communicates a negative impression. People interpret poor dress to be an indication of a person who is inferior in some regard. The poorly dressed person does not command respect; what he or she has to say, therefore, will be heard with prejudice if, in fact, other people even bother to listen.

Reputation is equally influential in conveying meaning. If our good reputation precedes us, people are more likely to make allowances if what we say is not clearly stated. On the other hand, what a person is may well cause his or her best-intended words to be distorted into an opposite meaning. Emerson expressed this point when he wrote, "What you are stands over you the while, and thunders so that I cannot hear what you say to the contrary."

A student who nods his head in class as his college professor lectures is communicating to the instructor that he is listening attentively. If he fails a subsequent examination, the instructor changes his interpretation of the meaning of the nodding head. The student has communicated that the nod of his head was merely feigned attention, and in reality was merely a device used by him to attempt to impress his instructor while at the same time trying to keep awake. The student's appearance, what he has done, and what he has said or not said communicate meaning. All of these forms of action and inaction say something.

The communication process, therefore, may include the use of any and every technique to convey meaning. Language, sounds, and other visual devices—such as signs, gestures, smiling, and frowning—all convey meaning. These are only some of the media used in communication.

SYMBOLS OF MEANING

Meaning, then, is transmitted and received by the use of symbols—things that stand for or suggest something else by reason of relationship, association, or convention. The symbol may also suggest another meaning by accidental resemblance. Symbols are numerous and of many types. These can be categorized into two general classifications—verbal symbols and nonverbal symbols.

Verbal symbols

Verbal symbols of meaning are words. The term *verbal* popularly refers to spoken words only, as in the case of the *verbal* or unwritten contract. The latter term is somewhat of a misnomer, for the term *verbal* refers to written words as well as to spoken words. Words themselves are merely symbols of meaning. We use words to convey meanings to others. We use language—a system of words and method of combining words—to communicate meaning.

Through the use of language, we frame written words into sentences and paragraphs, and these facilitate the process of written communication. Much communication in the commercial world is through written words in the form of letters. Books and documents record the history and much of the substantive knowledge of human beings. Were this not so, many of the teachings of the past would be lost to future generations. Each succeeding generation would have to rediscover simple principles which preceding generations had already discovered but had failed to record.

We are often more inept in our use of written words than we are in face-to-face communication. Through faulty words and poor composition, we fail to convey the meaning intended. The typical job applicant, for example, particularly feels the pressure when he or she must write a letter of application and submit it before an interview will be granted. The applicant cannot go first to the employment office in his or her best clothes, teeth brushed, and through good speaking ability acquire the job. The applicant must first sell himself or herself by using an inanimate object—a sheet of paper—the job application form or personal letter and resume. Poor sentence construction, poor spelling, messy erasures, and an inadvertent thumb print on that impersonal sheet of paper may close the door to further communication.

To communicate facts and information.   Selection of proper word symbols to convey the desired meaning is most important. If a person means one thing but uses a word or a combination of words which have an entirely different meaning, communication is thwarted in the very beginning. A headline once in a New York newspaper read "Former Prominent New Yorker Had Liver in Paris for Eight Years." A paper in Tennessee told of a meeting of a garden club: "The study subject will be 'Conservation of Native Pants.'" A Michigan paper declared that "Nudism would be bared in Michigan under a bill introduced in the House Wednesday." A Florida newspaper reported that "Mrs. G——, guild president, announces that the final meeting of the year will be hell, as usual, at her home, Tuesday at 3 P.M." The real meaning of such blunders is apparent with little study. Comparable errors, however, often crop up in written or oral discourse and create much more serious obstacles to communication. For example, U.S. multinational corporations have made some expensive and embarrassing blunders in their advertising of products in other nations because the word symbols they used in their advertising copy conveyed an entirely different meaning than that intended. General Motors's "body by Fisher" came out as "corpse by Fisher" in Flemish.[2] Pepsi's U.S. slogan "Come Alive with Pepsi" in German meant literally "come alive out of the grave."[3] Colgate-Palmolive's Cue toothpaste was marketed under the same name in France without knowing that "cue" is a pornographic word in French.[4]

Words must symbolize a well-understood meaning to those for whom the words are intended. We derive no meaning from language unless we are familiar with that language and with the specific meaning which each word symbolizes. A bottle labeled "Veneno" means nothing to most people in the United States. If the same bottle is labeled "Poison," the meaning is immediately grasped. Few people in Latin America would understand the meaning of the second word. They would understand the first word. Both the United States's citizen and the person from Latin America, however, would understand if the label was marked with a skull and crossbones. Although the label contained no writing, the meaning of such a symbol is universally understood in both geographic areas.

The significance of words as symbols of meaning is most apparent to us when we attempt to make ourselves understood in a foreign country. We must select symbols which communicate meaning to the native people. One person's language will have more or less universal acceptance within his or her particular geographical area. If a man walks into a store in the United States, however, and inquires, "¿Que hora es?" he will probably get a blank stare.[5] If he persists further in his attempt to communicate, he may ask, "¿Habla usted Español?" He will get the same response. The other person does not know the meaning of the words.

Unless the other person is in on the secret of the meaning which the first person has assigned to a word, communication breaks down. The story is told, for example, of the truck that was speeding down the

---

[2] Edward M. Mazze, "How to Push a Body Abroad Without Making It a Corpse," *Business Abroad* (August 10, 1964), p. 15.

[3] *Advertising Age* (May 9, 1966), p. 75.

[4] Howe Martyn, *International Business, Principles and Problems* (New York: Collier-Macmillan, 1964), p. 78. The GM, Pepsi, Colgate and other communication blunders are cited in David A. Ricks, Marilyn Y. C. Fu, and Jeffrey S. Arpan, *International Business Blunders* (Columbus, Ohio: Grid, 1974).

[5] Unless, of course, he is in Miami, Florida, or in one of the other U.S. cities where there is a strong Latin-American presence, and Spanish is in common use.

highway. A state highway policeman stopped the driver and inquired, "Did you know you were speeding?"

"No sir, I surely didn't," was the reply.

"Well, don't you have a governor on this truck?" asked the officer.

"No, sir," replied the truck driver, "that's a load of fertilizer back there."

To convey and arouse emotion. Symbols of language convey emotion as well as facts and ideas. For this reason some words or phrases become inextricably tied to certain emotional responses. Any word which vents emotion serves as a pressure valve for anger. That is why certain curse words or phrases are so popular. They act as safety valves for pent-up emotions, and at the same time, they permit the user to rebel against authority and against society-imposed standards of propriety. Further, they may act as a method by which the user can punish his or her enemies, causing anger or distress, by directing the language toward tormentors and using it in their presence. Obviously, the tormentors must understand the meaning of the words and the tone of voice utilized for the user to achieve the intended effect.

Words a person employs usually have no effect upon someone who does not attach a familiar meaning to them. If the word or expression has no emotional coloring for the listener, that person's response may be quite neutral. Our response depends upon the meaning we assign to a specific word or phrase. In some countries, to be called a "son of a jackal" would convey a most insulting mental image and arouse considerable emotion and animosity. In the United States it probably would be relatively inoffensive language. Jackals inspire no particular emotional reaction in this country. These beasts are not noted for their abundance in the United States, and we don't think about them one way or another. The use of such an expression, consequently, seems most quaint—right out of the "Arabian Nights." The fact that it bears some resemblance to an expression favored by one U.S. President would probably be lost upon the listener.[6]

Emphasis on verbal symbols. Children start to work with words

---

[6] Harry Truman was not averse to using "colorful" expressions, particularly following one music critic's evaluation of the voice recital of Margaret Truman, President Truman's daughter.

as soon as they enter school. Grammar is a rudimentary subject in the elementary school years. Logic and the organization of verbal expression, either oral or written, are introduced fairly early, and emphasis is placed upon the principles of grammar, logic, and syntax throughout a student's formal education.

Humans are obsessed with the power of words. We have come to rely upon words as absolutes. In our obsession we sometimes fail to recognize that words are mere symbols of meaning. Locke in his *Essay Concerning Human Understanding* wrote: "We should have a great many fewer disputes in the world if words were taken for what they are, the signs of our ideas only, and not for things themselves."[7]

Certain combinations of words have magic. This trait has given rise to what has been characterized as "the slogan society."[8] Slogans have been used most effectively in political campaigns and in advertising. They often serve as a substitute for logical argument. Repetition of a catchy phrase gives it familiarity, and familiarity lends respectability and credibility to an assertion which may or may not be true. Nebraskans some years ago elected to the U.S. House of Representatives a candidate whose campaign slogan was "Vote for ———— ————; he's got gumption!" Since we have a basic intolerance for ambiguity, complex issues can be resolved by adoption of a simple slogan which eliminates the necessity for analytical thinking.

Words come to be so important that they are sometimes thought to be the only means of communication. Thus, to improve communication, it is sometimes believed that one need only simplify language. The insurance business has concerned itself with contract simplification. "Simple" language, accompanied by clever drawings and illustrations, has been introduced to insurance contracts. In this way, the public is supposed to be better able to understand insurance policies. Surely this has some merit; but so-called simplification sometimes complicates the claims handling process and confounds the claims representative and insurance counsel. Some of the abandoned complex language had definite legal meaning interpreted by a body of court decisions. The new "simple" language is sometimes difficult to apply to the involved situations which arise in the complex legal world of insurance claims handling.

---

[7] John Locke, *An Essay Concerning Human Understanding* (Philadelphia: James Kay, Jr., and Brother, 1800), book 3, chap. 10, sec. 15.

[8] "The Slogan Society," *Time* (October 16, 1964), p. 96.

Sometimes in the rush toward simplification, a richness of meaning is lost. Rudolph Flesch in *The Art of Plain Talk* exhorts people to "write as we talk."[9] In the process of doing just that, great literature may be reduced to journalism, robbing it of its rhythm, rhetoric, and irony. There is merit, nevertheless, in clarifying ambiguous language and in eliminating conflicting terminology, particularly in the insurance business.

Nonverbal symbols

One see is worth a thousand tells.
────Chinese Proverb

Humans devote much effort to mastering the rules of verbal communication. Nonverbal communication, on the other hand, receives comparatively little attention. Some people seem to overlook the merit of the nonverbal symbols as communication tools.

The typical person often does not dwell on the value of the impressions, emotions, ideas, and meanings that are communicated to him or her through the media of music, the pictorial arts, the theater, the ballet, and all the forms of nonverbal human behavior. We are so wrapped up in our worship of verbal forms of communication that we have almost a complete naïveté and reliance on the power of words. Some people believe that all we need do to suppress unpopular or "immoral" ideas is to ban their expression in verbal forms. As a consequence, we censor and burn these books and like materials. This, we foolishly believe, will eliminate communication in certain subjects.

Humans have always turned to other forms of communication when verbal expression is outlawed. The nonverbal means of communication, for example, convey a wealth of meaning. Instrumentalities of symbolism are rich in variety; meaning has many outlets.

Bodily movement. "Every little movement has a meaning of its own," so go the lyrics of an old song. Meaning can be expressed by action of any part of the body. The lips purse, and the eyes wink to express meaning. Drumming of the fingers or tapping a foot nervously can show impatience or boredom. The master of nonverbal communication is the young baby who sucks, bites, clutches, cries, smiles,

---

[9] Rudolph Franz Flesch, *The Art of Plain Talk* (New York: Harper & Bros., 1946).

shouts, babbles, and laughs to express meaning. People often communicate with a smile, a frown, a shrug of the shoulders, a wink, or any other bodily movement or lack of bodily movement.

Certain symbols have fairly universal meaning, although the person using that symbol may not have specifically intended that meaning. Humans tend to equate a smiling countenance with a happy, friendly individual, even though that person may be an unfriendly, scheming scoundrel who merely wishes to display his new bridgework. On the other hand, the person who frowns is invariably characterized as an unfriendly, cheerless drudge. Maybe he or she is a pensive individual who frowns while thinking. In fact, he or she may be a person of good humor who loves people.

People tend to sympathize with the blind man tapping his way down a sidewalk with a white cane. He has communicated the fact to people that he is blind. The white cane is the well-recognized universal symbol of blindness. In addition, it is apparent from the hesitation and uncertainty of the blind man, as he takes his steps, that he is blind. He has used symbols of meaning to communicate with the world around him. That meaning is apparent. A stranger knows of the blind man's plight and asks him if he desires help. The blind man hears the offer of help and can answer.

Consider, however, the deaf-mute who depends upon sight for communication. Unable to hear, this person cannot create meaningful sounds. If spoken to while the back is turned, the deaf-mute receives no symbol of meaning. The person who speaks nevertheless interprets inaction of the deaf-mute to be a communication. The speaker feels rejected.

People expect responses to their conversation; they take offense if they are ignored. The rejected person avoids the deaf-mute as an unfriendly, undesirable person. The latter, living in the isolation of a soundless world, is further cut off when people purposely avoid him or her. Perhaps the deaf-mute should wear a sign which reads "I am a deaf-mute." This often creates more problems than it solves. Most people don't know how to communicate with a deaf-mute. It may be impractical to write a message to the deaf-mute, and few people know sign language. As a consequence, many will ignore the deaf-mute or simply stare in embarrassment, hoping that he or she will go away. If you feel compassion for the blind, consider the infinite sympathy which you should feel for the deaf-mute—a person cut off from verbal communication in a world where sound plays such an important role in communication.

Sounds. People can convey meaning by sounds not formed into words. A scream, a shout, a grunt, a sigh, or a whistle may serve as a symbol of meaning. Usually, however, the interpretation of the sound depends upon a previously established meaning connection. In other words, the person who hears the sound must associate a certain meaning with it.

A word, a sound, or any other symbol, has meaning only when the person has been previously educated to that meaning. A whistle by itself means nothing unless it has meaning. For example, a man can attempt to summon his small son to supper by whistling to him. He can whistle until he is blue in the face. The boy will simply ignore the sound or stare at his father, wondering why such a racket. The man must explain to his son that when the latter hears his father's whistle, he must respond in all due haste. The son then knows the meaning of the symbol, the whistle. If the son at first fails to respond in timely fashion, the man can strengthen the stimulus-response connection by paddling or otherwise chastizing the youngster. Subsequent whistles by the father will elicit accurate meaning interpretations and (hopefully) more rapid responses from the boy.

Signs or visual symbols. Human beings communicate meaning by visual symbols, such as paintings, photography, engravings, drawings, sculpture, and so forth. Besides using words to convey direct meaning, words also are used in a riddle-like manner so that they do not lend themselves to easy interpretation. People attempt to interpret meaning in poetry, books, paintings, or in other symbols of human expression. An 18th-century Englishman wrote a poem which created controversy at the time. Speculation raged so that the author was questioned about the meaning written into his poem. "No meaning," he answered simply, "I wrote it because I needed the money." Despite his answer, the poet could not eliminate all meaning from his poem, even if he tried.

A popular pastime of book reviewers, critics, and other intellectuals or pseudointellectuals is to ascertain the meaning incorporated in such books as Salinger's *Catcher In The Rye*. People are still trying to determine the meaning behind the famous smile of the "Mona Lisa," painted by the 15th-century painter Leonardo da Vinci. An artist friend of the author cut his artist's palette into a square, framed it, and entered it in an art contest at the county fair. The artist listened gleefully to people attempting to interpret the meaning expressed in the "painting."

A person's appearance serves as a symbol of meaning. Rightly or wrongly, we are judged by our appearance. Mention has already been made of the role played by proper dress in the process of communication. We are judged by our appearance. We are aware that society expects us to dress to fit the time, the place, and the occasion.

Failure to observe the conventions of society usually communicates negative impressions and meaning. The gaily dressed recent widow, for example, is assumed to display a shocking disrespect for the memory of her late husband. Her manner of dress is interpreted to mean that she had no love for the deceased and in fact probably is happy that he is no longer alive. The truth may be that she is deeply grieved by his passing but is trying to adjust and to ease the shock of his death for herself and her children by keeping up an appearance of cheer.

Certain "prestige" clothing stores are marked by the absence of casual dressers. The clientele of these stores are typically "dressed to the hilt." It is expected of them. They have an image to maintain. A woman customer who dares to enter such a store in flat shoes and simple housedress usually would feel conspicuous and out of place.

In today's world where college professors are expected to get out of their ivory towers and identify with the community, appearance is most important. If a male college professor, for example, should grow a beard and mustache, wear Bohemian dress, and ride a bicycle to and from campus, he might possibly be criticized by the university administration and passed over on promotions and salary increases. Dress standards undergo major changes, marked by occasional periods of acceptable informality, but the standards exist in every era. People's appearance must fit the time, the place, and the occasion. Convention demands it. Failure to conform conveys adverse meaning, and the nonconformist will receive his or her punishment through society's ostracism and by failure to achieve success in certain social or business environments.

COMMUNICATION AND INSURANCE CLAIMS HANDLING

Our primary job as a claims representative is that of communication. All of the functions which we are called upon to perform depend upon the ability to convey meaning and to receive meaning from others. Furthermore, in claims work the claims person should be held to a high standard of accountability in the performance of the communication process. This is because we are operating in an area of rather rigid rules pertaining to legal evidence, contracts, and principles of liability. The claims representative must work for a high degree of perception in understanding others and an exactness in being understood by others. Any other standard is unacceptable. Any difficulty experienced in conveying meaning or in understanding others reflects upon our ability to perform the claims handling job.

The claims person, therefore, must understand communication—in face-to-face relationships, in drawing, and in the written word. The words we choose, the way in which they are spoken, our facial expressions, body posture, mannerisms, and attire, all serve to communicate meaning to those people we meet. The ability to write intelligibly and report faithfully the exact words related by a witness will lend credibility to the latter's statement. Clarity in written communication is particularly essential as the claims representative prepares reports for the home office or assigning office. Investigation reports require clarity, conciseness, and completeness. Summaries of recorded statements and analyses of claims necessarily demand unusual skill in written communication. The claims representative must be able to communicate not only with words but with other written symbols as well. We must possess enough ability and talent to draw simple diagrams which clearly convey meaning, and photographs and other visual symbols must communicate clearly if they are to have any value in the claims handling process. Particularly important is the necessity of establishing the proper climate for communication with insureds, claimants, and witnesses, for successful communication can break down in a hostile environment.

Climate for communication—a philosophy

When Napoleon Bonaparte invaded Egypt, he stood before his vast army in the Egyptian desert in the shadow of the great pyramids and declared: "Forty centuries look down upon you!" His speech was designed to arouse the enthusiasm and loyalty of his army. When he first moved into Egypt, he immediately launched a newspaper, *The Courier of Egypt,* for purposes of improving his relations with the conquered public. Everywhere he went, he monopolized as many channels of communication as possible so that he could attempt to influence people to like him. He was his own public relations man, using words and action to win public approval. The British statesman, George Canning, summarized the role of public opinion in the events of the Napoleonic Wars as "a power more tremendous than was perhaps ever yet brought into action in the history of all mankind."

Public opinion is still the greatest power today. It molds public and individual thinking throughout the world. It is essential to the welfare of any government, any institution, and any individual. It creates great change. New laws come about by the force of public opinion; old laws are abandoned. Old institutions and ways of life tumble and are destroyed when public opinion turns against them. New institutions and concepts arise and become prominent.

Public relations are vital in every activity, whether it is business or personal activity. Our ability to obtain and hold jobs and our ability to attract and win husbands or wives is dependent upon public relations. Public relations is the ability to make friends, and just as important, the ability to retain friends.

Human beings are gregarious animals; we depend upon mutual aid. Our success in life is measured often by our ability to make friends and influence people rather than by our technical skill and our native and acquired intelligence. A psychologist states: "It is the individual who is not interested in his fellow men who has the greatest difficulties in life and provides the greatest injury to others. It is from among such individuals that all human failures spring."[10] The foregoing has great significance for the insurance industry and for the individual claims person.

Today's insurance claims representative, of course, should not look upon himself or herself as a great philanthropist whose primary job is to make people happy by bestowing upon them large amounts

---

[10] Alfred Adler, *What Life Should Mean to You* (New York: Grosset & Dunlap, 1931), p. 253.

of money in the form of claim payments. It is not within our province of proper activity to buy goodwill and otherwise to make payments which are not legally justified. The claims person's primary duty is still that of paying claims only where there is legal justification for such payment. It is important, however, for us to recognize that we can perform the claims handling functions only if we will create the proper climate and atmosphere.

The claims person must practice good public relations within a climate and atmosphere in which he or she can best communicate. Without communication, we can little hope to motivate and influence others to cooperate so that we can perform the claims handling functions. The claims representative must keep in mind this philosophy.

The claims person's personal appearance

We must at all times be conscious of our personal appearance. Since people judge other people by how they look, the claims person's appearance must always be proper in terms of time, place, and occasion. Extremes of dress must be avoided. Shabby appearance of a claims representative militates against our best efforts to gain confidence of insureds, claimants, and other people. You are the representative of a business and must meet the standard of appearance expected of businessmen and businesswomen—well-groomed and wearing modest, good-fitting clothes, neat shoes, and whatever other attire is dictated by the custom of your particular locality.

Overdressing is as out of place for the claims person as it is for any other businessperson. Anything that is ostentatious, or that is noticeably luxurious, should be avoided. Society sets the custom for dress for each occasion, and adherence to that custom and the standards dictated will result in society's acceptance. Deviation from the standard will produce adverse reactions. It communicates an unfavorable image. Commenting on proper attire for businesspersons, Dale Carnegie once said: "I love colorful clothes and regret that custom demands that I wear suits of somber hues; but when I crawl into bed at night, I wear pajamas of flaming red or canary yellow." The claims representative, similarly, must restrict his or her nonconformity in dress to leisure hours.

Some interesting studies have been conducted in recent years on the role of apparel in business success. Research indicates that people's wardrobes and accessories affect their careers and social success. The way you dress can move you up socially and in business, or it can hold you back. It can mask or overcome detrimental physical features, and it can make a man or woman more effective and more successful.

John T. Molloy, author of *Dress for Success* (a widely-read syndicated column) and *The Woman's Dress for Success Book,* contends that what you wear immediately establishes your authority, credibility, and likability. Molloy, a consultant who has devoted his career to studying the role of apparel in business success, writes: "The darker, more traditional the clothing, the more authority it transmits. So if you want to convey an image of power and prestige, your main garments should be dark blue or dark gray, and always of top quality. You should buy the best clothing you can afford."[11]

Young men and women who are just starting out on a job may be limited in their financial resources and feel restricted in their ability to buy quality clothes. Most of us don't have a lot of money to spend on clothes. It is not lack of money, however, that causes most people to fail to dress in a way that commands respect. It is a matter of judgment and unfamiliarity with the rules of dress. With a little care and effort, the average man or woman can easily create the look of success.

Obviously, the standard of dress for the successful and effective insurance claims representative does not entail dressing like the president of General Motors. If you dress like a top corporate executive and go out to speak to a housewife who's wearing blue jeans and chasing a couple of kids, your clothing will appear ostentatious. Molloy cites an example where a corporate executive of an aircraft company appeared on television to talk to the public about his firm's financial problems. The firm was seeking government aid—help from the taxpayers. He appeared on television standing on the plant floor wearing a $450 suit and a white hard hat, shiny and new and obviously never worn before. The image he presented was, "Look, I'm standing here in my $450 suit. I don't want to get my hands dirty, but I need your money."

----

[11] John T. Molloy, "Does What You Wear Tell Where You're Headed?" *U.S. News and World Report* (September 25, 1978), pp. 59, 62.

Use common sense. There is a standard of dress for all business persons—almost a uniform. The insurance claims person is not supposed to look like a director of AT&T or the chairman of the board of Bank of America. He or she, however, must dress like a serious, efficient, and "business-like" person. Rules of dress vary from one part of the country to another. The Northeast tends to be the most conservative. Dress becomes more casual in the Midwest and Far West, and in California, according to Molloy, "Everybody goes bananas, and the rules of the rest of the country just don't apply."

You have heard the expression, "The clothes make the man." That goes for women, too. The losers stand out like sore thumbs. Molloy states: "Many people believe that they get promoted on the basis of their efficiency, reliability, and hard work. But very often, it's the semblance of these qualities brought out in good dress and good grooming that helps success along."[12]

Good dress and grooming give the appearance that you are what you represent. It conveys the impression of authority, knowledge, and power. It impresses employer and customer alike. With the insurance claims representative, good dress is a positive asset that impresses employer, insureds, witnesses, claimants, attorneys and others with whom the claims person comes in contact.

Follow the rules of proper dress if you would be more effective and more successful. The rules of proper dress, according to the experts, are:

For everyone:

DON'T wear something "far out" or flamboyant (Carnegie's rule against nonconformity).

DO dress for the occasion. Keep your business dress and social dress separate. Business dress is often too conservative and severe for many social affairs, whereas most social dress is completely inappropriate for the conduct of business. There is no question that styles change, rules of formality may soften, and informality may creep into business usage. However, a staunch thread of formality always remains in the rules of proper dress. You might dress informally in your own business, but there is always a standard that must be met in the greater world of business, particularly

---

[12] Ibid.

where you work for other people, for corporations, and for other institutions. For people in business, there is a standard—almost a uniform—of proper dress, and the standard must be met if you wish to convey the image that will help you to become more effective on your job.

DO be mindful of colors of clothing. Dark, traditional clothing conveys an image of power and authority. Wear main garments of dark blue or dark gray, and always of top quality. Curiously enough, however, this rule does not apply to raincoats. A beige raincoat stamps the wearer as belonging to a higher socio-economic class than a black raincoat. Studies reveal that the wearer of the beige raincoat receives more deferential treatment from other people than if the raincoat is black.

DO wear high contrasts in clothes. There should be a high contrast between the color of one's suit and the shirt or blouse. For men, that means a white shirt with a dark suit. For women, a white blouse with a dark suit, perhaps set off with a bright scarf.

For Men:

DON'T wear a bow tie. Research studies indicate that bow ties convey negative impressions. Men who wear bow ties are considered to be unpredictable. Research conducted in the psychology of jury selection reveals a strong bias against men who wear bow ties. Some experienced trial lawyers who believe they have a good case will try to keep a man wearing a bow tie off the jury.

DON'T wear loud, gaudy ties; they have a cheap, "lower-class" look.

DON'T wear loud, gaudy shirts. Shirt colors should be restricted to white, pale blue, beige, pale yellow, pale pink, or any simple clean stripe against a white background. Molloy, however, advocates adoption of *the white-shirt-only rule.* Latest research, he reports, indicates that a white shirt lends credibility and authority to its male wearer.[13]

For Women:

NEVER wear sexy or frilly things to the office. You are sending the message: "I'm a sweet little girl; I'm here just to be charming."

---

[13] John T. Molloy, "Dress for Success," *Sunday World Herald* (September 21, 1980), p. 2–E.

This is always negative for a woman who is striving for credibility and the appearance of authority.

DON'T dress as an "imitation man." Don't wear a shirt and tie, a vest, a pinstripe or other wearing apparel that is currently male-associated. Such clothes on women generate negative reactions and strongly diminish a woman's effectiveness on the job.

DON'T carry a handbag or purse. A woman claims representative should carry an attache case, a file jacket portfolio, or whatever happens to be in current use by businesspersons.

DON'T wear fashion boots to work. If you must wear them because of inclement weather, change into more conservative shoes when you get to the office.

DON'T buy a fashion item as soon as it reaches the market. Be conservative and wait until the item has been generally accepted by women in business. If you buy and wear the item too soon, it may not "catch on" in the market, and you will be stuck with a useless item of apparel. Worse still, you will have the appearance of a nonconformist.

Bodily movement

Bodily movement plays an important role in the communication process. Since we as claims persons must motivate other people to respond in a desired fashion, we must be particularly aware of the meaning we communicate and the reaction caused by our body actions.

We may enter a house, for example, which may not measure up to our standards of livability. Odors, filth, and litter, personal uncleanliness of its occupants, and other factors may shock our sensibilities and repulse us. If we are not careful, we may by inadvertent cringing show evidence of this repulsion and disgust. The inhabitants of the house may notice this reaction and be offended. We have communicated adversely, and it probably will affect our efforts to handle a claim, obtain a witness's statement, proceed with negotiations, and so on.

Travelers in foreign countries often meet people whose values and standards are strange, forbidding, or repulsive. Having to eat some foreign foods and having to tolerate some accommodations can be most trying for the tourist. When we travel, we must be diplomatic if we are to avoid offending our hosts or foreign acquaintances. Insurance claims persons, likewise, must beware of allowing personal bodily movement to betray dismay or disgust about things which do not meet our standards.

Accidental or inadvertent communicating can be most unfortunate, for it confuses, misinforms, irritates, or creates dissension. A classic case of communication error took place during World War II. An aerial gunnery student was taking a training flight over the Gulf of Mexico. The pilot, enjoying the ride and the scenery, pointed over the side of the plane, in a friendly spirit, to call the student's attention to a speedboat below. The student, interpreting the gesture to mean "Bail out," hurriedly parachuted over the side. This drastic case of accidental communication resulted when the pilot attempted to communicate without fitting his symbols to the world of his student.

To avoid adverse communication, the claims representative must be careful in the approach to other people. Consider an actual example. A man walked into the showroom of a new car dealer and was met by a salesman. In the course of conversation, the salesman introduced his sales supervisor. The supervisor rushed up to the man, effusively addressed him by first name, grasped his elbow with one hand and his right hand with the other. To greet a stranger in this manner may be acceptable procedure in the supervisor's sales meetings, but such familiarity may be offensive to other people. As insurance claims representatives we must approach people with respect and consideration. If we meet a claimant and immediately assume a dominant and overbearing manner, we will in most cases communicate an adverse impression. We appear as high-pressured promoters. People may very well recoil with suspicion and distrust.

Later in this book the subject of motivation is explored. The claims person is instructed to use certain techniques—such as positioning—to communicate the correct impressions as he or she earns another person's confidence and respect and then begins the subtle process of wooing the other person over to a desired way of thinking.

Smiling and courtesy—An attitude

Two men look out through the same bars;
One sees the mud, and one the stars.
———Frederick Langbridge

A most important form of bodily movement is smiling. A person is required to use muscles to move a leg or to gesture with arms, hands, and fingers; smiling, too, requires the use of muscles. It is not coincidental that people who are most successful at communicating are also skilled at smiling.

Smiling is definitely a skill. Although people take the smile for granted as something which naturally results when a person is happy or amused, being able to smile when one does not feel happy or amused demands skill. This is why actors devote hours of practice to smiling and laughing. In their role playing they must be able to smile or laugh on cue. Their smiling, under these circumstances, usually has nothing to do with their personal feelings of happiness or amusement at the moment. Politicians, likewise, must know how to turn on a smile at a moment's notice, although they may be suffering from severe fatigue from the demands of a campaign. They fully recognize the truth of Nathaniel Hawthorne's admonishment: "A stale article, if you dip it in a good, warm, sunny smile, will go off better than a fresh one that you've scowled upon."[14]

The insurance claims representative must know how to smile, for as a goodwill builder, smiling has no equal. A mechanical, insincere smile, of course, is out of place. The reader might ask, "How can I smile sincerely when I don't feel amused or happy?" Dale Carnegie suggests the answer—a change of attitude. Think in terms of the happiness and amusement which you give to others and smile with that objective in mind. The more we smile to give happiness and amusement to others, the more it will redound to our own benefit.

The habit of smiling is even more successful when it is combined with unfailing courtesy. Courtesy and politeness are the essentials of considerate behavior, and considerate behavior produces rapport with others so that communication is facilitated. James Thomas Fields wrote: "Courtesy transmutes aliens into trusting friends, and gives its owner passport round the globe."[15]

Life sometimes seems to be a series of frustrations caused by other people. If we become upset and resort to discourteous and impolite action to vent our anger against those people who cause our frustrations, we erect barriers to future understanding and communi-

---

[14] From *The House of the Seven Gables*, chap. 4.

[15] From "Courtesy," contained in *The Shorter Bartlett's Familiar Quotations* (New York: Permabooks, 1953), p. 129.

cation. "To err is human, to forgive, divine" is not merely an altruistic platitude. It makes good sense. Although a claims person may be frustrated in dealing with other people, he or she will find that courtesy yields its reward. The people who presently confound the claims representative may, because of his or her considerate behavior, ultimately respond with consideration and make the claims handling job easier. People tend to reciprocate kindness, and they retaliate against meanness.

A natural reaction to mistakes and unreasonable action of others is anger, but we must realize that we, likewise, sometimes err and are unreasonable. It is important, therefore, that we maintain a mental attitude of courtesy and consideration for others. Such an attitude combined with a warm, sincere smile can work wonders for us. We will be better received, better liked, and more successful in our human relations, whether they be at home, at church, or on the job. Employing an attitude of consideration and good cheer, the claims person who smiles during contacts with insureds, claimants, and all others has a formidable tool for conducting successful communication.

The professional visit

Successful communication requires the claims representative to maintain a professional attitude in visits with insureds, claimants, and witnesses. Reference already has been made to the subject of overfamiliarity employed by some salespeople. The insurance claims person must be particularly careful about this point. We should always be sincere and friendly, but should never become "buddy-buddy" with the other person. One personal injuries attorney has described a case which he handled because a claims man arrived at a claimant's house at lunch time and boldly invited himself to lunch. The claimant (a housewife) graciously acceded to this demand. That evening, after learning of the incident, her infuriated husband called the attorney.

Another aspect of professionalism has to do with the length of the interview. A brief visit should be the rule. The claims person must not overtalk or overstay a visit. Overtalking and overstaying seem to produce distinctly unfavorable reactions on the part of a claimant, insured, or witness. A claimant, for example, may decide that the claim must be more serious than it appears or else it would not be discussed interminably. An alternative reaction is that which any door-to-door salesperson "pest" generates—the claimant becomes irritated at having his or her time wasted.

Written communication

Take away the dross from the silver and there shall come forth a vessel for the refiner.

——Solomon

A new claims person who has been an indifferent student of grammar and composition will be severely handicapped in the claims handling job. Dismissing these subjects as "dry" during our school years is a mistake, for it is these very topics which provide the claims representative with the tools required to convey meaning. The claims person becomes painfully aware of the importance of these subjects when undertaking to write a clear, concise letter or a complete, easily read, well-organized investigation report.

Nothing is more irritating to claims examiners and insurance counsel than to receive written communications which are poorly constructed, ambiguous, and strangling in a miasma of verbiage. An investigation report that is constructed of a series of long, rambling paragraphs, resembling the jumbled parts of a jigsaw puzzle, with incomplete and widely scattered statements of fact throughout, is a serious reflection on the office of its origin. Poor composition, irrelevant material, and poor arrangement and organization rob a reviewer of precious time and mental energy.

The claims person should work for clarity, simplicity, and completeness in all written communication. A letter or a written report may have several purposes—to inform, to persuade, and so forth. To accomplish these purposes, the writing must be clear, concise, and complete. *Clarity* requires that we write in such a manner that there is no ambiguity in meaning. We must examine our own written words to see if they actually express the meaning and the information that we wish to communicate. We must put ourselves in our reader's shoes and write from his or her point of view to make certain that the reader will understand.

Conciseness requires that the writer remove all superfluous or elaborative material from written expression. It requires that we be on point and to the point—expressing much in a few words. Our purpose is to allow the reader to understand quickly and easily. Wordiness, irrelevant details, and business jargon destroy conciseness. Suppose a field claims representative received a letter from the home office or assigning office which began like this:

> I have recently been reviewing the file regarding the above-captioned
> matter and note that in examining my letter to you of February 10th of
> this year that I indicated to you that it would be most desirable if you
> would approach the claimant, John Jones, on this matter and see if he
> might not now be persuaded to conclude final negotiations on his
> bodily injury liability claim, and I wonder if you would advise at your
> earliest opportunity if you have had the time to follow up on my
> suggestions?

The writer has merely inquired, "Have you settled with the claimant, John Jones?" To begin a letter with such a simple question may appear brusque and impolite to some readers. On the contrary, the monstrous wordiness of the first example is impolite, for it robs the addressee of valuable time and mental energy. When we send a personal telegram to a member of our family, we will work hard to reduce the redundancy of words. We do this because extra words in telegrams cost money. Similarly, claims persons must realize that excessive wordiness in letters and investigation reports is also costly.

Conciseness, of course, is not necessarily synonymous with brevity. *Completeness* is important. Claims correspondence must contain all of the vital information. A well-worn adage dictates that good writing is like a woman's skirt, short enough to be interesting but long enough to cover the subject. A message must not be so brief that it becomes ambiguous.

To satisfy the requirements of clarity, conciseness, and completeness is a difficult problem for a person who is not skilled in writing. It explains why poorly written communication is widespread in business, including the field of insurance claims handling. As claims persons, we must work hard to acquire competence in written communication. We must boil our letters down into well-digested and well-arranged messages. Investigation reports must be handled in a similar manner. They must communicate clearly, concisely, and completely. Since a report is merely a long letter, the writer must employ sound principles in the construction of the report.

Because of a report's length, however, the claims representative is well-advised to use subject headings in preparing it. One authority, for example, recommends that investigations involving automobile accidents be reported with the following headings and captions:[16]

1.	Enclosures	12.	Imputed negligence
2.	Coverage	13.	Liability
3.	Identification	14.	Collision loss
4.	Date, time, and place	15.	Third party—subrogation
5.	Locus	16.	Property damage
6.	Diagram	17.	Medical payments claims
7.	Description of accident	18.	Doctor
8.	Claimant data—suggested reserves	19.	Lost time and wages
		20.	Special damages
9.	Witness statements	21.	Settlement
10.	Police reports—official records	22.	Control
		23.	Risk
11.	Photographs	24.	Recommendations

Claims representatives are encouraged to use different or additional captions where indicated if the information submitted cannot be stated properly under one of the above subject headings. The important point is to communicate with clarity, conciseness, and completeness.

In written communication, whether it be in written letters or reports, there are a number of pitfalls to avoid. The following are examples:

1. *Routine and stereotyped openings—*
   We wish to acknowledge receipt of your letter of
   With regard to your letter of
   I have received your report
   Replying to yours of December 12
   I have your letter of December 12 at hand
   (Why not begin with "Thank you for your letter" or "We appreciate your letter"?)
2. *Trite, vague, and excessive words—*
   Along these lines (meaning is unclear)
   At the earliest possible moment (say "soon")

---

[16] Corydon T. Johns, *An Introduction to Liability Claims Adjusting* (Cincinnati: National Underwriter Company, 1965), p. 260.

Contents duly noted (unnecessary wordiness)
For your information (omit this)
This letter is for the purpose of requesting (omit this)

3. *Words which antagonize—*
    You claim, you state, you say (recast the sentence to soften the tone)

4. *Poor organization—*
    No logical order in presentation of ideas.

5. *Generalizations—*
    No facts or supporting evidence to justify conclusions.

6. *Poor closings—*
    Thanking you in advance (presumptuous—it antagonizes the reader because it assumes that he or she is going to do what you have requested. Say instead, "We shall appreciate" or "We shall be grateful for your help.")
    Thank you again (same criticism, also unnecessary repetition)
    Thanking you, I am (dangling participle, hackneyed)
    Thank you for your cooperation (again, presumptuous)

7. *Other trite and outworn expressions and business jargon—*

Beg to inform	Under separate cover
Allow me to	Up to this writing
As per	The undersigned
Attached please find	Yours of recent date
Each and every	Permit me to say

The insurance industry in recent years has sought to cull the legalese —wordy, highly formal and complex legal language—from insurance contracts in order to facilitate communication with the insuring public. Other institutions, however, have added to our store of rich examples of poorly written communication. The federal Occupational Safety and Health Administration (created in 1970), for example, has contributed the classic definition of an *exit:* "that portion of a means of egress which is separated from all other spaces of the building or structure by construction or equipment as required in this subpart to provide a protected way of travel to the exit discharge."[17] This absurd exercise in ostentatious verbiage insults the intelligence of any reader.

---

[17] U.S. Department of Labor, Occupational Safety and Health Administration, *Federal Register,* vol. 37, no. 202, part II, section 1901.35 (c) (October 18, 1972), p. 22130; see discussion, "Storm-Tossed OSHA," *The New Republic* (May 17, 1980), p. 5.

The claims representative must resist any temptation to substitute this type of writing for good communication.

Speech

Speech, although discussed last in this section on communication and insurance claims handling, is perhaps the most important medium of communication. Speech, because of the endless variety of word symbols available, is no doubt the most versatile communication medium used by mankind. Besides the variety of words in existence, a tremendous variation in meaning can be transmitted by the tone of the voice, its inflection and timing, its volume, and the rate at which words are spoken. Furthermore, our unique ability to connect words into phrases, sentences, and paragraphs allows us to convey our thoughts and ideas and to expand upon them and delve into them in great depth.

The ability to speak well is an important asset for the claims person. A person's ability to influence others is directly proportional to his or her speaking ability. Nevertheless, mere glibness and surface brilliance will not help the claims person accomplish the functions of the claims handling job. To achieve and maintain a position of influence in any field of endeavor, we must work to develop integrity in our speech habits—we must cultivate directness and sincerity in oral expression. We must have truth and thoughtfulness in our words. If we are good speakers, we ordinarily can make friends more easily than less articulate persons. Other things being equal, if we speak well, we will progress more rapidly in our profession than individuals less skilled in speech.

Men and women usually do not acquire competence in articulate speech without considerable effort. Some people seem to have been born to speak; others develop their abilities through extensive practice of the principles of speech. These principles were formulated centuries ago by such men as Aristotle, Plato, and Cicero. Their writings, together with the contributions of great leaders and speakers such as Daniel Webster, Susan B. Anthony, John C. Calhoun, and Abraham Lincoln, still serve as a rich source of instruction to the modern student of speech.

Probably the most important principle of speech is that communication is not restricted to words alone. All of the nonverbal symbols enter the picture and strengthen, weaken, modify, or completely distort the words being spoken. In other words, while the insurance claims representative is speaking, meaning is being communicated to the listener in many different ways. The listener is receiving meaning from the words being spoken, by the way in which they are being spoken, by the expression on our face, by our appearance, by the impression of friendliness or unfriendliness that we convey, by the trust or distrust that is stimulated in the listener, and by all of the many other symbols which serve to communicate meaning.

One must conclude, therefore, that effective speech requires skillful blending of all of the nonverbal symbols with the verbal symbols of meaning in order to communicate. The nonverbal symbols of meaning must be used to complement and strengthen the verbal communication of the claims representative.

Effective speech, then, is much more than the skill of putting words together and saying them. Words by themselves are lifeless; without complementation, they may be useless in communicating meaning. Effective speech contemplates the use of all of the factors of successful communication. The relations between words and their complementing factors are indicated as follows:

WORDS

Are enhanced by the "communication climate" created by:
    Reputation of the claims representative.
    Appearance of the claims representative.
    The manner of the claims person—are we considerate?
        Or are we over-bearing?
    Our consideration of our listener.
    The establishment of rapport with the listener.
Are strengthened by delivery because of:
    The claims person's self-confidence.
    Our conviction.
    Our enthusiasm.
    Our apparent sincerity.
    The support our body gives to our words.
        Lack of tension.
        Movement in harmony with the words spoken.
        Gestures.
        Smiling, frowning, and other facial expression.

Facility of oral expression.

Pleasant voice tone, manner, variation, and freedom from monotony.

Are supported by:

The claims person's sound argument and logic.

Our organized presentation.

Our apparent knowledge of the subject.

Words, implemented by all of these factors, construct a meaning and convey it to the sense receptors of the other person. Presence or absence of either positive factors or of negative factors can alter drastically the word meanings originally intended by the speaker. Through skillful speech, the claims person's meaning will be conveyed accurately and positively. Through clumsy expression, word meanings may undergo considerable distortion.

Whether it be verbal communication, written or oral, or whether it be nonverbal communication, the claims representative must be familiar with the process. We must know the mechanics of communication, and we must know the obstacles that confront communication. We must understand why meaning sometimes is transmitted imperfectly or not at all, and we must have a practical approach to remedying the obstacles or distortions that interfere with good communications. These problems will be explored in the following pages.

MECHANICS OF COMMUNICATION

Communication is the process of passing meaning from one place to another without losing or modifying it enroute. When meaning is lost, distortion takes place. Obstacles to communication enter in and distort or completely block the transmission of meaning.

Transmission in communication works in a similar fashion to the transmission of power in the automobile. In the automobile, power comes from the motor. It makes the gears turn and causes the drive shaft to revolve. In the conventional automobile, this in turn transmits power to the rear wheels. When they turn, the automobile moves.

Transmission of power in the automobile can be interrupted. A defective clutch which fails to engage the motor with the drive shaft, a broken drive shaft, or a worn-out set of rear bearings all will interfere with the transmission of power from the motor to the wheels.

Figure 4–1

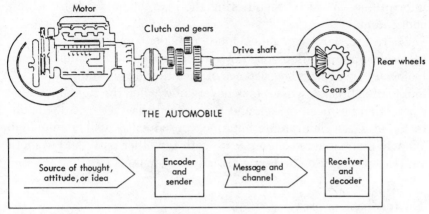

THE AUTOMOBILE

COMMUNICATION

The mechanics of communication work in the same manner. The similarity is shown in Figure 4–1. Meaning must be transmitted from the source of thought to the decoder of the message. The motivation for communication, rather than a gasoline motor, is a source of thought, an attitude, or an idea. This is encoded into symbols of meaning which are given expression by a sender. The expression, or message, follows a channel (speech, a letter, a gesture). It is transmitted to a receiver who must then translate or decode it into meaning.

Communication—a mechanic's nightmare

Unfortunately, the mechanical process of communication is not as simple as that of the transmission of power in the automobile. The communication process is fraught with problems of defective and misfitting parts. In short, it is a mechanic's nightmare. It obviously is a much more complicated process than getting the power of an automobile engine to the wheels of the vehicle. Meaning is tenuous and not easily harnessed and transmitted. Distortions creep into the communication process and result in breakdowns.

Some forms of communication breakdown are obvious to the claims representative. If we are talking to another party via long distance telephone, and the operator breaks the connection, there is a definite communication breakdown. We know how to remedy the telephone interruption. We need merely ring the operator and ask for a new connection.

There are, however, much more prevalent and more important types of communication breakdown which confront the claims person. Unless we recognize the existence of the other manifestations of communication breakdown, we may never know when the communication connection has been broken and how to remedy the breakdown. Effectiveness as a claims representative, consequently, will be impaired. We will be unable to communicate with the other party and to motivate the other person to respond in a desired manner.

The feedback process

It is critical in the communication process to know whether distortion has entered the picture, causing communication breakdown. We must determine whether our meaning has passed through the various steps of communication so that meaning has not been lost or modified enroute. This is accomplished by the *feedback* process.

Our automobile example illustrates the transmission of a thought, attitude, or idea by the encoder and sender, who sends a message through a channel to a receiver and decoder. We must ascertain whether the message has reached the other person and has been decoded accurately. This is where feedback enters the picture. Feedback is highly essential to guard against breakdowns in communication, assuring that the message is not distorted, for communication is "a two-way street."

An example perfectly illustrates the feedback principle. A common device used in communication is a radio transmitter-receiver set. Readers who have used the popular citizen's band (CB) radios, ham transceivers, or other two-way equipment have experienced the practical problems encountered in two-way communication. Distortions from noise, interference, faulty equipment, weak signal, the sender talking too rapidly or unclearly, and other problems affect the quality of the communication. Any CB user who has attempted to understand a trucker who is using newly adopted trucker jargon and is talking like he has his head buried in a bowl of wet oatmeal knows the true meaning of distortion.

The Federal Communications Commission has established rules and regulations for the operation of transceivers to discourage improper operation and to facilitate personal and business radio-communications. Proper use of equipment is prescribed, and a radiotelephone code is utilized. This code, the "10" signals, has been used for many years by the various radio services and is in common use by CB operators. After a message is transmitted, if the receiver-decoder responds with the familiar "10–4," this means "Okay, message received." This is the feedback. The feedback signal is commonly used in radio communications. Its use has not been formalized in everyday, ordinary conversation, and it is frequently missing in the communication process. That is why the insurance claims representative must obtain feedback and must take care to guarantee that the steps in the communication process are free of distortion.

Steps in communication

The reader will better understand the nature of the communication process and the problems confronted if the steps in the process are first explained and analyzed. These steps deserve considerable study by claims representatives.

The starting point in communication is the thought, attitude, or idea which exists in a person's mind. When we consider communicating, we must decide how best to express that meaning and pass it on to another. Just as important, however, we should consider how that meaning will survive the process of communication. If the sender's exact meaning is not communicated to the receiver, the purpose to be served by the communication may be subverted.

Suppose that a claims representative has a definite idea which he or she desires to communicate. Suppose a fire adjuster, for example, must explain to an insured why the insured's scorched wallpaper is not covered under the fire policy. The idea the claims person seeks to convey is the meaning of a "friendly fire" and its application to the insured's particular claim. The claims person in this case is said to be the *source of the idea.*

The next step in the process is for the claims representative to take that idea and encode it into a message which will be understood by the insured. The process of *encoding* is taking a meaning and phrasing it into *a message* by using symbols of meaning. When we select a language and phrase a message into that language, we encode it. Problems can arise for the decoder if the language selected is a difficult one. If an encoder uses the International Morse Code, and if the words formed are in English, the encoder will be unable to communicate to anyone except those people who know both the International Morse Code and the English language. If the claims person tries to tell the insured about *friendly fires* in English, and the insured understands nothing but Spanish, the claims person won't get the meaning across. Moreover, the claims person may have difficulty encoding the meaning in English even though the insured understands English.

Consider, for example, a conversation between a fire adjuster and a lady insured. "The fire in my stove ruined my wallpaper, and I'm putting in a claim," she declares.

"Well, Mrs. Smith," begins the claims person, "your claim wouldn't be covered, because your damage was caused by a friendly fire."

"Friendly, hell!" declares the insured, "Look what it did to my wallpaper!" She had no idea of the specialized meaning of *friendly fire*, a fire confined to its proper receptacle. The claims person erred in this case by encoding the meaning into word symbols which had a different meaning to the insured.

People often select words whose meaning is not fully understood by others. As a consequence, distortion results when the receiver attempts to decode these word symbols into meaningful thoughts. Shurter tells the classic story about communication failure concerning a plumber who had found hydrochloric acid excellent for cleaning drains. He wrote a Washington bureau to find out if it was harmless. Someone in Washington wrote the following letter to him: "The efficacy of hydrochloric acid is indisputable, but the chlorine residue is incompatible with metallic permanence."

The plumber wrote back, thanked the bureau, and said he was very glad that they agreed that hydrochloric acid was good for cleaning pipes. Back came the second reply: "We cannot assume responsibility for the production of toxic and noxious residues from hydrochloric acid, and we suggest, therefore, that some alternative procedure be used."

The plumber answered that he was getting fine results thus far, and the bureau might like to suggest the use of hydrochloric acid to other people. Finally, someone in Washington exploded into clear, simple,

understandable language for the reader: "DON'T USE HYDRO-
CHLORIC ACID! IT EATS HELL OUT OF THE PIPES!"[18] Someone had finally encoded the message into language which could be
understood by the plumber.

Once the meaning is encoded into a message, the next step is to
select *a sender* and *a channel* for the communication. Usually the encoder also acts as the sender. A claims representative in the course of a
conversation thinks of an idea (the claims representative is the source),
puts it into English words (encoding a message), and then sends it via
a channel. The channel of communication chosen is exceedingly important. The claims representative may transmit or send the message
by speaking or writing the words. If the encoder-sender uses speech
to transmit meaning in a message, he or she may be in the presence
of the receiver-decoder at the time. If the encoder-sender sees something going wrong with the communication—in other words, if the
communication is breaking down—the encoder-sender is in a superior
position to correct for error. This, obviously, is the value of the feedback process. The encoder-sender can detect whether the communication process is succeeding, and if not, he or she can correct for error.

Obtaining witnesses' statements by mail

The complexity of the communication process is one reason a claims
person should not attempt to obtain important witnesses' statements
by mail. In using a mailed questionnaire the claims person is confronted by a difficult situation. If he or she desires to obtain an accurate
account of an accident from a witness by mail, there are two separate
communications which must take place. First, the claims person must
come up with some good questions which will elicit the type of response desired. In other words, the claims person must encode a desired meaning into well-phrased questions which will bring forth specific detailed answers that will reveal and comprehensively and clearly
present the witness's knowledge and recollection of a specific fact situation, whether that situation is simple or complex.

After encoding questions, probably in English words on a questionnaire form, the claims person then composes another message

---

[18] Robert L. Shurter, *Written Communication in Business* (New York: McGraw-Hill, 1957), pp. 30–31.

(probably an accompanying letter) in which there is a request that the witness complete the form, write his or her name at the bottom and return it to the claims representative in the stamped, self-addressed envelope. The claims person sends the letter and attached questionnaire through the United States mail (the channel). It is then received by the witness and may or may not be decoded. If the witness is a busy person who does not like to fill out questionnaires, he or she may simply place the questionnaire aside to be completed later (at a later date, the witness may pick it up, rationalize that the request is so dated that it would have no value to the claims person, and the witness, therefore, destroys the questionnaire). Here is a good example of communication breakdown.

Suppose, however, that the witness fills out the questionnaire and returns it to the claims representative. The second communication begins to take place, and all of the steps of communication start again. The witness interprets the questions in the questionnaire, and the answers given may or may not respond to the questions (this, of course, depends upon the respective skills of the encoder in selecting appropriate meaning symbols and of the decoder in translating these symbols).

The witness then encodes answers in words and sentences. They may be intelligible, descriptive, and full of symbolic meaning. On the other hand, the witness may write unintelligibly with fragmentary sentences in a terse, perfunctory manner, which leaves the message of the witness susceptible to several interpretations. Whichever the case, the witness mails the questionnaire back to the claims representative, who then plays the role of the receiver-decoder. The extent to which the claims person is able to interpret the meaning the witness encoded into the message determines the success of the communication.

Needless to say, the procedure of mailing out questionnaires to witnesses should be used sparingly, and then only in relatively unimportant matters. It is much more effective for a claims representative to be face to face with the witness so that encoding and decoding can be done on the spot, thus helping to insure that communication will be effective. With face-to-face communication, the claims representative can immediately correct any errors in the communication. With today's widespread use of telephone recordings, the telephone can be used effectively and economically, and there is little practical value in securing witnesses' statements by mail. Nevertheless, some insurers still routinely send witness forms through the mail, and where a witness cannot be reached by telephone and personal contact is impractical, the practice is certainly sound.

DISTORTIONS IN COMMUNICATION

Distortions in communication can occur at any point in the communication sequence. Although it seems that we should be able to convey meaning to other people with a minimum of difficulty, distortions are common. The author once took a written statement from a man who was rather deaf. Like any new claims person, the author had a list of questions and subject matter which he wished to cover in the statement. After entering the man's house he was invited to sit down, and proceeded with the job of obtaining a statement.

Unfortunately, the man's wife was also rather deaf, and she was watching television. The volume on the television set was turned up high, and it was difficult for the author and the witness to hear one another. To add to the tumult, the man's wife kept shouting at her husband to ask him what the author was asking. The man shouted back the question to her, and the lady would answer it while the man remained silent. Meanwhile, two small children played cowboys and Indians in the center of the room, emitting bloodcurdling shouts and shrieks and tripping over the author's feet. The lady screamed her annoyance at the children. Although he finally secured his statement, the author left the premises a shaken person.

In the above case, the author acted as encoder and sender. Distortions probably existed in the encoding. Because of inexperience, the author had difficulty in phrasing questions and selecting appropriate words and sentences for questions. In addition, distortion crept into the physical aspect of sending the message through the speech channel because of the noise and distractions which were present. To aggravate the situation, the receiver and decoder had poor hearing ability compounded by the noise and distraction which were present. The overall effect was considerable communication breakdown. It took three times as long as necessary to obtain the statement. More experience made it apparent to the author that in similar situations it is of primary importance to suggest courteously and tactfully to the man that he turn off the television set (or arrange a time when the interview would not interfere with his television viewing); that the charming children be banished to other parts of the house; and that the lady of the house kindly refrain from interrupting.

Some writers have suggested that distortions can be placed in three categories: physical, semantic, and psychological.[19] Such a classification is helpful and will be discussed next.

Physical distortions

Physical distortions are obstacles which physically block the transmission of meaning. The preceding case gave some examples—the noise of the television set, the woman's loud conversation, and the children's shouts. Such noise and distractions are common channel problems. Conversations in the background and the television program created distractions which resulted in communication breakdown.

Particularly today, when so much emphasis is placed on recorded statements, the claims person is well advised to arrange to interview witnesses in a quiet, comfortable setting that is free from noise and distractions. This, admittedly, is extremely difficult in some situations. Oftentimes the claims person's only opportunity to interview a witness comes under unfavorable circumstances. Statements often must be taken from construction workers where heavy equipment is creating a din in the background; insureds are interviewed at places of business, where customers are coming in and out of a store and interrupting the interview; and the physical surroundings will sometimes make the conduct of an interview more difficult.

Before the introduction of reliable, light-weight portable recorders, the author once took a couple of written statements in a hard-rock mine. He donned a hard hat, slicker, and boots and was in water up to his knees. The only light came from the carbide lamp on his hard hat and from the lamps of two miners. Water dripped from the ceiling of the passageway in which he was standing. The statement pad was held to a clip-board as he wrote, and he attempted to keep water off the paper. This admittedly was not the ideal physical environment for statement taking, but because of the pressure of time and the circumstances, it was necessary in this case. One claims man took a statement

---

19 G. Hugh Russell and Kenneth Black, Jr., *Human Behavior and Property and Liability Insurance* (Englewood Cliffs, N.J.: Prentice-Hall, 1964).

in a slaughterhouse on a hot, summer day. The memory of the experience still causes him to turn ashen. The claims representative obviously should attempt whenever possible to avoid such situations and to maneuver the other person into an environment reasonably free from physical distortions and distractions.

Semantic distortions

. . . I had rather speak five words with my understanding, that by my voice I might teach others also, than ten thousand words in an unknown tongue.
——Paul's Epistle to the Corinthians

The difficulty of semantics has already been touched upon in the preceding paragraphs. Semantics is the science of meanings in words. It has to do with the meaning assigned to word symbols. Two people must assign the same meaning to the same word; otherwise communication between them is distorted. There is a breakdown in meaning. The problem of reducing insurance and legal terminology into language which the layman will understand continually plagues the insurance claims representative.

One of the practical semantics problems that has confronted the automobile physical damage claims person in past years was the adjustment of collision claims involving animals. What is a collision? Insureds were told that a collision is a collision, whether it be with another automobile, a tree, or an animal. Insureds countered with the argument that the animal collided with the car; the car did not collide with the animal (in some cases). The claims person replied, "A collision is a collision, regardless of whether the automobile collides with the animal or the animal collides with the car."

"Yes, but," continued the insured, "the deer that hit my car was leaping through the air and hit my car, thus he was a falling object. Damage from falling objects is covered under the policy, and there is no deductible."

"Well," rejoined the claims person, "conceivably, if a deer is on a ledge over the highway, and a hunter shoots the deer, causing it to fall on your automobile, then this would be a falling object and covered under your 'other than collision' coverage. Courts have ruled that objects impelled by the force of gravity are falling objects. If an animal, however, is impelled by its spring rather than gravity, it is not a falling object. If it runs into your car, it is a collision."

In this manner the battle rages over the meaning of a word, and it often requires a court decision to determine the legal meaning. Happily, the problem of collision with animals was resolved when the National Automobile Underwriters Association decided years ago to alleviate some of the communication problems of the claims representative by including collision with animals as a part of the automobile comprehensive coverage. Today the "other than collision loss" coverage ("comprehensive" coverage) specifically provides that contact with a bird or an animal is not considered a "collision" under the policy terms. In this way an extremely difficult problem of semantics was resolved by incorporating in the policy a definition of *collision* that is obviously contrary to the literal meaning of collision—the coming together with solid impact of two objects.

One of the big difficulties which confronts people in the selection of word symbols to represent meaning is the fact that a word never completely describes the object for which it stands. This inherent inadequacy of words causes people to become involved in controversy regarding word meanings. To resolve the argument, they turn to a dictionary. A dictionary, unfortunately, usually does not list all of the possible meanings of a word symbol, or it lists numerous conflicting meanings. Frequently it fails to resolve the argument. Webster, for example, lists a number of meanings for the simple word "great." It means "large in size; big; pregnant; numerous, long continued; remarkably adept or proficient; particularly favored; and excellent." Consider the word "acute." If the reader talks about an "acute situation," he or she may mean a critical situation, or perhaps the reader is referring to a situation of less than 90 degrees. The second meaning is rather ridiculous in this instance, but it indicates the problem where alternative word definitions are present. The 500 most-used words listed in the *Oxford English Dictionary* have an average of 28 meanings each. The word "round" has 73 meanings.

Because of great proliferation in word meanings and because of the human's basic lack of skill in using language, words frequently are improperly used by people. People grope for the exact word to express their meaning. In their groping, the misuse of words is common. Failing to find a suitable word, people often will select an unsuitable word to symbolize their meaning. Men and women are constantly firing off incorrect messages because of failure to select proper meaning-symbols.

Psychological distortions

If a man is partially deaf and has turned off his hearing aid, a physical distortion to communication takes place. There are additional cases, however, where no physical distortions or semantic distortions are present, but meaning is still distorted or blocked. These distortions are psychological in nature, resulting from selective listening (concentration on one sound to the exclusion of others), the failure to listen, or from certain defects of listening. The listener, for example, may hear what is said and there may be no conflict in semantics, but nevertheless, distortion exists because the listener colors listening receptivity with emotion or shades it according to personal frames of reference. This interferes with the listener's ability to receive and decode a message objectively.

Frames of reference. Frames of reference, as discussed in Chapter 3, are all of the background experiences, education, mental conditioning, ideas, prejudices, and moods which form the foundation used by all of us when we interpret phenomena. When we hear something or when we receive any other stimulus, we must interpret the meaning of that stimulus—we have to decode the message. Obviously, our efforts at decoding are handicapped or enhanced by the scope, depth, and fullness of our experience, our judgment, and our psychological makeup. We decode or interpret the stimulus with the tools at our command, and we, therefore, are limited to the peculiar makeup of our own personal frames of reference. Every person lives in his or her own world, and he or she has an individual and personal way of looking at things. The insurance claims representative's words and actions will be screened or filtered through other people's own frameworks of experiences and preoccupations. Sound, for example, may get through, but the meaning may be garbled.

People differ considerably in their frames of reference. Two employees working for the same employer may have entirely differing conceptions of their boss. Jones may consider his boss to be an excellent employer. When Jones finishes a piece of work, his boss may walk up to his bench, pick up the finished work, grunt, and set it down again. Jones may interpret from the tone of the employer's grunt and his action that his boss is well pleased with the work, and Jones is flattered by the attention that he has been given.

Smith, on the other hand, cringes when the employer looks at his work. He interprets the silence and the grunt to be disapproval. He thoroughly dislikes his employer; he dislikes his job; and he is completely unsure of his position on the job. The employer may in fact think that both men are doing excellent work. He is able to communicate easily with Jones but is failing to communicate with Smith. Smith has a different background and a different psychological makeup. He interprets things within a different frame of reference. The employer would do well to pat Smith on the back, smile at him, and tell him how much his efforts are appreciated.

Unintended meaning sneaks into the communication process. The encoder-sender may be entirely unaware that it is happening. He or she doesn't realize that the receiver-decoder puts a different construction or interpretation on what is being said or written. In effect, the receiver-decoder is "reading between the lines." As claims representatives, our meaning that is expressed in our letters or in our conversations may be entirely clear to us and the other person may clearly hear or see our words. However, since no word or message ever means exactly the same to any two people, the meaning may be lost. Our words and actions, remember, have to be filtered through the other person's idea of the meaning of the message transmitted.

Listening.   Skillful listening plays an exceedingly important role in the process of communication. Careful, attentive listening is quite a strain. Most people spend the time between their own utterances composing their next statement. The new claims person may find that he or she is so busy composing the next question that there is resultant failure to hear much of the reply to the previous question.

We often interrupt when another person is speaking. Interruptions constitute a common but nevertheless grievous form of poor listening. A person sometimes may talk just to keep the air full of sound—quiet periods are awkward for immature individuals. Another few seconds of silence might lead to a valuable revelation of information by the other person.

Claims representatives particularly must consider the effect of interruptions as they pursue their work. We must avoid interruptions which might serve to support what the other person is saying or might tend to moralize on what the other person is saying. Such interruptions can lead us further from the information we are seeking.

For example, if we remark, "I certainly agree with you there!" we may make the other person more comfortable, but it may also reinforce a line of thought which had been shaky in the mind of the person prior to our remark. The remark, "That wasn't a very nice thing to do!" moralizes and may serve to fortify the conviction of the other person. Remarks of this type may help to win the confidence of a claimant in the initial conversation, but they are dangerous to use, since they may distort the information received by the claims representative.

Good listening is imperative if one is to avoid psychological distortions to communication. Good listening is more than a matter of patience; it requires habits that must be developed through prolonged practice. Effective listening is a skill. The scientific principles underlying good listening are important to understand. Poor listening distorts communication just as effectively as if a partially deaf person's hearing aid is turned off.

Vacuous duologue and conversation

The distortion arising from failure to listen is common in everyday conversation. *Conversation,* according to *Webster's Dictionary,* is an "oral *exchange* of sentiments, observations, opinions, ideas." The author has added the emphasis to "exchange." Conversation involves *dialogue,* and dialogue contemplates conversation, an exchange of ideas and opinions between two or more persons.

Unfortunately, conversation frequently breaks down because of the absence of exchange. Two people may be talking *at* each other, but no exchange of sentiments, observations, opinions, or ideas takes place, because neither person is listening. This is called *vacuous duologue,* an empty, hollow dialogue between two people. Frequently in this situation, when we are not the person who is talking, we often can hardly wait for the other person to finish talking so that we can talk about ourself, our experiences, our problems, our opinions. Two people may be standing on a street corner talking *at* each other. Jones cannot wait for Smith to "shut up" so that he (Jones) can talk. Smith cannot wait for Jones to "shut up" so that she (Smith) can talk. Meanwhile, each pays little attention to what the other is saying. In essence, we have two *monologues.* Each speaker is alone because of a breakdown in communication resulting from failure to listen. There is no exchange.

People usually are poor listeners. They often are selfish conversationalists. Their conversation is characterized by an excessive use of the personal pronoun "I." People talk about themselves in order to achieve ego recognition. Self-directed conversation helps a person to feel important and is a vent for pent-up emotions. It is an excellent self-therapeutic device. It is cathartic. As claims representatives, we must resist the natural impulse to talk about ourselves. We must talk in terms of another person's interests. We must learn to use the pronoun "you." Fewer psychological distortions will interfere with the claims representative's efforts to communicate with the other person if he or she will only learn to listen.

Because of its vital importance to the subject of insurance claims handling, the art and skill of listening will be discussed in greater detail in subsequent chapters.

SUMMARY

There is considerable science and art involved in dealing with other people successfully. To understand other people the insurance claims representative must have a working knowledge of human behavior. In order to apply that knowledge to day-by-day claims handling activities, the claims person must understand thoroughly and be able to apply the principles and rules of good communication.

In taking statements, in negotiating settlements, in denying claims, in building files of evidence, in obtaining admittance to hospitals after visiting hours, in requesting a pay raise, and in explaining to his or her family or friends why present activities must be interrupted or sacrificed when the claims handling job demands, the claims representative must communicate effectively to be successful. This means that we must (1) understand the message we wish to communicate; (2) convey the message in terms understandable to the other person; (3) try to avoid physical environment or conditions which will distort the message; and (4) understand all of the other problems involved in bringing about meaningful and accurate communication. The effective claims person not only must be able to hear and to be heard; he or she also must be able to influence insureds, claimants, attorneys, insurers, garage personnel, physicians, and other people. As claims persons we must be able to communicate and to motivate others to accept our point of view.

Because of its importance, the communication sequence has been explained in this chapter. It has been observed that communication is the process of passing meaning from one person to another. The process itself requires the encoding of a message and a transmission of that message through a channel to a receiver who then attempts to decode the message. Whether the original meaning survives the process seems to be largely fortuitous because of the intervention of distortions. These distortions arise for a number of reasons, which have been conveniently classified as physical, semantic, or psychological distortions.

Sometimes a message is not transmitted effectively or received because of the presence of physical obstacles. If the battery in a witness's hearing aid is dead, there is said to be physical distortion. Likewise, if a television set drowns out a witness's remarks, no message reaches the claims representative. This is another example of physical distortion. If, however, a message is beamed loud and clear to us and we receive it with no distortion, communication may still break down if the word symbols selected to convey meaning are meaningless to us.

If an individual does not understand the other person's use of language, no oral communication takes place. If a person understands only simple language, and the claims representative uses technical jargon and legalistic phraseology, the two will find it difficult to communicate. This is an example of semantic distortion, which results when two people assign different meanings to the same word, phrase, or language.

Even if there is no physical or semantic distortion, psychological distortions can cause communication breakdown. We introduce such distortion into communication when we interpret in a biased manner what we hear. We interpret according to our frames of reference, derived from personal experience, attitudes, beliefs, and background. If an individual fails to listen to another person, such failure introduces a psychological distortion to communication, because it effectively interferes with the communication process.

There are many other examples of the three types of communication distortion, but the foregoing serve to illustrate to the claims person the practical difficulties confronted when he or she attempts to understand other people and induce other people to understand him or her. If we can remove the physical, semantic, and psychological distortions to communication, we can proceed with the process of motivating the people with whom we must deal. Communication and motivation go hand in hand in the day-by-day dealings of the claims person. Many principles and techniques used in motivation help in the process of communication, because they serve to remove blocks to communication. These principles and techniques will be explored at length in subsequent chapters.

5

Listening

The subject of listening deserves special emphasis and study because of its importance to the field of insurance claims handling. Failure to listen is one of the psychological distortions of communication, as observed in an earlier chapter. It either distorts communication so that incomplete information is passed from one person to another, or else it completely blocks the communication process.

Failure to listen is as effective in destroying good communication as is the physical act of turning off the hearing aid of a deaf person. No message is received. There is no communication. The symbol of meaning which was transmitted by the sender of information is lost. The sender or transmitter of the message is simply trying to communicate with a person whose receiver is either off or is tuned to the wrong wavelength.

GENERAL IMPORTANCE OF LISTENING

Human beings communicated by the spoken word for centuries before experimenting with written communication. Initially, humans expressed themselves with primitive cave drawings and other symbols. Hieroglyphs and written language systems came much later. Many centuries passed before the alphabet was developed so that people could further use written communication. Even then, speaking and listening were by far the most important means of communication. Until the printing press was invented and modern-day methods of mass production in printing evolved, the book was a luxury few people could afford.

Even in modern times many of us spend comparatively little time with the written word. In today's age of the telephone and rapid transportation the modern business person relies less and less upon the mails to send messages. Particularly in insurance claims handling in recent years, there has been a marked shift in emphasis from written communication to oral communication. Written communication is still critical to the proper conduct of insurance claims handling functions, but the emphasis in claims investigation has been strongly placed on oral tools. With the development of miniaturized electronic circuitry, replacing the bulky and less reliable vacuum tube, the reliable, inexpensive portable recorder is used extensively by claims persons. Prior to the widespread adoption of this useful tool during the 1960s, all important evidential material was reduced to writing.

The written statement, painstakingly written out in the claims person's own handwriting or prepared by the court reporter, was the focal point of the claims investigation. The developing written statement served as a point of reference, and as information was obtained from the insured, claimant, or witness, the claims person could constantly review whether the material was complete. A quick review of the material covered with a witness, for example, told the claims representative what new line of inquiry should be pursued.

Today's insurance claims handling offices, in pursuit of economic efficiency and expediency, rely heavily on the recorder for statement-taking, and a great premium and reliance is placed on listening skills. Skillful use of recording as a tool to acquire information and evidential material on insurance claims makes it absolutely essential that all claims representatives be accomplished listeners, a unique and acquired skill.

It is not only in insurance claims handling, however, that greater reliance is placed on the spoken word. Today's business person in every line of business endeavor finds it more advantageous to conduct business by the spoken word—a more persuasive medium. Contemporary humans rely primarily upon speaking and listening abilities to communicate. We depend greatly upon mass communication media, such as television and radio, to give us the latest news, to tell us about the latest products on the market, and to entertain us. If we are to obtain information from all of these communication media, we must have the ability to listen.

If we fail to listen, we lose our opportunity to gain information and knowledge in a simple manner. The same information and knowledge may take us weeks or months to acquire through reading. In addition, a knowledgeable speaker can reduce a complex subject to understandable terms for us, so that it is not necessary for us to read a great deal of background material in order to understand the subject. It is also possible that the information may be so recent that it is unavailable in written form. Furthermore, attentive listening helps us to appreciate language more and to acquire greater competence in our own speaking.

We spend much of our time in the role of the listener. Even as early as 1929, before the advent of television, a study revealed that 45 percent of the working day—more than five hours per day—was spent in listening to others talk.[1] From this it has been concluded:

We write the equivalent of a book in a lifetime;

We read the equivalent of a book in a month;

We talk the equivalent of a book in a week; and

We listen to the equivalent of a book in a day.[2]

It is apparent that the subject of listening is of prime importance. We must acquire an awareness of the vital role played by listening if we are to improve our ability to communicate.

GOOD LISTENING IS NOT TYPICAL

In spite of the fact that listening is so highly important in the lives of most humans, people tend to be poor listeners. It would appear that effective listening should be a natural trait. The evidence appears to be to the contrary. People frequently are not interested in sounds they hear, and they block them from their minds. Poor listening is typical because, in a sense, people work hard at being poor listeners. The world is so full of sound that we must use effort to block some

---

[1] Survey by Paul T. Rankin, supervising director of research and adjustment for the Detroit Public School District, 1929.

[2] Cited in "Listening—The Much Neglected Key to the Practice of Communication," *National Underwriter* (August 2, 1963), p. 2 (report on an address by Robert Haakenson, community relations manager of Smith Kline and French Laboratories).

sounds from our minds in order to concentrate upon those matters which are most important to us at a particular time. In this process of *selective listening,* we tend to shift our attention to extraneous matters if our interest diminishes in a conversation, a public address, or other source of sound.

We use both physical and psychological means to avoid the necessity of listening. We use physical means to avoid listening by staying away from a speaker or walking out of a meeting where the speaker may be talking. This is one of the problems that confronts political candidates. Surveys have indicated that most people will not turn on their radio or television sets to listen to a political candidate unless he or she happens to be their choice. They listen only to their favorite candidate. They thus effectively block listening in the case of other candidates.

Similarly, people use psychological means to avoid listening. Sociologists describe the typical listener as a stubborn, hard-to-change individual, who blocks out most messages. Raymond A. Bauer describes the typical listener as highly selective. The typical listener makes up "the obstinate audience,"[3] which accepts messages that support positions it holds already and shuts out everything else. People listen only to those ideas they expect to hear. Psychological studies indicate that many people ignore information that conflicts with their established patterns of thought.

We, therefore, get a great deal of practice in not listening. The more practice the individual gets and the more effort he or she devotes to not listening, the harder it is to listen effectively when the need arises. Confronted with the necessity of listening, our minds often are so cluttered with extraneous and unrelated matters that only through sustained effort or great interest are we able to concentrate upon the meaning of another person.

Listening and retention

Public addresses of various kinds, particularly after-dinner speeches, seem to be highly popular. The evidence indicates, however, that the

---

[3] The title of a paper by Raymond A. Bauer, associate professor at Harvard Business School, presented at a seminar of the Foundation for Research on Human Behavior at New York University, October 1964, cited in "The Art of Listening," *Business Week* (October 17, 1964), p. 76.

audience usually does not listen carefully to what is said. The author heard one after-dinner speech delivered before an audience of 150 people. The speaker's thoughts were disorganized and unrelated to one another, his meaning was often unclear, and his presentation was punctuated by incomplete utterances of thought. He did, nevertheless, deliver the address with great enthusiasm and voice inflection and with remarkable variations in volume. His gestures were vigorous and emphatic, and he often pounded on the speaker's lectern. The address was given without a prepared text, and it rambled on and on, accompanied by an amazing array of behavior on the platform.

After the speech, a well-known and skilled speaker who spends most of his time traveling the United States delivering public addresses, turned to the author and whispered, "Wasn't that terrible? What did the man say?" The author was astounded when several people came to the speaker's platform and congratulated the after-dinner speaker on his excellent address. "That was the finest talk I have ever heard," burbled one man. One can only wonder where the man's mind was during the delivery of the speech. He certainly had not tuned in on the subject.

Some time ago, James J. Chastain, former dean of the Insurance Institute of America, addressed a gathering of I.I.A. and C.P.C.U. students, suggesting to them ways in which they could best prepare for the national examinations. Said he, "You are almost certain to pass the examinations if you will faithfully employ the 'Four P's for Passing: Preparation, Participation, Practice, and Planning." He then placed the "Four P's" on the blackboard in the front of the class and proceeded to discuss them at length.

The following night he gave the same pep-talk in a different city. By coincidence, one of the people from the previous night's session was visiting that city and decided to attend. Recognizing him from the previous night, Dr. Chastain asked him to list the "Four P's." The man could remember only two of the four. Presumably, by failing to listen closely and to think about what was said, he found it impossible to recall such a simple subject. Poor listening resulted in poor retention.

Effective teachers often find that they must repeat important points several times during a lecture before they are heard. Before a point is heard, it often is necessary for the teacher to write it on the blackboard. Despite the efforts of a teacher in repeating an important point, and although he or she will write the information on a blackboard, some students still will not hear and retain this information.

Classroom teachers find that one of the greatest obstacles to the teaching process is the inability of the individual student to listen. A number of high school teachers once were asked to interrupt their lectures suddenly and record whether their students were listening. Students were allowed to respond with unsigned written answers. Three fourths of the students were not listening to their teachers.[4]

A study conducted by the University of Michigan some years past revealed that students tend to remember only 20 percent of lecture material.[5] Students frequently do not bring their minds to the classroom. They are not interested; they are not motivated to listen. If they don't listen, they won't have an opportunity to remember the lecture material.

Some successful teachers have employed unorthodox methods to obtain the attention of their classes. Rather than standing relatively motionless in front of a lectern while lecturing, the teacher may move disquietingly about the speaker's platform or move out into the audience and stare at individual students. One university professor begins his lecture in a standing position. As the session progresses, he places a foot on a chair; then he climbs upon the chair. A little later, he places a foot on the adjacent table, and he finally concludes his lecture standing on the table. The maneuver is so unexpected, students become unusually alert and entertained, anticipating the professor's next move. The subject being presented is usually one that can be dramatized with some histrionics.

A professor at the University of Oklahoma was known for his acrobatics in class. A former circus acrobat, he would walk across a table on his hands while continuing his lecture. Needless to say, all of the students' minds were focused upon his activities. Whether they also were listening to what he was saying is conjectural.

The classic case of poor listening on the part of an audience took place in 1938 when 6 million people in the United States heard Orson Welles' hour-long science-fiction radio program describing an invasion from Mars. Despite repeated announcements that the story was fictitious, an estimated 1 million people thought the program was a true news story. Telephone switchboards were jammed with calls; people rushed from their homes to respond to the emergency;

---

[4] Ralph G. Nichols and Leonard A. Stevens, *Are You Listening?* (New York: McGraw-Hill, 1957), pp. 12–13.

[5] Edwin S. Overman, *Teacher's Guide Book for C.P.C.U. Classes* (Bryn Mawr: American Institute for Property and Liability Underwriters, Inc., 1963 revision), p. 27.

and some suicides were reported. The program caused a panic of national proportions simply because people did not listen carefully.

Listening and the oral contract

Many of the contract cases that reach the courts result from poor listening. When the contract has not been reduced to writing, it often is necessary to prove the existence of the contract by reference to the oral communication which took place between the contracting parties.

Bitter controversies arise between honest people who have wide differences of opinion regarding the exact terms of a contract. Because of poor listening ability, Ms. Jones may agree to certain contract terms which she has not heard. When Mr. Smith subsequently requests performance of the contract according to the terms which he had spelled out to Ms. Jones in a previous conversation, Jones may accuse Smith of dishonest, shyster tactics. Smith, bewildered and outraged, takes the matter to his attorney, and a law suit ensues because Ms. Jones was not listening. It is for this reason that lawyers are quick to recommend that all important contracts be reduced to writing.

The great variation in testimony regarding the question of the existence or the terms of a contract also has brought about the enactment of laws which require that certain important types of contracts be in writing before they are enforceable.

Lack of training in listening

The poorly-trained ear works overtime, while the well-trained eye has only a part-time job.
———Ralph Nichols and Leonard Stevens

Despite its great importance, the subject of listening is given little attention. A notable exception is afforded by the Diamond Alkali Company of Cleveland, which has used programed learning to teach effective listening to its salespeople. The course material was placed on audio tape. Examination scores have indicated that the average company trainee in the course attained significant increases in listening skills after taking only two and one half hours of programed training.[6] Similar programs have been utilized by other corporations.

---

6 "Teaching Salesmen to Listen," *Sales Marketing Today* (November 1964), p. 12.

For the most part, however, there is seldom any attempt made to train people to listen. Reading-improvement, speed-reading, and reading interpretation courses frequently are available, but a class devoted to listening improvement is unique.

It is encouraging to note that some colleges and universities are offering listening courses. Today's educational system, nevertheless, is overbalanced in favor of the visual skills. Children are taught to read and write, while little or no attention is spent on the development of listening skills. From the first grade, a child is admonished to pay attention and listen. For some reason, however, the child is given no formal training in how to listen effectively.

The emphasis presents a real problem. As soon as we leave school, we discover that reading and writing are not as important in personal progress as are the abilities to speak and listen. We find that much of our academic information comes through the listening process.

Much attention has been devoted to the subject of communication through the medium of speech. This stress on speech, however, makes it appear that communication is a one-sided process. The speaker is frequently given the entire burden of communicating, while the listener is passive. One highly touted company handbook on employee communication, for example, defines communication as meaning "to inform, to tell, to show." Nowhere does it say anything about the highly essential aspect of listening. As a consequence, much of the so-called communication which takes place can be likened to the radio transmitter which beams out messages which are never picked up because all radio sets are turned off.

This narrow concept of the process of communication is self-defeating, for communication is a "two-way street." A transmitter indeed is important, but it is valueless unless there is also a receiver of the message. Speaking, by itself, is not communicating; speaking makes up only half of the process. Every speaker must have a listener in order to complete the communication process. The subject of listening, therefore, deserves equal emphasis with the subject of speaking.

LISTENING AND THE CLAIMS REPRESENTATIVE

Communication, above all, is vital to the claims handling job. Good investigation is impossible without it. Successful negotiations cannot be undertaken without it. Communication requires listening, for listening is one of the prime essentials of the communication process. The claims person must be particularly skillful in the art of listening. This is because the majority of our time will be spent in listening to others. If this is not true, we are talking too much.

Every word, every inflection of voice, every meaningful pause must register an impact in the mind of the insurance claims representative if he or she is to be successful in the claims handling job. Because the claims person is called upon to secure statements, he or she must have the uncanny ability to ask questions, interject meaningful comments, hear and absorb everything the other person says by analyzing and interpreting the information and remembering the recorded information, and use this material as the basis for the development of further information. In the case of recorded statements, we must be able to hear and retain everything said by the witness so that we can question the witness further on subject matter excluded by the witness as the latter relates his or her recollection of an occurrence or situation. While the recording is proceeding, effective listening on the part of the claims person facilitates the development of the statement by pointing the way for further questioning. The claims representative must continue to listen effectively while composing further questions and controlling or "steering" the interview. This requires continued response to the other person's words, through interjection of empathetic and interested comments.

By skillful listening, the claims person is able to develop fully the witness's narration and to expose, where possible, all pertinent information possessed by the witness. Imperfect listening, on the other hand, results in an imperfect recorded statement.

In today's age of reliance on the recording machine, listening and retention abilities are of paramount importance. Obtaining a good recorded statement is much like writing a book—information must be developed in an orderly, complete, and well-organized manner, and thoughts must flow from one to another with a certain amount of planned continuity and skillful transition. This cannot be accomplished unless the claims representative is listening with skill and with enough retention so that he or she can recall what already has been said and what must be asked in order to develop the conversation fully for the complete exposition of subject matter.

Although it may appear to the new claims representative that it is a difficult problem to be able to do so many things simultaneously, the skill is acquired through practice. The law of attention proscribes that we cannot devote attention to more than one thing at a time. Nevertheless, humans have the remarkable ability to shift attention with great speed and agility from one subject to another without losing continuity. Further, although we can speak approximately 125 words per minute, we can listen at the rate of 400 to 500 words per minute. Thus, with experience, a person can develop the ability to write a statement, ask questions, and remember what is being said as another person continues to speak.

This ability to accomplish the foregoing tasks is not inborn. It comes to some claims representatives only from months and years of experience. The superior, seasoned claims person who has achieved success in the claims field has developed a remarkable talent for listening and remembering almost everything that is said during a conversation. This person probably has an ability to recall minor points and detailed facts concerning a situation. He or she has had to acquire this ability in order to do a competent job in statement-taking so that the conversation can be developed for a full exposition of information. New claims representatives can acquire increased skill in listening by following the recommendations presented in this book.

Developing the conversation

Although the emphasis in this chapter is on developing listening skill, it should not be assumed that listening is the ultimate objective of the claims person. Listening is only a means toward an end. That end or purpose is to induce the other person to reveal information. The claims person's purpose is to accomplish an intelligent and complete investigation.

Accordingly, then, *as claims representatives, we listen so that we can develop the conversation so that information will be completely exposed.* All other purposes are secondary in the investigative process. Collateral objectives of listening, of course, are to obtain the confidence of the other person so that he or she will be easier to deal with and so that we can induce the other person to "let off steam" in order to dissipate obstructive emotions which cloud that individual's reasoning ability. An important purpose of the listening process, however, is to hear accurately and completely what the other person is saying so that the claims representative can detect what the other person is not saying. In other words, the witness's narration frequently may be so fragmentary, guarded, or implausible that it will give us important clues on whether information is being withheld, falsified, or exaggerated. Thus the claims person must be able to listen skillfully, record what he or she hears (either in a written statement or by recording machine), evaluate what is heard, and then *direct the interview or conversation in such a way that all the necessary information is divulged.*

It obviously is no problem to get the story from the other person if the latter is willing to talk. Steering the conversation so that there is a complete and orderly exposition of the subject matter is the prime problem. A claims person must know what questions to ask in order to fill in the blank spaces that an untrained witness is bound to leave.

An experienced claims representative may discount the emphasis placed on the subject of listening in this chapter. He or she may have developed listening skill over many years of experience. The experienced claims person may declare that sloppy work is not a matter of listening, but of analysis. New and inexperienced claims representatives, however, typically have not come from areas of activity such as insurance claims work or legal work where a premium is placed upon the ability to listen. They, consequently, do not have the listening ability, nor an initial awareness of the importance of the listening ability, to begin the process of analysis. Listening and analysis are inseparably wedded, but the former skill must be developed before the latter function can be performed effectively. This is why it is so important to emphasize listening skill early in the education and training of new claims representatives.

Receiving instructions

When the new claims person starts out on the job, his or her first inquiry will be, "What do I do first?" It is here that the ability to listen carefully first becomes important. The new claims person must be able to receive and retain instructions. He or she must be able to listen attentively and recall accurately so that instructions given by the claims supervisor will be followed precisely.

The instructions given the new claims representative by a supervisor are of particular importance. Instructions given by a supervisor pertaining to methodology of statement-taking are vital. Rapt attention and perfect recall will be of utmost value to the new claims person to avoid unpleasant personal situations on the new job. A good statement is essential and, if it is to be good, it must reveal all of the salient points necessary to establish or to rule out liability in a given case and, at the same time, lend evidential value to the statement.

Consequently, when we take our first statements on the job, we probably will find that it is a considerable challenge to cover all points which should be dealt with in a particular case. To meet that challenge, attentive listening is essential. We must pay attention to the instructions given by the claims supervisor. To aid in recall, we will find it helpful to take meaningful notes so that we can refer to them while interviewing an insured, a claimant, or a witness.

Failure to listen to a supervisor's instructions coupled with a failure to cover all of the necessary points while taking a statement reflect upon the performance and apparent competence of the new claims representative. If the new field claims person returns to the office with an incomplete statement, he or she probably will be sent out to obtain a supplemental statement requiring a second visit to a witness, claimant, or insured. If the initial contact was made by telephone, and inadequate and incomplete information was acquired by the "inside" claims person or by an "outside" field representative, a further contact will be required by telephone. Needless to say, some of these repeat visits and telephone calls will be fruitless, particularly where the claims person is attempting to obtain additional information from a claimant. By the time the claims representative makes the second call, the claimant may have developed serious reservations about the wisdom of talking to the claims person. The claimant may, in fact, now regret that he or she talked to the claims person in the first place. This feeling probably will be intensified by the fact that the claims representative is now anxious to obtain additional information. The claimant may now attach greater significance to the statements that he or she has already made or is now being questioned about. As a consequence, the claimant may become defensive in the further dealings on the claim.

Listening and taking statements

An official who must listen to the pleas of clients should listen patiently and without rancor, because a petitioner wants attention to what he says even more than the accomplishing of that for which he came.
————Ptahhotep, 2400 B.C.

People do not like to talk unless they have an audience. The more the listener reveals his or her interest and attention, the more the speaker will reveal personal thoughts, ideas, and opinions. This is well-known in the field of psychotherapy. The psychiatrist's most valuable tool is his or her ability to listen well. By effective listening and appropriate response, the psychiatrist is able to draw information out of the patient and better determine the patient's problems.

Earlier in this book the importance of listening was briefly discussed under the subject of communication. The self-therapeutic value of talking was mentioned. The more a person talks, the more he or she purges the mind of things which are personally disturbing. Talking gives us the opportunity to settle conflicts in our minds. By hearing our own words, we are able to evaluate our thoughts. We obviously must have a good listener while this process is taking place, for few people find it particularly helpful to talk when no one is present to listen. We need a listener; we need to bounce ideas off another person. We need the carthartic therapy of being able to vent emotions to a sympathetic listener.

In addition, speech provides the speaker with ego recognition. The sound of our own voice instills in us a sense of confidence and importance that is a vital requirement for maintaining mental health. Sympathetic listeners provide a means by which people can unburden themselves emotionally and at the same time raise their self-esteem.

The more responsive the audience, therefore, the more likely that the speaker will warm up to his or her subject and more fully express thoughts, ideas, opinions, and factual information. The point is simply this: through attentive and sympathetic listening, the claims representative will achieve success in inducing insureds, claimants, and witnesses to talk. The claims person's success in eliciting information will be directly proportional to his or her listening skill and to personal ability to show the other person that the claims person is a good listener.

As we undertake to obtain information, we must refrain from talking to excess, for this will inhibit and discourage the other person from talking. We must steer the conversation with pertinent, well-chosen questions and appropriate remarks as the interview unfolds. We should be prepared to interject these "steering" questions where it will be helpful to keep another person on the subject and where it is necessary to expose certain facets of a case.

The rest of the time, however, we must keep our eyes and ears open and mouth shut as we seek complete exposition of information. Our entire attention and concentration must be directed toward the other person and what that person is saying. The speaker's words must be heard and understood. When we do not understand what is said, either we are not completely attentive or else the speaker has not made his or her meaning clear. In either event, we will do well to ask the speaker to restate his or her meaning in additional or different words. Our request for a restatement must be handled skillfully to avoid offending the speaker by appearing to challenge the speaker's veracity.

Empathy and rapport

Skillful listening produces beneficial results for the claims representative in other ways. Besides making it possible to secure information, effective listening helps the claims person to relate to the subject and to the other person. This process of *relating to others* is called *empathy*. It is the projection of one's feelings into harmony with the feelings of another person. As claims representatives we are able to take on some of the feelings of another and place ourselves in the other person's shoes. In so doing, our ability to understand other people is enhanced. We can better comprehend the circumstances about which the other party is interested. Such comprehension on our part gives us greater insight in the handling of claims. It also stimulates our imagination so that we are able to arrive at claims solutions that will be satisfactory to the insurance company and to the claimant.

In addition, an accompanying result of skillful listening and the attainment of empathy is the establishment of "rapport." *Rapport* comes about when two people have arrived at a harmonious understanding. They understand each other and have a certain feeling of mutual trust. Through sympathetic and attentive listening we achieve a feeling of empathy so that we better understand an insured, a claimant, or a witness. Simultaneously, we have demonstrated interest in the other person. This encourages the other person to talk more. As a consequence, the latter is more likely to reveal personal ideas, opinions, thoughts, and information possessed.

Considerate listening impresses others that we are interested, attentive, and sympathetic. This creates a climate of goodwill. It molds other people's feelings toward us. This, in turn, establishes a climate of confidence which greatly improves communication and the opportunities for motivating others to respond in a manner desired by us. For example, if Mary Jones, a claims person, has the confidence of a witness, the goodwill generated enables Jones to steer the witness in a conversation. She can analyze the conversation, pick out open points, and, without irritating the witness, can bring him or her back to discuss uncovered subject matter. If, on the other hand, Jones is an impatient, unsympathetic, and clumsy listener, she is likely to create an irritated and recalcitrant witness.

Skillful listening may aid us considerably when we attempt to motivate another person to act in a certain manner. If we have established a pattern of attentive and considerate listening, the other person is likely to feel an obligation to listen when we begin our persuasive appeal. This desire to reciprocate courtesy may contribute appreciably to a claims representative's success in conducting claims negotiations.

Listening and the recording device

With the development of compact, portable recording devices and telephone recording techniques, and their increased acceptance as evidence by courts, there has been greater dependence upon such devices for statement taking. Unfortunately, with their greater use, there is considerable likelihood that new claims representatives might be less likely to develop the talent for good listening.

In the process of writing a complete, detailed statement, a claims investigator is required to listen intently and then reproduce what has just been heard into words on a statement pad. We also necessarily must cultivate the ability to recollect. We should have excellent recall so that we can write down another person's exact words or engage in skillful paraphrasing. Meantime, to develop the statement fully, we must devote considerable effort to listen and to recall what is being said as the statement progresses. The claims person does not receive this valuable practice and experience while using a recorder.

There is great value in the use of the recording devices. They can be invaluable in saving time and in securing statements which otherwise would be unavailable. However, the claims person may be so busy thinking about what question to ask next that he or she fails to listen to all that is being said by another person. There is some merit in requiring the claims person to develop listening talents by taking written statements before being permitted to use a recorder. It is for this reason that some claims managers do not permit a new claims person to use a recorder for taking statements until he or she has had some experience at writing statements. Nevertheless, some companies make extensive use of recorders, even for new claims personnel. Thus, the use of the recording device will be discussed in greater detail in a later chapter.

BAD HABITS IN LISTENING

Studies made at the University of Michigan have shown that the average person has an attention span of only two or three seconds at a time. A listener's attention is constantly interrupted by extraneous thoughts. Oftentimes the listener's thoughts are mixed in with what a speaker is saying, and as a result, a completely erroneous interpretation of the speaker's remarks results in the mind of the listener. Good listening takes much effort.

Another complicating factor works against good listening habits. The world is so full of sound that if we attempted to listen to everything, we would soon become confused. Consequently, we have found it necessary to be selective in order to hear those things which we believe to be most important.

Because of these and other factors most of us have developed a number of bad habits in our listening. Nichols and Stevens in their book *Are You Listening?*[7] have outlined a number of bad habits in the listening process. Several are pertinent to the field of insurance claims handling.

Dismissing the subject as uninteresting or too difficult

There is no such thing as an uninteresting subject; there are only uninterested people.

——G. K. Chesterton

The listener may dismiss the subject as uninteresting or too difficult. Here the listener's ears and mind are closed to the subject. He

---

7 Nichols and Stevens, *Are You Listening?*

or she therefore is able to avoid the effort that is required in order to listen effectively. This too often is the weapon of the sluggard—the lazy person escapes the work of listening. It requires much effort to absorb complex and difficult material by listening. It is easier not to listen.

Consider, for example, the problem that would confront a claims person if all personal lines insurance policies contained coinsurance clauses. Imagine the difficulty we would encounter in trying to explain the principles of and the reasons for coinsurance to a homeowner, for instance. The unsophisticated insurance buyer with an insurance loss might find our explanation of coinsurance theory much too complex and uninteresting to warrant an attentive ear. Furthermore, it probably would appear to some insureds that coinsurance is a tricky gimmick used by insurance companies to escape their legal responsibilities.

It is unlikely that a claims representative's legalistic explanation of a fine point of law will receive a full hearing. The complexities of law often are lost upon the layman, who may fail to listen to what appears to be a dull, technical treatise on an incomprehensible subject.

In ordinary daily conversations people often are not interested enough to listen to one another. We frequently wrap ourselves in self-interest. We may seek the company of others only so that we will have an opportunity to express ourselves. If a person listens attentively and agrees with the speaker, the listener probably will be characterized as an interesting conversationalist as well as an intelligent person. If he or she prefers to talk rather than listen, however, somewhat of a stand-off occurs.

Two people may talk *at* each other without listening to what is said. For example, Mr. Jones may tell Mr. Smith about his vacation experience. Smith hears the word *vacation,* and his mind immediately turns to more interesting thoughts—thoughts of his own vacation. Meanwhile, he stops listening to Jones. This saves the effort of listening. As Jones continues to talk, Smith is aware of the sound, and catches an occasional word or phrase. He can barely wait, however, to interrupt the other person with a narration of his own vacation experiences. When Smith begins to talk, Jones may catch snatches of Smith's narration which will stimulate his thinking in another direction about himself. He waits impatiently to talk and seeks the first opportunity to interrupt Smith. In this way the conversation see-saws back and forth with much talking and little listening.

That evening Smith tells his wife that he met Jones earlier in the day and heard all about the latter's vacation. Mrs. Smith inquires, "Where did they go? What did they do? How long did they stay?" Smith replies, "I believe they went to Canada and went fishing. He rambles on so, I didn't catch many of the details, but he said they had a lot of fun."

A friend of the author, a writer, has observed that people who frequently appear in reception lines often seem to be oblivious to the comments of those who pass through the line. The hardened greeter is more concerned with speeding up the line by the pressure on the elbow and the push with the hand which is doing the shaking. The small talk, the stereotyped greetings, and the repetition induce a state of boredom and disinterest which produces inattention. Poor listening results. The author's friend delights in making disarming remarks to people in these lines. At one reception she shook hands with a man and smiling broadly said, "I went shopping today, and my feet hurt." The man responded by smiling vacantly and remarked, "Oh, that's nice."

The claims person who fails to listen considerately and attentively to insureds or claimants will do little to gain their confidence. It is most unflattering to know that another person has not bothered to listen to you. Such inattentiveness is the mark of a careless, insensitive person who presents the definite impression of being indifferent and unconcerned about other people.

Tolerating distractions

The listener often escapes the work of listening by permitting background noise and movement to interrupt. A claims person who is interviewing an insured claimant or witness in the insurer's office and permits telephone calls or conversations with office personnel to interrupt the interview is guilty of rudeness. If we are dealing with a claimant, for example, we convey the impression that the claimant's problems are of secondary importance to the office routine. Tolerating distractions can adversely affect the outcome of negotiations. We should not allow distractions to interrupt the conversation. Secretaries or the switchboard operator should be instructed to hold all incoming telephone calls, and we should not permit office routine to disrupt conversations with others.

The subject of distractions already has been mentioned in connection with physical distortions to communication. Although it is impossible in some cases to provide ideal conditions for conducting interviews and negotiations, the claims person should make reasonable attempts to do so. A quiet, comfortable setting, free from distractions, can contribute much to effective listening and complete communication and understanding between the claims representative and another person.

Excluding generalizations

There is a tendency for claims representatives to exclude generalizations when they obtain statements or discuss claims with other people. As a consequence, they may be impatient in their listening habits and may not listen to another person's generalizations. They also may attempt to cut off the other person when he or she speaks in generalizations. The claims person is interested in distances in feet, speed in miles per hour, physical conditions, verbatim accounts of conversations, how fast a pedestrian was moving when struck by an automobile, and so forth. The claims representative must, by necessity, sift the chaff from a witness's oral expression in order to produce a clear, factual statement. Further, the claims person often may find it necessary to steer the conversation into an area of more relevant and material information.

It is always important, however, for us to realize that the specifics of a given case support and justify generalizations. It is equally true that any generalizations must be supported by specifics. If, therefore, we will gradually note the generalizations made by others, we may observe inconsistencies not borne out by specific facts. By calling them to the attention of a witness, we may cause the witness to recollect forgotten facts which support the generalizations. A story is told of a male defendant who was charged with mayhem; he was alleged to have bitten off another man's ear during a fight. The state's entire case rested upon the testimony of a person who reportedly witnessed the occurrence. During direct examination the prosecuting attorney asked the witness, "Did the defendant bite off the ear of John Jones?"

"Yes," replied the witness.

The defendant's attorney believed that the witness's testimony was too general. During the cross-examination, therefore, he inquired specifically, "But, did you *see* the defendant bite off the ear of John Jones?"

"No," answered the witness.

At that point the defense attorney was in an excellent position to dismiss the witness and point out the inconsistency of his general statement and the specific fact inquired into. The attorney, however, decided to make an example of this witness. He decided to ask one further question. "Well, then," he gloated, "if you did not see the defendant bite off the ear of John Jones, how do you know he did it?"

"I saw him spit it out," replied the witness simply.

In this case the witness's generalization was not corroborated by the known facts. Subsequent questioning, however, did reveal additional facts which supported the generalization. An inconsistency was brought to the attention of the witness, and he revealed a fact that supported the generalization, much to the chagrin of the defense attorney. The claims representative should pay attention, in the same manner (but with more satisfying results), to specific facts as well as to the generalizations made by others.

In addition to helping a witness to reveal additional facts, we can by noting generalizations help the witness to see inconsistencies and thereby help to correct his or her recollection and conception of a fact situation. We can accomplish this only by careful and attentive listening.

Letting emotions interfere

He that would govern others, first should be master of himself.
———Phillip Massinger (1583–1640)

Emotions color listening receptivity or block it completely. Emotions can interfere with the efficiency of the claims representative in two ways. Our emotions can impair our listening and communicating ability. Likewise, the emotions aroused in others can make it most difficult for us to communicate effectively. Both of these factors will be discussed in the following sections.

Inflating the insured's case. A new claims representative may grasp unduly upon favorable points of a liability claim in an eagerness to serve the insured and in a desire to believe the insured's version of an accident. The new claims person's attitude on the job is important here. We should come to the claims handling job with the objectivity and the willingness to give impartial consideration to both sides of a case. If we start out with a tendency to favor the insured, our listening ability will be impaired. This is because we tend to listen to things which support our beliefs. We may accept or change some of what we hear, or we may reject and block unpopular things from our hearing receptivity.

This emotional overemphasis may cause a claims person to overlook unfavorable aspects of the insured's case. If we hear conflicting stories from an insured and a claimant, and there are no circumstances to support either story, then we obviously should support and defend the insured's story. What the claims person must guard against is becoming emotionally involved in the case so that he or she listens only to favorable aspects of the insured's case and reads things into the insured's case which are not there. Proper analysis and disposition of insurance claims require that they be handled according to their true legal merits.

A claims representative who has the tendency to champion the insured and consider all claimants as antagonists is in for some bad moments. He or she soon will learn that some claimants are more honest and easier to believe than some insureds.

Coloring listening receptivity—the role of language. A further point regarding emotional coloring should be considered. We must not permit certain specific words, phrases, or language to influence and prejudice our ability to listen. We must realize that certain words, phrases, and language are emotion-laden as far as we are concerned. They will interfere with our listening ability.

Individuals respond differently to given words and phrases according to their particular backgrounds. Words that would shock or infuriate one person are common language to another and arouse no emotional reaction. Because of the nature of the insurance claims handling job, claims representatives come in contact with people from every conceivable social and economic level. Over a period of years a claims person becomes familiar with a wide variety of language—the socially "acceptable," the vernacular, and the obscene.

The claims representative hears the accents, the dialects, and the languages of many nationalities. If we judge the merit of insureds, claimants, or witnesses by the language used by them, our listening receptivity may be colored, thus reducing our effectiveness on the job. This is particularly true in the case of profanity if the claims representative has a propensity to blanch at such language. We, nevertheless, should not make the mistake of judging a person by the language that person uses so that we fail to listen objectively to what that person is saying.

We must likewise be aware of words which stimulate a feeling of prejudice in our own minds. Such "red-flag" words arouse mental pictures in the listener's mind and may color listening receptivity. Here again, a given word may or may not stimulate an emotional response; reaction depends upon the claims representative's background. A word need not be an apparently emotion-laden one. Hugh P. Fellows points out that a listener's reaction to a given word depends upon the association he or she consciously or subconsciously attaches to the word that is used.[8] Even if we are unable to find the reason why we dislike certain words, the fact that we have identified them and have recognized the words will enable us to deal with personal prejudice and emotions. We can guard against allowing red-flag words to block our listening. Possible emotion-laden words are: *teenager, politician, cop, yankee,* and so forth. We can all make our own list.

Most Americans believe they are tolerant. *Tolerance,* however, is a word which does not mean complete acceptance of other people and complete lack of bias or prejudice about a given subject. It means simply the quality of enduring or putting up with something.

In the "melting pot of the world," the United States, people have little choice except to be tolerant. Sociologists tell us, however, that most people are prejudiced to some extent about one or more nationalities, or religions, or other differences in the people around us. The point is simply this: we all must recognize our own feelings about ethnic, religious, or other subjects and not permit them to color our listening receptivity.

Coloring listening receptivity—the role of subject matter.   Closely allied to the topic of language is that of subject matter. We do not like to listen to ideas or facts which conflict with our mental patterns. Introduction of a given subject by a speaker may arouse us to such

---

[8] From Hugh P. Fellows, *The Art and Skill of Talking with People* (Englewood Cliffs, N.J.: Prentice-Hall, 1964).

an extent that in our listening process we will interpret what is said in such a manner that we will end up with a meaning completely opposite from the meaning intended by the speaker. We will tend to listen only to those things which conform to personal beliefs and attitudes. This situation presents a danger for a claims representative who is attempting to make an impartial and objective investigation of an insurance claim.

If, for example, a claims man has a poor opinion of teenage drivers or women drivers, he must guard against permitting this emotional coloring to influence his objectivity, causing him to arrive at erroneous conclusions. Emotional coloring must be eliminated from his listening process. Our approach must be objective, detached, and impartial when we are attempting to establish the circumstances of an accident or other occurrence. Allowing emotion to color listening receptivity is a practice that must be avoided by the claims person.

Blocking listening receptivity.   Equally important is the role that emotions play in blocking listening receptivity completely. Emotions cause deafness. We can become so disturbed at what we have just heard that we will fail to listen further to what is being said. The Orson Welles invasion-from-Mars incident proved the point. Shocked by the announcement that an "invasion" was taking place, people simply turned off their hearing apparatus and failed to listen to repeated announcements that the invasion was fictional. In like manner emotion frequently blocks listening receptivity in ordinary conversation.

Our prejudices, convictions, beliefs, and feelings often are disturbed by words which reach our ears. Our ability to listen, to analyze, and to evaluate critically may be completely erased momentarily by words which arouse our emotions.

In the claims world of adversary relationships the claims representative must guard against allowing his or her emotions to affect hearing sensitivity and listening receptivity. Although occasionally we may be the target of undeserved vituperation, we must learn to react coolly and unemotionally. In short, a claims person must have a "tough hide."

Emotions not only block the listening receptivity of the claims representative, but they also interfere with the listening ability of insureds, claimants, and witnesses. A claims person meets many people who are emotionally upset. Severe traumatic experiences sometimes cause a person to break down and cry when talking to a claims representative.

It is not uncommon for the claims person to witness displays of anger on the part of an insured or a claimant.

People in an emotional state of mind do not hear well. They often will not hear questions fully, and they are unlikely to listen attentively to complex explanations. Every claims representative, consequently, should recognize the effect of emotions on listening ability, for emotions can interfere considerably with the communication process. The claims representative is well-advised to make every attempt to try to reduce or eliminate emotional obstacles which block the listening ability of others.

Obtaining receptivity with a claim denial. A message which arouses anger or distress in another person will destroy communication and negate the claims person's attempts to influence others. If we are effectively to convince another person to act in a certain manner, we must be certain that the person "hears us out," or permits us to complete the explanation of a point or the reasoning behind the course of action taken by the insurer or the decision reached by the company.

This point is well illustrated in actual claims situations. Claims representatives often are instructed never to deny a claim directly, either orally or in writing. If a claims representative begins with the words: "Mrs. Jones: We regret that we cannot pay your claim," it is quite likely that Mrs. Jones will never bother to listen to reasons for the denial. The immediate, direct denial may stimulate outrage and anger. Although the reasons for the denial may be spelled out in a fair, reasonable, and most persuasive manner following the statement of denial, they may be entirely ineffective in abating the anger of the listener. The critical faculties of the listener's mind are disabled momentarily so that he or she is unable to comprehend or evaluate the reasons for the denial. Research has shown that if negative conclusions are stated first, people stop listening to the remaining conclusions, even if they are favorable. If desirable conclusions are stated first, the person is more attentive to all of your conclusions that follow.

A claims person, consequently, must begin oral or written claims denials in an indirect manner. The claimant should be informed that his or her claim has received "careful, painstaking attention" so that the insurance company could arrive at "a fair and equitable decision." Conciliatory and noninflammatory language, such as the foregoing can be used to good avail. In past years most claims persons have tried to make claims denials as noninflammatory as possible and have attempted to say as little as possible. Today, however, denial letters must contain more complete information in order to comply with "unfair claims settlement practices" laws (See Chapter 10). For example, referring to first party claims, typical statutory language provides that "no insurer shall deny a claim on the grounds of a specific policy provision, condition, or exclusion unless reference to such provision, condition, or exclusion is included in the denial";[9] or a typical state statute may condemn the "failure to promptly provide a reasonable explanation of the basis in the insurance policy in relation to the facts or applicable law for denial of a claim or for the offer of a compromise settlement. . . ."[10] If state legislatures and courts extend these protective provisions to third-party claimants, considerable care will be required in drafting denial letters to third-party claimants.

Whether a letter is directed to an insured or a third-party claimant, a foundation of conciliatory language should be employed before the actual denial is made. Conciliatory language is utilized, followed by a "reasonable" explanation spelling out relevant facts and applicable law bearing on the claimant's case. The most important thing is to point out to the claimant that he or she has received "fair and impartial" treatment; that the claim has been given "full and exhaustive consideration"; and that the insurance company has attempted to "appraise fairly and properly all of the circumstances surrounding the claim."

The handling of the exact wording of the denial itself is important. Although some claims representatives favor saying little or nothing in the way of explanation for the denial, others believe that they will forestall a telephone call or a personal visit from an angry claimant if they inject a brief word of explanation for the denial. Aside from the foregoing considerations, the law now requires a "reasonable" explanation of the basis for the denial. The following general statement may be helpful in making the denial in a state where contributory negligence is a bar to recovery or where it has been determined that the claimant's negligence was solely the cause of the accident: "The physical circumstances of your accident indicate negligence upon your part, which bars recovery under the law. We regret, therefore,

---

[9] Section 8 (a), *N.A.I.C. Unfair Claims Settlement Practices Model Act* (National Association of Insurance Commissioners, 1971).

[10] Section 44–1525 (n), *Revised Statutes of Nebraska, 1943*, 1978 reissue.

that we must deny your claim." The extent of detail incorporated in the denial will vary according to the practice and philosophy of the individual company or adjusting firm, but it must be adequate to comply with applicable statutes on the subject. Whatever the case, the denial should begin with conciliatory language, expressing goodwill; should present an explanation of your analysis and evaluation of the liability question; and then conclude with the statement of denial.

If a claims representative handles a denial in this manner, the critical faculties of the other person are given an opportunity to function for a while before the emotion-arousing decision is announced. If the case for the denial has been presented in a sincere and believable manner, much of the emotion-arousing potential may be dispelled before the claim is denied. As Bismarck observed, "You must apply the lather before you start shaving."

SUMMARY

It should be apparent from the foregoing pages that listening is a personal skill which must be developed by the individual claims representative. To achieve success in the field of insurance claims handling, the practitioner must be able to communicate effectively.

Unlike many other areas of activity, insurance claims handling requires a very high standard of listening performance. We must be able to listen to everything that is said by other people and, much like the court reporter, preserve that information in a permanent form as a written or recorded statement. The court reporter, however, records only what is said and has no responsibility for developing a conversation so that information will be exposed completely. We must be able to listen, record what we hear, evaluate what is heard, and direct the interview or conversation in such a way that all the necessary information is made known.

The requirements of the claims handling job, therefore, impose a high standard of listening skill upon the claims person. Unfortunately, a new claims representative often comes to the job with indifferent listening ability. The reason is simple. Good listening skill is not typical. People are generally indifferent or poor listeners, because they have had so much practice at not listening.

To become proficient at listening so that we will achieve success in claims handling work, we must purge ourselves of the bad habits which interfere with good listening. Some of these *bad habits which interfere with listening* are as follows:

1. Dismissing the subject as uninteresting or too difficult.
2. Tolerating distractions.
3. Excluding generalizations.
4. Letting emotions interfere with listening receptivity.

Not only must we recognize and eliminate bad listening habits from our everyday activities, we also should adopt affirmative techniques which will aid us in sharpening our listening skills. The following chapter will explore some of these techniques and provide possible suggestions for developing listening skills.

6

Developing listening skills

Good listening is a skill. It must be developed with practice. Like the skilled pianist, the skilled listener must devote time and effort to develop and retain necessary skill. Consider the job of the linguist at the United Nations who must hear every word of a speaker, understand its meaning well enough to convert it into another tongue, and simultaneously translate it into the other language. Telephone operators, likewise, must acquire the ability to listen effectively if they are to perform well on their jobs. More related to insurance claims handling, consider the highly competent court reporter who can sit in a room in which four or five persons are speaking, hear every word that is spoken, recall it, and record it in shorthand notes at 240–250 words per minute.

It is not entirely accurate to say that these individuals are listening with the objective of achieving comprehension in the subject matter. Court reporters, for example, indicate that quite often their job is somewhat of a mechanical process of converting oral words into written words. It is not unusual for the court reporter to have no comprehensive understanding of the subject matter; he or she is merely working with words. This particularly is true in cases involving complex, technical testimony of expert witnesses. Court reporters, furthermore, often perform their jobs in a highly competent manner while they are thinking about some other subject. This reportedly is more true if the reporter uses a stenotype machine than if he or she is pen-writing shorthand. When material is interesting to him or her, however, the court reporter is likely to listen attentively and to achieve a high degree of comprehension.

The claims representative must hear accurately so that he or she, like the court reporter, can perform the mechanical task of recording and recalling accurately everything heard. Since this function is not merely mechanical, however, the claims person also must comprehend what is being said.

ESSENTIALS OF GOOD LISTENING

The most essential ingredient for success in listening is the correct mental attitude—the desire to learn to listen. In every form of endeavor, the desire to achieve is paramount. Without this desire—without this motivation—people cannot succeed. To be a champion swimmer, for example, a boy or girl must resolve to succeed at swimming. He or she must be motivated to accept nothing but success in this activity. The swimmer may dislike the strain of practice—swimming hours every day; he or she may dislike the muscle-building exercises that must be undertaken; and the sacrifices which must be made in social life may be distasteful. The swimmer is willing, however, to put up with these disadvantages because of personal motivation to succeed at swimming.

A similar motivation and desire is necessary in order to succeed at listening. We may be disinterested in what is being said; we may find that it takes extreme effort and concentration to listen to what is being said; and we may find it distasteful to have to stop talking long enough in order to listen. If we are to succeed at listening, however, we, like the swimmer, must make sacrifices to acquire the desired competence.

Motivation and efficiency

Mental attitude is all-important to effective listening. Psychologists state that boredom occurs when a person is inadequately motivated. Unless a person has the motivation, desire, and interest to succeed at listening, he or she can easily lapse into boredom. Boredom destroys human effectiveness. This was borne out by exhaustive studies by

Joseph Barmack which revealed that boredom causes physiological changes in the human body.[1] Some of these changes are as follows:

1. Depression in oxygen consumption, either sustained or occasional.
2. Increased unpleasantness and irritability.
3. Increased inattentiveness.
4. Increased fatigue.
5. Decreased output.

Barmack concluded that these physiological changes are a function of attitude. Boredom produces them. Further, when these changes occur, they result in inefficiency.

On the positive side, Barmack's studies also revealed that interest sustains vital activity. Motivation and the interest generated by it cause the human mind and body to function more efficiently. Under the circumstances, we must maintain our motivation, desire, and interest if we are to obtain skill in listening, or for that matter, if we are to be good students and acquire competence in any field of learning.

Listening requirements

To be a good listener requires the proper mental attitude. This requisite includes the following elements:

1. Motivation to succeed at listening—a sense of purpose.
2. A willingness to stop talking and to start listening.
3. A willingness to listen even though the subject matter may seem uninteresting and dull.
4. Enthusiasm and pride in the achievement of having heard all that was said.

SUGGESTIONS FOR DEVELOPING LISTENING SKILLS

Once the claims representative has the proper mental attitude, he or she needs practical guidance in how best to develop listening skills. This section will present helpful suggestions to aid the claims person to develop skill in listening.

---

[1] Joseph E. Barmack, "Boredom and Other Factors in the Physiology of Mental Effort," *Archives of Psychology*, vol. 31, nos. 216–23 (New York: Columbia University, 1937–38), p. 29.

As mentioned previously, the human mind thinks four times faster than a person can speak. This gives the listener extra time which is not needed for listening. It permits us to think of other things while listening. This can be advantageous. The inherent advantage of thought speed permits us to obtain the ultimate benefits of the listening process. It enables us to review and summarize what has been said. It also allows us to plan questions which will encourage the speaker to expose the subject further. The danger is that it also may permit the listener's mind to wander aimlessly to other topics during this extra time. Ultimately we may shift our entire attention to other thoughts. The result is inattention—failure to listen.

We must avoid the "vacuous duologue," discussed in the chapter on communication. We must not interrupt the speaker, interjecting our own views, stifling informative and effective listening. Tuning out the speaker and shifting to our own opinions and ideas cuts off the communication exchange. The progressive tuning out of a speaker and shifting to another topic is common. It is a bad habit and destroys effective listening. The principal problem, therefore, is to pay attention to the speaker and to the subject. There are a number of things the listener can do to concentrate on the speaker's subject. These will be discussed in the sections which follow.

Analyze and evaluate the speaker's statements and conclusions

People tend to believe what they hear regardless of the merit of what is being said. We essentially are gullible listeners. The spoken word is intimate and persuasive. Although facts often are exaggerated or edited, there is little time to evaluate what is being said. As a consequence, we often fail to mentally attack unsupported conclusions, illogical statements, and inconsistencies uttered by others. We frequently accept half truths and untruths. The listener must analyze and evaluate the speaker's statements and conclusions. In this process he or she must seek answers to a number of questions, including the following:

1. Are the speaker's statements and conclusions founded upon sound logic, or are they raw appeals to emotion?
2. What authority or evidence does the speaker muster to support his or her conclusions? When the speaker quotes alleged experts or

authorities on a topic, are these people really competent authorities? Is the evidence current or is it out-of-date? Are the speaker's statements of opinion merely unsupported conclusions?

The listener must methodically and critically examine the words of others. We must hold ideas up to the light of intelligence and perspective and inspect them thoroughly and impersonally in the same manner that the entymologist looks at the bug on the end of a pin. We must be able to uncover the speaker's main thoughts and be able to screen inconsequential, immaterial, and irrelevant thoughts.

Accurate and critical listening enables us to listen for main and subordinate ideas. It helps us relate subordinate ideas to the main point and enables us to identify the sequence of ideas. This process makes it possible for us to evaluate critically the facts and evidence and arrive at our own conclusions. We then are in a better position to analyze and evaluate the speaker's statements and conclusions.

Anticipate the speaker

In analyzing and evaluating the speaker's statements and conclusions we should try to guess what the speaker is leading up to. We should think ahead and anticipate what is coming next. This keeps our listening on track. Equally important, this practice will help us in our analysis and evaluation. If we are able to anticipate the conclusions of the speaker, we learn by comparing the speaker's conclusions with our own anticipations.

There is some danger in anticipatory listening. The listener must be mindful of the tendency of people to hear what they want to hear. When we are listening to a speaker, we should attempt to anticipate the speaker, but we always must be ready to revise our mental impressions as the speaker's thoughts unfold. This can be accomplished only through attentive listening.

Analyze the speaker

Close scrutiny of the speaker and strict attention to what the speaker is saying and how he or she is saying it will help the listener to detect meanings suggested by vocal inflection, emphasis, and voice quality. Further, visual clues will aid the listener in evaluating appeals made by the speaker. Nonverbal messages may contradict what the speaker is saying. In analyzing the speaker, therefore, the listener will find it helpful to:

1. Watch the speaker's face and eyes—is he or she direct and straightforward, or does the speaker appear evasive?
2. Listen to the speaker's voice—does his or her voice have a ring of conviction, sincerity, and truth to it, or does it show hesitation and reflect artificiality? Voices often betray thoughts and emotions.
3. Is the speaker neutral or is he or she prejudiced on the subject? What will the speaker gain personally if his or her views are accepted?
4. Listen for information balance—does the speaker overemphasize or underemphasize information? This practice may reveal the speaker's biases or lack of knowledge; it may reveal the speaker's real opinions. What he or she leaves unsaid may speak louder than what is said. The speaker may be evading a pertinent point.

Observation and analysis of nonverbal messages are particularly important as the claims representative seeks to analyze the speaker. Utilization of nonverbal feedback is highly important. Frequently, the nonverbal messages may completely contradict what the other person is saying. For example, research studies conducted by forensic psychologists for law-enforcement agencies and trial attorneys reveal that nonverbal messages are highly significant. For instance, studies reveal strongly that the hand-over-the-mouth gesture is definitely significant—it frequently reveals that the speaker is unsure of or disturbed about what he or she is saying. Gerard I. Nierenberg, author of *The Art of Negotiating,* contends that the gesture of covering one's mouth while speaking indicates that the person is doubtful, unsure, lying, or distorting the truth. The claims person should be aware, however, that the speaker may be adjusting his or her bridgework, covering the gap left by a missing tooth, or trying to spare the claims representative from sharing the rich aroma of a garlic and pastrami sandwich recently consumed.

In a conversational situation the claims representative frequently can determine how well the other person is listening by closely observing the nonverbal feedback. If an insured, claimant, or witness, for example, folds his or her arm across the chest, the person is signaling defensiveness, resistance, or boredom. The person may not be receptive to what you are saying and may not listen closely to your message. To proceed with the same conversational pattern, therefore, may be futile in such a situation. The claims person is advised to try a new approach or change of pace in getting the other person into a more open and acceptive mood or stance.

Similarly, other body positions, actions of the other person (yawning, drumming the fingers, eye contact, and eye movements), and other nonverbal clues have an important bearing on the quality of the communication exchange. Thus, the claims representative must listen with the ears, the eyes, and the mind in order to fully utilize the listening function.

Review in summary form

As the speaker proceeds, we must be able to review and summarize in our minds all that has been heard. This particularly is true if we are taking a statement. By reviewing in summary form what has been said, we will know what points must be developed further and what new areas of information should be explored.

Use questions and appropriate comments

Questions obviously are important in developing an interview and in extracting as much information as possible from the speaker. They also have another great value to us as listeners. In the event that our attention is wavering, questions enable us to relate back to the speaker's subject matter. Questions reinforce our attention and help us to pick up information which we may not have heard or understood fully on the first telling. A question such as, "Would you mind explaining that a little more fully?" gives the listener a second chance to listen.

Skillfully interjected and appropriate comments serve the same purpose as questions in enabling the listener to relate back to the speaker's subject matter. Further, there are times when a direct comment concerning the speaker's words can cause the speaker to develop his or her thoughts more fully and help the speaker to express thoughts more adequately. Fully as important, however, comments also indicate to the speaker that the claims person is listening. To convey this impression, the claims representative will find it helpful to employ what has been called a series of "eloquent and encouraging grunts":[2] such as "Hmmm," "Uh-huh," "Oh," or "I see." This lets the other person know that we are listening, and it helps to establish and to maintain the confidence of the speaker.

React with bodily movement

In the skillful use of comments and questions, the listener is reacting to the speaker. The listener reveals interest in and attention to what the speaker is saying. Obviously, however, we cannot rely only upon interjected comments and questions to reveal interest. We must remain silent much of the time so that the other person may speak.

There are, nevertheless, other means by which we can reveal interest and attention and at the same time help relate to the speaker. We may use visual clues to let the speaker know that there is an audience present. We may smile, incline our body slightly forward in an alert attitude, or we may nod responsively. Our facial expressions and eye movements will help to indicate whether we are listening. The better the listener's response, the greater the likelihood that the speaker will be encouraged to talk. Skillful use of body language is important here.

A word of caution should be mentioned here. The interjected comment, or "eloquent and encouraging grunt," the alert attitude, and the nodding head often are misused. Reference has been made to the student who sits in class and nods the head up and down as an instructor lectures. The student, by every appearance, displays interest and rapt attention. In a subsequent examination the student also may display an amazing ignorance of the subject being discussed by the instructor. In short, the student is faking an appearance of attention and interest. Many people have the bad habit of doing this. They sit with their gaze riveted upon a speaker, a glazed look in their eyes, and their thoughts busily engaged in other subjects. This deception is a distinct liability when it is important to listen. The speaker's subject matter is completely missed. Further, feigned attention soon becomes apparent to the speaker.

---

[2] Ralph G. Nichols and Leonard A. Stevens, *Are You Listening?* (New York: McGraw-Hill, 1957), p. 53.

A DAILY EXERCISE IN LISTENING

Learning is hard by the yard, but a cinch by the inch.
———James J. Chastain

Educators have observed that knowledge dispensed in regular, systematic, relatively small portions over a considerable period of time usually is learned better and retained longer than knowledge dished out in hurry-up cram courses. Knowledge grows like plants; it requires sprouting time between each watering.

We cannot absorb large doses of information, ideas, theories, and concepts in brief periods of time. Likewise, in any program involving acquisition of skill and competence, progress comes a little at a time. Almost 2,000 years ago Plutarch recognized this elemental fact when he wrote, ". . . many things which cannot be overcome when they are together, yield themselves up when taken little by little."[3] The process of acquiring knowledge and skill spans a lifetime; formal education itself may stretch over a period of two and a half decades; and apprenticeship periods for even the simplest trades usually require several years.

Since competence grows little by little, a new student or apprentice begins by working on limited projects. This is the idea utilized by the Diamond Alkali Company in its listening course, mentioned earlier. The company used audio tapes to present a programed learning course on effective listening. The listener-trainee was presented with a series of taped statements of varying lengths and complexity. The statements were narrated in many voices: masculine and feminine; high-pitch and low-pitch; rapid and laconic. They were alternately grammatical, ungrammatical, clipped, rambling, organized, and disorganized. The program taught the listener to capture the main content while ignoring emotion and background distraction.

The trainee responded either verbally or in writing to the information presented in each statement. He or she answered pertinent questions or summarized statements, then had an opportunity to evaluate responses by comparing them with the correct answers. As the program progressed, the taped information became longer and more complex, requiring responses which reflected greater listening

---

[3] Plutarch, *Lives* (tr. John Dryden, revised by Arthur Hugh Clough, Modern Library Giant edition), Sertorius, p. 688.

skill. As the student gained competence, he or she moved forward to more difficult tasks and projects.

A series of graduated steps

Strength of mind is exercise, not rest.
        ——Alexander Pope

A program of gradual attainment of education and skill can be most effective for the claims representative. Although we may not have access to a company-sponsored course in listening, we can, nevertheless, gain competence in listening by employing a simple daily exercise. The exercise, in a series of steps graduated in degree of difficulty, makes it possible for the claims representative to practice listening. Furthermore, the exercise enables us to evaluate our performance at the same time.

An attractive aspect of this exercise in listening is that it calls for a minimum expenditure of time while at the same time providing for a systematic method for developing listening skills.

The program

In order to utilize the exercise the claims person must have the following requisites. He or she must:

1. Possess the motivation and the desire to improve personal listening capabilities.
2. Have someone (a relative or a friend) to help in the program.
3. Set aside a certain period of time each day to perform the exercise.

Briefly, each day we should have a relative or a friend read some preselected material to us. Following the reading we immediately should sit down and write what we have just heard. A comparison then should be made comparing what has been written with the content of the material read by the relative or friend. Essentially, then, the exercise consists of:

1. A reading.
2. A recall and a writing.
3. A comparison and an evaluation.

As we acquire competence, we should move on to material that is more difficult and of greater length. We will know how fast to advance as our evaluation advises us that accuracy is improving in recall and in writing the material heard.

The reading.   Particular care should be taken in the selection of material to be read. Since the student-listener obviously should not first read the material and select it, the relative or friend will have to make the selection. The material initially used should be chosen for its generality and should be relatively free of complex statements of fact, figures, and names. Magazines, newspapers, and books will provide a wealth of material that will vary in complexity of reading.

Of equal importance is the amount of material which should be read each day. It is suggested that the reader start out at a moderate rate of speed, (e.g., 90–100 words per minute). As the listener acquires skill, the reader can increase the reading speed to about 140 words per minute. The first day's reading should not exceed 20 seconds in duration. In this amount of time the reader will be able to read 30 to 35 words, and this will be a challenging initial test for the student-listener. As the listener gains competence in listening and recall on progressively harder materials, he or she then can move on to readings of greater length.

The recall and the writing.   The short period of time required to perform this simple exercise should make it possible for the listener to maintain intense concentration on the task at hand. Since we are able to listen at the rate of 400 to 500 words per minute, this should give the listener considerable time to hear what is being said, register it in the mind, and organize it in such a way that it should be possible to recall the information and write it down when the reading period is over.

In the process of recall the listener should not attempt to memorize words. Rather, the listener should search for and find the main ideas of each sentence and remember enough of the accompanying words to express those ideas as accurately as possible. As the listener moves on to progressively longer readings, he or she should concentrate on the main ideas and should be able to recall verbatim the significant facts, figures, and names. In writing down his or her recollection after each reading, these facts, figures, and names should be stated accurately, together with the main ideas contained in the textual material. All of these should appear in a skillful paraphrasing which closely resembles the original text in tone, grammar, and sentence structure.

The comparison and the evaluation. It is in the comparison and evaluation that the subjective judgment of the listener must be exercised. We are required to establish a personal standard of achievement, serving as our own taskmaster to judge whether our listening and recall have approached the degree of competence required by those personal standards we have established for ourselves. If we are to become skillful listeners, however, we should set those standards high.

A suggested schedule

As a means of aiding the student to utilize the foregoing listening exercise, it is suggested that he or she adopt the schedule shown in Table 6–1. In Step 1 the student will have a friend or relative select material of general nature (relatively free of complex statements and specific data—facts, figures, names), and this type of material will be utilized for 5 days. For the next 5 days the reader will read material combining general statements and specific data. Complexity of material can be increased as the student progresses from one step to the next.

If a student is not satisfied that he or she has acquired the degree of listening competence desired after the prescribed number of days at a given level, the student should remain at that step until he or she is satisfied with the level of competence achieved. In addition, as the student progresses to longer listening sessions (two minutes or longer), he or she will find it increasingly necessary to take notes to aid in recall.

With the great emphasis now placed on recorded statements, note-taking becomes highly essential. Before the recorder came into common usage, claims representatives relied almost completely on the handwritten statement. As an interview progressed, the salient facts were written into the statement. It was a simple matter to review the statement to determine whether all of the important points of the investigation were fully covered. Unfortunately, this review process is not possible with the recordings. As a consequence, the claims person must keep track of the progress of the interview, noting what subject areas and details have been covered and those yet to be explored. Obviously, unless one has a perfect memory, the best way to accomplish this task of recall is to rely on notes.

Note-taking ability or skill is an acquired trait. Strangely enough, it is not a skill that is fully developed by many college students today. After almost a quarter of a century of teaching experience, the author remains astounded that some senior college students have not developed competent note-taking skills during their school years. Unless the insurance claims representative has developed good note-taking skills, extra effort should be devoted to the task in order to enhance his or her performance on the claims handling job.

In note-taking the student must not make the fatal mistake of attempting to write down everything word for word. The student soon will discover that he or she will get behind and will fail to listen effectively. In note-taking as in listening, the student must search for main ideas and reduce them to writing by employing a system of abbreviations. Each student can develop a system to meet personal

Table 6–1

Step	Number of days	Length of reading	Nature of material
1	5	20 secs. (30–45 words)	General
	5	20 secs. (30–45 words)	General-specific
2	5	30 secs. (45–70 words)	General
	5	30 secs. (45–70 words)	General-specific
3	5	40 secs. (60–90 words)	General
	5	40 secs. (60–90 words)	General-specific
4	5	50 secs. (75–115 words)	General
	5	50 secs. (75–115 words)	General-specific
5	5	60 secs. (90–140 words)	General
	5	60 secs. (90–140 words)	General-specific
6	5	1½ mins. (135–210 words)	General
	5	1½ mins. (135–210 words)	General-specific
7	5	2 mins. (180–280 words)	General
	5	2 mins. (180–280 words)	General-specific
8	5	4 mins. (360–560 words)	General
	5	4 mins. (360–560 words)	General-specific
9	5	6 mins. (540–840 words)	General
	5	6 mins. (540–840 words)	General-specific
10	5	10 mins. (900–1,400 words)	General
	5	10 mins. (900–1,400 words)	General-specific

needs. An example of a system of abbreviations used in note-taking is as follows:

Words or phrases	*Abbreviations*
Plaintiff	P
Defendant	D
Contract	K
Attorney	atny
Adjuster	adj
Motor vehicle	mtr veh *or* mv
Personal injury or Bodily injury	PI *or* BI
Property damage	PD
Necessary	nec
Passenger	psgr
Claim	clm
Claimant	clt
General damages	genl dgs *or* gen dam
Question and answer	Q&A
Individuals	indivs
Judgment	jgmt *or* jgt
Significant	sig
Background	bkgrnd *or* bkgd
Litigation	litig
Settlement	setlmt or stlmt
Liability	liab
Negligent	neg
Collision	coll
Comprehensive	comp
Insured	I
Man	♂
Woman	♀
Excess coverage	xs cov
Driving while intoxicated	dwi
Couple	cpl
Evidence	evid
With	w/
Within	w/in
Original	orig
Imagination	imag
Court	ct

The reader no doubt has his or her own abbreviation system for taking notes, and if not, the above will serve as a starting point for developing one's own personal shorthand system. The author employed the above system in taking notes during his college years, and it served his needs admirably. Superior systems of abbreviation unquestionably exist, and the reader should develop a system that is personally helpful.

It obviously will help if the student will write down specific facts, figures, and names when taking notes. It should be mentioned that in the early steps of this suggested listening exercise the student must attempt to do without notes. This should effectively sharpen powers of concentration and improve recall ability. It is only as the student progresses to the longer listening sessions of two minutes or longer that he or she should rely on note-taking.

Following the completion of this exercise the listener will have gained a level of competence and skill to make it possible to listen to and evaluate most public addresses, whether they be after-dinner speeches, political addresses, or the sermons of the neighborhood minister. If claims representatives will follow faithfully this formal listening program day by day, they can improve their attentiveness and recall and intensify their interest in and awareness of the important role which listening plays in the communication process.

Supplemental programs

To supplement the formal exercise, the claims representative also may find it helpful to devote an hour each day to the task of actively listening to everyone seen during that hour. During that time, the claims person also should employ the various techniques suggested for developing listening skills—reacting to the speaker, using questions and appropriate comments, and so on. It is suggested that the claims representative pick an hour which is unrelated to the claims handling job. For instance, the claims person might well devote the hour to attentive listening at a church activity, at a service club function, at coffee with friends, or at home with family and friends. It is most likely that the conscious effort devoted to listening one hour per day in this manner will improve and enrich relations with acquaintances, friends, and most important, the family.

Needless to say, any activity which makes us appear more interested and friendly with other people will make them more interested in us. Furthermore, our increased ability to listen and recall will do much to enhance our value to our employer as well as to add to our own appreciation of the world of communications.

SUMMARY

The claims representative must recognize that good listening is a skill which is developed only through practice and through effort. Everyone who desires to be a skillful listener must work to acquire competence. It is essential, in the very beginning, for the would-be listener to have a proper mental attitude. We must have the desire to succeed at the difficult job of effective listening. Without motivation, we all tend to lapse into boredom, and boredom causes inefficiency; it causes physiological changes which prevent the human mind and body from functioning efficiently.

Mental attitude, therefore, is all-important if one is to become a skillful listener. *Correct mental attitude for proper listening requires* the following essentials:

1. We must be motivated and have the desire and interest to succeed at listening. We must have a sense of purpose.
2. We must be willing to stop talking and to start listening.
3. We must be willing to listen attentively even though the subject matter may seem uninteresting and dull.
4. We must have enthusiasm and a sense of pride in the achievement of hearing all that the other person may say.

If we have the proper attitude and are willing to put forth the necessary effort, we will discover that there are techniques which we can utilize to practice listening skills. These suggested techniques help us to maintain interest and to relate our mental processes to what is being said. Without the ability to concentrate upon our speaker's discourse, it will be easy for us to stray from the subject and ultimately to shift our entire attention to other thoughts.

To develop listening skill, it will be most helpful for the would-be listener if he or she follows a few simple suggestions. These suggestions enable the listener to concentrate on a conversation or speech, improve personal ability to listen constructively, and diminish the likelihood that his or her mind will stray from the subject. In addition, the utilization of these guides will enable the listener to better understand the speaker and the speaker's motives. Furthermore, the listener's attitude of alert, attentive, considerate listening will make it possible to gain the confidence of the speaker. A climate of confidence will enhance the listener's ability to influence and to motivate the speaker to respond in a fashion deemed desirable by the listener. The *suggestions for improving listening skills* are as follows:

1. As the speaker talks, analyze and evaluate his or her statements and conclusions.
2. Anticipate what the speaker is leading up to.
3. Analyze the speaker. Is the speaker sincere? Can you detect his or her biases and real opinions?
4. Continually review what the speaker has said.
5. Use questions and appropriate comments to guide the direction the speaker is taking and to encourage the speaker to talk.
6. React to the speaker. Make the speaker aware that he or she has a listener.

Progress in acquiring listening skill comes as a gradual process. Like every area of human endeavor it must be developed little by little. The important thing for the student to remember is that a regular and systematic program of self-improvement probably is the most beneficial in acquiring education, skill, and competence. The claims representative, therefore, may find it quite helpful to utilize some simple *formal program to develop his or her listening competence.* This program should make it possible for the claims representative to:

1. Work on a limited project.
2. Work on a controlled project, so that the subject matter may be systematically increased in difficulty.
3. Work on a project which permits the student to analyze and evaluate his or her progress.

A later chapter introduces the reader to the subject of motivation. An understanding of the factors of motivation will help the claims person perform the job of influencing other people, utilizing listening skills and other principles and techniques of successful claims handling.

CHAPTER

7

Communication techniques

Considerable attention has been directed in the preceding chapters to the general principles of communication, including emphasis upon the critical role played by listening. Striving for two-way communication is highly essential for the claims representative to achieve effective communication skills. This chapter directs attention to various communication techniques and the psychological principles that bear upon the subject of the communication process. Particularly, emphasis is placed upon the mechanics of interviewing, stressing types of questions utilized in the claims handling interview and in claims investigations.

Great changes have occurred in the area of insurance claims handling and the conduct of interviews and other factors of claims handling investigations. These have been brought about by the revolution in recording technology which makes it possible for claims representatives now to handle most claims by the telephone and to preserve the facts and evidence of a case by the use of the recording device. Thus, this chapter explores the subject of the recording device, telephone claims handling techniques, telephone personality, and other facets of this subject. Of particular importance, of course, is the problem of personalizing a media of communication, the telephone conversation, which by its very nature is impersonal because of the remoteness of the two parties in the communication exchange.

THE RECORDING DEVICE

Telephone recording devices have been in use to some extent since 1916. A substantial demand and use for such recording devices began, however, about the beginning of World War II. By 1945 three large manufacturers of recording devices estimated that a total of about 19,000 of their telephone recorder instruments were in use in the United States. Most of these devices were being utilized by the navy and the War Department, and by industrial plants engaged in the production of war materials under contract with the U.S. government.

Wartime experience gained with telephone recording devices resulted in an unprecedented commercial demand after the war. Telephone recorders were used for many commercial purposes and by many types of users including attorneys, auditors, physicians, engineers, banks, food processors, insurance companies and brokers, hospitals, printers, manufacturers, meat packers, railroads, bus companies, and welfare and trade associations.

The use of the telephone recorder has proliferated incredibly with the great technological improvements made possible by miniaturization and the general availability of reasonably-priced and reliable recorders. Among the primary users of the telephone recorders today are insurance companies and their claims handling personnel.

Recorders and the claims person

Most insurance claims offices are equipped with desk recorders, and telephone recorders are in common use by insurance company claims departments, independent adjusters, and the large insurance adjusting firms. One of the nation's largest insurance adjusting firms, for example, reports that fully 95 percent of all statements taken on workers' compensation cases and 50 to 60 percent of statements taken on liability claims are now accomplished through the use of the telephone recorder. Many insurance companies today utilize the telephone as the primary and principal tool of claims handling.

Increasingly, the economics of insurance claims handling has required companies and insurance claims firms to seek ways in which to reduce claims handling expenses. The telephone and the use of tele-phone recordings have provided a convenient and economically feasible expedient. As more insurance claims departments and adjust-ing firms turn to the telephone as the primary claims communication device, questions of the relative merits of such reliance on the tele-phone rather than on face-to-face claims handling are in issue.

One writer contends that it is 25 times more expensive to make face-to-face calls than to conduct the same business by telephone.[1] The increased pressures exerted upon claims departments to become more efficient and economical in their activities have forced claims persons to rely upon time-saving methods of handling insurance claims, but as a substitute for face-to-face negotiations, however, there are many critics of telephone claims handling. Critics contend that there is over-reliance on the telephone for claims handling, and much of the "personal touch" and the opportunity to accurately assess a claims sit-uation is lost when investigations and negotiations are conducted by telephone. One writer admonishes: "It must always be kept in mind that a telephone interview is at best only a substitute for personal interview and should be used as a last resort where a personal inter-view is not warranted either because of expense, distance, weather conditions, or other good and sufficient reasons."[2]

The telephone claims handling technique has many defenders, and telephone claims handling is the pragmatic innovation of today. The large majority of insurance claims are relatively minor in dollar amount, and reduction in the extent of person-to-person contact be-tween the claims person and insureds, claimants, and witnesses results in a great savings in claims handling expenses. Many companies have concluded that it is good business practice to settle claims over the telephone rather than expend the time of claims representatives in making personal contact. One insurer reports:

> We do not do anything in the investigation, negotiation, or settle-ment of a claim until we have attempted to accomplish it solely by the use of the telephone. If we cannot succeed in accomplishing our requirements by the use of the telephone, we will then arrange for a face-to-face visit with the individual involved. The adjuster actually

---

[1] Murray Roman, *Telephone Marketing Techniques* (New York: Amacom, American Management Associations, 1979), p. 11.

[2] Pat Magarick, *Successful Handling of Casualty Claims* (New York: Clark Board-man, 1974), p. 180.

handling and controlling the claim is the person that remains inside at a desk. If outside support facilities are required, we call upon the independent or staff field claims persons to make the contact and report back to the adjuster who has the file on the desk. In some few cases, the inside adjuster will go outside to make his or her investigation or attend settlement conferences.[3]

Telephone claims handling has been extensively adopted by some insurance companies, while others employ it sparingly and in the traditional manner utilized before the advent of the telephone recorder. Although the telephone has become a valuable tool in the insurance industry, its use at the present time is more prevalent at the company level, with some of the large adjusting firms making extensive use of it. Others attempt to limit reliance upon telephone claims handling.

There are many philosophies regarding the degree to which the telephone should be utilized. Those making extensive use of the telephone employ it to accomplish all claims handling functions—taking statements, negotiating, and making settlements by telephone.

Other firms require face-to-face dealings with bodily injury claimants, but these firms will use the phone extensively to obtain statements from insureds and witnesses, and also to secure other types of information. Other firms restrict the use of the telephone to making appointments, securing estimates, negotiating with attorneys, and other more traditional uses of the telephone. All important contacts with personal injury claimants and important witnesses are still performed on a face-to-face basis.

The past two decades have introduced a great variety of recording devices, many of which are highly superior to the early disc or belt-type recorders used by claims persons. The achievement of miniaturization and the improved fidelity of these instruments has now made it possible for claims persons to utilize highly portable and versatile recording devices for the taking of statements. So useful have these recorders become that many claims persons use them almost exclusively for taking statements and profess that they have little need of the court reporter's services, and that the written, signed statement has become an anachronism.[4]

---

[3] Letter from Richard H. Greene, vice president, The Maryland, November 13, 1979.

[4] Bernard L. Webb, J. J. Launie, Willis Park Rokes, & Norman A. Baglini, *Insurance Company Operations*, vol. 2 (Malvern, Pa.: American Institute for Property and Liability Underwriters, 1978), pp. 448–50.

Recorded telephone statements are useful in any type of claims situation for gathering information regarding the factual circumstances of a claim. Such statements, particularly, are of practical value in the liability claims handling process. They provide a simple and efficient method by which information can be obtained quickly and reduced to evidential form.

Evidential use of telephone recordings

The evidential use of telephone recorders is of particular significance to attorneys and to claims representatives and the claims examiners of insurance companies. Early use of these devices in connection with the investigation of legal cases usually required attorneys and claims persons to restrict telephone recording activities to the office, since recorders were bulky in size. The quality and integrity of the recording was also a major impediment to the extensive use of these devices. Further, initial use of the telephone recorders was restricted because of questions concerning the legality of these devices, and the admissibility of telephone recordings into evidence in court proceedings. Early use of the telephone recorders tended to be rather surreptitious, for users questioned the legality of the devices, particularly when the recordings were made without the "beeper" signal incorporated into the recording. Today, there is still great confusion in the minds of many claims persons and attorneys regarding the evidential use of telephone recordings.

The widespread practice of using telephone recordings as evidence is a recent phenomenon. Today thousands of insurance and legal investigators in the United States are using the telephone recorders to gather evidence. Consequently, we have entered an era of judicial testing of the evidential value of the statements taken by telephone recorders.

Recorded statements are subject to the same rules of evidence as written statements—recorded statements must be properly authenticated and a foundation for admissibility established. The requirements for admissibility of recorded statements are as follows:

1. It must be shown that the mechanical transcription device was capable of taking testimony.
2. It must be shown that the operator of the device was competent to operate it.

3. The authenticity and correctness of the recording must be established.
4. It must be shown that changes, additions, or deletions have not been made.
5. The manner of preservation of the record must be shown.
6. Speakers must be identified, and
7. It must be shown that the testimony elicited was freely and voluntarily made, without any kind of duress.[5]

When a proper foundation is established and the recorded statement is authenticated, the

> recorded witness's statement provides evidential, practical, and psychological values. It assures witnesses that their story is fresh, true, and preserved. It assists witnesses by refreshing their memory of facts and circumstances which have dimmed with time. It discourages fabricated claims and changed versions of fact situations. It will impeach lying witnesses so that the jury and the judge will not believe these witnesses when they change their story. It will guard against the inevitable influence that later events may have on recollection and on the witness's attitudes and opinions.[6]

The literature on the subject of telephone recording reflects a wide variation of opinion regarding the use of recordings where the beeper signal is absent in the recording. One writer contends that "there is the strong probability that telephone statements recorded without the automatic beeper might be ruled inadmissible in courtroom impeachment and other procedures simply because they were illegally obtained." He also implies that "applicable federal statutes" prohibit the recording of telephone conversations without the permission of the parties, so that the use of induction coil devices to facilitate the taking of recorded telephone statements "is in violation of statutes, administrative rulings, and tariffs." Supporting this viewpoint is the official position of the telephone company that "the signal is provided by the telephone company for your protection. Use of a recorder without recorder-connector equipment containing a tone-warning device is contrary to the company's tariffs and is not permitted."[7]

However, the cases would appear to support the right of any party to a telephone conversation to record that conversation irrespective of

---

[5] *Steve M. Solomon, Inc.* v. *Edgar,* 88 S.E. 2d 167 (Ga. App. 1955).

[6] Webb, Launie, Rokes, & Baglini, p. 320.

[7] *Northwestern Bell Telephone Directory,* May 1979–80, p. 5.

notice or permission given by the other party(ies). A line of federal cases supports the right of one party to a telephone conversation to record the conversation without consent of the other party. Federal statutes and those cases dealing with the subject in the federal courts pertain to "interception" of communication and were specifically addressed to illegal wiretapping on the part of third parties, usually law enforcement personnel. Interception "indicates taking or seizure by the way or before arrival at destined place and does not ordinarily connote obtaining of what is to be sent before or at the moment it comes into possession of intended receiver."[8] As for the admissibility of telephone recordings in evidence, a federal court ruled, "Evidence obtained by recording or by listening to a telephone conversation with consent of one of the parties but without knowledge or consent of the other is admissible."[9]

From a practical standpoint, recorded statements introduced into court proceedings are usually done for the purpose of impeaching the testimony of the witness. Thus, it is necessary to convince the jury that the witness's veracity is subject to question. It is also necessary to make a good impression upon the jury. From a psychological standpoint, therefore, it makes good sense to impress upon the jury that there has been fair play and proper conduct on the part of the claims person who took the statement. This impression is perhaps best achieved if there was obvious cooperation existing between the claims person and the witness. Consequently, there is wisdom in acquiring statements in an open and candid manner. Where, however, it appears doubtful that the witness would cooperate with the taking of a recorded statement, the cases support the acquisition and use of a recorded telephone statement without the knowledge of the other party to the conversation and without the presence of the so-called beeper signal. Claims representatives should check for the possible existence of restrictive state statutes regulating this subject.

Traditional telephone uses

The telephone has always played an important role in the handling of insurance claims. Certain functions have been routinely handled through the use of this important tool. A fast, economical means of

---

8 *Goldman* v. *U.S.*, 62 S. Ct. 993, 316 U.S. 129, 86 L. Ed. 1322, rehearing denied 63 S. Ct. 22 (2 cases), 317 U.S. 703, 87 L. Ed. 562.

9 *Carnes* v. *U.S.*, 295 F. 2d 598 (C.A. Ga. 1961).

communication, information can be speedily gathered through its use, and when a case must be assigned to a claims office in a distant city, instructions can be telephoned to claims personnel on those cases that require immediate attention.

It has always been common to receive first notices of accidents and claims by telephone, and sometimes it was possible in past years to handle all of the details of such a claim by telephone. The insured would be instructed to send in invoices or come to the claims person's office so that a damaged automobile could be inspected. In other cases a telephone call from an insured was all of the information a claims person required in order to proceed with the handling of the claim. It is true that insurance policies have required the insured to provide "written notice" as soon as practicable;[10] however, it has always been routine in the minor liability claims or in simple property damage losses for the claims representative to fill out the claims form.

In cases where accidents occurred in an area remote from the insurer's office, making it impractical and unduly expensive for the staff claims personnel to handle the claim, the telephone was always a superb device for communicating with claims representatives who serviced the particular area in which the accident occurred. Thus, a staff claims representative would contact an independent adjusting firm, an attorney, or other party in the area to handle the claim, providing that individual with coverage verification and details, initial information obtained about the claim, and instructions concerning its handling and disposition.

The telephone, of course, has always been the primary communication device used where time was of the essence and where it was believed unnecessary to obtain a signed statement from the individual providing information. Thus, *the overriding determinant of whether the telephone was used was a need or an absence of need to obtain a signed statement.* In those cases where it was believed that it was essential to secure evidential materials for later use in litigation, the telephone was ruled out as a communication device until recent years.

The need of evidence

The telephone was shunned wherever it was deemed necessary to obtain concrete evidential material. It was always believed, rightfully,

---

[10] Some of the newer policies no longer specify that *written* notice be supplied by the insured.

that information gathered by telephone would have little practical use in litigation. A claimant, insured, or witness, for example, could make statements by telephone and then completely contradict these statements in a later court action. Because the original conversation was oral and by telephone, defense counsel would be unable to use the original contradictory statements as a means to impeach the witness in court. The same was true of statements made on a person-to-person level. Thus, in past years when recorders were not in use, it became absolutely necessary for statements to be in written form, read, and then signed by the witness involved. The statement could then be used as a means to refresh the memory of the witness in a later court action, or it could be used to impeach that witness's inconsistent testimony.

There was also merit in making personal contact with a claimant, rather than telephoning the individual. It was believed to be a simple matter for a claimant to refuse to talk to the claims person by telephone; however, the presence of the claims person made it more difficult for the claimant to refuse the person-to-person conversation.

The following "traditional taboos" have been identified as reasons for not using the telephone in the past:

1.   Initial contact with a bodily injury claimant by face-to-face confrontation was always considered to be essential. Contact by telephone, according to traditional wisdom, would make it too easy for a claimant to refuse to permit an interview. The arrival of a claims representative unannounced provided an element of surprise. Thus, utilizing the telephone would permit a claimant to delay a face-to-face confrontation, giving the claimant an opportunity to think about the claim, secure expert and not-so-expert advice, and set the stage for exaggerated claims. Whereas if the claims representative knocked on the door unannounced, the element of surprise permitted the claims person to secure fresh, untainted information.

2.   The telephone was considered to be inappropriate for interviewing hostile witnesses. Adverse witnesses, like claimants, could not be depended upon to present the same version of the fact situations of claims in the initial interview that they subsequently presented in the court hearing. Thus, it became imperative to obtain a signed statement from the hostile witness as soon as possible in order to assure that the witness's statement was fresh and as truthful as possible. Here again, the surprise element entered in when a claims person could immediately confront the adverse witness and secure the statement. Lapse of time or an initial contact by telephone was considered to be

negative, because it afforded the witness an opportunity to delay the conversation and also made it possible that the witness would have time to reflect on the consequences of telling the truth about an accident or other claims situation.

3.   An investigation file had to be constructed, and this could not be done by securing information by telephone. Reference has already been made to the fact that witness's statements in court can be impeached when a previous authenticated statement is introduced which is contradictory to the witness's court statement. However, it was also necessary to reduce the file to writing or some other form that could be readily examined by claims examiners, supervisors, and defense counsel. All of these people had to be able to review a file and be able to evaluate the liability and valuation of a claim, and this could not be done unless concrete information was provided in the file. Since telephone statements were not reduced to any tangible form, they had little use in past years.

4.   The final disposition of a claim required a face-to-face meeting. It was unheard of to consummate a claim, particularly a bodily injury liability claim, by telephone. The negotiation process was tricky, and although it could be conducted somewhat by telephone, the final round of negotiations and the agreement to settle were done in a face-to-face manner in the usual case. Final execution of the formal release form made it desirable to have the two parties together to guarantee that a binding contract of release was executed. Thus, the claims representative would explain that the release was in full and final settlement of all claims of whatever nature; the claimant would understand the circumstances; and a contract would be in effect.[11]

Today, of course, the widespread use of the telephone for the investigation, negotiation, and settlement of cases largely disregards all of these considerations. Because of the evidential use of telephone recordings, it is possible to secure statements by telephone, and these statements can be used in later court proceedings for the purpose of impeaching the perception, integrity, and recollection of witnesses. The information is also available for review by claims examiners, supervisors, and defense counsel.

Likewise, the subject of requiring face-to-face confrontations in all settlement negotiations has changed tremendously. Because of the use

---

[11] Suggested by David Hinkle, *The Seventies and Change—Modern Use of the Telephone in Insurance Claim Adjusting* (Atlanta, Ga.: Crawford, 1970), a cassette learning program.

of "no release," "walk-away settlements," and "open release" techniques, the requirement for executing a formal release document has been greatly deemphasized. The most staunch advocates of the use of the telephone for insurance claims handling would argue that all aspects of insurance claims investigations, negotiations, and settlements can be handled by the use of the telephone.

Most insurance claims authorities, however, recognize the practical limitations of the telephone on some types of cases involving complex and strained personal relations between the parties. Even those insurers that use telephone claims handling extensively recognize that there are some situations where the claims handling requirements cannot succeed without a face-to-face visit with the individuals who are involved. There are still many claims situations where reliance on telephone usage is *not acceptable*. Particularly in heavy commercial-property and some personal-property and automobile physical-damage cases, personal contact is essential. Complex matters involving inspection, appraisal and determination of pecuniary loss, and highly sensitive negotiation situations frequently are handled more skillfully and successfully in face-to-face contact. Some of these situations cannot and should not be handled by telephone. Further, as discussed later in this chapter, complex physical circumstances in connection with a claim can be visualized with greater accuracy and clarity if there is direct contact with an insured, third-party claimant, or witness.

Irrespective of the diversity of opinions and personal philosophies expressed concerning the advisability and value of telephone claims handling techniques, it is clear that the telephone has come to fill and will continue to play a more dominant role in insurance claims handling. The great economies accomplished by the use of the telephone in terms of claims handling costs dictate that companies be committed to this form of claims handling technique, irrespective of the personal belief on the part of some claims experts that the quality of claims handling suffers appreciably from the loss of the personal element involved in face-to-face contact. The restructuring of claims offices to accommodate the use of large-scale telephone claims handling procedures, utilizing "inside adjusters" and "outside adjusters," signals a strong commitment to the use of the telephone technique. The growing sophistication of telephone recorders and judicial acceptance of the telephone recording provide a further reinforcement of arguments for the use of the telephone in insurance claims handling.

HUMAN RELATIONS AND THE TELEPHONE

The major emphasis in this book and in the practice of insurance claims handling in past years has focused on face-to-face interpersonal relations between insurance claims representatives and insureds, claimants, witnesses, and other people. The principles of communication discussed in this book, for example, have stressed the use of nonverbal techniques of communication, being aware of distortions that affect face-to-face communications, and the need to utilize body language in conveying interest and consideration in establishing rapport and empathy with the other person. The use of gestures, smiling, and walking, and the role played by an individual's personal appearance all are important factors in the face-to-face contact. In motivating another person, the use of various types of movement techniques, such as eye contact, deferential movement, positioning, and other important visual signals that can be communicated to an insured, claimant, or witness to influence that individual's actions, are all important in the personal contact situation.

However, we now address ourselves to the subject of the interpersonal contact through the remote device, the telephone. It would be a mistake to assume that the various person-to-person techniques are no longer applicable to the use of the telephone. The telephone conversation can still employ many of the same techniques used in face-to-face contact, and the principles of communication and the motivation techniques are clearly applicable to telephone claims handling. For example, deferential treatment and the establishment of rapport, by displaying consideration of the other person, are highly important in the telephone conversation.

Without the use of most of the nonverbal signals that can be employed in the person-to-person contact, however, greater effort must be utilized in the telephone communication to display consideration and to establish the rapport and the relationship with the other individual essential for successful claims handling. One writer observes: "Shut your eyes and listen to a conversation. How much you lose! Gestures, facial expressions, the lights and shades of meaning are gone. Several words were so blurred that you could hardly catch the speaker's views."[12]

---

[12] J. C. Scammell, *Use of the Telephone in Business* (New York: Ronald Press, 1924), p. 25.

Telephone claims handling is confronted by communication obstacles. The listener is obliged to depend entirely on our voice, since facial expressions and significant nonverbal movements of the hands and body are not visible. In addition, the listener's attention can easily be distracted by visible activities and other stimuli on the other end of the telephone line. Control of the voice and adherence to the important rules of good telephone communication are vital. We must rely entirely upon the voice to communicate, providing for a clear exchange of information; to establish rapport with the other person; to display empathy and consideration for the other person; to persuade and motivate; and to convince the insured or claimant that a certain course of action is in his or her best interest.

The voice, therefore, must have amazing versatility in the telephone conversation situation. With only the voice and the telephone as the communication tools, the claims representative must demonstrate that he or she is considerate, honest, competent, and interested in the problems of the other person on the telephone line. Some claims experts as well as general communication specialists believe that in today's age of consumerism, people are a "different breed from those of the past." Murray Roman writes: "They demand integrity and honesty in the approach. . . . Paradoxically, as the consumer has become part of a conditioned mass market, he or she has also become more demanding in insisting on being regarded as an unique individual whose own special personal needs must be catered to."[13]

Your telephone personality

The general rule for all difficult situations—speak with a smile.
——J. C. Scammell

Insurance companies and claims handling firms have reported widespread variations in the abilities of individuals to successfully use the telephone for claims handling work. One firm reports that those claims persons who are the most successful in using the telephone for claims work are primarily well-educated and articulate individuals who have a natural instinct for developing a rapport with a party on the other

---

[13] Murray Roman, *Telephone Marketing Techniques* (New York: Amacom, American Management Associations, 1979), p. 15.

end of the line. Education obviously plays an important role in achieving success in any line of endeavor, and this certainly holds true for the use of the telephone. Consequently, it is essential to spell out principles and techniques that are useful for developing the telephone personality. It is true that some people have a natural ability to project a warm, sensitive personality on the telephone, but much of the lack of success in using the telephone stems from ignorance.

When we have small children in our family, we devote considerable time to explaining to them how to use the telephone, stressing such things as courtesy, consideration, and the importance of obtaining the caller's name and telephone number so that we can return the call. An educational process for an individual who must utilize the telephone for business purposes is an extension of this process, but the principles are the same. A positive telephone personality must be developed, and the amenities of courteous and considerate behavior must be observed.

Put a smile in your voice.   The communication industry has long stressed the importance of proper telephone usage, and some of the principles of communication developed by telephone companies have been most helpful to other firms that wish to improve their telephone image. There are some excellent courses offered by the communications industry which address telephone techniques. The Bell System has long used the slogan, "put a smile in your voice," stressing the importance of pleasantness and conveying a warm, friendly, and courteous voice to the world.

The chapter on communication stressed the importance of facility of oral expression and the necessity to use a pleasant voice tone, manner, variation, and freedom from monotony. The enthusiasm and the interest that we project with our voice is more important in the telephone conversation than it is in face-to-face conversation because we do not have some of the other nonverbal tools of communication at our disposal while talking on the telephone. The sum total of the "face" that we project by telephone is our telephone voice—our telephone image. The first step in the telephone communication process is *image projection.*[14]

---

14 Hinkle, *The Seventies and Change.*

Image projection.   Image projection contemplates establishing in the mind of the other party on the telephone a visual picture of who you are. When we talk to a stranger on the telephone, we tend to form a visual picture of what this individual looks like. We see a face; we have an impression of the age of the individual; and we definitely decide whether the person is attractive or unattractive, all based upon the quality of the image projection extended by this stranger. People with warm, pleasant, considerate, and interested voices appear as smiling, friendly individuals. We form a positive viewpoint toward such individuals. Furthermore, the image we obtain is usually immediate. We respond immediately to the voice on the telephone, and the manner of response colors the entire conversation that follows. Thus, first impressions are critical in telephone communications.

Because we immediately form an impression of liking or disliking the stranger on the telephone (with intermediate feelings between these two extremes), we tend to respond according to the way we feel about the individual. Thus, the warm, friendly, courteous, and interested individual will elecit a response from us that is positive. On the other hand, if the voice on the other end of the telephone is flat, listless, unfriendly, discourteous, and inconsiderate, our response is predictable.

The primary objective in telephone communication is to evoke a favorable response. The claims person's image projection determines the quality of that response. One writer lists the following rules and principles for obtaining a favorable response while talking to other people on the telephone:

1. Make a good impression at the beginning of a phone call.
2. People will respond more favorably and quickly when they feel a sense of fair treatment.
3. People will respond positively to a caller who is friendly and courteous and who expresses the utmost integrity in his or her manner and activities.
4. People will respond more favorably to a positive statement than to a negative statement.
5. People will forget what you say but not how you say it.[15]

---

[15] Mona Ling, *How to Increase Sales and Put Yourself Across by Telephone* (Englewood Cliffs, N.J.: Prentice-Hall, 1963), p. 52.

Developing your telephone image. The claims representative should be most curious concerning his or her own telephone personality. What image do you project? The best way to judge your telephone personality is to listen to yourself and to ask other people how you sound on the telephone. Since we have telephone recorders available in most claims offices, it should be a simple matter for you to have your voice recorded on several occasions and then play the recordings back so that you yourself can judge your telephone personality. More important, however, will be to have others—friends, relatives, or business associates—evaluate your telephone personality to assist you in making improvements in your image projection.

Mona Ling recommends that we set aside some time each day to work on the development of our telephone voice. She suggests a number of questions that should aid the reader in evaluating his or her own telephone voice:

1. Is your voice weak?
2. Is your voice too loud?
3. Is your voice harsh?
4. Is your throat tense?
5. Is your voice monotonous?
6. Is your voice colorless?
7. Is your voice too nasal?
8. Is your voice shrill?
9. Is your voice irritating?
10. Is your voice and speaking manner affected and pretentious?
11. Do you use calm and controlled tones?
12. Do you have vitality in your voice?
13. Do you have variety in the pace and timing of your voice delivery?
14. Do you overuse or abuse certain words or expressions?
15. Do you overuse the personal pronouns ("I," "me," "my," and so on)?
16. Do you become emotionally involved?[16]

We cannot all be blessed with the same physical features in our voices. Some of us may have flat and monotonous voices. However, this is the purpose of education. Recognize your problems and work

---

[16] Ibid., pp. 63–67, 168.

to improve your image projection. Develop your telephone personality by incorporating the warmth, sincerity, courtesy, and enthusiasm that you admire in other people's telephone personalities.

You must also project the image of competence and confidence. This applies to both men and women claims representatives. It is a particularly important consideration for women who enter business careers traditionally dominated by men, and the insurance claims handling job is one of those careers.

During the 1950s and most of the 1960s the ranks of the insurance claims representatives were almost completely composed of males. This has changed dramatically in recent years as companies have turned more and more to women to handle insurance claims. There have been some interesting questions regarding the capability of women claims persons to handle difficult liability claims, negotiations with attorneys, and other complex claims situations. Can women claims representatives cope with the intimidation which sometimes arises in a "macho," male-dominated society? Are complex, difficult claims more of a problem for a woman to handle than her male counterpart?

The author has discussed the subject with a variety of experienced claims supervisors and long-time claims persons, both men and women. Although differences of opinion abound, there seems to be a consensus that women claims representatives, like their male counterparts, can accomplish the insurance claims handling functions with great success, and the key to that success is image projection.

Women at the present time in many business pursuits, including claims handling, perhaps have more of a problem with image projection because of societal stereotyping of women in certain occupations. However, the success of women or men claims representatives depends entirely upon how they are perceived by the insureds, claimants, witnesses, and other people with whom they must deal. On the telephone, as well as in person-to-person contact, there is a need to project competence, self-confidence, and a definite image of knowing your job. A claims person, male or female, who reflects timidity, indecision on the job, and lack of knowledge projects a poor image.

Some trainees have told the author that they have experienced situations where older attorneys would not deal with women claims representatives, and there have been other cases where men have told the woman claims person that they prefer to talk to her "boss." Male-female role stereotyping has been inbred in most of us, and despite our best intentions, it will undoubtedly persist for some time as a serious part of the sexist background conditioning of most Americans, both male and female.

The reader can evaluate his or her own sexist background conditioning by studying the following two stories:

Story number one:

A man and his son were hurt in a terrible accident. They were taken to a nearby hospital. The physician on duty saw the boy and exclaimed, "Oh, my God! I can't operate on him. He's my son."

Story number two:

George Smith met a friend whom he had not seen or heard from for over ten years. Accompanying his friend was a little girl, and Smith inquired,

"Is that your daughter?"

"Yes, I was married six years ago."

Turning to the little girl, Smith asked, "And what is your name?"

"Same as my mommy's," she replied.

Addressing the girl, Smith inquired, "Oh, how are you, Marguerite?"[17]

How many of you readers assumed in the first story that the physician on duty was a man? How did George Smith in the second story know the name of the little girl? Role stereotyping is common in American society today, and having read the above two stories, the reader can gain some insight into the extent to which sexist role stereotyping has been a part of his or her background conditioning.

Male-female role stereotyping is breaking down in American society, and there is no reason for women claims representatives to tolerate sexist treatment in claims handling situations. The best way to avoid such treatment is through image projection. If you project the image of incompetence, timidity, indecision, and subservience to the people with whom you are dealing, then you can expect negative treatment. However, if you project the image of self-confidence, personable but not personal behavior, and decisiveness, showing that you possess the knowledge and the ability to accomplish all of the functions of your job, then you are projecting the correct image. If the voice on the other

---

[17] Recounted by Inez Gonzales, Claims Training Specialist, Fireman's Fund Insurance Companies, communication workshop, January 7–11, 1980.

end of the line asks to see your "boss," that individual should be informed firmly, but courteously and good-naturedly, that you are the person in charge of the case; that you are prepared to negotiate settlement; and that you are prepared to take whatever action is necessary to bring the claim to a proper conclusion. If you don't have all of the information at your fingertips and need to make an additional call, inform the individual politely that you will get back to him or her and set a time for your next contact. Whatever you do, male or female, do not apologize or justify your lack of information because "I am only a trainee."

Mechanics of telephone communication

The technical achievement of telephone technology in the United States has provided us with a medium that is relatively free from the distortions which are common in some media of communication, such as radio communication. We are not usually bothered by problems of static, interference, and weak signals. We do, however, sometimes experience physical distortions to communication in long distance telephone calls. Ordinarily, however, the channel of communication is relatively free of distortion if it is utilized properly. This means that we must use the telephone in such a way that we can maximize its effectiveness. To do so, certain rules should be followed.[18] These are the mechanics of telephone communication:

1.   Identify yourself. Every telephone conversation should commence with the parties identifying themselves. There is nothing more confusing and inimical to good communication than to have to sit on the telephone and try to guess who the person is who is calling. Personal telephone calls sometimes commence with a "guessing contest," as the receiver of the call attempts to identify the voice on the other end. Such a circumstance in a business call is absolutely inexcusable. Immediate identification of yourself starts the communication off on a proper foundation, personalizes the telephone call, and immediately displays consideration for the person on the other end of the line.

2.   Mentally come to attention. Whether placing a telephone call or receiving one, it is highly essential to indicate that you are alert and ready to communicate with the person to whom you are talking.

---

[18] Suggested in part by the Bell System, "Your Telephone Personality," 999–600–101, issue 2.

3.   Be concise and clear, stating within the first few seconds an unquestionable and incisively stated reason for the call.

4.   Observe "the four Cs"—be clear, concise, conversational, and convincing. Work for simplicity. Telephone conversation should be couched in simple, straightforward language. This requires the avoidance of complex language or the use of technical terms that might confuse the listener. Simple and concise, uncomplicated language displays consideration for your listener. Simplicity and clarity displays consideration and facilitates communication. As part of your telephone personality and the task of image projection, you should always avoid language that would convey a negative impression of you as an individual. Thus, most slang words and other inappropriate language should be avoided.

5.   Be considerate in telephoning and answering. The Bell System advocates that we permit a number to ring for at least one full minute before hanging up. We are inconsiderate when we dial a number and fail to let it ring at least ten times. Most people attempt to answer the telephone in a timely fashion; however, people may be remote from the telephone at the other end of a large area and have some distance to walk in order to reach the telephone, or they may be out in their yard when the phone rings. Consideration requires that we give them time to answer the phone. Consideration also dictates that we answer our telephone promptly.

6.   Proper use of the telephone requires that we position ourselves in such a way that we can speak directly into the telephone transmitter so that we can be heard clearly. It also requires that we do whatever we can to eliminate any physical distortions to communication, such as eliminating background noises that will interfere with or impair the quality of the telephone conversation.

7.   Be aware of your voice quality and pace. The telephone user should talk at a moderate rate and volume. Voice inflection is highly important, since it avoids the problem of monotony and assists the caller in projecting a positive image. Lack of voice inflection causes the listener to hear a flat, listless, monotonous voice. Voice inflection provides emphasis and vitality and projects an image of enthusiasm.

8.   Be an active listener. As in the case of all listening, whether by telephone or otherwise, effective listening requires active listening. Particularly in telephone conversations, it is necessary to display and to project the fact that there is active listening. This can be accom-

plished by the interjection of questions and appropriate comments. Here also, the claims representative can employ what has been called a series of "eloquent and encouraging grunts:" "Hmmm," "uh-huh," "oh," or "I see" (already mentioned in one of the chapters on listening).[19]

Active listening can also be accomplished by the prominent employment of the other person's name. We all like to hear our name used, and it displays consideration, interest, and attentiveness when the claims representative uses the other person's name in the telephone conversation.

9.   Be courteous when terminating the conversation. The telephone conversation should not be terminated abruptly. Image projection is highly important here, for you must continue to display consideration and friendliness. All telephone conversations should be terminated with positive courtesy expressions such as "thank you," "I have appreciated," "I'm glad you called," "you're welcome," and other appropriate language.

The mechanics of telephone communication must constantly focus on image projection, and the claims representative must always keep image projection in mind while telephoning. Positive image projection establishes a smooth channel in which the telephone message can travel. The negative telephone personality, on the other hand, provides a rocky, imperfect channel for telephone communication. Thus, great emphasis must be placed upon image projection as the cardinal requirement of good telephone communication.

Once a smooth channel has been established by conveying a positive telephone personality, the mechanics of sending the message must be observed. Here the principles of communication, including speaking and listening, are of utmost importance. With the use of the telephone, however, there are many opportunities for communication "breakdown," and the distortions to communication are prevalent here.

TELEPHONE STATEMENTS AND QUESTIONING

Because of the great reliance placed upon the telephone for securing information, the telephone statement is the basis for the claims investigation. Telephone statements must take the place of the written

---

[19] Ralph G. Nichols and Leonard A. Stevens, *Are You Listening?* (New York: McGraw-Hill, 1957), p. 53.

statements, the court reporter statement, or the statement that is recorded in a face-to-face conversation. Because of the remoteness of the two individuals, however, care must be devoted to securing the telephone statement so that all of the essential facts are obtained and effective communication is accomplished.

Securing the facts and conducting a successful interview by telephone is highly essential as we place more and more reliance on the telephone to conduct claims investigations. It is particularly important in this process to secure the initial cooperation of the other person. That person must be willing to talk to us, and cooperation must be obtained if we are to be successful at obtaining a recorded statement by telephone. Thus, we must practice good human relations and practical psychology to get the other person—whether an insured, claimant, or witness—to agree to the taped interview. Once this cooperation is secured, questioning may begin, and the statement can be obtained.

Communication, of course, is the process of passing information from one place to another without the loss of meaning. Since it is a two-way street, information is exchanged between two parties without a loss of meaning enroute. In telephone communication, the parties must be particularly watchful for distortions in communications, since the parties are remote from one another. Consequently, to secure accurate information by telephone, as in the face-to-face contact, the claims person must be particularly careful in the use of the questioning technique.

Obtaining cooperation

With the increased reliance that is now placed on telephone claims handling, the claims person has a challenging responsibility to obtain a recorded telephone statement. As in the case of the face-to-face contact, difficulties may be experienced in securing the statement. In a sense, however, securing a recorded statement should be less difficult than obtaining a signed, written statement. The claims person needn't ask the other person to "sign" anything. Thus, there is a psychological advantage in using the recorded statement, particularly in the face-to-face contact.

Nevertheless, securing a recorded statement by telephone poses inherent disadvantages. The remoteness of the two parties to the conversation lends an impersonality to the relations of the two parties. The sense of obligation or intimidation that may be present in a face-to-face encounter is absent in the telephone encounter. Simply stated, it is easier to avoid someone who telephones us. We can refuse to talk; we can be taciturn in our cooperation. It is an easier personal confrontation to handle; it is less threatening.

Fortunately, most insureds, claimants, and witnesses cooperate fully when contacted by telephone. Relatively few persons refuse to cooperate in providing information and in agreeing to have the conversation recorded. Some people do refuse to cooperate, however, and some of these cases are unavoidable and irremediable. Despite the claims representative's best efforts, cooperation cannot be obtained.

Often, however, the intelligent application of a few motive appeals and techniques can turn an apparent uncooperative, recalcitrant witness into a cooperative and helpful witness. These "time-tested telephone tips" are helpful in obtaining a recorded statement in a face-to-face contact, but they are particularly helpful in the telephone contact.

Stressing the other person's needs. Experienced claims persons report that they experienced considerable rejection and lack of cooperation in their early attempts to record telephone statements. Claimants, particularly, would sometimes refuse to be recorded. Cooperation improved considerably when claims persons began to use telephone claims handling techniques that appealed to the needs of the claimant. Showing deference to the welfare of others increases the claims representative's success in securing the cooperation of the other party to the telephone conversation.

When making the telephone contact, the claims representative must relate to the needs of the other person. Never initially appeal to a witness's sense of cooperation by declaring, "Would it be all right if I record our conversation? I need this information to complete my investigation" or "The company requires me to get these taped interviews so that they can evaluate the case." The motive appeal here is, "Cooperate with me so that I can get *my* job done."

It is safe to say that if a claims representative uses these motive appeals stressing *his* or *her* needs, most people will cooperate fully. In fact, it is dangerous to categorically declare that such an appeal should *never* be used. The other person's sense of altruism to help a claims representative to do his or her job may produce cooperation. It is the difficult case, however, where psychology and skillful technique *must* be applied, because some people (particularly some claimants and witnesses) don't care about *your* needs. Claimants, for example, sometimes sense a personal danger in cooperating with you. In all cases, therefore, it is recommended that the claims person appeal initially to the needs of the witness, claimant, or insured, when requesting cooperation in a telephone interview.

Preserving YOUR story.   In an actual telephone claims handling situation, a claims representative asked a claimant if the telephone conversation could be recorded. The claimant responded, "No, I won't give you a statement. Absolutely not!"

Rather than giving up in this situation, the claims person reasoned with the claimant:

Claims person: Well, I can understand your reluctance, but let's look at it this way—If I record your statement today, it will protect *you*. *Your* version of the facts here—the way *you* saw it, and the way that *you* knew and believe the accident happened—will be preserved.

And once I take *your* statement, no one can ever change it.

Claimant: Well, that's right. I never looked at it that way before. Go ahead and record it.

A simple motive appeal stressing the best interests of this claimant resulted in full cooperation. The fact that the statement was taken in part to preclude the possibility of the *claimant* changing *his* own story did not enter into the claimant's deliberations. The motive appeal strongly focused on the claimant's best interests and welfare, and it was a successful approach in this case.

Saving YOUR time.   Likewise, when the claims representative asks another person for permission to record a statement, the approach can be directed to that person's needs in other ways. Rather than worrying about getting a statement, the claims person is concerned about saving time for the insured, claimant, or witness.

Approaching the statement-taking from the witness's standpoint, the claims representative inquires: "Will it be okay with you, Mr. Jones, if I record our conversation? I would like to save *you* time and inconvenience. In order to avoid taking a lot of *your* time in my having to write all of this down on paper, I would like to record our conversation to speed things up for *you.*"

This appeal to the other person's needs and time-pressures displays consideration and concern for the best interests of the insured, claimant, or witness. It is a strong motive appeal for busy people, and even if the witness is not busy at the time, the approach is considerate and selfless, reflecting genuine concern and interest in the other person's welfare.

Providing YOU with a copy.   Occasionally when a claimant or witness refuses to cooperate or will not agree to a recorded statement, another approach can be used if nothing else works. The claims representative can offer to give the person a copy of the statement.

This approach should be used infrequently and only when other approaches are unsuccessful, for it is not economically feasible to provide copies of recorded statements to witnesses. The cost of duplicating a tape or of having it transcribed to provide the witness with a transcript of the statement is prohibitive.

However, in difficult cases where a recorded statement is highly desirable, and the witness is refusing to cooperate, the technique has merit. The claims representative proceeds as follows:

> "Well, Mr. Jones, I can understand and respect your feelings on this subject, but let me suggest something. I will provide *you* with a copy of our recorded statement. Then *you* will have a permanent record of what happened. *You* can use it to refer back to, and *you* won't ever have to worry about forgetting any of the details of the accident or of having to write them down. It will preserve *your* recollection of the accident and will provide *you* with a permanent reference if *you* need it later."

These are a few illustrations and suggestions for securing cooperation from others in the telephone interview. They may be most helpful in dealing with the uncooperative and recalcitrant claimant or witness. They are useful guides and only a few of the approaches that the claims person can utilize.

Different people require different approaches. Whatever the approach utilized by the claims person, it is preferable in virtually all cases to approach other people from *their* standpoint, stressing *their* needs, *their* best interests, and *their* welfare when attempting to secure the recorded statement.

The types of questions

We have observed that the evidential value of a telephone recording has been well-documented in the courts, provided that the recording has been authenticated as truly the conversation of the witness and further provided that a proper foundation has been established for taking the statement. In order to establish the proper foundation for admissibility of recorded telephone statements certain requirements must be met. These were detailed earlier in this chapter.

Once the foundation has been established for the proper taking of the telephone statement, the claims representative can proceed to secure information. This requires an intelligent use of the questioning technique. There are many types of questions, and each serves its own particular purpose, both proper and improper. Reference has already been made in an earlier chapter regarding the use of leading questions and the fact, that through the use of leading questions, ideas can be implanted in a person's mind so that his or her perception of sensory impressions will be influenced. This, of course, can produce an erroneous recollection of the facts and circumstances of a situation and can result in inaccurate information. Various types of questions will be examined in greater detail in the following sections.

Leading questions.   The use of leading questions in securing statements or in examining the witness (discussed below) demonstrates rather forcefully the fact that the nature of the questions put to a witness can predetermine his or her response. Leading questions implant ideas and impressions in the mind of the witness. The effect of these implanted impressions is to distort the witness's recollection of an event to such an extent that the suggestion contained in the leading question is so strong that it will replace the original sensory impression received by the witness. Arne Trankell writes of "The witness's tendency to adapt himself to the expectations reflected in the examiner's manner and formulation of his questions. . . . The distortions of memory images, which are caused by the interrogation technique and later produce secondary memory images which appear to the witness as genuine recollections of the original occurrence."[20] The leading question leads a witness up to a desired answer. It is put in such a way as to suggest to the witness the answer that is expected or wanted.

Leading questions are proper if they are merely facilitative and utilized for the purpose of disposing quickly of preliminary information. Examples of such questions are those pertaining to residence, occupation, business relations, and so forth. For example, we can inquire, "Your name is John Smith?" It is clear this is the individual's name, and you merely ask the question in order to have the response placed on the recording. "And you live at 1422 East Washington Street?" Here again, it is known that the witness lives at this address, and the purpose of the leading question is merely to get the reply on the record as expeditiously as possible.

Examples of improper leading questions that will distort the quality of the information that you secured from witnesses are as follows:

1. "Did you fall because the floor was rough in that spot?"
2. "Did you see *the* broken headlight?"
3. "Did you see the child when he *ran* across the street?"
4. "When you saw the automobile approach, how much would you say the black car was exceeding the speed limit?"

A number of studies have shown that leading questions can definitely influence eyewitness testimony. Once an observer has seen an event, anyone who questions the observer can influence the way he or she "remembers" what was seen. In the reports of studies conducted by Elizabeth Loftus, she declares that "eyewitnesses can and will identify people they've never seen, and change their story according to the wording of questions they are asked."[21] Loftus reports a number of experiments that prove that changing even one word in one question can systematically alter an eyewitness account, revealing the inordinate influence of leading questions. In one story, for example, she showed 100 students a short film segment depicting a multiple-car accident. In the film a car makes a right hand turn into the main stream of traffic. The turn causes on-coming cars to stop suddenly, and there is

---

[20] Arne Trankell, *Reliability of Evidence* (Stockholm: Beckmans, 1972), p. 29.

[21] Elizabeth Loftus, "Reconstructing Memory: The Incredible Witness," *Psychology Today* (December 1974).

a five-car bumper-to-bumper collision. After the students viewed the film, they filled out a questionnaire containing 22 questions. Three of the key questions asked about items that had appeared in the film, while three others asked about items that had not actually been present. Half of the students were asked the question "Did you see *a* broken headlight?" The other half were asked "Did you see *the* broken headlight?" There was no broken headlight; however, the use of the word *the* caused over twice as many students to report that they had seen this nonexistent item than in the group that had been asked if they saw *a* broken headlight.[22]

In another study, Loftus tested to see whether the substitution of one word for another could affect quantitative judgments—such as eyewitness judgment of the speed of an automobile. The audience was shown a film of a traffic accident, and after the film was shown, subtle changes in wording were placed in the questionnaires that were distributed to the audience, with some members of the audience receiving one wording while others received a different wording. One group was asked "About how fast were the cars going when they *hit* each other?" For others, the verb *hit* was replaced with *smashed, collided, bumped,* or *contacted.*

Estimates of speed varied considerably depending upon which question was answered. Those members of the audience with *contacted* in the question gave the lowest speed estimates while those questioned with the word *smashed* gave the highest speed estimate. The results obtained are shown in the accompanying table.

Average speed estimates for different verbs

Verbs	Miles per hour
Smashed	40.8
Collided	39.3
Bumped	38.1
Hit	34.0
Contacted	31.8

Source: Elizabeth F. Loftus and John C. Palmer, "Reconstruction of Automobile Destruction: An Example of the Interaction Between Language and Memory," *Journal of Verbal Learning and Verbal Behavior,* 13(5) (October 1974), pp. 585–589, at p. 586.

---

[22] Elizabeth F. Loftus and Guido Zanni, "Eyewitness Testimony: The Influence of the Wording of a Question," *Bulletin of the Psychonomic Society* 5 (1975), p. 86–88.

The researchers knew exactly how fast the cars were travelling in the film. The study bore out the conclusion that people are not very good at judging the speed of a vehicle and that the results of eyewitness accounts of speed can be materially influenced by the wording of the question. The implications are clear for the insurance claims representative. Leading questions must be scrupulously avoided by the claims representative to avoid the otherwise inevitable distortion in witness recollection and narration.

"Wife-beater" questions. Similar to the leading question and equally improper is the question which assumes a fact is established and calls for an amplification of it. The wife-beater question sets up a fact situation that assumes the fact is established and calls for reinforcement and requires acceptance of the fact. The wife-beater question simply stated is "Do you still beat your wife?" or "Have you stopped loafing on the job, and are you putting in a full day's work instead?" A "yes" or "no" answer does nothing to disturb the existence of the established fact. Such questions are inappropriate and improper both in court and in the claims handling investigation.

In a Massachusetts case, a plaintiff filed suit for injuries arising out of a fall caused by water that had collected on the floor of a passageway leading from a subway station to the street. No evidence had been established that anyone had ever seen water come through the walls or ceiling of the passageway prior to the accident. An employee of the defendant subway station was asked how many years water had come through the walls and ceiling prior to the accident. The question assumed an established fact, and the court excluded the question as assuming a material fact of which there was no evidence.[23]

Multiple questions. Use of multiple questions to examine witnesses should be discouraged because such questions militate against preciseness in securing information. An example of such questions is the following: "Were you going east or west?" A witness could answer such a question with a "yes" or a "no." A witness could reply in a similar fashion to questions such as "Was there a man or woman in the car?" or "Was that the blue car or the green car that was approaching from the north?" The example can be made even more absurd by ask-

---

[23] *Reardon* v. *Boston Elevated Ry. Co.*, 311 Mass. 228, 40 N.E. 2d 865.

ing the question, "Was the airliner flying in from the east, north, south, or west?" One might quibble over intermediate compass points between the four directions; however, it would still be quite possible to answer such a question with "yes."

The claims representative should work for precision in his or her questioning technique. Obviously, the multiple question should be avoided for the sake of clarity and to expedite the interview.

Direct questions. Direct questions are commonly and properly used in the claims investigation. A direct response is requested of the witness. For example, a claims person might ask a series of direct questions as follows: "Was it raining at the time?" "Did anyone see you fall?" "Did you report the injury to anyone?" "Did you go to see a physician?" These all elicit direct responses to specific questions.

A direct question is commonly used in the claims handling investigation in order to fill out the narration of the witness, covering matters that were not previously mentioned in the narration but that are important in the claims investigation. If, for example, the witness is describing the circumstances leading up to an automobile collision, the witness may have stated that she was coming down the hill toward an intersection. At this point, the claims representative might wish to interject a direct question: "How fast were you going at this time?"

Reflective questions. Reflective questions are utilized in the claims investigation in order to provide a review or summation that enables the witness to develop the narration more fully or to get back on track on the subject matter. It is also used to encourage the witness to continue with the narration.

An example of the reflective question is as follows: "Okay, is this right? You said you were walking up the stairs at the time; reached for the banister; and your hand slipped off the rail. Is that correct?" This elicits further response on the part of the witness. The witness will either reply in the affirmative or make corrections and will probably be encouraged to continue with the narration of the fact situation. The reflective question technique is most helpful in steering the conversation along so that the complete details of the fact situation are developed and exposed, fleshing out the statement.

The reflective question serves another important function. It is sometimes helpful to "stall without fouling the record." Corydon Johns suggests that if the claims representative feels pressured, and it seems to him or her that there is insufficient time between questions to organize and develop the progress of the interview, then the reflective question is a legitimate and useful technique.[24] The claims person slowly and deliberately reviews a portion of the fact situation already covered by the witness, and this provides some precious moments to think ahead and further develop the interview. It also affords the opportunity to slow the tempo of the conversation if in the claims representative's best judgment a slower pace is desirable.

In the use of the reflective question technique, the claims representative must be most cautious to correctly review the fact situation narrated by the witness. Little is to be gained by interjecting erroneous material in the summation or summary process. The reflective question summarizes and recapitulates what the witness has already said. As a general rule, it should be accurate.

Open questions. The open question is considered to be the most reliable means to obtain the witness's recollection of the fact situation. Thus, the witness is asked to "tell his or her own story." In the open question technique, the claims representative scrupulously avoids questions in which the witness can respond with a "yes" or "no" answer. Instead, questions are open so that the witness responds with a narrative. The key to asking open questions is to begin the question with *when, who, what, where, why,* and *how.*

Examples of open questions are:

"When did you first notice smoke coming from the building?"

"Who was in the car at the time of the accident?"

"Where in the building was the focal point of the fire; where do you think the fire originated?"

"Why didn't you report this bond claim when you first discovered the loss?"

"How do you figure the water got on the floor?"

All of the above questions are open-ended, requiring the witness to respond in detail to each question. This is the best technique to utilize in eliciting detailed narrations. Where the narration does not reveal

---

[24] Corydon T. Johns, *The Adjuster's Guide to Taking Statements* (Cincinnati: National Underwriter, 1976), p. 6.12.

salient facts that are necessary for a complete investigation, then the claims representative must use the reflective question and direct question techniques in order to elicit information.

Obtaining comprehension

It is particularly necessary in obtaining telephone statements, a remote communication technique, to make certain that the witness always understands the questions and the subject matter. Communication is exchange of information, and comprehension is critical for proper understanding. Thus, the claims representative must always work to overcome any misunderstanding or ambiguities that might enter into the conversation, particularly on technical matters that may be confusing for the witness. Conversely, however, the claims representative must be certain that he or she understands technical information that the witness is explaining.

General considerations.   Reference has already been made to telephone mechanics and the need to employ the telephone in such a manner that no mechanical distortions enter into the communication process. Such mechanical distortions can enter when the speaker is too far away from the telephone or there is a poor connection so that the parties have trouble hearing each other. Other forms of distortions, of course, arise because the individual talks too fast or fails to pronounce words clearly and carefully.

Psychological distortions obviously enter the picture when one of the persons on the telephone is talking in such a way that psychologically he or she "tunes out" the other person. Lack of expressiveness of voice, listlessness, inconsiderate language, and other negative factors can create emotional responses and other psychological reactions that cause breakdowns in the quality of the communication.

Aside from the mechanical and psychological distortions to telephone conversations, there are other problems that interfere with understanding on the part of one or both parties to the conversation. These have been discussed previously and involve a lack of understanding and comprehension because of some facet of the conversation or subject matter, such as technical language. It is, therefore, helpful to employ certain techniques to obtain comprehension. The "point of reference principle" is most helpful in this respect.

The point of reference principle.   To facilitate comprehension and the communication process, the claims representative will find it most useful to employ the point of reference principle. The essence of this technique is common in any form of education. The teacher must begin at a common point of understanding before moving into unfamiliar territory. Thus, the claims representative must be able to find a common point of understanding to use as a reference point before explaining the subject in depth.

To illustrate, suppose the claims person advises an insured that the measure of damages on the loss of carpeting is *depreciated value.* Employing judgment derived from handling many similar losses, the claims representative considers the quality of the carpeting, the replacement cost of similar carpeting, and the wear on the carpeting in question. Much of this information can be determined by the claims person where a loss has not completely destroyed the property. In other cases, information has to be solicited from the insured in order to make an intelligent estimate of actual depreciation.

The insured states, "Mr. Brown, your carpeting is four years old. You have five people in your family, and the carpeting was in a room that received considerable usage. Your insurance policy covers the depreciated value of the lost carpeting, and it would appear in this situation that your carpeting has a depreciated value of 50 percent of replacement cost of carpeting of like quality."

The insured might respond, "Well, golly, my insurance premiums certainly don't depreciate each year. I don't believe it is fair that I am now required to pay the full purchase price of a new carpeting and only receive a 50 percent settlement on the carpeting. This is particularly onerous, since we intended to keep that carpeting for the remainder of its useful lifetime before we bought a replacement."

Employing the point of reference principle, the claims person might say, "Well, Mr. Brown, I can certainly understand your feelings on the subject. You didn't plan to lose your carpeting at this point, and it is an inconvenience and an unexpected expense to have to buy a new carpet. And it is sometimes hard for people to understand the idea behind depreciation."

"It might help if I explained the matter of depreciation on carpeting by comparing it with an automobile. You and I know that if our 1979 automobile is completely destroyed, that we are only entitled to receive the value of a 1979 automobile rather than a new car. The same thing is true in the case of the used carpeting. We are only entitled to the value of used carpeting. The thing that makes it difficult to understand is that we don't have a used carpeting market, but we do have a large used car market. We can go out and replace our automobile with an automobile of the same year and condition. But we certainly cannot and will not go out and find a used carpet to replace the one we have lost."

In the above illustration, the claims representative has taken the matter that is confusing to the claimant and made a simple comparison with a subject matter that is widely understood by the motoring public. If the claimant is a reasonable individual, he or she can see the parallel between used carpeting and used automobiles and the fact that the measure of the damages is the value of a used carpet and not a new one.

The example on depreciation reflects a claimant's lack of understanding of the rationale used to justify a claims evaluation. Equally serious is the situation where the claims person and the insured or claimant ascribe different meanings to a word or term used. For example, such a lack of mutual understanding can be illustrated in the following telephone conversation:

Claims Person: "You'll need special therapy." [*The claims representative is really referring to hot tub treatments that the claimant can receive on an outpatient basis.*]

Claimant: [*Claimant believes "special therapy" means traction and weeks in the hospital.*] "I'm not going to do that."

Claims Person: [*Claims person believes the claimant is malingering; he is obviously dragging out this claim.*]

In this case, there was a communication breakdown, resulting from a lack of comprehension. Each party to this telephone conversation assigns a different meaning to the subject of *special therapy*. The claims representative should have made certain that the claimant understood the meaning of the term, or at least the meaning intended by the claims person. In this case the point-of-reference principle should have been employed. The claims representative should have expanded on the subject of *special therapy*, explaining what was entailed in this type of treatment.

Thus, it is incumbent upon claims representatives to always be careful in the use of words in the conversation to make certain that semantic difficulties do not arise in the interpretation of language used by both parties. A simple elaboration and explanation of the subject of *special therapy* by the claims person in this instance would have avoided a breakdown in communication.

VISUALIZING THE FACT SITUATION

In every claims investigation it is important for the claims representative to visualize germane physical conditions surrounding a given situation. For example, accident locale, physical conditions, and features of the site of an occurrence are essential so that the claims person can obtain an accurate understanding of the circumstances of a given case. This has always been rather easy to accomplish in face-to-face questioning because the claims representative would draw a diagram of the accident scene or would actually examine the physical circumstances in an on-the-site inspection. In case of error, the insured, claimant, or witness was always there to correct the visual depiction of the subject matter.

In the case of the telephone conversation, however, it is more difficult to obtain an accurate picture of physical facts unless the claims representative is mindful of the procedures, techniques, and safeguards that will ensure accuracy in visualization. Careful attention must be devoted to these techniques and procedures.

Techniques and procedures

Mindful of the fact that it is highly essential to visualize the physical facts of the claim investigation, it is incumbent upon the claims representative to construct a visualization of physical facts that are detailed by the person on the phone. Thus, if it is an automobile accident that is involved, the claims representative should draw a diagram of the intersection or part of the street or highway where the accident took place, noting all important features of the immediate location. The claims person must understand whether we are dealing with a two-lane street, a four-lane highway, an interstate with median dividers, or a traffic circle. This should all be diagrammed by the claims representative, showing all lanes of traffic, intersection features, compass orientation, and so forth. The position of the involved vehicles should be accurately designated before impact, at point of impact, and following impact.

Constructing a visual picture for the record.   Visualizing the fact situation is a highly essential function, for the claims representative must have an accurate mental image of what happened in order to systematically and accurately develop the interview. Equally important, however, the claims person must construct a visual picture for the record. The statement must contain an accurate and vivid description of the physical facts so that anyone who reviews the statement will also be able to accurately visualize the situation.

The claims person's diagram serves a useful function in constructing a visual picture for the record. The physical facts shown on the diagram should be complete, accurate, and detailed, and these facts must be translated into verbal word pictures for the recorded statement. There must be a comprehensive word picture of the locale of the accident or other occurrence. There also must be a clear word-visualization of the physical forces and activities that gave rise to the claim situation.

Developing the interview.   Visualization entails a complete unraveling of a fact situation in connection with specific claims, and as in any claims investigation, there are specific techniques and procedures that are recommended. The use of situational checklists are most helpful in developing the interview, particularly in obtaining telephone recordings.

Checklists are widely used in insurance claims handling and are particularly recommended for new and inexperienced claims representatives. Even highly experienced claims persons find checklists to be invaluable in complex claim situations. The form of the checklists utilized varies enormously among individuals, with one claims person mentally noting a list of points that he or she wishes to cover and another claims person relying on a lengthy printed checklist.

Situational checklists exist to cover a host of claim situations and types of claims, and many of these checklists are available for general use. The reader is encouraged to examine the checklists and situational

discussions that are contained in some of the excellent general claims handling textbooks listed in the bibliography.

The visualization process must begin immediately as the claims representative seeks to obtain the facts of a claims situation. Otherwise, it is impossible to analyze a case, determine liability, or begin the evaluation process. When it is impossible because of the complexity and nature of the physical locale of an accident or occurrence for the claims representative to visualize what has occurred, an on-the-site inspection is mandatory. When an on-the-site inspection cannot give a complete visualization of the physical facts of the claims situation, the claims representative must rely upon the perception, memory, and narration of the individual witness. It is here that research on the human brain has provided some interesting insights into the ability of humans to visualize the physical facts of a situation.

The right brain-left brain phenomenon

Each half with its own way of knowing, its own way of perceiving external reality.

———Betty Edwards

Of great significance to the subject of telephone claims handling is the right brain-left brain phenomenon. It has particular importance in its effect on the visualization process. Remember that a critical objective in telephone claims handling is to obtain an accurate visual picture of the physical facts. The right brain-left brain phenomenon suggests that there are certain situations where telephone claims handling is clearly not advisable under the circumstances.

Research on the human brain has indicated that there is a marked difference in the two hemispheres of the brain, both of which have widely different functions. The integration of the brain's two halves is accomplished through the *corpus callosum,* the bridge between the two hemispheres. If the callosum is severed, the effect of two independent conscious brains in one person is produced. One brain, the left, will be creative, inventive, reasonable, and logical. The other, the right, will be altruistic, emotional, childlike, and superior at spatial interpretation, recognition of faces, and interpretation of environmental stimuli.

The left cerebral cortex is the language center (*Broca's area*) used when people communicate their conscious ideas to one another. "The left hemisphere analyzes, . . . plans step-by-step procedures, verbalizes, makes rational statements based on logic."[25] The left brain is logical, reasonable, analytical, and objective. It is the language-process center of the brain, processing language-information inputs. Deaf persons who have learned to communicate through American sign language process the unspoken language primarily in their left hemisphere even though the message is visual rather than spoken. This is the analytical function of the left brain. The brain tries to "make sense" of the visual language stimulus received.

Since the left brain is the language center, it is the hemisphere of the brain that we appeal to when we are asking questions on the telephone or face-to-face, and we appeal to the left brain when we expect people to describe and visualize *in words* the physical circumstances surrounding a claims situation. The person being questioned accommodates a claims person by giving logical, reasonable, and socially acceptable answers.[26] We question the witness's left brain, the language hemisphere, and ask for visual representations of physical circumstances expressed in words. However, visual images are stored in the right hemisphere of the brain.

The right hemisphere of the brain is subjective, emotional, creative, and analogical. Its mode of processing is rapid, complex, whole-pattern, spatial, and perceptual. It contains the deeper feelings of a person, and appreciation or creation of analogies, poetry, music, art, ballet, and metaphors are right brain functions and are powerful vehicles in conveying feelings. Spatial perception is an important function of the right hemisphere of the brain. The spatial function has to do with "seeing where things are in relation to other things, and how parts go together to form a whole"; there is an "awareness of things, but minimal connections with words" in the right hemisphere.[27] The right brain is the process center for visualization. Visual images result from this processing. When a person hears the sound *bee*, for example, the signal will be processed primarily in the left

---

[25] Betty Edwards, *Drawing on the Right Side of the Brain* (Los Angeles: J. P. Tarcher, 1979), p. 35.

[26] Thomas Sannito, *A Psychologist's Voir Dire* (Dubuque, Ia.: Thomas and C. J. Sannito, 1979), p. 2.

[27] Edwards, *Drawing on the Right Side*, p. 40.

hemisphere if the context suggests that the letter *B* is intended. The right hemisphere will be much more accurate in processing the sound as signifying a bee rather than the letter *B*.[28]

The significance of the right brain-left brain phenomenon to insurance claims handling is the fact that in those cases where visual depiction of the physical circumstances surrounding a claim are critical to the establishment of liability, the investigator should seek to obtain the most accurate depiction of those physical facts. Don't say to the witness, "Tell me what you saw." The witness will respond with a verbal description, using the left side of the brain. Rather, you should instruct the witness, "Picture in your mind what you saw," and *the witness should be asked to draw a picture, diagram, or visual representation of the physical facts. In this way the right hemisphere of the witness's brain is operating. This provides a much more accurate depiction of the physical facts.* Asking the witness to describe *in words* the physical facts requires the witness to use his or her left cerebral cortex, and the witness is more likely to describe a visualization that seems logical, reasonable, and socially acceptable, rather than the way it actually may have been.

SUMMARY

There are various communication techniques and psychological principles that can be used to improve the quality of the communication process. A particularly important aspect of communication from the standpoint of the claims representative is the subject of interviewing. Therefore, the mechanics of interviewing are critical to claims handling in general and claims investigation in particular.

Interviewing has been revolutionized because of great advances in recording technology so that it is now possible for insurance claims persons to depend heavily upon the recording device for the conduct of investigations. Technological improvements made possible by miniaturization and the general availability of reasonably priced and reliable recorders have resulted in a dependence on the use of recording devices by most insurance claims offices today. Insurance company claims departments, independent adjusters, and the large insurance adjusting firms, in varying degrees, rely upon the recorder.

---

[28] Harold M. Schmeck, Jr., " 'Two Brains' of Man: Complex Teamwork," *The New York Times,* January 8, 1980, pp. C1, C3.

Increasingly, the economics of insurance claims handling have required companies and insurance claims firms to seek ways in which to reduce claims handling expenses. A convenient and economically feasible expedient has been the use of the telephone together with the time-saving recorded interview. There are many uses, as well as misuses, of the telephone for insurance claims handling, and each individual claims office employs its own philosophy regarding telephone use for claims handling. Today, however, because of the judicial acceptance of recorded telephone statements, it is practical to secure statements by telephone, and these statements can be used in later court proceedings for the purpose of impeaching the perception, integrity, and recollection of witnesses. The information is also useful for review by claims examiners, supervisors, and defense counsel.

Telephone interviewing introduces an interpersonal contact through a remote device, the telephone. Consequently, great care must be employed in telephone communication to display consideration and to establish the necessary rapport and relationship with the other party to the telephone conversation in order to expedite successful claims handling. Psychological distortion to good communication and the obstacles that are presented in the impersonal telephone device require that conscientious attention be devoted to the development of a warm, sensitive telephone personality. "Put a smile in your voice" is a slogan that connotes the use of a warm, friendly, and courteous voice.

Successful use of the telephone requires the skillful projection of a positive image. We must be warm, pleasant, considerate, and interested in order to seem to be smiling, friendly individuals. We must evoke a positive response by projecting an image of competence and confidence. A positive telephone image can be facilitated by paying attention to the mechanics of good telephone communication, including utilization of good verbal skills and making whatever adjustments are necessary for the lack of nonverbal means of communication.

Certain techniques are helpful in obtaining the cooperation of other people so that statements can be obtained, investigations can be completed, and negotiations can be carried through to a successful culmination. Of vital importance is the proper use of the questioning technique, recognizing the uses of the various types of questions, and avoiding those techniques, such as the use of leading questions, that are detrimental to the conduct of the claims investigation. This requires primary emphasis upon the direct question, reflective question, and open question techniques.

The claims representative's focus must be directed toward the attainment of understanding between the parties to the telephone conversation. Care must always be taken that the insured, claimant, or witness understands the question and the subject matter. Likewise, it is essential that the claims person be able to visualize the factual physical circumstances surrounding any given case. This is important in order to provide for the development of the interview, and it is also a vital factor in insuring accuracy in obtaining the physical facts of a loss situation. Further, it provides a visual picture for the record so that a file can be reviewed by a claims examiner, defense counsel, or the claims representative at a later date.

Where it is impossible or difficult for a claims person to visualize the claims situation, an on-the-site inspection is sometimes essential to obtain a complete visualization. In addition, where the visual depiction of the physical circumstances surrounding the claim are critical to the establishment of liability, the claims representative should be aware of the "right brain-left brain phenomenon," making a personal contact with a witness desirable so that the witness can draw a picture, diagram, or other visual representation of the physical facts of the case.

Other communication techniques and principles are outlined in the chapters on communication and listening. The claims representative should study these and employ them in day-to-day claims handling activities.

PART
III

Influencing people

8

Motivation

The insurance claims representative must understand people and be understood by them before he or she can hope to influence their thoughts and actions. Thus, as we have learned, effective communication is a prerequisite to successful human relations. Through knowledge of the process of communication, we can talk and listen with minimum distortion. We can convey information, and we can receive information. Like the salesperson, however, we still must motivate people if we are to be successful.

The character of human behavior and the principles and techniques of successful communication have been discussed in preceding chapters and have helped the claims person to understand himself or herself, the insured, claimants, witnesses, and other people. In this and the following chapter some of the principles of motivation are explored. This examination will help us as claims representatives to understand more about the nature of human behavior and will aid us in the task of influencing other people. It will also permit us to assess our own job performance and behavior patterns on the job, because job success in insurance claims handling is inextricably bound to the claims person's own motivations.

The claims representative works hard and sincerely attempts to do his or her job in the best possible manner because of pride, a desire to enhance reputation, and a hope to receive justified praise. In some cases, however, the individual may be motivated only to do a "passable" job, content to receive a paycheck, viewing the claims handling job as a temporary expedient until a better job comes along. All of the motives that will provide skill, proficiency and superior performance may be entirely lacking in this individual.

The emphasis of this chapter and the book is necessarily placed on motivating other people and bringing insurance claims to a satisfactory conclusion. Nevertheless, the claims representative's motivation is critical in this process. Our motives as we undertake each claims handling function color the entire picture. Thus, we must understand the subject of motives and motivation and recognize how our own motivation affects job performance and the failure or success that we realize in the insurance claims handling job.

NATURE OF MOTIVATION

Although a claims person may be effective in communicating with other people, he or she must motivate people to respond in a desired fashion. If a fire adjuster informs an insured that the low bid on the insured's damaged building is $436.50, and the insured understands that the low bid on his building damage is $436.50, the claims person has communicated. This doesn't mean that the insured will be motivated to accept $436.50 to settle his loss. On the contrary, the insured may have serious doubts that the contractor who submitted the bid is competent to do the work satisfactorily and in a reasonable time. The claims representative still must motivate the insured to accept the amount of the bid. To help the claims person in this task of influencing others, it will be helpful to discuss the nature of motivation and why and how people are motivated.

Essentially, *motivation* is the impulse or stimulus which accounts for activity. The word *motivation* comes from the Latin word, *movere* —to move. Motive forces are stimuli which cause motion. An automobile engine is motive when it is running. If it is not running, it will remain passive until it is motivated to move by an outside force or stimulus.

The stimuli which cause an automobile engine to run are relatively simple. A driver supplies those stimuli when he or she turns the key and engages the starter. A familiar response usually occurs. The starter turns the crankshaft, and the ignition shoots an electrical impulse into gasoline vapor causing it to fire. A sequence of firings or timed combustions in the automotive engine causes the motor to turn. The wheels will turn when the driver provides a further stimulus. The driver engages the clutch (or the automatic shift), and the engine causes the drive shaft to revolve, turning the wheels.

The insurance claims representative, in the job of motivating people, is simply trying to find the right key to activate another person. The claims person then hopes to steer that person in a desired direction. It has been observed, however, that a person often responds to a host of different stimuli, and he or she already may be moving in a direction which may or may not be desirable from the standpoint of the claims person. The latter must possess the knowledge and skill to direct the behavior of others into a path which will facilitate the successful conduct of the claims handling job. As claims representatives we, therefore, must understand the mechanics of the motivation process. We must recognize that a number of keys or stimuli fit the figurative lock of the human mind and influence it to move and that a great number of stimuli or outside forces can steer the direction of the response.

The mechanical steps which can be taken in getting an automobile to move and in steering it in a certain direction are relatively simple. In the job of motivating human behavior, however, we are confronted by a much more formidable task. Human motivation is a complex subject, since behavior is influenced by many forces, making it difficult to formulate principles which apply to all kinds of situations. Nevertheless, there are step-by-step procedures which may prove helpful to the claims representative for use in motivating people.

MOTIVES AS DETERMINANTS OF BEHAVIOR

All behavior is motivated. It is causally determined. Freud, for example, stated that behavior such as slips of the tongue, breaking and losing objects, forgetting names, failures to keep appointments, and other irregular behavior are not pure accidents but are dependent upon mental causes. These causes or determinants of behavior are the result of present and past conditions. The conditions themselves may be physiological or they may result from social relations and come about by the previous experiences of individuals.

We believe ourselves to be "free agents," capable of making rational decisions and acting in a rational manner. Whether we know it or not, however, the manner in which we think or act usually will fit within a predetermined framework of subconscious and conscious motives, urges, and desires according to each individual's own mental makeup. Our behavior results from a myriad of causes. Although it is impossible to discover all of the causal determinants of a human act, some of the determinants can be identified. Once identified, certain human behavior can be predicted. More important, the reason for specific human behavior can be explained.

If human behavior, then, manifests itself in a cause-and-effect pattern, one need only point to the cause, the determinant of human behavior, in order to anticipate certain effects—the human behavior. Although this conclusion oversimplifies the subject of motivation, it nevertheless explains how certain behavior can be stimulated in other people. Its practical significance to the claims representative is clear.

BASIC PRINCIPLES

Motives control human behavior. People behave in a manner which is instrumental in satisfying a need, drive, or motive. Just as the pianist must be able to identify the keys on the piano and know what response will come forth from each individual key when played upon, the claims person must know the human motives which make up the keyboard of human behavior. Like the pianist, the claims representative must be able to play upon each motive and produce a fairly predictable response. He or she must understand the motives which behavior seeks to satisfy.

The comparison of a pianist and the piano keys to an insurance claims representative and human motives again seems to oversimplify the underlying principle of human motivation—that there is a cause-and-effect relationship between motives and behavior. The concept, nevertheless, is based upon a solid foundation which is utilized daily by propagandists, salespersons, and all other people who influence human thought and action. Accordingly, then, the claims person must play upon human motives like the pianist plays upon the piano keys. Whether the claims representative and the pianist each come up with discordant results or with harmonious results depends entirely upon their knowledge of their subject and the skill which they possess and apply.

The following pages will prove of value in helping the claims representative understand those motives which may have the most direct application in insurance claims work.

Equilibrium state of people

People in their normal state, as a general rule, follow the line of least resistance. They follow familiar paths. Since they fear the unknown, they avoid strange and new situations. Most of us stay on the same job or pursue the same vocation not because we are perfectly satisfied with the job circumstances but because we may abhor change and the concomitant insecurity of change. Faced with a job decision, a person may undergo days or weeks of indecision, worry, conflict, and frustration before being finally able to arrive at a decision.

The normal condition of people has been characterized as one of physical relaxation, mental inertia, and emotional equilibrium. This is merely an extension of a fundamental principle of physics—that of the law of inertia. *Inertia* is defined as being "A property of matter by which it remains at rest or in uniform motion in the same straight line unless acted upon by some external force."[1] The external force in motivation is the stimuli which disturbs the relaxation, mental inertia, and emotional equilibrium of an individual and results in some sort of responsive behavior. The external force motivates the person. James A. Bayton, psychology professor at Howard University, wrote: "Motivation arises out of tension-systems which create a state of disequilibrium for the individual. This triggers a sequence of psychological events directed toward the selection of a goal which the individual anticipates will bring about release from the tensions and the selection of patterns of action which he anticipates will bring him to the goal."[2] A human being tends to remain in a state of inertia until some external force causes the person to respond with a different type of behavior which he or she anticipates will produce a satisfactory result.

---

[1] *Webster's New Collegiate Dictionary*, 1977.

[2] James A. Bayton, "Motivation, Cognition, Learning—Basic Factors in Consumer Behavior," in *Marketing and the Behavioral Sciences*, Perry Bliss, ed. (Boston: Allyn & Bacon, 1963), p. 44.

The insurance claims representative usually must deal with people whose physical relaxation, mental inertia, and emotional equilibrium have been disturbed or influenced by some external circumstance (such as the happening of an accident). We must be prepared to recognize the nature of the human behavior which usually results and to know the motive or motives which prompt that particular behavior. In a specific case we may discover that we are faced with behavior which does not enhance the opportunities to handle a claim successfully. For example, the happening of an accident may have disturbed a claimant to such an extent that his or her emotions are aroused. The claimant's goal for the moment may be to vent considerable anger. In such a case, the claims person must do something to neutralize that anger. In addition, the claims representative must play upon other motives of the claimant which will produce more compatible behavior.

On the other hand, an accident may motivate a claimant to react with behavior which makes it easier for the claims person to perform the claims handling job. The accident may have stimulated an irrational fear in the claimant, an otherwise normal, rational man or woman. A fear of not having his or her wrecked automobile repaired and anxieties about unknown troubles may produce considerable distress in the claimant. When the insurance claims representative approaches the man or woman in a friendly, sympathetic manner and tells the claimant that the automobile damages will be taken care of, the claimant may lose the former anxieties and respond in a most cooperative and appreciative manner. This contrast between the two claimants does not mean necessarily that the first claimant is a troublesome, vexatious person. It merely reflects the fact that an event acts upon different motives of two people and results in dissimilar behavior. As soon as the claims representative can cool off the first claimant's anger and start appealing to other motives, the claimant may be most pleasant and cooperative.

To make these general observations helpful, it is necessary to reduce the discussion to specifics and to introduce additional examples.

Motives and motive appeals

Each mind has its own method.
——Emerson

Any attempt to list all of the factors which potentially influence human behavior would be a foolhardy gesture. Nevertheless, there are some common motives which cause people to act or not to act in a given set of circumstances. The claims person should become familiar with these common, basic motives.

We are all well aware that we possess basic *physiological or biogenic motives*, needs, urges, or wishes. The most important of these motives is the urge to obtain physical comfort. To obtain physical comfort, we seek to satisfy our desires for food, water, sleep, and sex. In addition, we respond to stimuli which cause us to be too warm, or too cold, or which subject us to pain. We will engage in behavior which will permit us to obtain comfort and relief.

When our basic motives are unsatisfied, we resort to a great variety of behavior, and much of this behavior may appear to be violent, irrational, or strange. Morgan tells of extraordinary cases of pregnant women who ate plaster off the walls or ate mud, presumably to obtain some of the minerals they needed but could not obtain in their ordinary diets.[3] If the male reader of this book, consequently, should return to his home some evening and find his wife gnawing voraciously on a part of the house, he should not immediately commit her to a mental institution. First he should examine her motives. She may only be pregnant.

Emotional motives are powerful determinants of human behavior. Emotion is a "stirred-up bodily state"[4] in which the body's physiological functions may be affected. The breathing, the heart rate, and the circulation, for example, may undergo considerable change during a moment of emotional stress. Emotional motives are such things as pleasure, anger, and fear. The motive of pleasure causes people to seek pleasure-fulfilling experiences; anger makes a person strike out against the source of torment; and the motive of fear causes an individual to avoid undesirable situations or to protect himself or herself against real or fancied dangers.

Psychologists tell us that we all have *ego-defensive needs*. We need to protect our individual personalities; to avoid physical and psychological harm; to avoid ridicule and "loss of face"; to prevent loss of prestige; and to avoid or to obtain relief from anxiety.

---

[3] Clifford T. Morgan, *Introduction to Psychology* (New York: McGraw-Hill, 1956), p. 64.

[4] Ibid., p. 88.

A third group of motives has considerable influence upon human behavior. This group involves urges, wishes, or drives which are called *social motives*. They appeared when humans developed into social creatures, and they are a natural outgrowth of our concern for our position in society. They influence human behavior, because we are all concerned with the society within which we live. That society exerts external pressure upon us and has caused us to adopt the social motives. We worry about what other people think, and we are concerned with other people's reaction to our behavior.

Primitive men and women wrested directly from nature the means for personal satisfaction and existence. The chief concern of primitive human beings was to adapt individual physiological needs to what nature provided and to adapt what was found in nature to personal needs. As soon as the human being developed into a more gregarious creature and learned to depend upon the exchange of goods with fellow humans, each individual had to consider the motives of others. Each person not only had to communicate personal wants to those who possessed the means of satisfying them, but also, the individual had to induce others to give up something they possessed for something that he or she had to offer in return.

Early in their development men and women employed simple motive appeals. If an individual wanted something belonging to another person, he or she would appeal to the other person's fear motive. One man would threaten to hit another with an axe. This appeal still works amazingly well in contemporary society. Because of restraints imposed by society, however, individuals today usually must employ other techniques of motivation. In addition, there is the possibility that today, as well as in the past, the other person may be larger, stronger, and in possession of a sharper and heavier axe. Every person today, therefore, is subject to many social motives, urges, and drives which smooth personal relations with other people and help each person to achieve personal objectives.

Since we depend upon other human beings, we respect the customs of the society within which we live. Social pressure exerted by our society makes us adopt social values. These values set standards for us and act as the guideposts which enable us to get along with other people. If we ignore social values and the established standards, our society metes out its punishment in the form of imprisonment, fines, rebuke and chastisement, ostracism, and so forth.

Fortunately, we have been taught social values almost from birth, and the learning process continues throughout our lifetimes. From birth through adulthood our social values develop and we acquire motives, urges, or drives. We worry about our reputations, because the status of our reputation has a strong bearing upon our feelings of self-respect. In seeking prestige, we obtain power—the power to influence the behavior of others. Power enables us to obtain security, and it bolsters our self-respect. We cooperate and we compete in order to obtain power.

MOTIVES AND CLAIMS HANDLING

A great many human motives become intimately involved when an individual is confronted with insurance claims situations. A person may be injured in accidents and suffer physical discomfort and pain. Personal injury and property losses cause trauma, confusion, and uncertainty, and these generate emotions. The person is thrown into contact with other people under unfamiliar and often strained relations. In these relations he or she is forced to behave in a manner which will produce both personally and socially acceptable results. Within this environmental framework the claims representative must understand human motives, and he or she must have a knowledge of the appeals which can be made to those motives.

In the following pages we will examine some of the more common motives which may be involved in insurance claims situations. In addition, we will explore a number of useful appeals for obtaining favorable behavior in other people.

Pride

The only way to make a man trustworthy is to trust him; and the surest way to make him untrustworthy is to distrust him and show your distrust.
———Henry Lewis Stimson

The strongest tendency, emotion, or drive confronting contemporary human beings is that of the social motive of pride. Gratification of physical motives is often postponed and sometimes renounced entirely in favor of this social motive—even at the point where survival itself is at stake.[5] Pride influences behavior in every way, because it is tied

---

[5] Bernard Berelson and Gary A. Steiner, *Human Behavior—An Inventory of Scientific Findings* (New York: Harcourt, Brace & World, 1964), p. 243.

to the two-pronged subjects of self-respect and reputation. Our personal view of ourselves influences what we do. We are besieged constantly by doubts about our self-worth, and we work hard at proving to ourselves that we are meritorious and talented, and that we possess admirable traits. The best way for us to prove to ourselves that we are good, talented, and admirable, is to have someone tell us that we are. This is called *ego recognition.*

Ego recognition.   Men and women direct their daily efforts almost always toward activities which will result in recognition, commendation, and acceptance by other people. Recognition of the ego nurtures us and drives us on to greater activity. Anything which gives us a feeling of greater importance nourishes our pride and our feeling of well-being.

The tremendous importance of ego recognition often is overlooked. Some employers, for example, believe that the best way to keep workers happy is to pay them well. Studies reveal, however, that although compensation is an important factor in job satisfaction, and men and women talk a lot about it, employees are much more concerned with ego recognition.[6] They want to be complimented on their work; they want the boss to tell them that he or she appreciates their work efforts and achievements; they want a pat on the back and a feeling of belonging.

We all want to feel important. It is essential to our mental health. Without self-respect we cannot live with ourselves. Self-respect is not generated from within; it comes from other people—what they say, what they write, and what the individual believes they think. As a consequence, we all fish for compliments, because compliments bolster our feelings of self-worth. People like to take psychological tests because the test reveals some good things about the individual taking it. Millions of people read astrology and go to palmists, phrenologists, or other fortune tellers in order to be told something good about themselves.

---

[6] See *Management Review* (June 1954), p. 362; and Michael J. Jucius, *Personnel Management* (Homewood, Ill.: Richard D. Irwin, 1955), pp. 298–99. © 1955 by Richard D. Irwin, Inc. Also see William Foote Whyte, *Men at Work* (Homewood, Ill.: Dorsey Press, 1961), p. 8. © 1961 by The Dorsey Press. Also William R. Spriegel, *Principles of Business Organization and Operation* (New York: Prentice-Hall, 1952), p. 466.

We are driven by curiosity to know what others think of us—if we hear a report that is good, it makes us glow with satisfaction. On the other hand, if we are attacked with criticism and receive unfavorable reports about ourselves, our feelings of importance are damaged. Our self-respect diminishes. Severe blows to our self-respect may cause us to react in a socially reprehensible manner. In an attempt to recover our self-image, we may act irrationally. We may attempt to destroy whatever or whoever threatens our self-respect. A damaged self-image may cause severe melancholy. Failing to make an adjustment to obtain vital self-respect may even cause a person to commit suicide.

Closely allied to self-respect is the subject of *reputation*. One's reputation acts directly on a person's feeling of self-worth. The better the individual's reputation, the more effort he or she will expend to preserve and enhance it because of the vital role it plays in the person's feelings of self-respect. We will usually work hard to improve our own reputations. We will go to great lengths to defend our reputations. Threats to reputation often cause greater concern to a person than threat of bodily harm. If our self-concept tells us that we are not as good as we are reputed to be, we will strive harder to improve ourselves. The greater our success in convincing ourselves that we are as good as our reputations indicate, the greater our feelings of self-respect.

Appeals to pride in claims handling.   The motive of pride plays an important role in successful insurance claims handling. If a claims representative can appeal to that motive, he or she may significantly influence other people's behavior. To obtain a person's confidence, for example, we should express sincere admiration for something about that person. If we are talking to a witness, for example, we must talk in considerate terms, thanking the witness for taking time from a busy schedule to talk to us. This makes the witness feel good. It appeals to the pride of the witness—the important feeling of self-respect.

As in the case of the witness, the claims representative must appeal to the motive of pride in negotiating with all other people. We must show deference to others' opinions, listening with patience, interest, sympathy, and consideration. We should understand the logic of another person's case, at all times conveying the distinct impression that we respect the other person's comprehension of the case and the latter's good sense in understanding the various ramifications of the case that have a bearing upon the issue of liability and the evaluation of damages. Finally, the claims representative must appeal to other people's fairness, good judgment, and sense of justice.

Insurance claims handling stimulates a certain amount of skepticism and cynicism in the claims person, and he or she well may question the wisdom of placing too much trust in insureds and claimants. Used wisely, however, the principle of ego recognition has direct application in insurance claims situations. Often an appeal to the self-esteem of a claimant or an insured will result in dividends. In certain situations and in certain types of claims the claims representative can give a claimant or insured considerable freedom in determining the outcome of negotiations. The claims person, for example, may put the claim into the hands of an insured, but at the same time, the claims person will retain control. This procedure is recommended only in those cases where the insured or a claimant is qualified to make an accurate appraisal and evaluation *of the factors* that will determine the extent of damages. Since there are few situations where a claimant or insured possesses the expert ability to appraise and evaluate factors of damages, the principle should be used with discrimination.

An illustration of the principle's application would be in a case involving property damage where the measure of damages is "actual cash value"—replacement cost minus depreciation. The claims representative will not approach the insured and inquire how much the insured wants to be paid; rather, the claims person will guide the insured into revealing the factors that will aid in the final evaluation of damages. For example, the insured will be guided in the process of determining the extent of depreciation of the property.

The claims representative perhaps will lay the stage by saying, "Mr. Jones, we have property here that appears to be fairly old. Now, Mr. Jones, I know that you are a reasonable and fair person; what do you think would be fair depreciation under the circumstances?" Before the insured has a chance to answer, the claims person outlines certain factors—original cost, the number of years this property usually would last, how old it now is, the obvious wear, how much it would cost to replace it now, and so forth. Then the claims representative repeats, "What do you think would be reasonable depreciation?" Mr. Jones is on the defensive; it has been placed in his lap. The claims person has stated that Mr. Jones is a fair and reasonable man. In all likelihood, Jones will now want to prove that he is reasonable and fair. Appealing to Jones's ego recognition gives Mr. Jones two things to be concerned about as he negotiates a settlement amount. He wants to be treated fairly on the settlement, but equally important, he wishes to preserve his pride by not altering the impression and image of respect and confidence in his integrity which the claims person apparently has of him. A brusque, impersonal, "strictly business" approach by the claims representative, on the other hand, might elicit a completely different response on the part of Mr. Jones. His preservation of his pride may focus on making certain he is not made a fool of by being cheated on his just claim by this brusque, impersonal claims person.

The principle can be illustrated further in another example. A contractor in an actual case sustained extensive damage to his tractor. The problem of evaluating the amount of the loss was complicated by the factor of depreciation. The claims attorney who handled this claim knew that the insured was a shrewd businessman and approached him with this comment, "Now look, Mr. Brown, you're a businessman, and I know that you understand depreciation, because you're up against it as far as the government is concerned. The government expects you to justify depreciation claimed as a business expense when you file your tax forms. In the case of your tractor, the depreciation, of course, will depend upon how much use you have had, and that is something you must decide. I've always found you to be a fair and reasonable man, so I would like your opinion of what is fair."

The insured in his desire to prove his fairness stated a higher depreciation figure than the claims attorney had in mind. Later the insured remarked to one of the officers of the insurance company, "That guy surely is a shrewd operator. He let me set my own depreciation, and I beat myself out of a lot of money." An inadequate settlement was not calculated on the part of the claims representative, but the case illustrates the application of the principle of ego recognition. By placing it into the other person's hands and relying upon the other person's sense of fairness, the result is sometimes better than if the claims representative went to the insured and declared, "Now this is what I am going to pay you." An insured may resent and resist such an approach.

Some authorities believe that a claims person should not ask a claimant how much money he or she wants in order to settle a claim.

These authorities contend that a person obviously cannot be expected to propose a figure which he or she honestly believes to be fair if he or she does not possess the expertise to evaluate fair value. Not knowing fair value, a claimant's instinct for self-survival—triggered by the understandable fear that asking for too low a figure will result in an inadequate and unfair settlement—will cause the claimant to ask for an amount that allows for a wide margin of error. It is only when the other person, either a claimant or an insured, is in a position to know the factors of value of the claim that the claims representative should appeal to the other person's sense of fairness and ask for an initial expression of opinion on factors entering into the determination of value.

Suppose an insured or a claimant is invited to state a fair figure, and he or she presents an amount in excess of that figure the claims person has in mind? The claims representative still is in the position of being able to withdraw and try a new approach. For example, if the contractor in the preceding case had stated a figure which did not fully acknowledge the amount of betterment realized in the tractor repairs, the claims representative would take a stronger position and say, "Now let's take a look at that again, Mr. Brown, because you may not have taken into consideration this particular aspect or that particular aspect, and so on." A reconsideration by the insured may result in a more realistic valuation.

Character of the claims representative. Because of pride, we all want to be respected. More important, however, we want to be respected by people whom we respect and whose opinions may reflect upon our reputation. People in one's own immediate business and social community figuratively make up the depository for our reputation and self-respect. A person may act in a most prudent manner at home, but at a convention in a distant city, away from the prying eyes of people who "count," he or she may act in an entirely different manner.

It is well known that some people bring out the worst in us; others bring out the best. We cheat those people whom we believe would cheat us. "Faith begets faith, and confidence begets confidence." We are most trustworthy around those people who heighten our feelings of self-worth and self-respect by trusting us.

The significance of the foregoing is that as insurance claims representatives, we must obtain the confidence and respect of the people with whom we deal if we expect to be able to influence these people in a desirable manner. To do this we must convince insureds, claimants, witnesses, and other persons that we are worthy of their confidence and respect. The claims person must be sincere in dealings with other people. Aristotle wrote, "The character of the speaker is the most important element in persuasion." A Roman educator, Quintilian, in his writings, stated, "[People] are influenced quite as much by their confidence in the person as they are in what he says. The man who is honest and sincere and who has his facts well in hand and speaks the truth, he is believed in when he speaks. He influences his listeners by his own character." To Quintilian, the influential speaker was always the good and able person speaking well.

The keynote of effective insurance claims handling, therefore, is the attitude, sincerity, honesty, and frankness of the claims representative. This does not mean, of course, that we should be so frank as to open claims files to claimants and their attorneys for inspection, although this can be done in some cases. It would be naïve to think that the claims representative should reveal the fact that the insurance company may offer a higher settlement figure on a case if the claimant should refuse the first offer. It does mean that a claims person's attitude toward other people is the determining factor in personal success in handling insurance claims. Deceit, dishonesty, sharp dealing, arrogance, condescension, and other human foibles have no more place in the claims representative's job than they have in any other area of human relations.

Penny foolish and pound wise. In the evaluation of special and general damages we are able to achieve better results if we are mindful of the important role that the motive of pride plays in negotiations. An affront to a claimant's pride can complicate unnecessarily the negotiation process.

The amount to be paid for general damages, that is, for pain and suffering, usually causes the most difficulty in personal injury settlement negotiations. This is because general damages usually are approximations and crude estimations at best. They are not directly related to actual dollars-and-cents expenditures and are not verifiable by reference to invoices and documentation, as in the case of special damages. As a consequence, general damages vary considerably on almost identical cases of personal injury. Realizing this, the claims representative often will find that the special damages (hospital and medical bills, lost wages, damaged clothing, damage to automobile, etc.) are relatively unimportant compared to the amount of general damages that is claimed by the claimant.

Negotiating general damages requires skill to induce the claimant to accept a figure that will be agreeable to the insurance company and to the claims representative. It is here that psychology enters in and can facilitate the making of an acceptable settlement figure. Remember that the claims representative must maintain the respect and confidence of the claimant throughout the period of negotiations. We must demonstrate sympathy, consideration, and most important, fairness in dealing with the claimant. This sort of approach will do much to prevent a claimant from withdrawing from the negotiations and seeking the aid of an attorney. This approach also is most likely to induce the claimant to respond in a considerate, fair manner, particularly when the subject of the general damages is broached.

If the claims person ignores human relations and combs through the listing of special damages with a hypercritical eye, being picayunish on every little exaggeration present in the listing, he or she may destroy the atmosphere which is necessary to proceed on to the monumental task of reducing the general damages to an acceptable figure. If we question every small item of special damages, we injure the self-respect of the claimant. Injury to the claimant's pride makes the claimant react with antagonism against the claims representative. In such a climate of hostility we can expect little success in appealing to the claimant's sense of fairness and justice.

The claims representative can "bend over backwards" in generosity in allowing certain items of special damages. We, of course, must demonstrate that we are being fair and not merely stupid in allowing inflated amounts for certain small items. In establishing the fact that we are unusually fair in dealing with the claimant, we are more in position to prevail upon the claimant to be unusually fair when the subject of general damages is broached. Noting that we have been fair in handling special damages, the claimant may reciprocate when the large item of general damages is negotiated. The claimant's pride—self-respect and the desire for a good reputation—will induce the claimant to want us to think well of him or her. Accordingly, the claimant is more likely to be reasonable and fair in negotiating than he or she would be if an atmosphere of hostility and suspicion existed between the claimant and the claims representative.

The British have a saying "penny wise and pound foolish" which applies to the claims person who haggles interminably over every little item of special damages in a personal injury case to the point that the claimant becomes quite hostile and resolute in the figure demanded for general damages. If the claims person has appeared to be fair and liberal in handling the special damages, that appearance carries over when general damages are discussed. The claimant is more likely to believe that he or she is being offered a fair and liberal amount when the claims representative presents an offer for general damages. There is, of course, a distinction between "fair and liberal" and paying for excessive or unsubstantiated special damages. If you pay excessively on special damages, the claimant probably will expect you to do likewise on general damages. Don't "nitpick," but also don't be over-liberal. There must always be a reasonable basis for your fairness and generosity on special damages.

The successful claims representative always must keep in mind the motive of pride when dealing with other people. The claims person must use skill in handling controversies and be sensitive to the feelings of others. He or she must protect the self-respect of others. We cannot bulldoze our way through to a successful conclusion of claims. A swimmer who is entangled in seaweed very well may become more ensnared if he or she attempts to thrash a way out of the predicament. If, however, the swimmer attacks the seaweed piece by piece, he or she ultimately will be free of the seaweed. The insurance claims person, likewise, will do well to go slowly in working to obtain successful results.

First, we should recognize a claimant's sense of pride by expressing a knowledge of the strong points of the claimant's case. We should discuss all of the salient points with no attempt to gloss over the strengths of the claimant's case. With respect and sympathy we can analyze and evaluate the claimant's argument. We then will work naturally into those areas of evidence and logic that tear down the claimant's case. At the same time, we will continue to work on the claimant's self-respect by appealing to the claimant's judgment and sense of justice.

Fear

The emotion of *fear* is a strong and compelling motive. It is a powerful force in stimulating response designed to avoid the situation which evokes the fear. It is intrinsically wedded to the basic and fundamental law of self-preservation. The motive of fear can cause dramatic physical and psychological changes. Fear, for example, causes the body to speed up certain body functions. The glands secrete adrenalin during times of stress when a person experiences strong emotion. This secretion stimulates the body and aids humans and animals to take flight at times of immediate danger.

Fear also can cause people to think and to respond irrationally. For example, fear causes people to do foolhardy and dangerous things. A person in a burning building may become so irrational from fear that instead of reacting intelligently to the situation and seeking out the best avenue of escape, he or she may select the poorest possible exit. People have been known to leap from windows during a fire when they could have escaped harm by walking to a safe exit nearby.

Fear also may prevent a person from doing a dangerous thing. An individual may refuse to mount a rickety ladder because of fear of falling. The person's fear in this case leads to rational behavior. Likewise, fear of social disapproval or punishment causes people to conform to the rules established by society. Social pressure is the strongest regulating factor in organized society. People dress, talk, and act according to the rules. Although some nonconformance is possible, too much deviation is frowned upon, and most people fear the consequences—disapproval and punishment. Because of the basic motive of pride, we all experience fear or anxiety if our self-respect or reputation is endangered. We, therefore, attempt to protect our pride by avoiding behavior which may endanger our self-respect and reputation. An insurance claims representative often can appeal to a person's self-respect and motive of pride to induce socially responsible behavior on the part of the latter. With such an appeal the claims person often can obtain cooperation and can effect prompt and reasonable settlements.

A claims representative frequently sees cases where insureds and claimants resort to falsehoods to cover up conduct that might reflect adversely upon their reputations, thus hurting their self-respect. A motorist who causes an accident because he or she is heavily intoxicated often will lie about the extent of his or her drinking because of fear of disapproval and punishment. The motive makes it difficult for claims representatives to secure accurate facts about accidents from insureds or claimants. This particularly is true where some clandestine activity is involved, as in the case of an insured (a married man) who insisted that he was alone at the time of an accident. The key witness in the case was a woman who got out of the insured's automobile and fled the scene of the accident. The insured's reluctance to tell the truth was understandable; the woman wasn't his wife. Moreover, she was a prostitute.

Anxiety. Closely allied to fear is the feeling of tension and discomfort called *anxiety*. Whereas fear is a reaction to specific situations, anxiety is a general state of apprehension or uneasiness that occurs in situations which may be ill-defined or general in nature. Anxiety is rather a vague or "objectless" fear. It may be less intense than fear, but, nevertheless, it has a profound influence on human behavior. Anxiety particularly is generated in legal controversies and insurance claims. This is because most people are uncomfortable, uneasy, and apprehensive in unfamiliar circumstances that can materially affect their welfare. People fear the unknown. Anxiety, consequently, results from this fear. Most people in their everyday existence are not engaged in work that involves a contest between two adversaries, in which appreciable sums of money hang in the balance, and in which there is the strange, unfamiliar, and complex world of contract or tort law that will decide the outcome of the contest.

The claims person, accordingly, must be cognizant of the importance of the emotions of fear and anxiety. In some respects we must eliminate or reduce the fear and anxiety present in other people. In other respects we can capitalize upon that same fear and anxiety and turn it to advantage in investigating and settling claims. When we approach another person, whether that person be an insured or a third party claimant, we must realize that an atmosphere of suspicion and distrust may be present. Since such an atmosphere is not conducive to good communication and successful claims handling, we must do all that is possible to reduce or eliminate the other person's fear and anxiety.

The insured or claimant, for example, quite naturally may have considerable anxiety over money (medical bills, damage to automobile, loss of income caused by disability, continuing household expenses, and so forth). There may be worries over lack of transportation or a concern about rehabilitation prospects following a severe, disabling injury. There may be anxiety over signing authorization or release forms. The claims person can do much to allay this anxiety and to facilitate good communication with the other person by making timely assurances of payment or using advance payments, a "walk-away" settlement, or other techniques. Allaying or eliminating anxiety over money in such circumstances is a primary responsibility of the claims person and one that should be accomplished without delay. The emphasis is placed on securing a desirable response from the other person—an amicable relationship where the claim is under control or where settlement is satisfactorily consummated.

We have learned from an earlier chapter that all behavior is purposive—caused by some motive or human drive. Thus, there are "stimulus-response relations," which, if identified by the claims person, can be successfully utilized in claims handling. One of the overriding or dominant stimuli in the case we are describing is money anxiety. It is easy to identify, because the individual frequently verbalizes concern over money worries—bills piling up, loss of income, continuing expense at home, and so on. The other person is uncomfortable, uneasy, and apprehensive. Payment of money or assurance of payment is a stimulus that will produce a positive response in reducing or eliminating the money anxiety of the other person.

Identification of nonmoney anxieties is more complex. However, the claims representative can frequently ferret out specific worries of an insured or claimant by engaging in considerate, interested, and concerned conversation, making solicitous inquiries that will often reveal the other person's anxieties. Concerns over rehabilitation prospects, for example, afford the claims person the opportunity to provide assurance about the type of rehabilitation services that are available in the area, other people's successful experiences at rehabilitation following similar injuries, and so on. With such considerate behavior—demonstrating empathy, sincerity, openness, and honesty—the claims representative can do much to reduce or eliminate the other person's fear and anxiety.

On the other hand, there are occasions where the claims representative can utilize the fear and the anxiety of a claimant to the claims person's own advantage. In insurance claims negotiations the claims representative explains to the claimant how the proposed settlement will eliminate the fear and anxiety which the claimant has. At the same time the claims person can intensify fear and anxiety by subtly suggesting how unfortunate and difficult things will be for the claimant if he or she does not accept the proffered settlement. Suppose, for example, the claims person is attempting to negotiate settlement on a bodily injury claim. The conversation might go somewhat like this:

Claims Person: Mr. White, I know that you must be anxious to get all of this off your mind. It no doubt will be a relief to you to get your car damages taken care of as well as to have all of your other expenses paid for—hospital bill, doctor's bill, and so forth. They probably are a great worry to you. My company has authorized me to pay for all of the bills that you have submitted to me. In addition, Mr. White, I am authorized to pay you an extra $725.

Mr. White: Well, I don't know. I had expected to get paid more than that. It doesn't seem like enough.

Claims Person: Frankly, Mr. White, your injuries would have justified a greater payment had they been more serious and of a permanent nature. You have told me, however, that you have made a complete recovery, and this is confirmed by your family doctor's report.

Mr. White: Yes, I know. But I've heard where people get paid more on accidents like this, and that's why I'm not sure that you are offering enough.

Claims Person: It is very true, Mr. White, that some people receive sizable insurance and court settlements. The cases you usually hear about are those that reach the courts and are finally decided after months of litigation. The spectacular ones are reported in the newspaper. They make great news, and people often get their impressions about the value of claims from these sensational cases reported in the newspapers. You seldom hear about the cases that are settled out of court—nor do you hear about thousands of cases that are tried in court and are lost by the people who bring the suit.

Most important, Mr. White, you don't hear about the delay, expense, and inconvenience of law suits. Then there is the fear and anxiety of wondering whether you will win, and if so, whether you will receive enough to cover all of your expenses, including 33⅓ percent or more to your attorney, and still end up with as much as the insurance company offered you in the first place.

It has been our experience, Mr. White, that many people who sue end up with less money after paying the expenses of their law suit and their lawyer than we offered them before the court action. In the meantime they have had the months of delay, inconvenience, and worry.

These are the things which must be decided by you, Mr. White. It is your claim and your decision. I don't want to force you to decide one way or the other. I know you possess the judgment to make the right decision. I can only point out the problems which present themselves if we are unable to get together on a figure. If we break off negotiations, and you hire a lawyer, I will have to turn my file over to our firm of defense attorneys. You and I would go our separate ways.

I wouldn't like to see this happen, Mr. White, because I believe that most lawsuits are only for people who cannot intelligently resolve their difficulties without trouble.

Mr. White, you and I have been in constant contact since your accident, and I believe that you are an intelligent, honest, and reasonable man. Recognizing this, I have been open and above-board with you. I have in all sincerity offered what I and my company believe is a fair and reasonable offer.

In this example the claims representative has used motive appeals. The claims person has appealed to the claimant's self-respect; he or she has used moral suasion by appealing to logic; further, an attempt has been made to reinforce the claimant's confidence and respect for the claims representative; and the claims person has stimulated the claimant's fear and anxiety about the consequences of refusing the offer that has been made.

Although the claims representative has utilized the various techniques and appeals to logic, the claimant still may hesitate to settle the claim, deciding first to secure a better bargaining position by using a common threat. Thus, the conversation may continue as follows:

Mr. White: Well, I appreciate your efforts, but I still don't believe you are offering enough money. I don't want to be unreasonable; I only want to receive a reasonable amount for all of my damages and the inconvenience that I've suffered. I really have tried to be reasonable about this, but I think I had better get an attorney.

Claims Person: Well, I am sorry to hear that. Be sure to have your attorney telephone me so that I can discuss the case with him (her). If your attorney and I can't arrive at some understanding, then I will refer my file to our firm of defense attorneys.

After the claimant has threatened to obtain an attorney, the claims person's reaction introduces an element of reality, showing the claimant that the claims person is not alarmed at having to deal with an attorney. This has shock value. It may induce the claimant to make a sudden change of position and decide to settle, for the claims representative has introduced a note of finality to the conversation that should effectively accentuate the anxiety experienced by the claimant. However, again the claims person should not "paint himself or herself into a corner." There should be a further attempt to salvage the situation to prevent the case from going to an attorney.

When we utilize the motive appeal of fear in order to motivate others to respond as we wish them to, we must take care that we do not work the situation into an irreversible position. In other words, use of this appeal can backfire. The claims representative must leave open reasonable alternatives. There is considerable wisdom in the words uttered by Plautus two centuries before the birth of Christ: "Consider the little mouse, how sagacious an animal it is which never entrusts its life to one hole only."[7]

Thus if the claims person has still not succeeded in persuading the claimant to settle after introducing the motive appeals of fear and anxiety, he or she should still leave the door open for further negotiation. The conversation might go as follows:

Claims Person: Mr. White, I would like you to do what you think is best for you. I don't want to discourage you from going to an attorney, since this is your right. But you might wish to think the matter over for a few more days before making a decision. How would it be if I called you again next week at this time, and we can continue our discussion about a possible settlement, and this will give you time to think about the matter further. Will this be all right with you?

In using this type of technique, capitalizing upon the motive appeals of anxiety and fear, the claims representative must be most careful in selecting the words used in talking to claimants. Under no circumstances should the claims person use language advising a claimant not to secure the services of an attorney. This would be improper and would subject the insurer to legal liability. Rather, throughout this type of dialogue, the claims representative must make it clear that he or she is merely trying to point out all of the advantages and disadvantages of not dealing directly with the claims representative. Further, if the claimant decides to obtain the services of an attorney, the claims representative must make it clear that he or she is ready and willing to negotiate further with the claims attorney.

Retreat, delay, and the remote opponent. There are occasions when an insurance claims representative can make good use of a

---

[7] Plautus *Truculentus*, Act 4, Sc. 4, line 15. Found in Ritschl's second edition, Bohn Classical Library, translation by Henry Thomas Riley.

tactic which can be called the retreat, delay, and remote opponent technique. In its use the claims person appeals to the motive of fear and anxiety—the claimant's apprehension of the unknown, remote, and unfamiliar. If the claims representative has been unable to effect a reasonable settlement after considerable effort and utilization of various appeals already discussed, he or she may find it helpful to advise the claimant that the matter must be referred to the home office.

The claims person might say, for example, "You understand, Mrs. Brown, that I am only an employee of the company. I cannot write a check and make payments which would be difficult to justify with the company. I would quickly be brought to task if I did. The figure that you have in mind is in excess of the amount that I believe the company will accept. I will have to submit this to my home office superiors and let them decide."

The claimant can argue with the claims representative, because the claimant is facing the claims person, or the claims person is the other party in a telephone conversation. If the latter submits the question to the insurer's home office, however, the claimant is exposed to a distasteful delay. It also introduces an element of uncertainty which produces anxiety in the claimant. Furthermore, the claimant is not in a position to argue with the company, the remote opponent, because it is back in the "home office" somewhere. This maneuver often is quite effective. The claimant is faced with delay, and he or she then must contend with a decision by some impersonal thing with which it is impossible effectively to argue. Under the circumstances, the claimant may come to terms with the claims representative.

A claims representative should *not* use this tactic merely to delay justifiable claims with the motive of forcing claimants to accept partial settlements when they are entitled to full payment. Such a practice may reflect favorably upon the insurer's loss experience, but it is bad business. Unjustifiable delay gives the industry a "black eye"; its continued use probably will result in increased litigation and remedial government regulation. The "unfair claims practices" and "unfair trade practices" laws that have been enacted by individual states were designed specifically to discourage this type of "sharp" and unconscionable conduct on the part of insurance claims representatives (see also Chapter 10). Probably more important, such unjustified tactics should effectively lower a claims person's feeling of self-esteem and pride in his or her work. Delay in those cases of questionable or disputed liability, however, is quite justifiable, particularly where it is apparent that the claimant's latest demand is unreasonable.

The principle of the "remote opponent" can be illustrated further in the insurance bargaining process. It is common in insurance claims negotiations to have a certain amount of "horse trading" between some claimants and claims representatives. Oftentimes this trading can be conducted on a strict two-party relationship—that is, the claimant and the claims representative bargain back and forth with the understanding that the claims person has some latitude in settlement authority. In this role the claims representative evaluates the claim, and he or she then makes an offer and responds to counteroffers of the claimant within a certain range of draft authority. If the claims person agrees to a higher figure, it is because he or she has decided that the figure is within the range of valuation that has been placed on the claim by the home office examiner, the home office supervisor, the assigning office (for an independent adjuster), or by the claims person himself or herself.

There comes a time however when we must take a firm stand on the amount that the insurer is willing to pay. It always must appear to the claimant that there is a rather narrow range of valuation within which we are willing to negotiate. Otherwise, the bargaining process deteriorates into a not-so-amusing game in which the claimant believes that it is only necessary to continue the bargaining over a lengthy period of time in order to elicit successively higher offers from the insurer. We must take a stand somewhere along the line. At the same time, however, we want to be able to control the claimant. *Control,* of course, refers to the objective of deterring the claimant from turning to an attorney—the channel of communication must be left open with the claimant so that settlement can be consummated directly with the claimant. This control is essential, because it generally is true that cases in the hands of attorneys will cost more to settle than those in which settlement is made directly with the claimant.

Consequently, if we hold fast on a certain "final offer," we must weigh the consequences. Should we deliver an absolute ultimatum? It is here that the remote opponent can be utilized in the bargaining process. We deliver the company's "final offer," perhaps in the following fashion, "Well, I am sorry, Mr. Jones, but the company's home office medical staff and legal department have evaluated the available medical information and all of the circumstances concerning your claim, and the amount that I have offered you is all that I am fairly justified in paying."

If this ultimatum is accepted, it is all well and good. If it is rejected, however, we are in danger of losing control and of having the claim referred to an attorney. It is here that the following homey quotation has some application: "If you are leaving home to set the world afire, don't slam the door too hard; you may have to come back for more matches."

If the claims representative has reason to believe that the insurer's "final offer" was a little premature and that a little more bargaining might save the case from litigation, he or she needs a graceful way to continue the negotiations. When the claimant rejects the "final offer," the claims person might respond as follows: "Well now, Mr. Jones, you have opened up a new facet of the case which perhaps I have not evaluated fully. You have told me that you still have some lower-back pain, and it may be that this residual deserves more consideration than I have given it. Let me write or telephone the company and emphasize this particular point. It may be that they will give your claim further consideration."

The claims representative assures the claimant that the insurance company is still interested in negotiations and is paying attention to the claimant's claim, and this assurance paves the way for a further offer. In some cases, obviously, the two parties will be so far out of line on the claimant's demand and the claims person's offer that it appears that a further offer would be useless. At this point, the claims representative might try the "think it over until Thursday—I'll see you then" technique. Even this may not help. In some cases loss of control and litigation cannot be avoided. It is not infrequent or surprising in such cases to learn that the claimant already has been to see an attorney and already has decided to have the attorney handle the claim.

An appeal to the motive of fear and anxiety of a claimant surely has its legitimate uses in many claims, and the retreat, delay, and remote opponent tactic can be used to good advantage on occasion. If we play upon the fear and anxiety of a claimant, however, we must use sincerity, subtlety, and skill in applying this motive appeal. We must use tact. "Tact is the knack of making a point without making an enemy." Heavy-handedness can produce results completely opposite from those intended. Unless great care is taken, we can antagonize and anger the claimant and arouse entirely different motives than those intended.

Anger and aggression

If you are patient in one moment of anger, you will escape a
hundred days of sorrow.
——Chinese proverb

People usually do not like to be pushed or forced to do things. Throughout our lifetimes we must submit to authority. We recognize that many requirements are natural and proper. Organized society requires that we all obey laws and submit to authority. Force in some cases, however, appears unnatural and improper. In such cases we dislike it, and we rebel. Rebellion results in behavior which is hostile, destructive, retaliative, and aggressive. With adults, hostility may be suppressed and not manifested openly as it is with small children.

Usually an individual's rebellion is minor because of his or her dominant tendency to maintain reputation and self-respect. Nevertheless, a person will flout the law with minor violations of traffic or parking laws, he or she will sometimes cheat a little on the annual income tax return, and the individual will sometimes break the work rules prescribed by an employer. We all possess an innate "cussedness" when our sense of right and wrong is outraged. We react to fancied or real grievances. Further, we seem to derive a peculiar pleasure and satisfaction from a certain amount of conflict. We enjoy a good fight or contest, if not as a combatant at least as a spectator. Instead of throwing Christians to the lions, today's "proper" citizens watch boxing, wrestling, soccer, ice hockey, or football. Occasionally today's spectator personally will fight, particularly when angered by some opposing force or person.

The insurance claims representative must be mindful of this tendency of other people. Any person who believes that he or she is being cheated, insulted, or attacked will strike back in defense or for revenge. Since society frowns on assault and battery, or because the individual's adversary may be physically more powerful, he or she may use other methods of attack. A person may vent anger and aggression with vituperative language. In some situations an individual may decide to hire an attorney and institute legal action to punish his or her enemy.

Competition and aggression

Closely allied to anger and aggression is the tendency of men and women to want to compete. This is another fighting tendency of society. We often enjoy the struggle of the contest. We frequently argue for the fun of it. The popularity of athletic games, bridge, poker, and other parlor games clearly reveals this tendency. Even though we may not become angry with our antagonists, we enjoy pitting our strength and intelligence against an adversary.

An acquired motive. It has been argued that humans are instinctively competitive and that for that reason there is little that can be done to increase cooperation and reduce competition in human affairs. Psychologists disagree with this conclusion, however, and point out substantial scientific evidence against this viewpoint. Societies range all the way from extremely competitive to extremely cooperative in nature, and it is concluded that the competitive drive or urge is an acquired motive. Before civilization intruded upon their territory, the African Bushmen, for example, had eliminated all competition from their society. Constantly threatened by famine and drought, their survival depended upon a completely cooperative attitude with no quarreling or fighting of any kind. The few possessions owned by the Bushmen were constantly rotated among various members of the tribe to make certain that no one started an argument because of jealousy. By contrast, the American and Western culture, although cooperative in some respects, is highly competitive.

In associations with other people, the claims representative sometimes sees the competitive tendency assert itself. Some insureds and claimants handle their claims in a highly competitive manner. Of course, the element of competition probably is present in some degree in all insurance claims because of the adversary nature of the activity. There are some people, however, who enjoy the negotiation process, because it gives them an opportunity to pit their wit and intelligence against that of the claims person.

Competition and attorneys. Competition particularly is present in many cases where a claims representative is negotiating directly with a third-party claimant's attorney. Many attorneys revel in the negotiation process. It is an exciting game. They plunge into claims negotiation with a vigor and bravado which may terrorize, or at least unnerve, the new claims person. The latter may discover that certain attorneys appear to be particularly assertive, positive in their declarations, and difficult to deal with. It is for this reason that the new claims representative often approaches his or her early contacts with attorneys with serious reservations.

The claims trainee can approach these confrontations with attorneys more confidently by recognizing the fact that claimants' attorneys, as a general rule, are fierce competitors and practitioners of the rule that "the best defense is a strong offense." "Reason against passion!" Albert Einstein wrote. "The latter always wins if there is any struggle at all . . . ." One of the author's law professors, the late Dean William Leary of the University of Utah College of Law, admonished his students: "If you are weak on the law, argue the facts; if you are weak on the facts, argue the law; and if you are weak on both the facts and the law, shout like hell!" This frequently is what a third-party claimant's attorney will do, and such tactics sometimes succeed in winning a weak case before it ever goes to trial. This particularly is true when used on a new insurance claims person. The technique is well known to experienced claims representatives; they use the technique themselves. It can be a source of considerable anxiety and consternation for new claims representatives who are thrown immediately into negotiations with claimants' attorneys.

Some insurance claims representatives will never be involved in these types of negotiations; others will not become involved until they have accumulated considerable experience. Every claims representative, however, should recognize that attorneys, and especially those who specialize in automobile liability and general personal injury cases, work in a world of adversary relationships. Even the new lawyer has spent the past three or four years reading cases which highlight adversary relations in every conceivable situation. Unlike the ordinary layman, the practicing lawyer may be dealing constantly with opponents in legal problems. If he or she has the temperament to stay in those areas of legal practice where controversy and conflict rage, the attorney has learned to enjoy the challenge of competition, and he or she thrives on the day-to-day forensic discussions which mark the course of claims negotiations.

It is because of these factors that insurance claims negotiations between the attorney and the experienced claims person often take on a gamelike quality of give and take, in which each party pits his or her skill, reasoning, argument, bravado, and exaggeration against the adversary. It is a game of applied psychology that often is played to the hilt. In other cases, this atmosphere of open aggression and competition may be almost absent. It will be helpful to the new claims representative, nevertheless, to recognize that negotiations with some attorneys have this similarity to a fencing match, where the adversaries circle one another, feint, parry, and thrust. As the claims person gathers experience and develops skill in this competitive aspect of insurance claims handling, he or she will find that it affords some of the most challenging and delightful moments of the claims handling job.

Acquisition and saving

The sooner the insured or claimant hears the word "money" the easier communication becomes.

———Gordon L. Berger
GAB Business Services, Inc.

A strong basic motive is that of acquisition and saving. Human beings have pack rat tendencies. We all like to acquire things. This motive is a most fundamental tendency or urge which causes us to acquire the basic needs—food, shelter, and clothing. The motive, however, has developed further than that of satisfying basic needs. It is a highly sophisticated motive that involves acquiring things simply for the sake of acquisition. This more sophisticated type of acquisition is an acquired motive. This we will call the *money motive*.

Much acquisition is related to the motive of pride—self-respect and reputation. We acquire money and property in order to enhance our feelings of importance. The more money and property we possess, the more important we are. In our world, money and possessions bring power. As Heilbroner points out:

> Land, Labor, and Capital are not just functional parts of a mechanism but are categories of social existence that bring vast differences in life chances with them . . . private property is not merely a pragmatic arrangement devised for the facilitation of production, but a social institution that brings to some members of the community a style of life qualitatively different from that afforded to the rest. In a word, the operation of capitalism as a functional system results in a structure of wealth and income characteristic of capitalism as a system of privilege.[8]

---

[8] Robert L. Heilbroner, "The Future of Capitalism," *Commentary*, April 1966, p. 24.

The wealthy person can buy prestige, reputation, and the power to command deferential treatment because of acquisitions. Contemporary humans place great importance on acquisition because society places it in high esteem. In our society the rich man or woman is admired and envied; the poor are pitied. Whether a person is rich or poor depends upon acquisitions.

The acquisitive drive of our society is in marked contrast to the philosophy which prevailed among the nomadic tribes of the American Indians.[9] The American Indian felt a great sense of kinship with the land. "The land is our mother," said the traditions of the Iroquois and the Northwest Nez Perces. There was, however, no private real property ownership. The idea that land could be bought and sold was an alien concept. The Indians clung possessively to certain chattels, but lands nearly always were held in common. An individual might have the use of a farm plot, but at his death it reverted back to the community. The irreconcilable concepts of landownership which existed between the two cultures helped to bring about the great tragedy of the American Indian.

People in the United States begin to acquire things as soon as they receive their first infant toy. As children they save dolls, bottle caps, empty beer cans, and photographs of baseball and football heroes. As they grow older, they begin to acquire things of greater value— stamp, coin, and record collections, clothes, and automobiles. When they mature, they acquire furniture, a bank account, stocks and bonds, and a house. Regardless of the relative economic advantages or disadvantages of renting versus buying, homeownership carries with it the important motive of pride—prestige and self respect. Of paramount importance, of course, is the acquisition of money. Money makes all of these things possible.

As insurance claims representatives, we always should remember that we are dealing in dollars and cents terms. Money is something almost everyone understands, and the desire to acquire and to spend or to save money is a strong motive in the claims handling picture. How much importance a person places upon a dollar depends upon the strength of his or her money motive. The strength of this money

---

[9] See Stewart L. Udall, *The Quiet Crisis* (New York: Holt, Rinehart & Winston, 1963), p. 5.

motive, in turn, is determined largely by how much money and property we now have, the size of our income, and other factors.

Money needs.   As a general rule, it will be easier to settle with a person who needs money than with one who doesn't. A given dollar settlement figure offered to claimant number one for a personal injury will be less attractive to this claimant than the same dollar figure offered to claimant number two for an identical injury—if claimant number one has more money, more income, more property, a higher standard of living, and so forth, than claimant number two. As a consequence, an extra dollar or $100 or $500 is correspondingly of less value or utility to claimant number one than to claimant number two. In other words, an extra dollar to claimant number two looks bigger and is of more value to him or her than it is to claimant number one.

People in lower income brackets, with little or no financial reserves, have a higher propensity to spend than people of higher income and greater financial resources. That is, they will spend a greater percentage of their income than will people of greater financial resources and incomes. The lower their income, the closer their propensity to spend will tend to approach 100 percent. Thus, people at a marginal level of subsistence spend all of their money as soon as they receive it in order to provide themselves with the basic necessities.

On the other hand, people with higher incomes and greater financial resources have a higher propensity to *save* and consequently spend a smaller percentage of their income as it is received. As a general rule, the greater their income the more likely they are to save a correspondingly larger percentage of it.

This suggests the theory that $10 offered to a claimant living at subsistence level will have more attractiveness to him or her than will $10 offered to a person of considerably higher income with a high propensity to save. One must necessarily conclude that the human desire to provide subsistence (i.e., food, shelter, and clothing) is greater than the mere desire to save money.

The practical implication of this theorizing is that in those claims where there is considerable haggling and delay in settling, more money will be paid per average claim to settle the claims of claimants with considerable income and financial resources than will be paid to settle claims of claimants of meager circumstances for injuries of comparable severity. This conclusion is borne out further by the fact that people with financial resources and high incomes have greater "waiting power" than do people with limited or no resources and low incomes.

Waiting power. Because of greater financial need, a person of meager circumstances is more apt to need money immediately. With this person, possession of a small sum of money at once may be more appealing than a possibly larger amount in the future. This individual feels a time pressure because of immediate financial need. A claimant with greater financial resources, who is not pinched for money, has more "waiting power" and is less apt to be pressured by economic necessity into a settlement, while a claimant with less resources at his or her disposal may be in comparatively greater need of money. Accordingly, this claimant will be more likely to settle sooner and at a lower figure, because of that lack of "waiting power."

Aside from the basic inequity resulting from this phenomenon, experienced claims representatives contend that their experience bears out the conclusion that, as a general rule, it is easier and less expensive to settle claims with persons of meager circumstances than with persons of affluence. There is an impressive body of experimental findings in psychology that supports their contention. Scientific studies affirm that psychological needs and personal values can affect an individual's perception of economic values. In a classic study conducted in 1947, Jerome Bruner and Cecile Goodman determined that children tended to overestimate the size of coins as compared with discs of the same size. The tendency was much greater among children from low socioeconomic backgrounds—because of the greater value the coins have for the poor children. A given coin literally looks bigger to them. The relationship is shown in Figure 8–1. The conclusion reached in this study and in others is that the variable of social class mirrors a need for money that is reflected in perceptual reactions.[10]

Most authorities believe that overwhelming evidence favors the interpretation that value and need, working through perceptual mechanisms, are determinants of size judgments. In many insurance claims, therefore, there is excellent psychological reason for the claims representative to have the settlement check prominently displayed.

---

[10] Also see W. W. Lambert, R. L. Solomon, and P. D. Watson, "Reinforcement and Extinction as Factors in Size Estimation," *Journal of Experimental Psychology,* vol. 39 (1949), pp. 637–41.

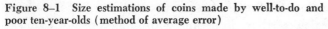

Figure 8–1   Size estimations of coins made by well-to-do and poor ten-year-olds (method of average error)

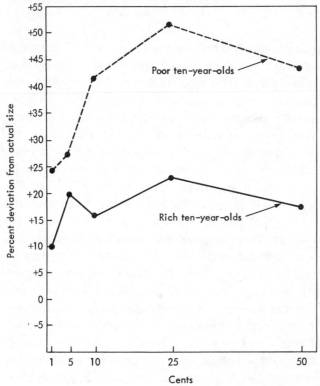

For example, we can clip the check to the outside of a file jacket or place it somewhere else within the vision of the person with whom we are negotiating a settlement. If a claimant can see the amount of the settlement check and can see his or her name as payee on the check, there is good psychological basis for believing that it will influence the claimant's judgment of whether to settle at the time.

Unfortunately, with so many bookkeeping functions computerized and centralized in home offices today, there appear to be fewer and fewer claims representatives who are given draft authority so that they can utilize this motivational technique. Without authority to issue a settlement check on the spot, the attraction of a settlement check displayed prominently in a file jacket is a lost opportunity. We have lost the chance to add a motivational assist to a claimant's wavering indecision as to whether to settle his or her claim in a timely fashion. The claims person may be required to make additional contacts to urge the claimant to settle. The lack of opportunity to utilize this motivational technique of capitalizing on a claimant's perceptual reaction to a displayed check robs the claims person of an important motivational tool.

The problem can be resolved in part if the insurer will issue a check prior to settlement so that the claims person can prominently display the check. Here, however, the home-office claims supervisor or examiner will issue the check for an exact amount, and this gives the field claims representative absolutely no flexibility to evaluate the immediate situation and to estimate the probable dollar figure that will produce a favorable response from the claimant.

Of course, this motivational technique has no value whatsoever in those claims negotiations conducted exclusively by telephone. Whatever the situation, however, because of the centralization of many functions at the home-office level, there appears to be a marked trend to give the insurance claims representative less and less flexibility in draft issuance. Indeed, claims representatives have complained to the author that the frequent delay of insurers in issuing a check after a settlement has been negotiated presents a major problem for the claims person in his or her relationships with the public.

The observation that money and the quantity thereof is judged differently by different socioeconomic groups suggests that there are some significant trait contrasts between two social groups. Pierre Martineau ascribes the following characteristics to members of middle-class and lower-status groups:

Middle class

1. Pointed to the future.
2. Viewpoint embraces a long expanse of time.
3. More urban identification.
4. Stresses rationality.
5. Has a well-structured sense of the universe.
6. Horizons vastly extended or not limited.
7. Greater sense of choice-making.
8. Self-confident, willing to take risks.
9. Abstract in thinking.
10. Sees himself or herself tied to national happenings.

Lower status

1. Pointed to the present and past.
2. Lives and thinks in a short expanse of time.
3. More rural in identification.
4. Essentially nonrational.
5. Vague and unclear structuring of the world.
6. Horizons sharply defined but limited.
7. Limited sense of choice-making.
8. Very much concerned with security and insecurity.
9. Concrete and perceptive in thinking.
10. World revolves around family and body.[11]

The reader can conclude from this list of traits that the middle-class claimant on a given claim is more prone: (1) to weigh alternatives, (2) to evaluate damages with relative rationality, (3) to delay making settlements until all of the facts are in, and (4) to assume the risks of litigation. The middle-class claimant's lower-status contemporary, on the other hand, is more apt: (1) to be concerned with present money needs, (2) to be less rational in evaluation of his or her damages, (3) to dislike the risks of litigation, (4) to want to dispose of problems immediately, and (5) to give less attention to potential alternatives.

Great variations exist in the opinions of experienced claims representatives as to the validity of the foregoing theory. This is because there is a dearth of meaningful scientific studies on the subject conducted specifically in the field of insurance claims handling. The theory, nevertheless, is soundly grounded in psychological theory and supported by empirical evidence. Its application to insurance claims handling is indisputable.

WANTS VERSUS NEEDS

Where passion leads or prudence points the way.
——Robert Lowth

Human beings tend to gravitate in the direction of activity that satisfies them. We all seek to satisfy needs and wants. Our motivation is directly tied to satisfying needs and wants. This in itself involves a

---

[11] Pierre Martineau, "Social Classes and Spending Behavior," *Journal of Marketing*, American Marketing Association, vol. 23 (October 1958).

process with many conflicts. Oftentimes a person finds that his or her needs and wants contradict one another. A man may need a new overcoat, but he wants a new hunting rifle. He tends to be motivated to buy the overcoat because of his recognition of a need. On the other hand, his wants push him toward a decision to buy the rifle. Needs and wants lend complexity to motivation and add to the frustration and conflict faced by people.

The claims representative often sees manifestations of needs-wants frustration and conflict. A person's decisions require resolving this conflict. Anything we can do to help resolve the conflict will increase our effectiveness in handling claims. A claimant, for example, may have both bodily injury liability and property damage liability claims against an insured. The claimant may want to wait further before settling the bodily injury claim against an insured. On the other hand, the claimant needs his or her automobile, and it is in the repair shop, already repaired, and with a storage bill running up. The claimant has no money to pay the bill, and the garage won't release the car until the bill is paid. The claimant wants to settle on the property damage claim so that the car will be released, but the claimant also wants to hold the personal injuries claim open.

It was standard operating procedure before the advent of unfair claims settlement practices legislation to insist that the entire claim of a claimant be settled at one time in a single settlement. Thus, in handling this type of claim, the claims representative would usually refuse to settle the property damage claim while the bodily injury claim was left open. Moreover, from a legal standpoint, it was sound practice. It certainly was justifiable in cases involving disputed liability.

Knowing that the claimant had a serious conflict between needs and wants, the claims person was in a position to influence the claimant to choose immediate needs over wants. The claimant often would settle the entire claim for both property damages and bodily injuries in order to release the automobile from the repair shop. In this case, the claimant was motivated to give priority to immediate needs instead of wants. This was a classic case of wants-needs conflict, and it worked to the advantage of the claims person and the insurer and to the detriment of the claimant. Whatever its merits, the psychology of this claims practice was sound in theory and in practice.

Even in those days when this claims handling technique was in common use, some insurance commissioners condemned the practice of deferring the settlement of property damage claims where there were outstanding bodily injury claims in cases of clear liability. From a public relations standpoint there has always been merit in advancement of funds to take care of a claimant's property damages, medical bills, and other expenses, without release, even though bodily injury claims are still pending. This practice has contributed substantially toward improving the image of the business. As claims representatives, however, we must become familiar with our own company's philosophy concerning the subject. We also should be familiar with the prevailing sentiment of the regulatory officials and have a thorough knowledge of applicable unfair claims practices legislation in the area.

It certainly is justifiable in cases involving disputed liability to withhold all payment until a complete release of all claims can be obtained. Even in cases involving clear liability, it would appear that there is little *legal* merit in making payment on a part of a single claim, leaving the remainder of the case open. In some cases, for example, making partial payment on a single liability claim might serve as an apparent admission of liability which would serve to encourage other claimants (such as injured passengers of the insured's vehicle whose claims are not justifiable under guest statutes) to press their claims against the insured. The law is changing rapidly in this area, however, and little justification remains to discourage partial payments on claims of clear liability.

This trend to provide a partial settlement is an example of the evolutionary nature of law, where the rules of conduct imposed by society constantly change to meet prevailing sentiment of what is or is not justice. A strictly legalistic approach to the subject of insurance claims handling, consequently, is fraught with danger, for law changes to meet the temper of the times.

Nevertheless, by understanding the principle it is apparent that the claims representative can cause other people to select between needs and wants. The claims person often is able to motivate people to act as he or she wants them to act in a given case.

The nature of needs and wants is complex. Some human needs may be well recognized by the individual—the needs for food, shelter, sex, sympathy, and social recognition. Other needs may go unrecognized. It might be said that most people need life insurance, but some people would argue the point. Wants, on the other hand, usually are well recognized. They are, moreover, more transitory in nature than needs.

Wants often arise on the spur of the moment. Advertisers recognize this when they appeal to impulse buying. Wants, likewise, may diminish in intensity quite rapidly and may disappear. Further, it is often true that a given need and a given want may be identical—there is no contradiction. If we need food, the chances are very good that we also want food. If an insured needs transportation, and he or she also wants a damaged automobile repaired, the insured's need and want both will be satisfied if the claims representative pays for the repair of the automobile.

In addition, frustration and conflict may occur because of competing needs and competing wants. A study is told of a donkey that starved to death because it was standing mid-way between two piles of hay and could not make up its mind which pile to choose. The donkey needed food and it wanted food. Its need and want were identical, but it was faced with the dilemma of having two competing need-wants. It needed and wanted to go to one pile, but, on the other hand, it needed and wanted to go to the other pile. We could resolve the conflict of the donkey by making one alternative less desirable than the other. We could explain to the donkey that one pile of hay is mildewed and bad tasting. We then would place several lumps of sugar on the other pile. The donkey would then resolve its conflict. We have motivated it to act in a certain manner.

The claims representative must approach the claims handling task in a similar manner. We must know enough about human behavior to recognize when frustration and conflict exist in other people. We must know the nature of that frustration and conflict and the factors that cause it. This the claims person is able to perceive through effective communication. Through communication the claims representative likewise is able to motivate others through persuasive techniques in order to help others to resolve their conflicts. This communication and motivation must be accomplished by the claims representative to carry out effectively the functions of the claims handling job.

FRUSTRATION AND CONFLICT

The insurance claims representative, because of the nature of the claims handling work, often deals with people who are experiencing frustration and conflict. *Frustration* is the thwarting of motivated behavior directed at a goal. When a highly motivated individual finds a barrier blocking the path toward accomplishment of a desirable goal, the person is said to be frustrated. An obstacle blocks the way. The obstacle is the result of one's environment or one's subjective characteristics. For example, a person may be frustrated because he or she has goals that are unattainable, because there is too great a discrepancy between the individual's level of aspiration and his or her level of performance.

If frustration is prolonged, emotional behavior may result. The blocking of purposive behavior produces annoyance and anxiety. The anxiety may result from actual frustration or from the threat of frustration. Purposive behavior is characterized by zest and eagerness. Behavior determined by frustration often is marked by resignation and by stereotyped and rigid behavior, unchanging in pattern. Under some conditions, however, frustration may result in increased effort in carrying out a task, to greater impetus, to a higher level of performance, and to problem-solving.

Under other conditions frustration is extremely disturbing. Sometimes frustration results from motivational conflict where a person is confronted with the need to choose between alternative courses of action. *Conflict* is a clash between two or more competing motives which results in the frustration of one of the motives. For instance, when a well-motivated person is compelled to choose between two goals, he or she is said to be in a state of conflict. Morgan discusses three kinds of motivational conflicts in his book,[12] and an examination of these will help to illustrate practical claims handling situations.

Conflicting attractions

Between two stools one sits on the ground.
　　　　　　——Rabelais

In the case of conflicting attractions, the individual is attracted by two positive goals which are incompatible with each other. The donkey starving to death between two piles of hay is a perfect example. It was unable to choose between the two alternatives.

This type of conflict often is present in insurance claims situations. A claims representative, for example, may have offered a third-party claimant $1,000 to settle her liability claim against an insured. The

---

[12] Morgan, *Introduction to Psychology*, pp. 250–53.

claimant would like to take the $1,000 now, but she reasons also that if she retains an attorney and sues the insured, she may end up with $5,000. Torn between the two alternatives, she experiences frustration.

An intelligent claims representative will recognize the conflict and will attempt to make one of the positive goals less attractive than the other. The claims person will point out to the claimant that "a bird in the hand is worth two in the bush." It is not improper to mention to the claimant that the latter will have to wait months before her case will be heard; that she will have to pay her attorney 33⅓ percent to 40 percent or more of her recovery; and that she may lose the case and not recover anything at all. If the claims person honestly spells out the claimant's alternatives, there is nothing unfair in this approach, because, quite frankly, the uncertainty, delay, inconvenience, worry, and expense of litigation of one's insurance claim is not a wise course of action in the vast majority of insurance claims. Claims are usually handled fairly, and the settlement figures offered by insurance companies are in most cases proper and adequate. If the claimant has strong feelings about the inadequacy of a proffered settlement, however, and is convinced that he or she is being treated wrongly by the claims representative, then recourse to an attorney and litigation may be the only course left in the case, unless the claims person is able to dispel the suspicion and doubts the claimant has about the claims person's offer of settlement.

It is here that the claims representative can examine, in an atmosphere of open communication, the alternatives available to the claimant. The claims person admits that some claimants who proceed with litigation frankly *do* end up getting more money for their claim than was offered by the claims person, even after they pay their attorney's fees. The claims person might explain:

> But that is why we attempt to be reasonable and fair in our claims settlements, because we attempt to avoid this type of situation where the case goes to litigation. We know that if we don't pay a fair amount on claims, and the case goes to court, we will have to end up paying the attorney's fee and court cost if we lose, and we have to pay the fees for our defense attorney, win or lose. That's why we try so hard to offer a fair settlement figure in all cases. Frankly, Mrs. Brown, we have found that in most cases where a claimant goes to court, we both lose. We don't like to litigate cases, and we have found that most claimants end up with less money after litigation than we offered them in the

first place. Some end up without *any* money and they all have the worry, inconvenience, uncertainty, delay, and expense of a lawsuit. But, it's your decision to make, Mrs. Brown. I have made the highest offer I can make, and I know it is a fair and reasonable amount for your claim. I honestly believe it would be in your best interest to accept it. We can settle your claim without further delay and worry for you, and you would have your money now, instead of months from now when your case finally reaches the courts. What do you think about it, Mrs. Brown?"

Conflicting repulsions

The second type of conflict, conflicting repulsions, involves the individual in a situation where he or she must choose between two unattractive or undesirable alternatives. A man who has witnessed an accident may be involved in such a conflict. He may have been a passenger of a third-party claimant's vehicle. He may believe that his friend, the claimant, was at fault for the accident. He reasons that if he tells the truth, his friend, the claimant, will be unable to collect on his claim and, further, will dislike the witness for testifying against him.

On the other hand, if the witness lies, his conscience will bother him. As a consequence, he may vacillate in his decision of what to do. The thought of testifying against his friend makes him consider strongly the telling of a lie. The more he thinks about it, the more his conscience disturbs him, leading him to consider strongly the telling of the truth. Rather than making a choice between the two unattractive or undesirable alternatives, the witness may react through *regression*. Regression is the act of retreating to primitive forms of behavior, frequently encountered in children and adults faced with frustration. Rather than making a choice between the two unattractive or undesirable alternatives, the witness may flare up in anger at the claims representative and completely refuse to cooperate with the claims person.

By recognizing the alternatives and making one appear less undesirable than the other, the claims representative may help the witness eliminate conflict. For example, we might appeal to the witness's motive of pride. We also might appeal to the witness's fear motive by pointing out that he may be required to appear in court as a witness, thereby exposing him to a possible perjury charge if he fails to tell the truth.

Repulsion-attraction conflict

Repulsion-attraction conflict perhaps is the most important of the three types of conflicts, because it is the most difficult to resolve. In this conflict, a person is both repelled and attracted by the same goal object. The claims representative who wishes to approach a supervisor for a raise is repelled by the fact that it will take some courage to perform the act. In addition, there is the likelihood that the request for a raise will be turned down, and along with the refusal, the supervisor might tell the claims person that he or she has not been too satisfied with the claims person's work.

On the other hand, the claims representative is attracted by the possibility that he or she will be given a raise, and maybe the supervisor will praise the quality of the claims representative's work. If both the positive and negative aspects of the situation have considerable strength, and if the individual is equally motivated to both forms of stimulation, the claims person vacillates in making a decision to act until he or she has generated a great deal of anxiety.

When anxiety reaches a high level, anything that can serve to swing the balance to one alternative or the other can do much to produce a decision on the part of the anxious party. A claims representative who is able to detect the presence of anxiety in a claimant where settlement negotiations are in progress, will do well to attempt to discover and analyze the alternatives which confront the claimant. Then, if we can figuratively place a few lumps of sugar on one pile of hay or the other, as we did in the donkey case, we may experience considerable success in obtaining the desired response from the claimant and accomplish the desired objective, the settlement of the claim and another closed claim file.

Situational reactions—traumatic neuroses

A good application of "green poultice" is the best cure known for many injuries.[13]

---

[13] *Miller* v. *U.S. Fidelity & Guaranty Company*, 99 So. 2d 511 (La. App. 1957).

Repulsion-attraction conflict sometimes manifests itself in mental disorders of varying intensity. There are a number of terms utilized to describe a mental disorder that an individual may develop from an injury caused by another person. The trauma results from an unexpected and overwhelmingly disruptive stimulus, and the stimulus need not be a major one. Two people react differently to the same stimulus, with one person greatly disturbed, and the other, hardly affected. Some psychiatrists commonly call the disorder *traumatic neurosis* and believe it is a true neurosis caused by a specific event or psychic insult, such as an accident. Most psychiatrists, however, consider it indistinguishable from the common neuroses, such as anxiety, or believe it is a complex of symptoms, rather than a neurosis. It goes by many names, depending upon the attitude of each person who does the labeling—*accident neurosis, triggered neurosis, hysterical paralysis, compensation neurosis, unconscious malingering,* and so forth.[14] The term, *traumatic neurosis,* is the wartime successor to the old term *shell shock.*

Even war-caused neuroses, however, go by different names. The Veterans Administration and the American Psychiatric Association have officially recognized a neurosis called *posttraumatic stress disorder* (PTSD); the person experiences mental flashbacks of combat experiences and has feelings of guilt and helplessness. Peacetime stress situations—such as divorce or loss of job—reportedly cause the veteran to respond with combat instincts, and he might commit crimes in the process. Attorneys have used the existence of the posttraumatic stress disorder in their clients as a defense to seek acquittals or reduced sentences in a sizable number of cases.[15]

Whatever we call it, or whatever our attitude may be regarding its authenticity, the accident or event from which it emanates causes emotional responses on the part of the injured person. The injury producing the emotional response usually is actual physical injury. The injury, however, may be unaccompanied by objective evidence of actual physical injury.

These traumatic neuroses, or situational reactions, occur frequently in insurance claims handling situations—in tort claims arising out of accidents (particularly automobile accidents); workers' compensation

---

[14] Ralph Slovenko, *Psychiatry and Law* (Boston: Little, Brown, 1973), p. 294.

[15] "Pleading PTSD," *Time,* May 26, 1980, p. 59; also see "The Troubled Vietnam Vet," *Newsweek,* March 30, 1981, pp. 24 and 29.

claims for disability; and various types of claims for benefits under disability and health insurance policies. The mental responses to accident and injury complicate the claims handling situation, particularly where it is alleged that the mental distress has aggravated the physical condition and prolonged recovery, or where the mental disorder itself is disabling. The problem is one of distinguishing between a case of true mental disability and one of malingering.

Psychiatrists readily admit the difficulty and complexity of assessing these types of cases where the claimant displays the symptoms characteristic of the traumatic neuroses. Detection of malingering has become increasingly difficult as people become more sophisticated in psychology. It presents a difficult problem in insurance claims handling. The emotional reactions to the trauma of accidents complicates the claims handling situation and must be handled skillfully and imaginatively by the claims person.

The claims representative's best defense against a case of suspected malingering is a thorough and perceptive investigation, for it is here that an investigator has a better opportunity to distinguish between genuine mental distress and malingering on the part of another person. According to Slovenko:

> Often the information must come from the spouse or other family member, since the person with the disability labeled "traumatic neurosis" is often verbally unproductive, unimaginative, and a poor observer of his own feelings and behavior.[16]

Common symptoms found in traumatic neurosis are anxiety, blackouts, changes in personality patterns, changes in sleeping patterns, decrease in appetite, decrease in sexual drive, depression, dizziness, exaggerated ideas and behavior, fatigue, fearfulness, headaches, hysteria, insomnia, irritability, nightmares or repetitive dreams of the accident, palpitations, startle reactions, excessive sweating, and so on.[17] A person who is malingering usually displays a more physical set of symptoms, such as paralysis of a limb or a marked limp. He or she will often display a "benign and even good-humored lack of concern . . . toward his (her) difficulty." Even here, writers disagree whether the

---

16 Slovenko, *Psychiatry and Law*, p. 301.

17 E. D. Luby, "Traumatic Neurosis and the Jury," *Michigan State Bar Journal* 39 (December 1960), p. 10; H. C. Modlin, "The Post-Accident Anxiety Syndrome; Psychological Aspects," *American Journal of Psychiatry* 123 (1967), p. 1008.

neurosis is real, as in the case of hysteria ("la belle indifference"), or is evidence of malingering.[18]

The malingerer usually doesn't want to submit to a medical examination. Further, the alleged injury won't interfere with the malingerer's social life if he or she believes the injury is unrelated to the social activities or if the activities are away from public view. Thus, covert surveillance of the individual is frequently helpful in ferreting out the insurance fraud. The author once sat with binoculars in his automobile one half block from a house, watching a workers' compensation claimant with an alleged back injury vigorously engaged in gardening in his back yard.

Experienced industrial physicians frequently take sharp issue with the opinions of neurologists and psychiatrists and contend that malingering is fairly common in industrial accidents. Cases in which there is no objective evidence of injury sometimes involve alleged blindness, deafness, back injury, and a number of claimed nerve impairments. Variously labeled "hysterical blindness," "nervous breakdown," and so on, blatant cases of malingering have been observed when surveillance has been utilized.[19]

A bizarre case occurred when a 62-year-old man, Edwin Robinson, was struck by lightning on June 4, 1980. Previously deaf and blind for nine years, Robinson claimed that the lightning bolt restored his sight and hearing, and hair began to grow on his bald head. Dr. George Garcia of the Harvard Medical School and president-elect of the American Ophthalmological Society, stated that it was impossible for the lightning to have such an effect. Discounting Robinson's previous condition as traumatic neurosis, Garcia observed, "The hysterically blind get better when it is no longer in their best interest to be blind." He remarked that Robinson belonged to a group of people that see "whether they think so or not."[20] The insurance claims handling implications of similar cases is quite clear and presents difficult problems for claims representatives.

"Whiplash" injuries to the neck have been a common problem for insurance claims representatives and defense counsel. Psychoneurotic

---

[18] See Roland P. Mackay, "Post-Traumatic Neuroses," *Adjusters Reference Guide* (Louisville, Ky.: Insurance Field Company, 1981), misc. 16.

[19] Walter Z. Baro, "Malingering after Industrial Injuries," *Adjusters Reference Guide*, misc. 17.

[20] "Physicians Reject Lightning Cure," *Omaha World Herald*, July 15, 1980, p. 5.

symptoms are prevalent in abundance, although initial evidence of injury seems to be trivial or minor. Indeed, many times, the patient will remark, "I didn't think I was hurt," or "I thought nothing of it." Symptoms usually follow a pattern. At the time of accident, the person may be dazed or bewildered. A few minutes to several hours later, there will be headaches and nervousness, with neck soreness and tenderness. Accompanying these symptoms, profound emotional reactions appear, such as nervousness, instability, insomnia, and sweating of the hands. These may grow progressively worse over a period of weeks.

It is clear from the research done on whiplash cases that the symptoms often do not respond well to treatment and at times actually get worse, but the settlement of the insurance and legal claims in many of the cases profoundly improves the person's condition. Nevertheless, this is not always the case, and irrespective of the suspicion we may have of the whiplash injury, it is generally recognized as a profound post-traumatic neurosis resulting from a curious mixture of physical injury, apprehension, nervous tension, and anxiety.[21]

In the case of ulcers, it is not what you eat, but "what is eating you" that causes the problem. The situation is frequently similar with whiplash and other situations. Overload can break a leg, or it can overwhelm the central nervous system. The damage is genuine in both cases. We have not yet been able to X-ray a headache, and the medical assurance that "there is no objective evidence of injury" is no basis for smugness on the part of the claims person who is attempting to evaluate a claimant's damages. Psychosomatic injury and illness account for a majority of the hospitalizations in the nation, and traumatic neurosis is receiving increased attention in the medical literature. Litigation demanding damages for mental distress in bodily injury cases has been with us for many years and shows no sign of abating.

SUMMARY

There is a direct connection between a person's motives and his or her response to a set of circumstances or to a situation. A person's activity or lack of activity is the result of personal motives, urges, wishes, or desires. The interplay of motives, the conflict which often

---

[21] Nicholas Gotten, "Survey of 100 Cases of Whiplash Injury After Settlement of Injury," *Adjusters Reference Guide*, Misc. 18.

occurs, and the frustration experienced by a claimant may produce seemingly strange behavior.

Apparent irrational behavior, however, can be explained if we understand the motive forces that cause a person to act as he or she acts. Irregular behavior does not result from accident but is dependent upon mental causes. These causes, or motives, are complex and of great variety. The physiological or biogenic motives are well known, because they impel us to seek food, water, shelter, sleep, and sex. Other motives which are less well-known are the emotional motives and the social motives. Among these motives are urges and drives which are dominant in the everyday affairs of human beings.

Humans, for example, are concerned with society's reaction to various manifestations of behavior. Thus, one of the most powerful forces which mold our behavior is that of pride—our reputation and our feeling of self-respect. Our efforts almost always are directed toward activities that will result in recognition, commendation, and acceptance by other people.

We also are driven by other motives. Fear and the feeling of tension and discomfort called *anxiety* influence our reactions to life situations. Anger and aggression cause us to react to others with hostile behavior patterns. Aggression also manifests itself in human relations in our desire to compete. The motive of anger in such relations may be entirely absent. Finally, a strong basic motive of contemporary human beings is that of acquisition and saving. Men and women like to acquire things.

A claimant may blame an insured for an automobile accident which was caused by the obvious negligence of the claimant's wife. Not daring to blame his wife for the accident, the husband strikes out with displaced aggression against the insured. The husband's motive of anger has been stimulated, and he responds with aggression. At the same time, however, his motive of fear has been stimulated. Furthermore, his motive of acquisition and saving money has been stimulated; he sees a possibility of losing something of value. The interaction of these stimulated motives results in what appears to be irrational behavior.

Sometimes two motives will act with equal power upon an individual. This person wants to do one thing, but at the same time, he or she wishes to do a second thing. Frustration and conflict result when the individual realizes that he or she cannot respond to both motivations at once.

It is most important that the insurance claims representative learn about motives and their relation to human behavior. We must study the subject of motivation—the discipline which seeks out all of the determinants of human activity. With a knowledge of motivation and an understanding of motives as determinants of behavior, the claims representative can seek out the true motives for what appears to be irrational behavior. This should help us to accomplish the claims handling functions. Equally important, an understanding of motivation will better equip us to understand ourselves. Our own motives, oriented toward goal-fulfillment or conflicting with one another in a state of frustration, can be analyzed and directed toward productive and satisfying activity.

9

Motivation principles
and claims handling techniques

Motivation and communication are closely allied. Communication must be effective before we can motivate other people to respond in a desired manner. Techniques of motivation also contribute to the process of communication. This mutual interdependence aids us in our efforts to influence other people.

Special techniques can be used to bring about better communication. Better communication, in turn, will convey meaning more effectively and stimulate other people to act favorably. Good communication creates stronger stimuli which are more apt to produce stronger stimulus-response connections. People, consequently, are apt to respond more quickly and favorably to the stimulus, making them more amenable to influence. The claims representative, of course, must acquire sufficient knowledge and skill to be able to produce positive responses in other people. The claims person must guard against producing strong, negative responses. The techniques for accomplishing this objective will be explored in the pages that follow.

The techniques which will be explained are nothing more than specific applications of the motivation principles previously discussed. They are intended to be more suggestive than prescriptive. No pretense is made or implied that this discussion of claims handling techniques presents the final, complete list of insurance claims handling skills and techniques. The behavioral science of psychology and its application to human relations is constantly unveiling new practical applications. In addition, many effective applications of the known basic principles undoubtedly await further discovery. Further, it should be understood that no approach is infallible. None of these procedures will work every time. They may, however, give the claims representative some good ideas for practical application in the every-day world of insurance claims handling and the many problems that arise in this vital area of human endeavor.

OBTAINING FAVORABLE BEHAVIOR

It was observed earlier in this book that certain basic stimuli cause certain general behavior traits. Personal contact, for instance, may cause a person to respond with consideration, or it may cause the person to act in a negative and highly assertive manner. If a young man, for example, places his arm around a young lady, with whom he is not acquainted, on a street corner (in a good neighborhood), there is a possibility that she may respond in a positive manner. It is much more likely, however, that she will pull away from him and scream for help. The young man soon learns that technique is all-important. He first must obtain her confidence before introducing his own assertive behavior. He learns that he must introduce himself and engage in small talk. Over a period of time, he may acquire the lady's confidence. In this manner, he will be able to eliminate her potential negative response to his overtures which a premature encounter might elicit. He establishes a foundation of rapport and clears the way for assertive behavior. He then can approach the lady at a meeting place on the same street corner, place his arm around her, give her a little hug, and then walk hand in hand with her, leading her down the street to the nearest theater or restaurant and ultimately down the aisle.

In dealing with the public, the claims representative, likewise, should discourage and eliminate negative assertive behavior in others. Since an unresponsive or assertive individual can confound us with many difficulties in our attempts to perform the claims handling functions, we, like the young man in the example, first must establish rapport before taking an insured or a claimant by the hand and leading the latter down the aisle to the successful conclusion of a claim settlement.

It is difficult to communicate with a hostile witness or an unfriendly claimant, let alone motivate such a person to act in a desired manner when this individual is asserting himself or herself by dominant and negative behavior. A person who is hostile to the claims representative possesses a psychological block to communication. This person is an unsympathetic listener. The individual's hostility causes him or her to be unreceptive to the claims person's attempts to negotiate a settlement. The hostile witness or claimant may seek to dominate a conversation by expressing personal opinions to the exclusion of other viewpoints. It is virtually impossible to arrive at a mutual agreement with a person in this frame of mind. Assertive behavior of others prevents the claims representative from communicating information and from concluding settlement negotiations. Such behavior also prevents us from motivating and influencing others so that we can conduct successful insurance investigations.

A claims representative might handle a case, for example, where preliminary information indicates that liability probably should be disputed. If no attorney represents the third party, we might approach the claimant and attempt to obtain a statement. If we can tie down the facts immediately in evidential form, it is much more possible to forestall any further activity on the claim of the third party

In an actual case a claims person was confronted by a situation that required imaginative and sensitive handling, as well as the ability to withstand the onslaught of a partially hostile interviewing environment. The claims representative called at the home of a man and wife. The husband, the claimant, had been seriously injured on the insured's premises, and an "on premises" liability claim was pending. The insured believed that the accident and resultant injury were the results of careless conduct on the part of the claimant. It was important for the claims representative to secure a statement from the claimant.

The claimant responded with *consideration* and friendliness, willing to tell the claims representative all of the facts about the accident which gave rise to the insurance claim. His wife, however, responded with hostility and *assertive behavior.* "Don't talk to him, honey," she instructed her husband. Turning to the claims person, she asked, "Why don't you leave? We don't want to talk to you."

The claims representative responded with a "Jack Webb-ism,"[1] "I'm

---

[1] Jack Webb was an investigative police detective in an early television series called "Dragnet."

just trying to get the facts, Ma'am," explaining to the wife that "a routine investigation" is always necessary in cases such as this so that a report can be sent to the company, thus making it possible for the claims person to give the claimant a prompt decision on his claim.

Meanwhile, the claims person continued to question the husband. If the consideration of the husband won out over the assertiveness of the wife, the claims representative would get a statement of the facts. It is important in such a case that the claims representative establish and maintain the confidence of the claimant and at the same time attempt to quiet the hostility and reduce the assertive behavior of any third party present. Fortunately, in this case the claims man got his statement. Because of disputed liability and a belief that the man's claimed damages were excessive, the claim resulted in litigation, and the statement proved to be invaluable in the case.

In addition to obtaining consideration and reducing assertiveness in a claimant, the claims representative will want the claimant to understand the claims handling process and the relative rights, duties, and responsibilities of the parties involved, as contemplated by the insurance contract. This comprehension is necessary to obtain agreement and also to convey the appearance of proper and fair dealing. *Comprehension* itself is a form of human behavior or response which has been defined in Chapter 2 as the tendency to understand situations and problems quickly and effectively so that a person recognizes that a certain solution is most feasible under a given set of circumstances.

In our contact with a claimant, we should communicate enough information to facilitate comprehension while playing upon the motives of the claimant to induce the claimant to reach a definite solution —that solution suggested by us. This, in essence, is the same function performed by any salesperson—inducing people to act in a manner satisfactory to the salesperson. If the complex problem of another person, however, causes the person to use his or her own imagination to solve the problem, rather than using information communicated by a claims person, the handling of the claim may be prolonged.

Imagination is defined as the formation of new images or ideas which are not perceived by the senses. Through imagination new and alternative solutions to problems are produced. These solutions may be entirely unrealistic and unworkable, but they nevertheless may appear in abundance unless the claims person assumes the dominant role in facilitating comprehension in the claimant, motivating

the claimant to accept the solution proposed by the claims representative. An illustration may prove helpful here. A claimant, Mr. Smith,
may decide that he will not settle for the amount of the estimate of
damages on his wrecked automobile. He demands a higher amount.
The claims person refuses to pay more than the estimate, explaining
that the claimant's measure of damages is that amount.

The claimant becomes angry, starts to leave the insurance office,
and threatens to sue. The claimant's complex problem is solved quickly
and effectively when the claims representative introduces assertive
behavior that shocks the claimant and helps him to obtain comprehension. The claims person simply states: "If you sue, our attorney will
defend our insured. All we need do is bring in the estimator who
prepared the estimate of damages. He will tell the judge that the car
can be repaired for the amount I offered you, and this will establish
the measure of damages. We will admit liability and tender the
amount of the estimate, and you will end up paying your own
attorney's fees and our court costs. Now I ask you, as a reasonable
man, don't you think it is in your best interests to accept my offer?"
Weighing the disadvantages of his threatened course of action in his
mind, the claimant may well respond with comprehension and agree
to settle for the amount of the estimate.

The foregoing is an exceptional case where the peaceable approach to communication and motivation does not help. An adversary approach produces better results in this situation. It has been
said, however, that "you can catch more flies with honey than with
vinegar." This ordinarily is true in insurance claims handling. We,
therefore, will find it helpful in most cases to avoid the adversary
relationship. We should approach other people with friendliness and
warmth. The best atmosphere for developing compatible relations
with other people is one in which the claims representative obtains
the confidence of other people. A discussion of these concepts follows.

A two-sided conflict

People usually have some preconceived notions about the insurance claims representative. A claimant or an insured already is
experiencing anxiety because of the loss which he or she has suffered.
This person's notions about the claims representative may serve to intensify that anxiety because of the conflict which is inherent in the

personal contact with the claims person. The conflict, essentially, is this: on the one hand, the claims representative is seen as the person who can solve the loss problems of the insured or claimant. On the other hand, however, the claims representative also may be perceived as a hard-hearted, sharp dealer bent on paying only a bare minimum.

Many people contacted by the claims person will experience this conflict. An insured or a claimant knows that the claims representative has the means to remove the anxiety which the insured or claimant is experiencing because of monetary loss. We can pay their claim. They, nevertheless, also are suffering anxiety because they often doubt that they will be treated fairly in the settlement negotiations. Such a conception may develop even before we appear on the scene. A large segment of the public has a preconceived notion about insurance companies and claims people. This preconception can create a major stumbling block to successful negotiations.

Obtaining another's confidence

We must establish a state of harmonious, friendly understanding between ourselves and other people. This is highly important for two reasons. First, it clears the air for communication by eliminating potential obstructions or distortions to the communication process. Second, when the climate or atmosphere is favorable for communication, it obviously makes it easier for the claims person to motivate another person to respond favorably. It is helpful, therefore, for us to take certain positive steps to eliminate or reduce appreciably the distrust which other people may possess initially.

As already mentioned, we must approach others with the realization that they often view the claims representative as an opponent. Our conduct will either reinforce another person's feeling of distrust and increase the inherent hostility of that person or it will allay his or her fears and establish the climate of confidence which is essential for insurance claims negotiations.

A relaxed air of courtesy.   A sincere, relaxed air of courtesy will help to put other people at ease. The claims person, accordingly, should greet others with a warm smile. An ancient Chinese proverb reads, "A man without a smiling face must not open a shop." It seems to be true in any job entailing public contact that doors open for a person who displays a genuine, warm smile. Dale Carnegie in his famous book has stated, ". . . a man with a smile is always welcome."[2]

After the greeting we should concentrate on winning the other person's confidence. Following a warm greeting we might launch directly into a discussion of a claimant's problems. The circumstances, however, may dictate that we delay the discussion and talk briefly about extraneous matters. For example, suppose we wish to obtain a statement from a claimant, and if the situation warrants, consummate a settlement. If we arrive at the claimant's home and discover the claimant working in his tool shed, it would be impractical to launch immediately into a discussion of the claim. Rather, as the claims representative, we should suggest that the conversation or interview be held in a place where there will be no distractions. (Remember that communication is most effective when it is free from psychological and physical distortion). Noise from the operation of an electric drill in the tool shed introduces physical distortion. A psychological distortion also may be present if the claimant's attention is distracted by the activities of operating the drill.

While the claimant is terminating his activity in the tool shed, we are accomplishing two important things. One, we are establishing a climate of confidence, and two, we are preparing the stage for effective communication. We should display consideration at this time, introducing no assertive behavior. The claimant should be encouraged to talk about those things which interest him—his hobby in the tool shed, his prize roses, or his other interests. It is in similar situations that the claims representative must be an astute and skilled observer in order to determine the interests of the claimant, regardless of the claimant's age, sex, or circumstances. A sincere demonstration of consideration is possible if the claims person can empathize with others, and this requires an attitude of courtesy and genuine interest in other people.

The compliment.   The claims representative can make excellent use of the compliment. William James once said, "The deepest principle in human nature is the craving to be appreciated." This is

---

2 Dale Carnegie, *How to Win Friends and Influence People* (New York: Pocket Books, 1936), p. 74.

nothing more than a restatement of the motivational principle that we all crave ego-recognition. We are motivated by appeals to our pride—our self-respect and our reputation. Consequently, a spontaneous, sincere compliment, delivered in an atmosphere of genuine interest, can accomplish much in establishing a climate conducive to effective communication and negotiation. Spontaneity and sincerity are vital, for they ease the way for effective complimenting and help ensure success of the claims person's efforts. Without these two traits, a person must be a highly effective actor, skilled in the arts of insincere flattery and deceit. The fact that sincerity and spontaneity ease the task of the claims representative further suggests that our mental attitude toward others indeed is important.

Everyone enjoys a well-placed compliment, for everyone needs ego-recognition. By appealing to that ego recognition, the compliment can do much to obtain the necessary confidence of another person. Considerate behavior lowers the guard of claimants and witnesses and makes them more amenable to subsequent assertive action in the form of persuasive appeals. The compliment is part of the process of anesthetizing the "patient's" potential negative assertive behavior so that the "operation" of claims handling can be performed painlessly and successfully.

The use of compliments in insurance claims handling, obviously, must be well placed and appropriately and discreetly used. Effusiveness is out of place. People must not be overcomplimented. Economists would explain that the principle of diminishing marginal utility sets in. Each of the succeeding units of input results in correspondingly smaller appreciation or output. Ultimately, the addition of an extra unit of input produces negative results—a decrease in output. The insurance claims representative, accordingly, is admonished that he or she must not overuse compliments.

The proper use of compliments does not contemplate taking advantage of another person, nor does it involve the use of deceit. The compliment and all other forms of considerate behavior are legitimately used only to establish a friendly and warm atmosphere between two people. It is used to establish the atmosphere for communication. It is this proper atmosphere for communication which is beneficial to the claims representative and to insureds and claimants alike. Each has the opportunity to present his or her viewpoint in the most advantageous light. In no sense does it involve taking advantage of other people. By talking in terms of a claimant's interests and by the judicious use of the compliment, we can do much to establish a climate of confidence before we and the claimant finally sit down and discuss the serious business at hand.

Displaying consideration

The claims representative usually should refrain from any pronounced assertive action early in the first meeting. If he or she immediately begins to introduce assertive behavior, the other person may react negatively. A case will help to explain this point. An insured had a canopy which extended out from the exterior walls of his drive-in cafe. Although there was insufficient clearance, someone drove a truck under the canopy, damaging it. The damage was covered under the extended coverage of the insured's fire policy. The claims representative hurried to the store, inspected the damage, filled in a Notice of Claim form for the insured, told the insured that she would send over a couple of contractors to bid on repairs, and quickly departed.

She sincerely believed that she had gone about the job in a completely efficient manner. Imagine her surprise when the agent for the insured later complained to her that the insured was insulted by the summary handling of his claim. When the claims representative reviewed her actions on the claim, she concluded that she *had* in fact made no effort to establish rapport with the insured. The thought had not even occurred to her that it was particularly necessary. The agent was present at the time and, in his usual loquacious manner, had dominated the conversation. The claims representative confined her conversation with the insured to business at hand.

The claims representative in this case should have chatted briefly with the insured about his business, the state of the weather, or asked him how he spent his holidays. After establishing rapport, she could then have launched into assertive behavior—handling the details of the claim. Some conversation, unrelated to the claim, usually is helpful in establishing a friendly atmosphere even when handling claims of insureds. It can be extremely important in dealing with third-party claimants. Whether he or she is dealing with insureds or with third-party claimants, the claims representative, by displaying consideration, can do much to create a friendly atmosphere for claims handling.

Some simple suggestions will aid the claims person to display consideration. These suggestions deal with eye contact, walking, and talking about and handling objects. These are highly important in insurance claims handling, and although the experienced claims representative may do most of these things automatically, the new claims person may make costly mistakes before he or she begins to practice these simple principles.

Eye contact.   The subject of eye contact is most important. Eye movement, the reader will recall, is one of the nonverbal symbols of meaning discussed in an earlier chapter. Whether we like it or not, the movement of the eyes carries meaning to another person. An unsteady eye contact or frequent avoidance of eye contact interferes with attempts to communicate and to motivate. We often distrust or have little confidence in people who will not look us in the eye. To be most effective, we should utilize a steady eye contact, as long as we don't try to "stare down" another person.

The reader may recall some instance where lack of eye contact destroyed rapport. The story is told of a company president who walked up to the desk of a junior executive. The latter, thinking that the new arrival was *only* a customer, continued writing and without looking up, inquired, "May I help you?" "Yes," replied the president, "you can damned well look at me when you address me."

Walking.   A person's posture and demeanor when walking are extremely important in conveying an impression to others. The way we carry ourselves; the self-confidence that we project; and the alert purposiveness of our walking style and characteristics all convey important clues to what we are as persons. Gerard I. Nierenberg, author of *The Art of Negotiating*, contends that the walking features of an individual give us a clear insight into the character as well as the current mood of a person. For example, an adult who walks rapidly, with arms swinging freely, tends to be goal-oriented, assertive, and aggressive in pursuing objectives. On the other hand, one who habitually walks with hands in pockets, even during warm weather, tends to be secretive, critical, and inconsiderate of others. A self-satisfied, pompous person may walk with chin raised, arms swinging in exaggerated manner, with a deliberate, measured stride.

People signal their moods by pace, length of stride, and posture. Shakespeare described the young "cock-of-the-walk" in *Troilus and Cressida,* "a strutting player who's conceit lies in his hamstring." A dejected or depressed person walks with head down, in listless and inattentive fashion. Men and women who are aware that they are attracting admiring attention adopt a lilt to their steps, a springy, buoyant movement that projects vibrancy and effervescence. The positive reinforcement received from the approving attention generated from the personal walking style is ego-building and salutary to a person's sense of self-being and self-worth.

Experts in *kinesics*—the study of communication through body motion—stress the vital communication role played by nonverbal communication, and walking expresses definite message signals to other people. The claims representative must convey appropriate walking messages to adjust to each situation. If the claims person is approaching an obviously busy insured in the latter's place of business, the approach gait should be somewhat accelerated, business-like, and must project an image of promptness in deference to the time pressures of the situation. A claims representative who enters the home of the claimant who has just experienced a grievous loss of a loved one in an automobile accident involving an insured must use a different approach gait, not unlike one that would be used to console a surviving family member at a friend's funeral.

Approaching other people is a matter that requires tact and consideration in any circumstances. In the claims handling situation, particularly, it requires great care. Proximity to others, for example, must be measured according to the circumstances. When the claims representative meets another person, he or she should walk toward the other person and halt at arm's length. In halting at arm's length, the claims person eliminates any element of threat or discomfort that arises when someone is too near. People often enjoy close proximity with their friends or relatives, but close contact is out of place with strangers. It is uncomfortable to many people to have a stranger too near.

Movement, however, can promote a climate of respect and goodwill. Under some circumstances, a person's movement toward others demonstrates deference and respect. For example, it is bad psychology for an automobile driver who has violated a traffic law to sit in the automobile and await the approach of a police officer. The police officer must move toward the driver with the disagreeable task of informing the motorist that he or she has just run a stop sign. In addition, the police officer is confronted with physical danger when approaching the motorist's vehicle. Police officers have been killed in such situations when irate motorists or fugitive felons have whipped out firearms and shot the approaching officer. It is good psychology for the driver to get out of the car, walk directly to the police car, and exclaim, "Golly, I'm sorry, officer! I just didn't see that stop sign." This technique has worked well in the experience of many people. It shows a courtesy and complaisant regard for the police officer and creates a good impression.

If in the course of everyday work the claims representative is able to take a few extra steps to greet another person, he or she may find that such movement reaps dividends in establishing goodwill. In addition, the claims representative will find that movement will help in maintaining that goodwill and the friendship and confidence of other people. If, for example, another person is about to leave the claims representative's office, the claims person should walk with the other person to the door or for some little distance. Such movement shows respect and eliminates the abrupt break and strained feelings which may occur when a conversation is ended and a back is turned immediately.

Over-familiarity—laws of proxemics. The claims representative must always observe the laws of *proxemics*—everyone has a "space bubble" that must not be violated. The bubble—the inviolate buffer space that exists between two individuals—may appear to be entirely absent in the case of lovers, and this is surely the case in part of that relationship. However, the bubble is there part of the time, even with lovers, although the inviolate space of each of them may be small most of the time. The size of the bubble varies according to the closeness of the relationship. Personal contact—touching, embracing, kissing—may be acceptable occasionally between relatives and friends, depending upon the relationship. Between strangers, however, a sizeable inviolate space bubble usually exists, and undue familiarity may be offensive. The law considers unauthorized familiarity—encroachment or violation of another person's space bubble—to be assault and battery, a criminal act.

Some salespersons, goaded on by archaic "rah-rah" sales pep talks, assume that if they immediately employ assertive, familiar behavior with a customer, a sale is much more likely to take place. Using a "buddy-buddy" approach to demonstrate how friendly they are, they rush up, place an arm around the customer's shoulders or shake hands, grasping the customer by the elbow with the opposite hand, simultaneously radiating presumptuous and malapropos camaraderie toward the customer.

Some people may respond favorably to this behavior. Others feel threatened and uncomfortable. They may bristle with antagonism. Such over-familiarity can adversely affect the relations between two people, making it difficult to create an atmosphere of mutual respect and trust. The claims representative must respect the inviolate space of others and be wary of over-familiarity. He or she can be considerate and friendly without being familiar.

A potential problem area of behavior involves the personal habit of smoking. With numerous research studies documenting the health hazards of tobacco smoke, considerable public attention has focused on the subject. Since researchers contend the tobacco smoke is injurious to nonsmokers who are forced to breathe secondhand, ambient smoke expelled by smokers, legislation has been enacted in many jurisdictions to attempt to provide segregation of smokers from nonsmokers where either objects to the other's presence. It is an emotion-charged issue. Here again, the laws of proxemics enter the picture. A person with respiratory health problems, or one who dislikes the smell of tobacco smoke, resents the encroachment of tobacco smoke into his or her space-bubble. It invades that person's inviolate buffer zone; it can create harsh feelings and strained relations between individuals. The smoker may have a strong conviction that he or she has an inalienable right to smoke. The nonsmoker believes that the smoker has trespassed on the nonsmoker's right to breathe.

An insurance claims person who is also a smoker should always be careful not to create a situation that may aggravate his or her relationships with insureds, claimants, or witnesses. To light up a cigarette or pipe in another person's home or office without permission may be perfectly acceptable, or it may be interpreted to be inconsiderate, selfish, antisocial behavior. Some nonsmokers have become quite militant in what they perceive to be their right to breathe smoke-free air. Whether this militancy manifests itself in vocal form or in smoldering resentment, the claims representative who unthinkingly or deliberately "lights up" in the nonsmoker's home or office creates an immediate obstacle to the task of attempting to handle a claim amicably and efficiently. If the claims person must smoke while conducting interviews, a simple inquiry by the smoker can do much to avoid any potentially damaging situation. A better rule would be to avoid the situation entirely by refraining from smoking while conducting interviews or claims negotiations.

Over-familiarity can take other forms, and the claims representative must always be mindful of the dangers of such conduct. "Be personable, not personal" is sound advice. Courtesy and respect for the privacy and the space bubble of others should be a part of one's normal relations with other people, not a feigned affectation. Uninvited invasion of privacy is not considerate behavior and has no place in claims work unless an inquiry is germane and essential to the conduct of the claims investigation.

Respect for others' property.   An individual's property, no matter what it is, usually is important to that person. People identify themselves with their belongings. Property of others, therefore, can serve as an excellent device for the claims representative in his or her attempt to establish goodwill. In some cases the claims person may enter a home that contains a valuable collection of figurines. In other instances the photographs on the top of the piano, an individual's pet, or flower garden may serve as conversation pieces. In any event, the claims representative should be sincere in the respect and attention directed to another person's property.

In a dirty, ill-kept home, the claims representative might believe it is difficult to admire anything. We, however, might reflect upon a quotation from Emerson: "But in the mud and scum of things, there always, always something sings."[3] We can always find something to admire, if we are observant and if we will put forth the effort. It is always possible, for example, to comment about another person's bright-eyed little child, a housepet, a family photograph, or some feature about the other person.

If the insurance claims representative can spend a little time to work these various techniques into the business at hand, he or she may find that the claims business is much easier to transact. For the new claims representative the utilization of these techniques may seem rather artificial and mechanical. For the experienced claims person

---

[3] Ralph Waldo Emerson, from "Fragments."

these steps may come naturally. They are an important part of being a human being. Displaying consideration and establishing goodwill should be a natural part of the everyday existence of anyone. These techniques are highly essential to the successful conduct of any type of social or business relationship. They will facilitate the claims handling function, for after a climate of confidence is established, the claims person then can proceed with the task of trying to influence behavior. This requires assertive behavior.

PRINCIPLES AND TECHNIQUES

Socrates was a Greek philosopher who went around giving people good advice. They poisoned him.

Few people in their jobs have the responsibility to influence human behavior under the trying circumstances that confront the insurance claims representative. He or she must learn to use assertive behavior effectively to influence the behavior of others. *Assertiveness* has been defined in an earlier chapter as the tendency to dominate social contacts. In using assertive behavior, a claims person must put personal thoughts into words and through the use of persuasion must attempt to convince the other person that the claims person's ideas and conclusions are meritorious. This can best be accomplished if those ideas and conclusions are indeed meritorious. The claims person must try to motivate another person to act in a certain way that will facilitate the conduct of an investigation or the negotiation and settlement of a claim.

Many situations confronted by the claims representative require the use of assertive behavior. We may be attempting to secure information through questioning. We may be trying to persuade someone to affix a signature to a document; or we may be trying to induce an insured or a claimant to agree with a suggested valuation of a loss. We always must keep in mind that assertive behavior on our part will facilitate the claims handling process only if the proper atmosphere is established first between ourselves and the other person. While using assertive behavior, therefore, the claims representative must simultaneously maintain rapport and continue to allay fears of the other person.

There are definite techniques for using assertive behavior. Books on salesmanship are full of them. Some are good; many are out of place in the insurance claims handling job. A few simple, but helpful, techniques will be mentioned in the following pages.

Plant and cultivate ideas

One of the simplest techniques of introducing assertive behavior is to provide a gentle transition from behavior which is essentially considerate to conduct which displays mild assertion. In other words, the insurance claims representative has, up to this time, devoted efforts to establishing a climate of confidence. This is considerate behavior. The emphasis is on consideration, and there is an absence of assertive behavior. The stage has been set for the introduction of assertive behavior. The climate of consideration must be maintained, but there must now be the introduction of behavior that will begin the motivation process. The claims person must now begin to introduce assertive behavior. We are able to effect this simple transition by beginning to introduce some new ideas or suggestions in an offhand manner. At the same time, we must keep courtesy and interest in the other person in the foreground.

The phrase *plant and cultivate*[4] describes the best sequence to use in presenting almost any point of view. The essence of this principle is to present new ideas as inconspicuously as possible at first. We must plant the seeds of new ideas. If they take root at all, it will be easy to cultivate them later.

If we relate new ideas or suggestions to the wants or needs of another person, we may find that the other person will pick up the idea as his or her own and repeat it. By doing so, the person reinforces the idea in the mind, and the idea can begin to serve as a strong stimulus to bring about the response we desire. Suppose, for example, we are talking to a man who was struck by an insured vehicle in a pedestrian lane. The claimant suffered a broken leg. We visit the claimant from time to time to keep the case under control.

As the leg heals, we maintain friendly relations and inform the claimant that a final settlement is forthcoming as soon as the claimant is ready to talk money. At the same time we hasten the process by remarking, "I'll bet you will be glad to get out of that cast and get back on your feet." We also state, "I imagine that it will be a real relief to

---

[4] Donald A. Laird and Eleanor C. Laird, *Practical Sales Psychology* (New York: McGraw-Hill, 1952), p. 282.

have all of the financial aspects of your claim cleared up." We all have financial worries, and a person with a broken leg is aware of the interruption that such a disability has introduced to one's earning capacity, social schedule, and other activities. In most cases it creates a financial strain. The claims person's assurance that settlement is forthcoming immediately upon the agreement of the claimant is the seed of an idea that germinates as the claims person cultivates the idea with frequent contact and assurances of payment.

Another example illustrates how the claims representative can begin to introduce ideas and suggestions without being overly assertive. The claims representative may be handling a claim under a bailee-customer's policy. Assume, for example, that the bailee somehow tore a button from a lady's coat. Part of the fabric came off with the button. The claims person may know that it will be less expensive to pay for a reweaving job than to pay for the value of the coat.

When the claims person confronts the woman, he or she handles the coat with respect and admiration, declaring, "This is a lovely coat. The color and fabric are beautiful, and the style is excellent! Say! I'll bet it would pay you to have it reweaved! Would you like me to see if it could be done to your satisfaction? I want you to be perfectly satisfied." In this manner the claims person plants an idea in the other person's mind while simultaneously displaying consideration for that person's best interests. At the same time the claims representative introduces further mild assertive action by cultivating the idea and suggesting a course of action to be followed by the other person.

The claimant in this case, however, may have already decided that she wants to be paid for her loss, and the claims person's idea may not have taken root. The planting may be unsuccessful at this point. The groundwork is not favorable for a successful planting of the idea of a reweaving job on the coat.

The claimant may resist the introduction of the idea that a reweaving job will be acceptable. She declares, "No, I don't want it sewed; a patchwork job will not do."

Therefore, the claims representative must continue with the effort to get the "seed"—the suggestion—planted and cultivated. Whereupon we continue to reflect concern and consideration for the claimant's feelings by stating:

> I don't blame you; I personally wouldn't want a patchwork job done if it was my coat. But reweaving is not patchwork. These people do a

marvelous job of fixing holes in fabric like this. It is not a mending job, and they don't sew on a patch. They take some turned-under material from a hem or other area of your coat that is not visible, and weave these threads into the area where the hole is. The fabric is from your own coat, so it matches perfectly. I have seen holes in fabric like this where the reweaving is done so expertly, it is impossible to tell where the hole was after the reweaving job was completed."

"Let's see if reweaving will do the job here. Then, I'll leave it up to you to judge the quality of the reweaving. I believe you will be delightfully surprised with the results. Shall we go ahead with it?

In this case the claims representative combined the "seeding" process with some necessary educating, accompanied by assertiveness, and all within a framework of consideration and concern over the claimant's well-being and satisfaction. Ideas planted and cultivated in this manner are destined, in most cases, to bear fruit. A reasonable person in this type of situation ordinarily will acquiesce in the course of action—the solution—proposed by the claims representative.

A balance between consideration and assertiveness is essential to facilitate effective contact with others. This is why assertive behavior, if properly handled and introduced at the right moment, can fortify and reinforce the claims representative's display of consideration. Although pronounced assertive behavior early in the first meeting may cause a claimant to respond with antagonism, once the claimant's confidence is obtained, we will find that assertive behavior will help the claimant resolve personal conflicts.

The reader will recall the example of the donkey that was faced with a problem. It could not decide which of two piles of hay to approach. Confronted with a conflict, it was in danger of starving. Through a display of consideration the claims representative could sympathize with the donkey, but this would not resolve the latter's conflict. Only through the use of assertive behavior could the claims person help the donkey. By telling the donkey what to do and convincing it of the wisdom of such action, the claims person could resolve the donkey's conflict.

Principle of introjection. The principle of introjection is based upon a curious phenomenon. The claims person interjects his or her ideas into a conversation with another person, and through a psychological process called *introjection*, the other person adopts and incorporates those ideas into his or her own viewpoint. As we listen to a claimant's ideas, it will be helpful for us to remember those ideas with which we agree. When the time comes for negotiation, we will find it helpful to refer to points which have been mentioned by the claimant. Using the latter's words and phraseology, we then begin to interject our own ideas into the conversation. These ideas should be made to follow logically from statements made by the claimant. The same principle, obviously, can be used while handling an insured's claim.

Suppose, for example, that an insured has had a fire loss. As Paul Thomas points out in his monograph "Checking Personal Property Claims,"[5] an insured often will list certain items of contents as total losses, when actually they can be reconditioned or repaired readily. The sight of a water-soaked rug, covered with plaster and soiled by persons trampling over it, may cause the insured to declare, "Look at that rug! It was a beautiful thing. We shopped for months trying to find a rug that would look good in this room. Now that we found one, it's ruined. Look at that mess!"

Although the insured is convinced that the rug is a total loss, the claims representative's inspection reveals that it hasn't been burned. From training and experience the claims person knows that the rug probably can be reconditioned completely if removed promptly to a rug cleaner before mildew occurs. Utilizing the principle of introjection, the claims representative remarks, "It certainly does look a mess now, Mrs. Brown, but it is possible that we can do something with it. As you say, it sometimes takes months of shopping to find a rug you like. Fortunately, this rug has not been burned. I have an idea that a rug cleaner can restore it to its original beautiful condition. Let's see if it can be done. We want you to be perfectly satisfied, Mrs. Brown. If it can be cleaned successfully, it will surely save you the inconvenience of trying to find another that will look as nice in your home."

If a claims person interweaves his or her own argument within the framework of ideas, words, and language of the other person, the latter is more likely to accept the conclusions drawn by the claims representative. Thomas Staton declares, "With his own ideas given flattering, prominence in the concept of the case that you are developing,

[5] Paul I. Thomas, "Checking Personal Property Claims," *Adjusters Reference Guide* (Louisville, Ky.: Insurance Field, 1981), Fire and Allied 13.

recognizing his own words, thoughts and expressions, often through introjection the claimant will accept some of your ideas as his own and incorporate them in his own future concept of the case."[6]

Consider, for example, an actual intersection automobile accident. A motor vehicle driven by the insured, proceeding north in the outside lane of traffic of a four-lane street, entered an intersection. The insured made a left-hand turn in front of an automobile driven by the claimant. The claimant's automobile was proceeding south in the outside lane of traffic. The front end of the claimant's vehicle struck the right side of the insured vehicle (see Figure 9–1), and the impact caused the claimant to sustain personal injuries.

The negligence of the insured was clear. He turned from the wrong traffic lane; further, he turned when it was unsafe to do so. The question that had to be answered in this case was whether the claimant was contributorily negligent. (The accident occurred in a state that still recognized contributory negligence to be a bar to recovery in a negligence case). If there were contributory negligence the defense

Figure 9–1.   Diagram

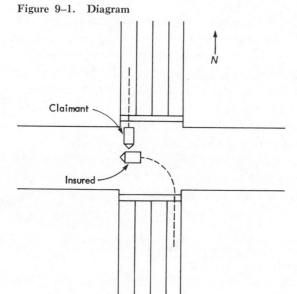

---

[6] Thomas F. Staton, "How to Get People to See Things Your Way," *Psychological Factors in Insurance Law* (Houston, Tex.: Federation of Insurance Counsel Foundation, 1963), p. 19.

potentialities of the case were enhanced. The claims representative wanted to know why the claimant did not avoid the accident. Didn't the claimant have sufficient warning to avoid the accident? (Remember that the insured turned across the inside northbound lane and the inside southbound lane before he was struck).

The claims representative asked the claimant, "How far, in feet, was the other car away from you when you first saw it?"

Suppose the claimant replies, "It was directly in front of me—a couple of feet away. I didn't expect him to turn."

If there were no visual obstructions preventing the claimant from seeing the insured automobile, the claims representative has a talking point. The claimant probably should have seen the insured vehicle before he did. Nevertheless, because of the claimant's personal injuries, in addition to the relative degrees of negligence of the two parties, this is a case which probably should be settled, particularly in states using the comparative negligence standard. In any event, it is likely that a jury's sympathy would favor the claimant if the case were litigated, thus even in a contributory negligence state, claims have frequently been handled as if comparative negligence rules applied.

The claims representative, however, will use the apparent contributory negligence of the claimant to settle the claim as economically as possible. To do this, the claims person must be able to convince the claimant of his contributory negligence and to show how it might prevent recovery in a lawsuit. Even in a comparative negligence state the claims person will be able to hold down the settlement figure appreciably if the claimant can be convinced that his lack of attention was a major contributing cause of the accident that occurred.

Using the principle of introjection, the claims representative might remark, "You say that you didn't see the car until it was two feet away? Not expecting the driver to turn, you probably were not particularly watching the other car, or you may have been thinking of something else at the time."

The claimant replies, "Yes, I think that's right. I didn't once expect him to turn there. It really surprised me."

The claims representative at this point might continue, "Well, Mr. Smith, the law requires everyone to be particularly alert when approaching an intersection. The unexpected causes accidents. We can't always rely on other people to drive as we expect them to. A careful driver must always be ready to avoid the unexpected. Because, as you say, you did not see the other car until it was a couple of feet away, you probably were not as alert as the law requires you to be. You perhaps should have noticed him when he started his turn rather than when he had completed it. This failure to keep a proper lookout could very well bar you from recovery, irrespective of the possible fault of the other driver. We want to be perfectly fair with you though, Mr. Smith, and would like to pay you, even though, as you say, you didn't see the other car as soon as you probably should have."

By interjecting our personal arguments in the words and language of the claimant, we strengthen the defense case and make it more likely that the claimant will accept the logic of our statements. The foundation now has been established for us to attempt to dispose of the case as economically as possible.

The secret of Socrates—The habit of agreement

Assertive behavior can be used effectively by employing knowledge of another psychological principle which Dale Carnegie referred to as "The Secret of Socrates." The Socratic method introduces the insurance claims representative to the "yes, yes response"—the habit of agreement.[7] The idea is to ask questions with which the other person must agree. The claims representative should not begin the discussion by talking about points over which there is bound to be disagreement. Emphasis should be placed on points of agreement so that a claims person at the outset secures a number of "yes" responses.

If we can continue to obtain agreement, we may ultimately lead the other person into accepting a conclusion that the person would not have accepted previously. The chain of agreement will cause a forward movement which, from a psychological standpoint, becomes more difficult to reverse. It is comparable to the state of inertia in physics: A property placed in motion will continue in the same direction until acted upon by some external force. The greater the impetus of the motion, the stronger the force must be to interfere with the motion. Thus, applied to an insurance claim situation, with every "yes" response on the part of the claimant, it becomes increasingly difficult to answer succeeding questions in the negative.

Salespeople constantly use this principle in their sales efforts. They have learned to keep choices simple and to lead a person to a complex decision by breaking it down into a series of relatively

---

[7] Carnegie, *How to Win Friends,* p. 144.

simple propositions which can be decided on a "yes" or "no" basis. For example, if a man goes into a men's furnishings store to buy a shirt, the salesperson may greet him and offer to be of service. The man declares that he is looking for a dress shirt. The salesperson begins to help the man make his choice by employing assertive behavior. The salesperson asks a series of questions with only one possible answer. The conversation may run as follows:

Salesperson: Are you looking for a shirt that will launder well?

Customer: Yes.

Salesperson: And do you want a shirt that will be wrinkle-resistant?

Customer: Yes.

Salesperson: I imagine that you want a shirt that is well-tailored and of good quality?

Customer: Yes.

Salesperson: Here is a shirt made of excellent material, launders easily, and is wrinkle-resistant. It is an excellent buy for the money (states the price), and I have it in your size. May I wrap it up for you?

The salesperson has covered the points most likely to be of interest to the customer. The customer has been motivated to respond with affirmative answers to the salesperson's questions. After a series of affirmative answers the customer most likely will answer in the affirmative to the salesperson's last question, and a sale is made.

The claims representative, likewise, can introduce this approach in handling insurance claims. Suppose, for example, that a claims representative is handling a personal property loss. As we have observed in Chapter 7, claims representatives know that it is virtually impossible to convince some people that there should be a depreciation deduction on a personal property loss. If a man loses his woolen suit, the claims representative probably will inquire when and where the suit was purchased and will ask how much it cost. The claims person may decide that the suit has a lifetime of five years, and since it is three years old, the claims representative will offer a 40 percent settlement figure. It is amazing how a person suddenly may turn red with anger and accuse the claims person of attempting to cheat. Such a reaction is not surprising in light of the clumsy claims handling on the part of this claims representative. The concept of depreciation must be explained, and in detail, to many members of the public.

The lay public readily understands why an insurance company should not be required to replace an old automobile with a new model. The public is accustomed to buying used, partly depreciated automobiles. This is well understood. The public does not, however, fully sympathize with the idea of deducting depreciation from a lost article of clothing. Very little used clothing is purchased by the public and replacement of a lost item with clothing of like age is relatively unheard of. It is in the adjustment of this type of claim that the Socratic method has excellent application.

Consider the case of a claimant who has lost his overcoat in a fire at a dry cleaning plant that is insured under a bailee liability policy. The conversation may go something like this:

Claims Person: With cold weather coming on, I'll bet you are anxious to replace your coat.

Claimant: Yes, I certainly am.

Claims Person: I imagine that you were somewhat dismayed when you heard about the fire and realized that your coat was gone.

Claimant: Yes, I was. With cold weather coming on, I was planning on using that coat real soon.

Claims Person: Well, let's get the necessary information together so that we can handle your loss. Okay?

Claimant: Yes.

Claims Person: Did you purchase the coat yourself? And how long ago?

Claimant: I bought it. It was about three years ago.

Claims Person: The coat was three years old?

Claimant: Yes, that's right.

Claims Person: From what store did you buy it, and how much did it cost?

Claimant: I paid $135 for it at the XYZ Men's Store—downtown.

Claims Person: Downtown St. Louis? (insured's city)

Claimant: Yes.

Claims Person: And that was $135?

Claimant: Yes.

Claims Person: How much would it cost to replace the same coat today?

Claimant: Well, with inflation the way it is, it would cost me $150 today.

Claims Person: You think $150 would do it?

Claimant: Yes.

Claims Person: About how long does an overcoat last you?

Claimant: Oh, maybe four or five years. That was a good coat and was holding up pretty well. It was showing some wear.

Claims Person: Then would you say this coat would have lasted you about five years?

Claimant: Yes, I think that's about right.

Claims Person: Then if it would last you five years, and it was three years old, you would have gotten another two years' wear out of it?

Claimant: Yes, that's about right.

Claims Person: Then, since the coat had given you three years of service and you could have worn it another two years, would you estimate that the coat had about 40 percent of its original value left at the time of the loss?

Claimant: Well, yes, I suppose that's right.

Claims Person: Well, Mr. Jones, you are entitled to be paid the value of the coat at the time of the loss—$60. Would it be fair and okay with you if I write you a check for $60?

Hopefully, at this point, the claimant will answer yes and the claims representative will be able to settle this claim in an amicable manner. It is usually the case that these settlements will be handled more smoothly, amicably, and expeditiously if the claims representative will lead the other person systematically through the reasoning process of understanding "actual cash value" and depreciation while simultaneously employing the "secret of Socrates." It is important to get the other person into the habit of agreement before the settlement figure is introduced into the conversation.

It is important to note that when this technique is being utilized, particularly on the initial questions asked of the other person, the claims representative should not ask the other person to agree with the claims person's views or opinions. It should be a natural agreement. The claims person should place emphasis on points where there is obviously mutual agreement. This will establish a foundation of agreement and make it easier to broach those matters where there is apt to be a difference of opinion. The Socratic method is well grounded in principle and works in many cases. If the other person falls into the "yes, yes response," or habit of agreement, the individual is less apt to take issue on a point on which he or she does not thoroughly agree.

All insurance claims handling, however, is not as simple as selling a shirt or settling a simple personal property loss. The conflicts which confront the other person often are of a much more serious nature. Our approach, consequently, must be subtle. If we attempt to use the Socratic method in an obvious, step-by-step approach, we may be doomed to failure. The principle, nevertheless, is good and can be used with effectiveness.

The key to success, of course, has been the use of assertive behavior by the claims representative. We have used it throughout by leading the other person through a series of steps to a logical conclusion. Further, we have accomplished the foregoing without appearing to be overbearing or high-pressured in the method utilized. The intelligent use of consideration has maintained rapport, while at the same time we have introduced an inoffensive but, nevertheless, highly effective type of assertive behavior.

Principle of completeness

Good fences make good neighbors.
————Robert Frost

In using assertive behavior, the insurance claims representative should make certain that he or she suggests what appears to be a complete solution to a claimant's loss problem. Staton points out that "the human mind and the human eye like to perceive things as complete, tidy packages with everything accounted for and nothing left over."[8] This is the principle of completeness—wanting everything neat and sewed up. The desire for neatness, simplicity, and completeness is a fetish of much of humanity. People like packages. They buy the travel tour because they needn't worry about the details of travel and accommodation reservations, tickets, itineraries, and so forth. The details all are handled by someone else. The homeowners insurance policy, as another example, is popular today largely because it takes care of prime insurance needs of the individual—direct damage to the insured's home and contents from the common perils and legal liability in one package. There is no need to worry about buying several separate policies.

The principle of completeness likewise accounts for the fact that so many people have fences or walls. They may not have livestock, pets, or children to enclose, but they have a fence or a wall anyway. They like to see the property line neat and well defined. They want well-established boundaries. There must be no ragged edges.

If we arrive at the scene of an accident, we will do much toward obtaining the claimant's confidence and controlling the case if we make use of the principle of completeness. Suppose, for example, that the

---

[8] Staton, *How to Get People to See Things Your Way*, p. 20.

accident involves a collision between two automobiles, and it is a case of clear-cut liability. The claimant is stopped at a stoplight. As the insured approaches the intersection, her foot slips off the brake and onto the accelerator, causing her automoblie to collide with the rear end of the claimant's automobile.

The man in the other car is jarred by the accident, and as he glumly surveys the damage to his car, his mind struggles in an attempt to determine what he should do about the situation. It is not uncommon for people who have just been involved in an accident to be suffering a certain amount of shock even though they are otherwise unharmed. That in addition to the fact that they are confronted with a situation which usually is novel for them often produces much confusion. Even an experienced claims representative may have an automobile accident and may experience confusion from the trauma of the accident. An experienced claims person, for example, may step out of a wrecked automobile and lean against the door in a rather bewildered state of mind. Although we have been handling automobile accident claims for several years, we are likely to find it difficult to think of what action we should take first under the circumstances. It is not surprising, then, for a lay claimant to be experiencing similar confusion.

If an insurance claims representative can come into this type of situation and use assertive behavior, advising the claimant of the steps he or she should take in ascertaining the damage to the automobile and presenting a claim, showing the claimant how all of the problems arising out of the accident can be resolved, the claims person can do much to remove the confusion in the claimant's mind. What we must do is to present a package of solutions. We may outline how we and the claimant can go about handling all of the problems—finishing the investigation, getting medical treatment (if necessary) and obtaining medical reports, getting damage estimates and having the automobile repaired, assembling all of the bills, and finally sitting down and working out a settlement.

When approached in such a helpful manner, the claimant may not deem it necessary to call an attorney for advice. This particularly is true if the claims representative has established rapport with the claimant by treating the claimant in a friendly, sympathetic, and considerate manner. It is here that prepayment of expenses often can yield favorable results. Following such treatment, the alternative of calling an attorney whom the claimant perhaps does not know will be less attractive.

The same principle is applicable when we are negotiating with a claimant to settle a personal injury claim. We itemize and evaluate items of special and general damages not only to prove damages but also to show a claimant that all the factors and loose ends of the claimant's case are being considered and evaluated. The claimant receives assurance that he or she will receive a neat package settlement for all of the items of the damages incurred.

Positioning

One interesting form of assertive behavior is known as positioning. Positioning refers to the relative place position of communicating parties. The role of positioning is well known in the area of dramatization. Actors speak of being "upstaged," "downstaged," or "center-staged." The relative position of each player on the stage will serve to make the player appear more or less dominant to the audience. Thus, if Hamlet delivers his soliloquy near the audience and in the center of the stage, his delivery tends to have more strength than if he delivered it elsewhere on the stage.

In this same manner, people who communicate with one another in personal contact tend to assume dominance or lack of dominance. It is difficult, for example, for a salesperson to perform effectively if he or she is seated and the customer is standing. The person who is standing somehow tends to dominate the one who is seated.

The insurance claims representative can use this principle in two ways. In attempts to establish rapport and develop consideration and comprehension, it probably is best for the claims person to stay at the same level as the other person or to assume a subordinate position. A new idea or suggestion, however, may be more readily accepted if it is presented from a dominant position.

The role of intervening objects also is important in positioning. Desks and chairs function as shields, creating an air of defensiveness and formality. If the claims representative desires to obtain a statement or secure initial cooperation from another person, he or she will find it better to talk beside a desk rather than across it. On the other hand, it may prove helpful in a given case to utilize intervening objects in order to effect a settlement.

Consider an example where positioning can be used effectively. A claims representative may have found it difficult to deal with a claimant at the latter's house. The claimant is on his own home ground, surrounded by his friends and relatives who give him moral support. Settlement negotiations sometimes can be carried on more successfully if the claimant is lured away from his familiar surroundings. He therefore, is invited to come to the office of the claims person. Seated and with hat in hand, he confronts the claims representative in the latter's office. The claims person is seated behind his or her desk with an imposing pile of claims files on the desk and a diploma or two tacked on the wall. If, during the ensuing conversation, the claims person stands and leans over the desk toward the claimant and displays a check made out to the claimant, such assertive behavior can often produce excellent results. The claimant may be willing to sign release forms and settle on the spot.

Agreement

A soft answer turneth away wrath; but grievous words stir up anger.
                           ——Old Testament, Proverbs, XV, 1.

Another principle which can be used effectively in combination with positioning is that of agreement. If a claims representative is aware of some strong attitude or interest of the claimant, it may be wise for the claims person to show agreement on this point if he or she doesn't have to compromise the insured's legal position by starting with agreement.

The application of the principle of agreement and that of positioning can be illustrated by an example. Suppose we enter the home or the office of a third-party claimant. The claimant may be filled with rage. The claimant may direct this rage at us. Two problems confront us—one, we must try to calm the claimant, and two, we must be able to reason with the claimant and influence the claimant's actions. Harvey Highbaugh compared the role of the insurance claims representative in such a situation to that of the anesthetist and surgeon team.[9] When the anesthetist and the surgeon approach the patient on the operating table, the anesthetist must keep the patient in a manageable state while the surgeon proceeds with the operation. The claims representative must perform both functions. We first must calm the claimant. Once the claimant is docile, we proceed to reason with the claimant to attempt to influence the claimant's actions.

---

[9] Harvey Highbaugh, *How to Control the Human Element in Claim Handling and Elsewhere* (Knoxville, Tenn.: Jackson Publishing, 1938), p. 18.

Faced by an irate claimant, the claims representative must take first things first. We cannot immediately proceed to reason with the claimant. First, the anesthesia must be administered. It is here that positioning and agreement become important. Through positioning the claims representative can assume a subordinate position by sitting down and then beginning to nod the head in agreement or to remark agreeably as the other person continues his or her tirade. If the claimant is an extremely assertive individual, it may be necessary to be particularly considerate, at least initially. Hopefully, as the meeting continues, rapport will develop. In some cases we may find that we must devote more time to a situation—the longer the session, the greater the opportunity we will have to be assertive without precipitating a crisis. As we patiently use positioning and agreement to create a more compatible atmosphere, we will discover that another factor will work to help create an atmosphere conducive to successful communication and good claims negotiations. This is a psychological phenomenon explained by the principle of catharsis.

Principle of catharsis

When angry, count four; when very angry, swear.
———Mark Twain

The principle of catharsis affords the very foundation for psychoanalysis. The psychoanalyst prevails upon the patient to talk about his or her problem. By completely airing the circumstances giving rise to the problem, the causes of the problem are exposed to analysis by the patient and the psychoanalyst. As a consequence, it sometimes is possible for the problem to be purged from the subconscious mind of the patient, and a cure is obtained.

When people orally express things which are emotionally bothersome, they vent the pressure of emotions by expressing thoughts in words. Figuratively speaking, they blow off steam. A boiler without a safety pressure valve may rupture its seams and blow up. Some people have the same problem. They keep their turmoil hidden, without releasing it. Pressures build up and before long, they blow up. They come apart at the seams, suffering heart attacks, developing ulcers, or exhibiting other manifestations of too much pressure because they are unable to purge themselves of the injurious internal pressures arising from anxieties and emotions.

A knowledge of the foregoing has practical value for the claims representative. We should recognize that it is difficult to reason with an angry claimant. We probably will find it well worth the time to persuade the claimant to "talk out" emotions—to blow off steam. In so doing, the claimant will express feelings and will be able to hear his or her own arguments rather than just feel strongly about them. The cold exposure of hearing one's own words enables us to analyze the logic of our feelings. We therefore accomplish two things. We dissipate the bottled-up emotions that have clouded our reasoning, and, at the same time, we are able to see our side of a question with more perspective.

While the claimant is airing emotions, the claims representative should maintain an attitude of considerate behavior. No attempt should be made to introduce assertive behavior at this point. We should not argue with the claimant, nor should we dispute the inaccuracies of the claimant. Such a course of action at this point would be unwise, because contradicting the claimant at this time would create more anger. Rather than purging the pressures created by the claimant's emotions, the claims representative actually aggravates the problem, nullifying the advantages of utilizing the principle of catharsis. Rather, the claims representative should listen sympathetically, agree where agreement is possible, and encourage the claimant to exhaust his or her emotions on the point in question.

The rage of the claimant, when confronted with tolerance, patience, and agreement, tends to dissipate rather rapidly, often giving way to a display of tolerance. As a matter of fact, the claimant may unconsciously regret the display of rage and will attempt to atone for it by becoming particularly amicable. With his or her rage dissipated, the claimant may decide to take a chair. The actions of the claims representative have produced rapport. The time is now ripe to introduce assertive behavior.

To introduce assertive behavior, the claims representative may find it useful to utilize the principle of positioning. Remember that a new idea or a suggestion may be accepted more readily if it is presented from a dominant position. The claims representative, therefore, stands up, walks toward his or her briefcase or recorder and remarks to the claimant, "I'm certainly glad you have told me all of this, Mr. Smith. Let me get my equipment (or statement pad), and we can get your version of what happened, if it is okay with you." The claims representative then proceeds to get a written or recorded statement. In most cases it is unnecessary to go through all of these preliminaries before starting to write or to record a statement. In some cases, however, skillful application of the foregoing principles will mean the difference between success and failure.

PSYCHOLOGY OF NEGOTIATIONS

In negotiating insurance claims settlements the claims representative must exercise great skill in the use of assertive behavior. It will require the use of assertive behavior to induce a claimant to accept a proffered settlement, but that same behavior can produce settlements which are not satisfactory to either the claims person or the claimant. For example, in the process of negotiations one of five things may occur:

1. The claims representative may make a settlement which the claims person, the insurer, and the claimant believe is fair and adequate. In this case the claims representative has utilized assertive behavior in a skillful and tactful manner, or he or she has been fortunate enough to have an unusually considerate and docile claimant with whom to negotiate.
2. The claims representative may make a settlement which is satisfactory to him or her but leaves the claimant disgruntled. An overbearing, high-pressured manner may succeed in settling claims, but it produces a bad impression and leaves a bad taste for years with the claimant, who believes he or she has been forced to accept an inadequate amount for the claim.
3. The settlement may be satisfactory to the claimant, but the claims person may believe that he or she has paid too much. In this case the claims representative perhaps failed to make a reasonable settlement because of a clumsy use of assertive behavior. Instead of motivating the claimant to settle for a reasonable figure, the claims person irritated the claimant, causing the claim to drag on interminably. To dispose of the claim the claims representative paid an excessive amount.
4. The claims person may be convinced that he or she paid too much, while the claimant may believe the amount paid was inadequate. Although this situation can occur despite the best efforts of a skilled claims representative, it usually results because of a break-

down in communication and lack of persuasive skill on the part of the claims representative.

5. The claimant may withdraw from negotiations and seek the services of an attorney, and litigation may ensue. Here again, this situation results in many cases despite the best efforts of a skilled claims representative, but most cases of such loss of control are caused by claims men and women who lack communicative and persuasive skills.

It is apparent that four of the five alternatives above will not please both the claims representative and the claimant from either an economic or a human relations standpoint. It is only the first course of action which satisfies both parties, and it is the satisfaction of both parties which should always be the ultimate goal of a claims representative.

Preliminaries to settlement

In every case involving settlement of insureds' losses or of the claims of third parties, the claims representative has to decide when to start the negotiation process. When should we introduce the assertive behavior which calls for the discussion of money?

In the case of insureds, it usually is possible to broach the subject without much delay. A certain amount of preliminary educating, however, sometimes is necessary with insureds. The subject of depreciation, we have noted, often gives rise to spirited discussions. Most insureds, for example, believe that their property, especially their automobile, was above average in value before a loss occurred. In the insurer-insured relationship, however, the situation is one of comparative mutual trust. Human relations problems are not quite so difficult in first-party claims as they are in liability cases.

As mentioned earlier in the book, the third-party claimant often views the claims representative as an opponent. We represent the insured, the person responsible for the claimant's misfortunes. Often, too, the claimant will have a basic distrust of insurance companies, and he or she may suspect that we are not entirely honest in the sense that we are viewed as an employee or representative of an insurer dedicated to making a profit and settling claims just as cheaply as possible. This latent hostility, distrust, and suspicion will vary among claimants and will be entirely absent in some.

The problem of timing the negotiation, therefore, will differ according to the individual claimant and to the nature and severity of the claimant's damages. On simple property damage claims or superficial bodily injuries (such as minor bumps, cuts, and bruises), a first-call settlement may be in order. On severe personal injury cases, however, the claims representative probably will have to spend considerably more time before introducing the assertive behavior preliminary to settlement. Because of severe and permanent injuries, there may be large medical bills and other special damages. Further, bills may be continuing, and this fact, together with the severity of the injuries, presents a thorny problem of how to evaluate the damages.

It is possible in such cases for the claimant's hostility, distrust, and suspicion of the claims representative to intensify unless the claimant believes the claim is handled properly. The claims person, consequently, must be able to assure the claimant that his or her claim will be handled fairly and promptly. Until we have established this initial assurance in the mind of the claimant, we cannot expect successful results when we introduce the assertive behavior necessary to consummate a settlement. It is here, especially, that we must employ our knowledge of the principles of human behavior, communication, and motivation.

The offer

Once a groundwork of mutual respect and confidence is established, the stage is set for negotiations. Before an offer can be made, however, the claims representative must have a knowledge of

1. The extent of the special damages—"out of pocket" expenses.
2. The nature of any continuing, progressive, and permanent injuries.
3. The peculiar psychological makeup of the individual claimant, the presence or absence of belligerence, the claimant's announced intentions, and other factors which give some indication whether the case is in danger of being referred to an attorney.
4. Whether the claimant, his or her family, and perhaps the claimant's physician believe the claimant is ready to talk about a settlement.

5. The legal ramifications of the case—whether it is clear-cut or disputed liability.
6. Whether the available witnesses for the defense would make favorable impressions on the witness stand.
7. The reputation of judges and juries in the jurisdiction for favoring either plaintiffs or defendants on personal injury liability cases.
8. Other factors which give some insight on whether litigation could be successfully prosecuted by the claimant.

To properly evaluate some of these factors requires a good working knowledge of human relations.

Who makes the offer?   After the foregoing factors are properly considered by the claims representative, and it appears timely to enter into negotiations, an important question arises. Who makes the offer—the claims person or the claimant?

There are two schools of thought on the subject. The fact that experienced claims representatives are divided in opinion suggests that there is no proven rule to follow on this point. The division of opinion also illustrates the fact that the industry follows no well-defined principles of human behavior and motivation to guide claims representatives in their handling of claims. It will be helpful to the reader to be exposed to the two schools of thought and to the theory advanced in support of each viewpoint. Following this exposition, the claims person should be able to decide for himself or herself which viewpoint appears most valid.

The first school suggests that the better procedure to follow is to determine from the claimant what he or she has in mind in the way of a settlement figure. In other words, the claimant initiates the offer—the claimant introduces the assertive behavior. The second school advocates that the claims representative initiate the offer—the claims person should tell the claimant what the insurance company is willing to pay. James H. Donaldson, in his text *Casualty Claim Practice*, states that most claims men subscribe to the first school.[10]

Claimant initiates the offer.   Those who favor the first viewpoint

---

[10] James H. Donaldson, *Casualty Claim Practice*, 3d ed. (Homewood, Ill.: Richard D. Irwin, 1976), pp. 818–19. © 1976 by Richard D. Irwin, Inc.

—letting the claimant initiate the offer—believe that there are the following advantages in this approach:

1) The claimant must reveal his or her position and take the initiative by making the offer. This, it is contended, gives the claims representative a superior bargaining advantage. The claims person has not had to expose his or her thinking as to value.
2) By not initiating the offer, the claims person does not risk overpaying on the case or losing the case to an attorney because the offer is too low. This risk of overpaying or offering too little can be avoided if the claimant makes the first offer, according to this viewpoint.
3) If the claimant expresses a figure, the claims representative has the option to accept the offer, make a counteroffer, or not make an offer, according to the reasonableness of the claimant's figure.
4) When a claimant is invited to reveal his or her thinking, oftentimes the claimant will ask the claims representative what the latter usually pays in similar cases. The claims person then can list the items of the claimant's damages and ask the claimant what he or she thinks of the figure arrived at after all the items have been added together.

Claims representative initiates the offer. Equally experienced practitioners argue convincingly that the claims person should make the initial offer. These claims representatives point out the fact that a good claims person is an expert in the job of evaluating damages and that he or she abdicates responsibility by turning that job over to a person who has had neither the training nor experience to evaluate damages and the complex factors that must be weighed in most claims situations. The claims representative who does not initiate the offer is saying, in effect, that the claimant is perhaps better qualified to evaluate money damages.

The expert claims person is educated in personal injury and property damage appraisals. The claims person's experience and the experience of the insurance company have permitted the claims representative to become familiar with comparable cases involving comparable damages. The claims person is in a superior position to evaluate a claim. Why should he or she turn over the job of valuation to someone whose concept of damages may have been obtained from the information picked up from the publicity attendant to high jury and court awards? Further, with the advice the claimant has received from other uninformed people such as relatives and friends, is the claimant not more likely to place an inflated and excessive value on the claim?

There is another argument to consider. When a claimant is invited to reveal personal thinking as to value, a definite monetary figure is established in the claimant's mind. The more the claimant thinks about it, the more he or she believes the amount to be reasonable. If the claimant thinks about a certain sum of money over a period of time (and many claimants do this), the repetition of thought concerning that amount, reinforced by an oral expression in the form of a demand, solidifies the claimant's belief that the figure is justified. After the claimant states an offer orally, any rejection of the figure by the claims representative may cause the claimant to defend the figure more vigorously than if it had never been expressed. Once the claimant has submitted the demand, he or she may be inclined to defend it because it is a personal affront to be contradicted rather than because the claimant is convinced of the inherent fairness of the amount stipulated. The claimant is motivated by pride. He or she has been asked for an opinion of the value of the claim. If the valuation is not accepted by the claims representative, it is an affront to the claimant's pride—an offense to the claimant's self-respect.

Whatever the case, when the proposed settlement figure is initiated by the claimant, it must now be accepted, rejected, or modified by the claims representative. If the claimant's demand is excessive, all three alternatives are unattractive. We don't want to accept the claimant's figure, and to reject it may cause us to lose control of the case. If we attempt to modify the demand, we are placed in the position of contradicting the claimant and setting the stage for haggling. It would appear that we are in a worse position than if we had made the first offer.

Those claims representatives who want the claimant to make the first offer believe the technique has merit, because the claims person can first condition the claimant's thinking and educate the claimant's understanding of damages by pointing out the out-of-pocket expenses and suggesting that the claimant's overall demand should bear a reasonable relationship to those expenses and to the injuries. This argument, however, surely is not limited to this school of thought. Where we make the first offer, we obviously will go through the same procedure to establish a reasonable foundation for the forthcoming offer. Furthermore, by laying the foundation and by making the first offer, we condition the claimant's thinking and may lower the figure the latter has in mind. This conditioning, happily, can be done without subjecting the claimant to the necessity of exposing his or her thinking on a subject about which the claimant may feel a definite inadequacy and ignorance.

There is a more important reason for arguing that the claims representative should make the first offer—he or she is using assertive behavior. Young men and women in military training are taught that battles often are won under great odds by the combatant who takes the initiative. "The best defense is a strong offense." Irrespective of the military aspects of who does or does not take the initiative, if an insurance claimant is asked how much he or she wants in order to settle, the claimant is invited to use assertive behavior—the claimant gains the initiative.

. If, on the other hand, the claims representative makes the offer, *he* or *she* introduces the assertive behavior. If the groundwork has been established for the introduction of assertive behavior, we should have an advantage. When we make the offer, and if the figure is supported by sound, clear-cut, persuasive reasoning, the claimant may accept the offer without haggling. If the latter does decide to haggle, the two parties are in no different position than they would be if the claimant was initially invited to make the offer, and he or she asked for an amount totally unacceptable to the claims representative. More important, however, in making the first offer, we have: (1) taken the initiative and used assertive behavior—a form of behavior, incidentally, which throughout human history has been utilized successfully by Alexander the Great, Napoleon, the leaders of the American Revolution, and successful salespersons and politicians of today, and (2) demonstrated that we believe that we are qualified to evaluate damages. The importance of this point should not be overlooked. Authoritative texts on selling and salesmanship present a unanimous view that the cardinal requirement of persuasion is the demonstrated knowledge of your subject matter.

Evaluation—the liking-leniency hypothesis

Evaluation of personal injury claims presents a complex situation. The concrete items of money loss are fairly easy to assess. However, the claims representative must give adequate consideration to evaluating all of the consequences of an injury. These include such things as permanency of disability, disfigurement, pain or mental anguish, inconvenience, loss of job, loss of promotion, loss of business or professional opportunity, adverse effects on marriage possibilities, deprivation of recreational and socioathletic lifestyle, and other forms of life enjoyment.

Aside from these factors, there are other considerations which weigh heavily on the subject of evaluation. Thus, there are many psychological aspects to claims evaluation. One psychological phenomenon that is well documented is called the *liking-leniency hypothesis*. In essence, it means that how well we like an individual bears a significant relationship to how well we treat that individual.

From a legal standpoint, how attractive a plaintiff or defendant is to the jury should be irrelevant to court judgments. Unfortunately, this probably is not the case. Researchers contend that there is strong evidence that jurors favor a plaintiff or defendant who is likeable or attractive, or who possesses attitudes similar to those of the jurors. This is the liking-leniency hypothesis. A number of studies purport to document preferential treatment to the party considered to be attractive to the jury. In criminal cases, for example, a male jury tends to judge an attractive woman defendant to be less guilty, recommending more lenient prescriptions for punishment, than in the case of the not-so-attractive defendant.[11]

Jurors identify with and favor a defendant or a plaintiff where there is attitude similarity between the party and the jurors, and the research has shown that ethnic differences play an important role in jury evaluation of parties. Jury critics are probably correct in claiming that jurors are inappropriately influenced by extralegal factors.[12]

The liking-leniency hypothesis carries over into nonjudicial settings. There is nothing mysterious about this phenomenon. We tend to favor those people whom we like or who are attractive to us. Studies have revealed that a person who is liked will receive much more favorable

---

11 M. G. Efran, "The Effect of Physical Appearance on the Judgment of Guilt, Interpersonal Attraction, and Severity of Recommended Punishment in a Simulated Jury Task," *Journal of Research in Personality* (1974), 8, 45–54.

12 See discussion in James H. Davis, Robert M. Bray, and Robert W. Holt, "The Empirical Study of Decision Processes in Juries," *Law, Justice, and the Individual in Society*, ed. by June Louin Tapp and Felice J. Levine (New York: Holt, Rinehart, & Winston, 1977), pp. 327–33.

judgments, such as approval of a loan or hiring, than one who is not liked.[13]

The significance of these studies on insurance claims evaluation should be apparent. Juror sympathy for a highly attractive, likable personal injury claimant-plaintiff may have an appreciable inflating effect upon the jury's evaluation of the plaintiff's damages. This phenomenon must be considered in the insurance claims evaluation. Further, the claims person's assessment of potential jury identification with and preferential treatment of a claimant should be communicated to insurer claims examiners or supervisors who must evaluate the case and establish dollar limitations on settlement. When the claims examiner or supervisor is remote from the scene and has not met the claimant, insured, and witnesses, and has the task of evaluating the case based solely on the objective evidence submitted in the investigation report, it is highly essential for the field claims representative to advise of other factors that might influence the evaluation of the case. The claims person's subjective assessment of the extralegal factors that might influence valuation should be communicated to the examiner or supervisor.

Likewise, the liking-leniency phenomenon applies in the claims person's assessment of whether witnesses to an event will make good or adverse impressions on jurors. Obviously, a likeable, attractive claimant who has likeable, attractive, and believable witnesses presents a difficult situation if the decision has been made to deny a claim and defend the case in court.

Dealing with claimants' attorneys

After all, advocates . . . are like managers of pugilistic and election contestants in that they have a propensity for claiming everything.
——Felix Frankfurter

A knowledge of human relations and an appreciation of the importance of assertive behavior in settlement negotiations is highly essential for claims representatives who deal with claimants' attorneys. Whenever it is clear that a claimant has retained an attorney, we, of course, should no longer deal directly with the claimant in the settle-

---

[13] See D. Byrne, *The Attraction Paradigm* (New York: Academic Press, 1971).

ment negotiations. When an attorney enters the picture, the claim is momentarily "out of control," and we must negotiate with the attorney. We must "regroup our forces" and work toward the objective of settling the claim without litigation, if possible.

To accomplish this task, it will be helpful for the claims representative to understand the position occupied by the attorney. The attorney was employed because the claimant did not want to negotiate directly with the claims representative, or it may be that (if an offer was made) the claimant did not like the settlement figure proposed by the insurance company. On the other hand, perhaps the claimant merely wants the attorney's opinion of whether the offered amount is fair. In many cases the attorney will recognize that the offer is reasonable and adequate, and in the attorney's own mind he or she sincerely believes that the claimant should accept the figure.

Other factors must be considered by claimants' attorneys. There always is the prospect that a case may be lost. There is a well-known adage among attorneys: "There is no case so bad that it cannot be won, and there is no case so good that it cannot be lost." It can be an embarrassing nightmare for a lawyer to explain to a seriously injured client why there was no recovery in a personal injury suit the attorney has just lost. It is even worse after a case has been lost for an attorney to have to explain to the client why he or she recommended refusal of an offer by an insurer or why the attorney did not insist that an offer be accepted.

Oftentimes, however, attorneys have as much trouble educating their clients to the economics of insurance claims values as do claims representatives. In addition, attorneys also must make a living, and when they agree to represent a claimant, it is important for them to demonstrate their monetary value to their client. Furthermore, there are many cases where an attorney believes that the insurance claims representative has been niggardly in the evaluation of a claim and must be educated to realities.

Whatever the case, most attorneys recognize the fact that they usually must ask for too much in order to obtain what they think a case is worth. This rather universal belief also carries over into the field of litigation. Attorneys find it expedient and wise to demand a higher sum in their complaint than they expect to receive.

There is good reason for this approach. It is well-recognized in the American system of litigation that both judges and juries resort to "averaging" techniques to arrive at judgment and verdict values.

Confronted by an ultraconservative valuation of damages presented by the so-called expert witnesses of the defendant and the over-generous appraisal of damages made by the plaintiff's witnesses, judges and juries often find themselves bewildered by the conflicting testimony, and they resort to a process of roughly averaging out the two widely varying values. They will throw their favoritism to one side or the other, depending upon the effectiveness of the individual witnesses, the relative social and economic positions of the two parties, their attitude toward plaintiffs and defendants in general, and a host of other factors. With this everyday phenomenon of human behavior rampant in the courts, and further reinforced by a general, and not entirely unjustified belief that insurance claims representatives never offer initially as much as they are prepared to pay ultimately, it is to be expected that a personal injuries attorney will frequently demand more than he or she expects to receive.

After the attorney's first demand, there usually follows a process of haggling and bargaining, bluffing, and contrived delays. Some cases will be disposed of swiftly and painlessly with little or no jockeying. Other cases seem to drag on interminably, often due to serious and honest differences of opinion regarding issues of liability and damages. In these cases litigation frequently is the only way to resolve the matter.

Forearmed with a knowledge of the practical considerations which motivate claimants' attorneys in their handling of insurance cases, a claims representative can approach negotiations with confidence and a greater likelihood for success in such negotiations. We should not be intimidated by the claimant's attorney, for we often know more about the facts of the case than the attorney does. We always must be mindful of the fact that most claimants' attorneys revel in a competitive world of adversary relationships. Our use of assertive behavior in such negotiations frequently offsets the attorney's aggressiveness and often provides us with the necessary balance and measure of success in the handling of insurance claims. (The reader at this point will find it helpful to review the subsection entitled "Competition and attorneys" in the chapter on motivation.)

Releases

The final step in negotiations is the execution of a release and the payment of consideration. In this transaction we must continue to use assertive behavior, but at the same time, we must retain the confidence of the claimant and continue to assure the claimant that the latter is being treated fairly.

The release probably is one of the least understood legal devices used in the insurance claims handling process. The general public commonly has little understanding of the nature, legal effect, and limitations of this device. After reading the awesome language embodied in the release forms used by many insurance companies, the average person is convinced that once the release is signed, he or she has entered into an unalterable, irrevocable, and ironclad relationship. This feeling carries over to such an extent that claimants sometimes will express a genuine fear that unless· they receive their money simultaneously with the act of signing the release form that there is some question whether the insurer will be required to make the promised payment at a later date. Such fears of a claimant can be easily dispelled if we explain to the claimant that a release is nothing more than a simple contract, and it is not binding on the claimant unless the promised money payment is made.

It would be untrue to say that the release is not a final legal disposition of a claim in the majority of cases. Nevertheless, some releases are "broken" because of the manner in which courts interpret the agreements of men and women. Whenever the validity of a release is examined in a law suit, the court will consider the past legislative and judicial history, the surrounding factors that are unknown to the parties, the subsequently occurring circumstances that could not at the time of the agreement be known to anybody, and the requirements of justice as reflected in the mores of contemporary society. In obtaining releases, therefore, we must take the initiative to make certain that a claimant not only reads the release but that he or she understands that he or she is giving up all legal rights in connection with the insurance claim involved. This assertive action of explaining the effect of the release as a full and final settlement will help avoid misunderstandings which cast uncertainty upon the contractual relationship.

In a large number of cases the release has greater psychological value than legal value. This particularly is true in the case of *parent-guardian releases*. A minor is an incompetent party, and special rules apply to minors in the area of contract law. Because of children's legal disability under the law, parents commonly believe that they possess the authority to settle their children's legal claims. Exploiting this misconception, insurers employ language in the typical minor's "release" form which states, for example, that the parent or guardian does "forever release, acquit, and discharge" the insured from "any and all claims or rights of action for damages which the said minor has or may hereafter have," and so on.

Parents have an independent cause of action for the loss of services of the child, and they also have a claim for the medical expenses which they have incurred on behalf of the minor. Parents, however, do not possess the legal capacity to settle the legal claim of the minor for the latter's injuries, including pain and suffering, and permanent injury, if any. Such a release can be consummated only by the court of proper jurisdiction wherein the minor resides. Usually there is a petition for letters of guardianship, and, after a hearing, a parent or another natural guardian is empowered by the court to execute a binding contract on behalf of the minor, releasing the minor's legal rights arising out of the injuries which he or she sustained through the wrongful acts of an insured.

The psychological value of the parent-guardian "release" and the misleading language which is incorporated therein and which purports to release the legal rights of a minor suggests, therefore, that the psychology of this type of instrument rests upon deliberate deceit and exploitation of the ignorance of the uninformed person. Perhaps the end justifies the means. To require general guardianship proceedings in all cases involving third-party minors would not be of benefit to society. As long as the insurance industry uses these release forms only in cases involving slight and temporary injuries where the amount of settlement will be small, and refers all serious cases to the courts for approval, perhaps the public interest is adequately served.

For the individual claims representative, however, it would appear to be desirable, from a personal standpoint, if he or she would avoid stating that such releases constitute full and final settlements of minors' claims. In our use of assertive behavior, we would do better to emphasize the positive aspects of the release transaction. We should point out that (1) the minor's injuries were minor and temporary in nature; (2) the minor has recovered or will recover shortly; and (3) a payment is being made to the parents in consideration of their release of *their* claims and as reimbursement of expenses incurred by the minor. By stressing the above positive points, the claims person avoids the misrepresentation that still appears in some insurance companies' release forms.

Today, insurance companies employ considerable flexibility in utilizing releases. Since a release is nothing more than a contract, the contract can be much more informal than it was in years past. Oral contracts, of course, are as binding as written contracts. Because of the importance of handling claims and the desire to provide substantial evidence that a contract had actually been consummated, insurance companies in the past employed the formal, written release form.

The liberalizing trend toward claims handling, however, has caused the insurance industry to adopt more informal claims handling techniques. Thus, the claims representative has the option in many cases of settling a claim without utilizing the formal release—a written agreement. This informal technique has been variously called *settlement without release, no release settlement,* or *walk-away settlement.* These latter settlements in which no release instrument is utilized are typically made when there is no permanent injury and when the value of the claim does not reach major proportions, including both special and general damages. In a no release situation, the claim is settled informally, and the agreement to release the insured of any and all liability results from the oral, informal understanding of the parties that the claims settlement has been satisfactorily consummated.

Another technique that is used in settling claims is the *open release.* In the cases of liability with serious injury and protracted disability involving uncertain prognosis, many companies now utilize conditional settlements with the understanding that future expenses or developments will not foreclose additional payment. Such an agreement makes the insurer responsible for future expenses, including medical bills and other expenses. It is customary to place a time limitation and a limitation of amount on these expenses, including salary loss.[14]

PEOPLE APPRECIATE ASSERTIVE BEHAVIOR

People may well appreciate the assertive behavior of the claims representative. Earlier in this chapter it was pointed out that a person,

---

[14] See Pat Magarick, *Successful Handling of Casualty Claims* (New York: Clark Boardman, 1974), p. 293; also see discussion on releases, Bernard L. Webb, J. J. Launie, Willis Park Rokes, and Norman A. Baglini, *Insurance Company Operations,* Vol. 2 (Malvern, Pa.: American Institute for Property and Liability Underwriters, 1978), pp. 462–66.

whether he or she is an insured or a third-party claimant, views personal contact with a claims representative with anxiety. The person may have a conflict. He or she may distrust the claims representative, but at the same time the claims person is seen as the individual who can solve the loss problems of the insured or third-party claimant. If we can dispel a claimant's distrust, we then immediately can begin to help solve the loss problems. It is here that the claimant may well appreciate being told what to do. Confronted by a situation which is novel, the claimant has no past experience upon which to draw, and he or she feels helpless. The claimant will likely be most amenable to suggestions—if he or she trusts the claims representative.

An actual case will illustrate the point. An insured dairy truck has struck a small boy, causing a head injury. The claims representative arrives at the home of the parents and finds the mother so distraught that she will hardly acknowledge the presence of the claims person. The latter sits down and talks at length with the father. Finally, the father asks, "All right, what should I do? Nothing like this has ever happened to us before. You seem to be honest. Can I trust you to tell me what to do?"

This is a refreshing and surprising approach. The claims representative decides to use a refreshing answer. There is no question in the mind of the claims person that the insured will be required to pay the claim. The child, at his age, under the law is presumed to be incapable of negligence. Whether the dairy truck driver has satisfied his duty of care is open to speculation. The claims representative weighs the possible consequences of his or her next words. The boy has not yet received a complete medical checkup. To attempt to settle the case on the spot, in the judgment of the claims representative, would be foolhardy. The claims person firmly believes that rapport has been established with the father and believes just as firmly that if an immediate offer of settlement is made, that climate of confidence and respect will be destroyed.

The claims person, therefore, decides to buy additional rapport with time, and therefore, answers the father as follows: "I appreciate your confidence in my honesty. I, therefore, will be perfectly honest with *you*. If I were the parent of that boy, I would have only one thought— the welfare of my son. I would not rush into anything. I would have him examined completely. Then I would wait a little while before I decided to do anything. May I drop back again Thursday and see how the young fellow is, and we will talk further about this? Meanwhile, why don't you have him examined completely?" The father agrees, and the claims person departs.

The claims representative calls again the following Thursday. The boy has been examined, and the attending physician believes that the youngster is all right. The physician has advised the father to wait another two weeks, however. The claims person and the father again have a friendly conversation, and they agree to meet at the claims representative's office in exactly two weeks.

Two weeks later the father greets the claims representative and states, "All right, the physician says my boy is okay. I don't have the slightest idea as to what his claim is worth. You tell me what you believe will be a perfectly honest amount, and that will be okay with me."

The claims person again discusses the matter candidly with the father and offers an amount that is adequate to cover the medical bills and an additional amount to cover the intangible aspects of damage as well as consideration to support a parent-guardian indemnity agreement. The father immediately agrees to the settlement figure. The climate of confidence established by the claims representative has borne fruit.

Experienced insurance claims representatives have discovered that most people respond well to assertive behavior when a claims person suggests how their claim should be handled. This, of course, is a conclusion based upon the assumption that the claims person has been skillful in establishing rapport and in obtaining the confidence of the other person before the assertive behavior is introduced. People generally appreciate displays of consideration and a candid, honest approach, followed by assertive behavior. There are, of course, always exceptions. Some fathers will capitalize on a simple injury, such as that just described, and will allege that their injured child is suffering from grievous pain, mental retardation, and/or continuing and permanent psychological disturbance. In some cases the claims representative won't even have the opportunity to talk to the father; the latter already will have called his attorney.

SUMMARY

The reader no doubt is convinced at this point that our relations with one another are indeed complex. The insurance claims representative is particularly conscious of this, for the success or failure which he or she experiences is intimately connected to the ability to handle human relations with skill and effectiveness.

Thus, if it is assumed that a claims representative is able to communicate effectively, there still remains the problem of motivating or activating another individual to respond in a desired manner. Our communication with another person must serve to set the stage for the use of successful motivation principles and techniques.

It has been observed that a person's motivation is directly tied to the satisfaction of needs and wants. If we can show another individual how those needs and wants can be satisfied, we can motivate the other person to respond affirmatively. Since the other person's needs and wants often conflict with one another, we can use persuasive techniques to help resolve that conflict by making one alternative action more desirable than another. In this unique position we can control things that other people need or want. For example, our specialized knowledge enables us to give compelling reasons why another person should select one course of action over another. Further, our authority to disburse money often enables us to influence others to select a given response.

In the role that we assume in attempting to influence others, we will find that certain specific techniques will enable us to establish a climate of confidence and mutual respect with other people. To avoid controversy initially and at the same time obtain rapport with another person, we can utilize such principles and techniques as positioning, agreement, and catharsis.

As soon as a friendly atmosphere is obtained, we then may begin to employ assertive behavior. Through assertive behavior we can introduce ideas and persuasive suggestions which motivate and influence another person to respond in a desired fashion. It is important to note, however, that while we introduce assertive behavior, we still must maintain an atmosphere of mutual respect and confidence.

Here again, there are techniques for introducing assertive behavior to influence other people. Usually, assertive behavior will be more effective if it is employed in a gradual manner. New ideas and suggestions, therefore, are introduced as inconspicuously as possible. We "plant and cultivate" ideas, interjecting our own ideas into another person's ideas, and we lead the insured or claimant into the "yes, yes response"—the habit of agreement.

The new claims representative may suspect at first that there is something phony and mechanical about using specific techniques to communicate with and to motivate other people. The claims person may believe that he or she is being asked to use a "canned" approach. He or she will discover, however, that as experience is acquired in handling insurance claims, these techniques are nothing more than the procedures which successful people use in all walks of life as they go about communicating with and influencing other human beings. They are based upon a few simple scientific principles of human relations. Understanding them is a vital and integral part of the claims representative's responsibilities.

In conclusion

A philosophy

Human relations requires the development of a philosophy.
——Keith Davis[1]

"**P**hilosophy" is a highly ambiguous and vague word. Any definition of it, therefore, tends to be arbitrary. Nevertheless, the following may well be as accurate and unbiased as a definition of philosophy can be expected to be: "A critical reflection on the justification of basic human beliefs and analysis of basic concepts in terms of which such beliefs are expressed."[2] Essentially, *a philosophy*, in a popular sense, refers to a system of value judgments or concepts relating to a given human activity. A philosophy of handling insurance claims relates to a viewpoint of how to properly conduct the claims handling function.

All human activities are conducted by human beings within the framework of divergent philosophies. The insurance claims handling occupation is no exception. Different philosophies exist in theory and in practice because of the development of individual claims representatives' attitudes over a period of months or years of experience. Variations also exist when individual insurers differ in their procedures and philosophies for handling claims.

Further, different claims philosophies result because of variations in the recruiting policies and practices of individual insurance com-

---

[1] Keith Davis, *Human Relations at Work* (New York: McGraw-Hill, 1962), p. 12.

[2] Paul Edwards and Arthur Pap, eds., *A Modern Introduction to Philosophy* (Glencoe, Ill.: Free Press, 1957), p. 3.

panies. One large automobile insurer, for example, rejects those claims job applicants whose selection tests reveal that they show "too much" interest in other people. Other insurers emphasize the need for "socially responsive" claims representatives. These vague subjective standards defy precise interpretation, but they nevertheless reflect different ways of looking at things. Some companies, moreover, insist that job candidates possess college degrees and prefer applicants with legal educations; other insurers will hire high school graduates and have a policy against hiring attorneys as claims representatives. The resulting wide variation in education and experience backgrounds of claims persons invariably results in divergent viewpoints on "proper" claims handling philosophy.

PHILOSOPHY AND SOCIETY

To do that which society believes to be against its best interest, though legally allowable, is but to invite the enactment of more laws.
————Ganong and Pearce[3]

How does a philosophy originate? Individuals set forth a body of principles according to the way they relate to their experiences. The element of subjectivity, therefore, is an intrinsic part of a philosophic system.

For an institution such as the insurance industry to ensure its continued existence in the framework of society, it should establish a rational philosophy. Since rationality is a relative term, whether something is rational depends upon the judgment of society. To the extent that "irrational" principles are adopted and kept in practice, society looks at such principles as onerous. The philosophy giving rise to the body of principles will be condemned. To the extent that a company's claims philosophy is inharmonious with the demands of society, it will be judged invalid, and sanctions will be taken to modify it.

Changing standards—Changing law

Standards of validity change with the changing conditions of individual and social life. Men and women change their ideas, and

---

[3] Carey K. Ganong and Richard W. Pearce, *Law and Society* (Homewood, Ill.: Richard D. Irwin, 1965), p. 39. © 1965 by Richard D. Irwin, Inc.

principles of human relations are modified to meet contemporary standards of society.

A claims philosophy must be dynamic and in harmony with the times. Today, probably more so than at any other time in our nation's history, there is national soul-searching concerning the relations of humans with one another. There is concern about equality, fairness, and justice. The bigot, the intolerant, the cheat, and the sharp practitioner are more openly criticized. Less attention is devoted to long-standing legal dogma. Such dogma often is swept aside and replaced by laws which reflect current thinking. For example, for many years automobile manufacturers and dealers sought to eliminate the liability imposed by the law of sales by substituting in the sales contract a warranty which proved to be of little value to the consumer. In one of a number of cases upsetting this type of limited contract, the court discussed the grossly inferior bargaining position occupied by the consumer. The court remarked that limited remedies for automobile purchasers are inimical to the public welfare. The judge declared: "The obligation should not be based alone on the privity of contract. It should rest . . . upon the demands of social justice. . . ."[4] The impact of this type of judicial thinking has caused the automobile industry to institute considerable reforms in its handling of automobile warranties. Meanwhile, it continues to be beleaguered by a society aroused by issues of automobile performance, fuel economy, safety, and air pollution.

The meaning is clear in its implications to insurance claims handling or to any other type of business activity. The challenge to today's businessperson to understand and to apply noneconomic values mounts, and the relevance of the judgment of other value-giving institutions becomes critical. Eells and Walton state: ". . . business as an institution is aware that a concern with intrinsic values—with good in its most sublime sense—has to have a place in its scheme of things."[5]

A philosophy directed only to the meeting of legal obligations without regard to concepts of morality and justice is not a realistic philosophy within the bounds of contemporary society. A rule of law is a fleeting thing. It has validity only if it fits within society. The law

---

[4] *Henningsen* v. *Bloomfield Motor, Inc.* (N.J.) 161 A.2d 69, 78, 86 (1960).

[5] Richard Eells and Clarence Walton, *Conceptual Foundations of Business* (Homewood, Ill.: Richard D. Irwin, 1969), p. 587. © 1969 by Richard D. Irwin, Inc.

of the land is dynamic; it constantly changes to fit the temper of the times. A great jurist and legal scholar once wrote: "The moral code of each generation, this amalgam of custom and philosophy and many an intermediate grade of conduct and belief, supplies a norm or standard of behavior which struggles to make itself articulate in law."[6] The validity of principles which make up a philosophy of conduct are always subject to examination and change. Principles will be challenged; onerous conduct will be condemned. The demands of social justice will be met. The law will change to reflect these demands.

It, therefore, is imperative that we examine the insurance claims handling philosophy. Are the principles underlying existing practice morally, as well as legally, sound? Do they comply with the demands of society? If a claims philosophy is not realistic in this context it is without merit.

Philosophy of the legal mechanic

Many rules of "fair play" appear . . . as a joke. Such as the English formula, "do not hit a fallen enemy!" . . . When would it be better and more advantageous to hit him?

———Luigi Barzini

It was standard practice not too many years ago for some claims departments to "let sleeping dogs lie"—don't "stir up" any quiescent claims. These claims departments followed the philosophy of the "legal mechanic." The legal mechanic believed that relationships between insurers, claims representatives, insureds, and claimants should be confined to a strict and narrow interpretation of the legal responsibilities dictated by contract and tort law. This philosophy was expressed by one claims executive as follows: "A liability insurance policy is prepared and sold by a corporation for *no other purpose* [author's italics] than an attempt to make a profit . . . the only proper approach to the adjustment of any insurance loss is by means of the policy contract."

This seemed to be a good philosophy to many claims people and defense counsel. It is an asocial philosophy. It ignores the social and political realities and the dynamic nature of the law. This philosophy was the breeding ground for the "unfair claims settlement practices" laws that states enacted in the mid-1970s and thereafter. The philos-

---

[6] Benjamin N. Cardozo, *The Paradoxes of Legal Science* (New York: Columbia University Press, 1928), p. 17.

ophy was narrow, absolute, and dangerous. Taken literally, such a philosophy means that claimants must be treated as legal adversaries in the strictest sense. Thus, the claimant had to make the first contact and initiate his or her claim, even though the claims representative already had received a full report from the insured on all of the circumstances giving rise to the claim. Particularly on minor property damage claims, the claimant was not contacted. Since, under the law, the burden of proving damages is upon the claimant, he or she was unaided in the procedure or task of proving damages, without help from an insured's liability insurer.

The legal mechanic defended this philosophy by pointing out that there was "no privity of contract" with a claimant. The claimant doesn't pay the premium, thus no legal duty is owed the claimant. Why contact the claimant? Until the claimant brings a claim against an insured, or unless the severity of personal injuries clearly portend a future claim of increasing potential severity, the company has no legal interest in the claimant's misfortunes.

Furthermore, the claimant and the insured are legal opponents, according to this theory, and the claims representative owes allegiance only to the insured. Thus, little is to be gained by helping a claimant to prosecute a claim. The fact that some claimants with legitimate claims may be discouraged from pressing a claim or may not know that they have a claim is a concomitant of such a philosophy, and incidentally, probably reflects favorably upon a company's loss ratio. It also creates bad will for the insurance industry.

An extreme of the legal mechanic philosophy is to deny all liability claims, regardless of merit. Since the claimant is viewed as an adversary, a small minority of claims representatives have attempted to reduce loss experience by placing every possible impediment into the claims settlement path of claimants, justifying such behavior by the fact that no legal responsibility is owed to claimants. The practice of denying all liability claims, regardless of merit, usually continued until a state insurance department intervened and expressed its disapproval of such a practice.

SOCIAL RESPONSIBILITY

The idea of incorporating a vaguely defined doctrine of social responsibility into the handling of insurance claims is foreign to the logic of the legal mechanic. The idea that claims representatives ultimately may turn into an army of "social servants" disbursing money according to vaguely conceived "social responsibilities" frightens the legal mechanic. It should frighten any responsible insurance claims representative. If interpreted broadly, the doctrine of social responsibility, which has been characterized as "a pious intonation of 'social service' doctrine and Christian brotherhood,"[7] could result in a perversion of corporate economic goals and functions and would surely signal the deterioration of sound contract law.

The strict interpretation of the insurance contract, similarly, is fraught with grave political, economic, and social implications, as discussed in preceding pages of this chapter. The problem is one of balance. The issue we must face in years ahead is how we can strike a balance between what is sound business practice in the interpretation of liability insurance contracts and what is good for the public interest. Without such a balance, we invite further governmental sanctions and statutory standards, such as the unfair claims settlement practices laws.

Unfair claims settlement practices laws

During the decade of the 1970s most states and Puerto Rico enacted legislation dealing with the subject of unfair methods of competition and unfair and deceptive acts and practices in the business of insurance. These laws, variously labeled "unfair trade practices acts" or "unfair claims settlement practices acts," have formalized public expectations for the handling of insurance claims. The laws are similar in their provisions, in large measure following the model legislation proposed by the National Association of Insurance Commissioners in 1971. The legislation prohibits misrepresentation and requires insurers to act "in good faith to effectuate prompt, fair, and equitable settlements of claims in which liability has become reasonably clear." In addition, the laws condemn "failing to promptly settle claims, where liability has become reasonably clear, under one portion of insurance policy coverage in order to influence settlements under other portions of the insurance policy coverage." Responsibilities of insurance companies and their claims representatives are spelled out in detail, and each claims person should become thoroughly familiar with the ap-

---

[7] Theodore Levitt, "The Dangers of Social Responsibility," *Harvard Business Review*, vol. 36, no. 5 (September–October 1958), p. 44.

plicable legislation in force in those jurisdictions in which he or she is handling claims.

The case law is still developing as courts construe the new unfair claims settlement practices laws. Not surprisingly, the courts that have considered these laws are not in agreement regarding the application of the legislation which has been enacted on the subject. For example, in one California case, a claimant sued an insurance company directly, alleging that the insurer had failed "in good faith to effectuate prompt, fair, and equitable settlement of claims in which liability has become reasonably clear," in violation of California law.[8] The court ruled against the claimant, since the claimant was not a party to the contract. The court interpreted the law as applying only to insurer-insured relations, including a "covenant of good faith and fair dealing which requires an insurer to effect reasonable settlement of the claim against the insured within his policy limits 'arising' out of the contract of insurance."[9] The court in a footnote also ruled out the idea that the claimant could recover as a third-party beneficiary of the contract. The California Supreme Court, two years previously, had unanimously held that the insurer's duty to settle runs to the insured and not to the injured party (the claimant).[10]

However, the results were different in another California case in 1979. In this case the claimant alleged that the insurance company had refused to exercise good faith in making a claims settlement, and that the claims person had allegedly advised the claimant not to obtain the services of an attorney, which was in violation of the California law. The California Supreme Court (by a four-to-three majority) held that a third-party claimant may sue an insurer directly for violating the California statute.[11] The court majority saw a statutory duty owed by insurers to third-party claimants to achieve good faith settlements of claims brought by the third-party against an insured.

Reflecting a different philosophy, two 1978 Oregon cases ruled that the Oregon Insurance Code was intended to be administered and en-

---

[8] California Insurance Code, Section 790.03 (h) (5).

[9] *Scheuch* v. *Western World Insurance Company*, 82 Cal. App. 3d 31, 145 Cal. Rptr. 294 (June 21, 1978).

[10] *Murphy* v. *Allstate Insurance Co.*, 17 Cal. 3d 937, 132 Cal. Rptr. 324, 553 P. 2d 584.

[11] *Royal Globe Insurance Company* v. *The Superior Court of Butte County et al.*, 153 Cal. Rptr. 842, 592 P. 2d 329 (March 29, 1979).

forced by the State Insurance Commissioner, and the unfair claims settlement practices legislation did not afford any cause of action to private parties.[12] An Illinois court ruled likewise, holding that a third-party claimant was not within the class for whose especial benefit the unfair claims practices statute was enacted. The court ruled that the statute was enacted for the benefit of the insured as well as to provide an administrative enforcement mechanism for the benefit of the public at large. The court declared "that a more explicit legislative intent to extend the duty to settle to third-party claimants should be required where imposition of such a duty would be in derogation of so much common law . . . the duty to settle has always been construed as running only to the insured, whether in first or third-party claimant situations."[13]

The Florida Supreme Court, nevertheless, held in a 1980 case that a direct action can be brought against a tortfeasor's insurer by a tort claimant for the insurer's alleged bad faith to settle the claimant's suit against the tortfeasor. The injured party becomes a third-party beneficiary under the policy.[14] Thus, Florida and California have permitted the unfair claims practices legislation to serve as the basis for a private suit for damages brought by a third-party claimant. California has been considered a legal "bell wether" state, thus its legal decisions sometimes establish precedence followed by other legislatures and courts in the United States.

It is foolhardy to predict the future, but the trend is apparent that government is being asked to apply extralegal consumer protection measures to serve the needs of the public. The unfamiliar direction in which the law is moving is unsettling, and the rapid pace of change imposes responsibilities that are foreign to traditional contract relations. Nevertheless, society is changing rapidly; societal expectations frequently do not honor tradition; and the law ultimately will mirror those expectations. As one writer states: ". . . the law derives from the social group; legal rules express the way in which the group considers that social relations ought to be ordered. . . . Statutory law is not essen-

---

12 *Susan E. Thorpe* v. *Wabash Life Insurance Company*, Civ. No. 78–347 (August 23, 1978); *Farris* v. *U.S. Fidelity & Guaranty Company*, 284 Or. 453, 587 P. 2d 1015 (December 5, 1978).

13 *Scroggins et al.* v. *Allstate Insurance Co.*, Ill. App. Ct. (September 14, 1979), 74 Ill. App. 3d 1027, 393 N.E. 2d 718.

14 *Boston Old Colony Insurance Co.* v. *Gutierrez*, Fla. Sup. Ct., No. 54, 769 (April 10, 1980).

tially different from custom; both are the expressions of the will of the group. . . . a legal rule is an expression of the collective will."[15]

Hopefully, insurance companies and claims personnel will be able to adopt standards that reflect societal expectations. This is necessary to obtain public acceptance of industry claims handling practices. Failure to do so will result in even more restrictive legislation.

A realistic standard

So, in our own body of law, the standard to which we appeal is sometimes characterized as that of justice, but also as the equitable, the fair, the thing consistent with good conscience.

———Benjamin N. Cardozo

In recent years a strong trend has developed among insurance companies to treat claimants in a morally responsible manner. With the enactment of the unfair claims settlement practices laws, this trend has become much more pronounced. All valid claims are handled as soon as circumstances permit. When an insured reports that he or she has had an accident resulting in damages to a claimant, the claimant is contacted and notified of procedure to be followed in submitting a claim. In addition, more and more companies are making prepayments on claims to help claimants meet pressing expenses; final settlement and release of claims may not be forthcoming for months on such claims. This prepayment philosophy is in sharp contrast to the policy of withholding all payment until a final release is negotiated.

An ideal standard contemplates the practice of good human relations, maintaining goodwill, paying all justified claims promptly, and rendering gratuitous service where possible, provided, however, that *it does not involve the compromising of legal principles or the buying of goodwill.* Legal rights are not abandoned when this standard is applied. The only thing abandoned is the strict adversary approach to handling liability claims. Just liability claims are paid voluntarily rather than forcing a claimant into a legal jousting match before consideration is given to the claim.

From an ideal standpoint, all justified claims should be paid promptly and in full. In borderline cases where there may or may not be liability, if legal prudence suggests an immediate compromise

---

[15] Henri Levy-Bruhl, *Sociologie du droit,* 2d ed. (Paris: Presses Universitaires de France, 1964), pp. 39–40, 60.

settlement to forestall a worsening situation, such a compromise should be negotiated immediately. In other cases of questionable liability, good claims practice might suggest an immediate denial of liability with the doors to compromise open in the event that a denial does not terminate activity on the claim. In cases where, in the opinion of the claims person, there is no liability, those claims should be denied. If further activity, such as litigation, ensues, it would be ideal to contest vigorously and defend the case to the utmost.

If all insurers defended against all unjustified claims, it no doubt would decrease loss frequency and severity. It would discourage claimants and some attorneys from pressing "nuisance claims." Payment of nuisance claims has given foundation to the belief that the American standard of "liability for fault" has degenerated into a standard of "liability through insurance."

The foregoing is a reflection of the fact that insurance settlements often are made irrespective of liability. Economic considerations dictate that if it will cost $500 to contest an unjustified claim but only $250 to settle it, the latter course probably should be followed. Occasionally, this degeneration of moral and legal principles infuriates the claims department of an insurance company, and it will defend a case at a monetary loss. Such a defense teaches an object lesson to an attorney who specializes in litigating meritless liability cases. It, however, may be a costly practice for an individual insurer. Without the cooperation of an insurance industry working in concert to eliminate this immoral practice, little can be done by individual companies, regardless of their best intentions.

The *realistic standard,* the standard based upon good human relations, militates against the practice of thwarting the just claim. There, obviously, is no moral nor legal justification for "stirring up" a claim where none existed nor for encouraging a claimant whose claim lacks merit. Where there is no validity to a claim, it certainly is acceptable business practice to deny the claim and to resist attempts on the part of a claimant to prosecute such a claim. It is the legitimate claim which deserves prompt and proper attention.

Failure to treat claimants in a morally responsible manner creates public hostility and antagonism and adversely affects the image of the whole institution of insurance. Further, it largely accounts for the small but significant volume of claims which are referred to attorneys. A prominent member of the American Trial Lawyers

Association (ATLA), Robert A. Collins, stated that many of his clients came to him with damning denunciations of their previous relations with insurance claims representatives.[16] He contended that the failure to observe proper liability claims handling fundamentals is the single factor that most frequently causes a normal claim to turn into a lawsuit.

In defense of the insurance claims person, it should be stated that no amount of contact and responsible conduct on the part of the claims representative seems to deter certain claimants from retaining attorneys to represent them. Some claimants, motivated by greed and the opportunity to "make the most of a good thing," seek out an attorney in order to exploit personal avarice. Other claimants have so little hope of being treated fairly that they see their lawyer before the claims person can make contact. A claimant's preconceived lack of confidence in claims representatives and insurance companies, obviously, is a public relations problem for the industry.

Nevertheless, claimants turn to attorneys for help when they believe they are being treated unfairly and are ignored by an insured's claims representative. This particularly is the case when they are not contacted within a reasonable period of time following an accident or occurrence and submission of a claim.

The immediate contact rule

*As in a theatre, **the** eyes of men,*
After a well-graced actor leaves the stage,
Are idly bent on him that enters next,
Thinking his prattle to be tedious.
      ——Shakespeare

In most cases claims men and women should establish immediate contact with claimants. Nobody likes the feeling of being ignored. Our feeling of prestige, of importance, of ego recognition, is damaged if we are avoided by other people whom we believe should be paying us attention. A claimant with a just claim expects attention; he or she is impatient for attention and is insulted if the claim is ignored. If the claimant is not immediately contacted, this damages the claimant's

---

[16] Robert A. Collins, an address given at a seminar of the Michigan Adjusters Association, reported in *National Underwriter*, February 24, 1961.

self-respect. He or she feels the need to do something to restore that damaged self-respect. The claimant may feel the need to retaliate—to strike out in anger. Sometimes that anger, plus the real need for legal services, causes the claimant to turn to an attorney for aid.

Immediate contact is the most important factor to keep third-party claimants from turning to attorneys for advice and counsel. A claimant immediately contacted by a claims representative who indicates willingness to give proper attention and consideration to the claimant's claim, usually will not feel impelled to turn to a lawyer for assistance. If the claimant is ignored, however, or if there is undue procrastination in the handling of the claim, that is another matter. According to Collins, some of his largest fees have come from cases where claimants sat at home for a week or more waiting for the claims person's visit. He comments: "My observation is that I rarely have cases involving certain companies whose claim supervisors really enforce the immediate contact rule."[17] Although a member of the ATLA, an organization which has been accused of aggravating the loss frequency and severity experience of the insurance industry, Mr. Collins expressed great interest in proper insurance claims handling procedures. He explained that both the members of the ATLA and insurance claims representatives have a common stake in the preservation of the negotiation process. According to Collins: "If the bulk of personal injury claimants are not fairly and adequately compensated through the orderly processes of negotiation, and we are required to rely on the vicissitudes of jury verdicts, we may well see the advent of a state-controlled arbitrated award."[18]

This "bureaucratic invasion" of both professions would be a distinct threat to the livelihood of attorneys and claims representatives alike. The continued expression of interest by legislators in the subject of automobile insurance, and the discussions relating to automobile compensation schemes, scheduled awards, and other subjects having to do with the valuation of damages indicate that Collins's statement is not mere conjecture.[19] For example, according to annual legislative

---

[17] Ibid.

[18] Ibid.

[19] See, for example, Robert A. Rennie, "An Experiment in Limited Absolute Liability," *Journal of Insurance,* vol. 29, no. 2 (June 1962), p. 177; Robert E. Keeton and Jeffrey O'Connell, *Basic Protection for the Traffic Victim* (Boston: Little, Brown, 1965); and Willis Park Rokes, *No-Fault Insurance* (Santa Monica: Insurors Press, 1971).

ts within society and how he or she can best influence
ls within that society. As discussed in the early chapters
story teaches us that we can best influence behavior of
e demonstrate social sensitivity. The wisdom of socially
vior is apparent when we examine the social, political,
c environment in which the insurance claims represen-
e insurance industry must live.

ance industry is confronted by a remarkable degree of
. New methods of distribution have caused a marketing
which has challenged long-established structures and
ense reevaluation of traditional relationships in marketing
Meanwhile, the industry, which frequently has been indif-
livious, and even callous to the concept of public relations,
ened to the fact that it is operating in a hostile environment.
s environment, values are scrutinized, modified, and adapted
the exigencies of the times. These values are expressed for-
r informally in the day-to-day handling of insurance claims,
ey vary from company to company. In some cases the concept
al responsibility occupies no position of importance in the hard
etitive world in which everyone strives to make a profit. Sharp
ng and obstructionism have been employed to reduce loss pay-
ts.

other cases, a so-called legally justifiable philosophy has been
pted. That philosophy, embraced by the legal mechanic, proscribes
t all activities of insurance claims representatives must be con-
cted strictly within the framework of responsibility dictated by
ntractual obligation. According to that philosophy, concepts of
cial responsibility not grounded in legal relationships of privity of
ontract cannot be justified in the harsh world of competition. Altruism
is for the impractical moralist—the do-gooder who sits back, insulated
from realities, and tells other people how to run their business.

It is apparent, however, that new laws are having a marked impact
on traditional contractual relations. This is not a new development.
Rather, it is a continuing evolution of contract law within the particular framework of insurance law. The insurance contract, unlike most
contracts, is created within an environment where virtually no bargaining and haggling takes place between contracting parties. The insurance company offers a contract package, and the insured, in the
usual case, can take it or leave it, but the insured cannot change it.

surveys conducted by
is each year accelerate
ance.

There is much to be sa
ophy relating to insurance
stated, is to pay all justifie
helping to remove the obstac
direct losses or liability claims
public. All claims, whether ju
prompt consideration. Those in
denied or compromised as the cir
no liability according to the judgm
insurance counsel, should be firmly,
claims, unfortunately, the decision w
ultimately must be made with a realisti
be practiced. Hopefully, the day will c
denied and then vigorously contested if

SUMMARY AND CONCLUSIONS

Considerable variations in philosophy a
United States on the subject of proper handl
Generally accepted theory dictates that an i
prompt service, as specified by the insurance co
liability claims, however, controversy exists whet
be contacted when liability exists, particularly
minor damages.

Further variations exist in philosophy and p
claimant presents a claim against an insured, there
the manner in which the claim is handled. The clain
dled in a prompt and considerate manner, or the clai
viewed as a natural adversary, and all of the weapo
handling warfare may be utilized to impede the claimant
ering against an insured, provided, of course, that the con
not violate applicable provisions of unfair claims settlement le

In light of the wide variations in the philosophy of handlir
ance claims, a claims representative must decide which philos
most realistic and will survive the test of time. Success in choo
personal philosophy requires a claims representative to be awa

In conc
how he or she f
other individua
of this book, h
others when v
sensitive beh
and economi
tative and th
The insu
competition
revolution
caused in
practices.
ferent, o
has awa
In thi
to mee
mally
and th
of soc
comp
deal
men
I
ad
th
du
c
s

The contract is complex and has frequently been viewed by the public as one-sided, favoring the insurer. As a consequence, legislators have required mandatory provisions and coverage in insurance policies, and the courts have often favored the public when contracts are interpreted. Thus, ambiguities in insurance contracts are construed against the insurer and in favor of the insured. Further, the doctrines of waiver and estoppel are applied in many insurance contract situations to the detriment of insurance companies. The insurance company's traditional contract right to cancel a contract or to refuse to renew a contract has been severely curtailed in recent years because of public opinion. These and similar developments in insurer-public relations have heralded and traced a continuing evolution in the legal revisionism of insurance contract law.

With the enactment of the unfair claims settlement practices acts, further major changes in contract relationships and the law relating to contract duties are to be anticipated. When the courts permit a third-party claimant to sue an insurer directly for alleged violation of the unfair claims settlement practices statutes, insurance claims representatives must be particularly mindful that rights comparable to contract rights may now be owed to third-party claimants because of these laws. One writer has observed, "Today's consumer-oriented society creates ever-increasing pressures on insurance companies to explain and justify their claims handling procedures. Many states . . . have opened the floodgates to extra contract liability on insurance companies, including punitive damages, under what are generally referred to as 'bad faith' first party theories of recovery."[20]

Insurance claims representatives and the insurance companies they represent must be ever aware of societal expectations. This may require claims persons to adopt a concept of social responsibility in their claims handling philosophies. The legal mechanic may be today's short term pragmatist but does not understand or else ignores the intrinsic character of the law. The legal mechanic fails to recognize the long-term fluid nature of a legal system. Law is not a static and immutable factor. Law is a mercurial thing which changes to meet the temper of the times. Champions of the social responsibility creed declare that insurance companies operate within a fluid environment and that

---

[20] Douglas G. Houser, "Unfair Claims Settlement Practices Act—How the Courts Have Interpreted the Act," *The Forum*, vol. 15, no. 2 (Fall, 1979), p. 336.

business institutions are nurtured, restricted, or terminated in response to societal pressures.

Because of this pattern of continued transition, some insurance companies subordinate present short-term profit objectives in order to assure long-term survival and acceptability within society. Spokesmen for these insurers believe that insurance claims handling is the first line of defense in winning society's approval. They accordingly believe that socially responsible behavior, not behavior dictated by a narrow interpretation of a highly vulnerable contract of adhesion, is more compatible with long-range objectives.

Such a social-responsibility creed holds that the free-enterprise, maximum-profit philosophy makes little sense in today's society where huge corporations play not only a vital economic role, but also an important political and social role. Insurance companies cannot avoid having a major and conspicuous impact on society, which society will either approve or disapprove, permit or prevent.

Thus, the variation in insurance claims handling philosophies in the American insurance business should be of major concern to every claims representative in the industry. The behavior of the insurance business inescapably affects the general welfare; it is properly a matter of public concern. As such, it is a target for further governmental interference, and all of the supposed sanctity of the written contract will not escape the ravages of that interference. Government will intervene to curb selfishness and irresponsibility which militate against the public interest.

The maintenance of a climate of social responsibility based upon the application of good human relations principles is essential for successful insurance claims handling. It is within this framework that the insurance industry and the job of the claims representative will best survive in the years to come.

Bibliography

Bibliography

COMMUNICATION, PERSUASION, GENERAL

Abelson, H. I. *Persuasion.* New York: Springer Publishing Co., 1959.

Berlo, D. K. *The Process of Communication.* New York: Holt, Rinehart & Winston, 1960.

Carnegie, Dale. *How to Win Friends and Influence People.* New York: Pocket Books, 1936.

Cherry, Colin. *On Human Communication.* New York: John Wiley & Sons, 1957.

Crocker, Lionel. *Argumentation and Debate.* New York: American Book, 1944.

Dean, Howard H. *Effective Communication.* New York: Prentice-Hall, 1953.

Fellows, Hugh P. *The Art and Skill of Talking with People.* Englewood Cliffs, N.J.: Prentice-Hall, 1964.

Flesch, Rudolph Franz. *The Art of Plain Talk.* New York: Harper & Bros., 1946.

Ling, Mona. *How to Increase Sales and Put Yourself across by Telephone.* Englewood Cliffs, N.J.: Prentice-Hall, 1963.

Monroe, Alan H. *Principles and Types of Speech.* New York: Scott Foresman, 1955.

Nichols, Ralph G., and **Stevens, Leonard A.** *Are You Listening?* New York: McGraw-Hill, 1957.

Roman, Murray. *Telephone Marketing Techniques.* New York: Amacom, American Management Associations, 1979.

Ruesch, Jurgen. *Nonverbal Communication.* Berkeley and Los Angeles: University of California Press, 1956.

Russell, F. A.; Beach, F. H.; and **Buskirk, R. H.** *Textbook of Salesmanship.* 7th ed. New York: McGraw-Hill, 1963.

Scammell, J. C. *Use of the Telephone in Business.* New York: Ronald Press, 1924.

Shurter, Robert T. *Written Communication in Business.* New York: McGraw-Hill, 1957.

Whorf, B. L. *Language, Thought, and Reality.* Ed. by J. B. Carroll. Cambridge, Mass.: M.I.T. Press, 1956.

Whyte, William H., Jr. *Is Anybody Listening?* New York: Simon & Schuster, 1952.

INSURANCE CLAIMS AND THE LAW

Cardozo, Benjamin N. *The Paradoxes of Legal Science.* New York: Columbia University Press, 1928.

Cote, John L. "Recorded Statements." *Insurance Law Journal* no. 449 (June 1960).

Crist, G. W., Jr. *Corporate Suretyship.* New York: McGraw-Hill, 1950.

Donaldson, James H. *Casualty Claim Practice.* 3d ed. Homewood, Ill.: Richard D. Irwin, 1976.

Fryer, William T. *Selected Writings on the Law of Evidence and Trial.* St. Paul, Minn.: West Publishing, 1957.

Ganong, Carey Kierstead, and **Pearce, Richard Warren.** *Law and Society.* Homewood, Ill.: Richard D. Irwin, 1965.

Goodhart, A. "A Changing Approach to the Law of Evidence." *Virginia Law Review* 51 (1965).

Highbaugh, Harvey. *How to Control the Human Element in Claim Handling and Elsewhere.* Knoxville, Tenn.: Jackson Publishing, 1938.

Hinkle, David. *The Seventies and Change—Modern Use of the Telephone in Insurance Claim Adjusting.* Atlanta, Ga.: Crawford, 1970, a cassette learning program.

Houser, Douglas G. "Unfair Claims Settlement Practices Act—How the Courts Have Interpreted the Act." *The Forum* 15, no. 2 (Fall, 1979).

Johns, Corydon T. *The Adjusters Guide to Taking Statements.* Cincinnati: National Underwriter, 1976.

———. *An Introduction to Liability Claims Adjusting.* Cincinnati: National Underwriter, 1965.

Magarick, Patrick. *Successful Handling of Casualty Claims.* New York: Clark Boardman, 1974.

Meehl, Paul E. "Law and Fireside Inductions." In *Law, Justice, and the Individual in Society.* Edited by June Louin Tapp and Felice J. Levine. New York: Holt, Rinehart & Winston, 1977.

Moore, William C. *A Primer on Adjustment.* Indianapolis, Ind.: Rough Notes, 1957.

Rees, Fred H. *Claims Philosophy and Practice.* New York: Spectator, 1947.

Rokes, Willis Park. *No-Fault Insurance.* Santa Monica: Insurors Press, 1971.

Ross, H. Laurence. *Settled Out of Court.* Chicago: Aldine Publishing, 1970.

Thomas, Paul I. "Checking Personal Property Claims." *Adjusters Reference Guide,* Louisville, Ky. Insurance Field 1981. Fire and Allied 13.

Thomas, Paul I., and Reed, Prentiss B., Sr. *Adjustment of Property Losses.* 4th ed. New York: McGraw-Hill, 1977.

Webb, Bernard L.; Launie, J. J.; Rokes, Willis Park; and Baglini, Norman A. *Insurance Company Operations.* 2 vols. Malvern, Pa.: American Institute for Property and Liability Underwriters, 1978.

Wellman, Francis L. *The Art of Cross Examination.* Garden City, N.Y.: Garden City Publishing, 1931.

Wigmore, John H. *Wigmore on Evidence.* Chicago: Foundation Press, 1935.

Winter, William D. *Marine Insurance.* New York: McGraw-Hill, 1952.

ANTHROPOLOGY, PSYCHOLOGY, SOCIOLOGY, AND PHILOSOPHY

Adler, Alfred. *What Life Should Mean to You.* New York: Grosset & Dunlap, 1931.

Allport, G. W., and Odbert, H. S. "Trait Names, A Psycholexical Study." *Psychological Monographs* 47, no. 1, whole no. 211 (1936).

Allport, G. W., and Postman, L. F. "The Basic Psychology of Rumor." *Transactions of the New York Academy of Sciences,* Series 11, vol. 8 (1945).

Barmack, Joseph E. "Boredom & Other Factors in the Physiology of Mental Effort." *Archives of Psychology.* New York: Columbia University, 1937–38.

Baro, Walter Z. "Malingering after Industrial Injuries." *Adjusters Reference Guide.* Louisville, Ky.: Insurance Field, 1981.

Berelson, Bernard, and **Steiner, Gary A.** *Human Behavior—an Inventory of Scientific Findings.* New York: Harcourt, Brace & World, 1964.

Bliss, Perry, ed. *Marketing and the Behavioral Sciences.* Boston: Allyn & Bacon, 1963.

Bruner, J. S., and **Goodman, Cecile C.** "Value and Need as Organizing Factors in Perception." *Journal of Abnormal and Social Psychology* 42 (1947).

Buckhout, Robert. "Eyewitness Testimony." *Scientific American* 231, no. 6 (1974).

Byrne, D. *The Attraction Paradigm.* New York: Academic Press, 1971.

Davis, James H.; Bray, Robert M.; and **Holt, Robert W.** "The Empirical Study of Decision Processes in Juries." *Law, Justice, and the Individual in Society.* Edited by June Louin Tapp and Felice J. Levine. New York: Holt, Rinehart, & Winston, 1977.

Davis, Keith. *Human Relations in Business.* New York: McGraw-Hill, 1957.

————. *Human Relations at Work.* New York: McGraw-Hill, 1962.

Dulany, Don E., Jr. "The Place of Hypotheses and Intentions: An Analysis of Verbal Control in Verbal Conditioning," in Charles W. Eriksen, ed. *Behavior and Awareness.* Durham, N.C.: Duke University Press, 1962.

Edwards, Paul, and **Pap, Arthur,** eds. *A Modern Introduction to Philosophy.* Glencoe, Ill.: Free Press, 1957.

Eells, Richard, and **Walton, Clarence.** *Conceptual Foundations of Business.* 3d ed. Homewood, Ill.: Richard D. Irwin, 1974.

Efran, M. G. "The Effect of Physical Appearance on the Judgment of Guilt, Interpersonal Attraction, and Severity of Recommended Punishment in a Simulated Jury Task." *Journal of Research In Personality,* 1974.

Eriksen, Charles W., ed. *Behavior and Awareness.* Durham, N.C.: Duke University Press, 1962.

Gagne, R. M., and **Fleishman, E. A.** *Psychology and Human Performance.* New York: Holt, Rinehart & Winston, 1959.

Gotten, Nicholas. "Survey of 100 Cases of Whiplash Injury after Settlement of Injury." *Adjusters Reference Guide.* Louisville, Ky.: Insurance Field, 1981.

Statements—*Cont.*
  Rule of Past Recollection Recorded, 60
  Rule of Present Recollection Revived, 61
  telephone; *see* Telephone
  timely statement, 60
  uses, 61, 199
Staton, Thomas F., 67, 76, 306, 313
Stereotyping, 66, 211
Stevens, Leonard A., 166
Stimulus
  adequate stimulus, 56
  defined, 41
Stimulus-response relations
  behavioral trait classification, 48
  connections, 288
  defined, 40
  examples, 36
  money anxiety, 258
  programmed stimulus-response reaction, 40
  "red flag" words, 36, 37
  value in claims handling, 40, 41, 48
Stress
  role of, 84
  telephone voice stress analyzers, 96
  traumatic neuroses, 281–84
Submissiveness, 46
Suggestion
  conditioning process, 66
  identification, 78
  leading questions, 69
Superior children, characteristics, 17
Surveys
  legislative, 350, 351
  public opinion, 22, 23, 91
Swift, Edgar James, 60, 64
Swift, Zephania, 70
Symbolism, instrumentalities of, 114
Symbols of meaning
  insurance contract simplification, 113
  nonverbal symbols
    instrumentalities, 114
    signs, or visual symbols, 116
    sounds, 116
  slogan society, 113
  verbal symbols
    to arouse emotion, 112
    defined, 109
    errors in use, 110, 111
    nature of, 109
  word meanings, 143

T

Tact, 264
Techniques of motivation, 288

Telephone
  critics, claims handling by telephone, 197
  economy in claims handling, 197
  evidential use of recorders, 199
  human relations, 206
  image projection, 209
  mechanics of communication, 134, 213
  obtaining comprehension, 226
  obtaining cooperation, 216
  put a smile in your voice, 208
  questions, types, 220
  right brain-left brain phenomenon, 231
  statements, 215; *also see* Statements
  traditional taboos, 203
  traditional uses, 201
  visualizing the fact situation, 229
  voice stress analyzers, 96
  your telephone personality, 207
Tension-systems, 243
Therapeutic value of talking; *see* Catharsis, principle of
"Think it over until Thursday," technique, 261, 264, 333
Thomas, Paul I., 306
Threats to reputation, 248, 249
Thresholds, 56
  differential, 57
"Time-tested telephone tips," 217
Tolerance, 172
Traits; *see* Behavior traits
Trankell, Arne, 70, 220
Traumatic neuroses
  defined, 281, 282
  malingering, distinguishing, 283
  posttraumatic stress disorder, 282
  symptoms, 283
  whiplash injuries, 284

U

Unconscious partisanship, 78, 87
Unfair claims settlement practices laws, 344
Unsupported conclusions, 181

V

Vacuous duologue and conversation, 147, 181
Value system, society's, 24
Visual acuity, 55
Visualizing the fact situation
  importance, 229
  situational checklists, 230
  visual picture for the record, 230
Voice and speech qualities, 133, 134

This book has been set in 11 and 10 point Caledonia, leaded 2 points. Part and chapter numbers are 30 point Venus Extra Bold; part and chapter titles are 30 and 16 point Venus Bold respectively. The size of the type page is 27 by 44 picas.